Sophia Geography

Exploring Spirituality,
Landscape
and Archetypes

J.P. ANTILL

Harpagornis
Publishing LTD

Harpagornis Publishing Limited
P.O. Box 20342,
Bishopdale,
Christchurch 8543,
New Zealand
www.harpagornispublishing.com
info@harpagornispublishing.com

First paperback edition 2015

ISBN-13: 978-0-473-26286-0
ISBN-10: 047326286X

Cover design: Mirabelle Thomas, Independent graphist
mirabelle.thomas@sfr.fr

Front cover photo: Roslyn Taylor
Kina Penninsula Rd, Tasman, Nelson, New Zealand.

Back cover photo: Tyler Roberts
tyler.roberts23@gmail.com thewoventhreads.blogspot.com/

Graphic design: Simon Gregory
simon@antenna.net.nz

ISBN: 978-0-473-26286-0   (Pbk)
ISBN: 978-0-473-26287-7   (Epub)
ISBN: 978-0-473-26288-4   (Kindle)
ISBN: 978-0-473-26289-1   (iBook)

For all those who have glimpsed
their landscapes in themselves,
and themselves
in their landscapes,
and wondered…

Foreword

One's ideas must be as broad as Nature if
they are to interpret Nature.
– Arthur Conan Doyle.[1]

IS THE EARTH CONSCIOUS? Does she feel our footsteps, sense our joys, understand our sorrows? Might she be calling us to harmonise with her energies and save the world from global collapse? These questions are not just metaphysical ones, they are emotional ones, and our answers may determine the earth's survival. For this reason, *Sophia Geography* is a topical book.

I first met the author, J.P. Antill, on a sunlit day in 1992, at Victoria University, New Zealand. We were both doctoral students in Religious Studies, pursuing research we loved despite the lack of employment opportunities in the field. Antill introduced me to Jane Robert's Seth books, lending me thick, well-thumbed paperbacks with tiny print, which promised to reveal the mysteries of the universe. In those days, Religious Studies scholars usually dismissed spiritual books as intellectually unsophisticated, and channeled writings as particularly suspect. Antill and I discussed the Seth ideas in secret – the covert nature of our discussions adding to the exhilaration.

Now, decades later, there has been a worldwide resurgence of interest in the sacred. Divine passion is no longer – to use Lord Alfred Douglas's phrase – " the love that dares not speak its name."[2] On the academic front too, intellectual thought has expanded, and traditional ideas that the universe is purely mechanistic are falling away.

Sophia Geography is part of this scholarly expansion. Antill takes readers on a journey to redefine the earth and their relationship to it, and the book is a veritable *tour de force* of philosophical, mystical, geographical, ecological and psychological writings. Antill knows the territory well, and uses Jungian archetypes as signposts to help the reader navigate the terrain.

The volume begins gently, but soon gathers momentum, with fascinating sections on the earth as mother archetype and technology as the trickster archetype. However, it is the final three chapters that are the most compelling, as they transport readers to the promised land where the outer landscapes of the earth and the inner landscape of the psyche merge. This fusion could best be described as enlightenment.

Any writer will tell you that the most heart-felt messages are usually the hardest ones to write. It is not easy, particularly in a scholarly work, to bathe the reader in the sacred; such a task is more easily accomplished by photographers, artists, musicians and poets. Antill succeeds by proposing that our physical landscape helps us rediscover our own psyche. In other words, when we see a snow-capped mountain, or feel the warm sun on our face, or catch the scent of a flowerbed, what we are really experiencing is our soul.

Why read this book? First, you may never see landscape in the same way again; after reading it, even the most run-down patch of garden may seem enchanting. Second, the book awakens readers to the beauty and fascination of the landscape *within*. Third, we live in a time when those in power are exploiting the environment to satisfy their own greed. Their actions threaten to destroy life on earth. The scientific community has repeatedly warned of the dangers, but the voice of reason has not been loud enough to bring about sufficient change. What is needed now are new narratives that inspire each of us to live in harmony with earth's energies.

Sophia Geography employs one such narrative – the earth is our mother and we are all connected. We are connected, not just to each other, but also to the cry of the wild, the scent of the forest, the leap of the tiger, the song of the bird, and ultimately to our own soul. Whether we see heaven in a grain of sand, as Blake did, or fear in a handful of dust, as Eliot did, ultimately we are seeing deep within.

Dr Heather Kavan
Senior Lecturer
Massey University
New Zealand

Contents

All the primitive emotions are ours –
hunger, thirst, heat and cold, triumph and fear –
as yard by yard we win our way to stand
as conquerors and survey our realm...
Spirit, imagination, name it what you will,
it steals into the heart on the lonely silent summits
and will not be defied.

FREDA DU FAUR, 'BETWEEN HEAVEN AND EARTH'

Once I thought the land I had loved and known
Lay curled in my inmost self; musing alone
In the quiet room I unfolded the folded sea,
Unlocked the forest and the lonely tree,
Hill and mountain valley beach and stone,
All these, I said, are here and exist in me.

But now I know it is I who exist in the land;
My inmost self is blown like a grain of sand
Along the windy beach, and is only free
To wander among the mountains, enter the tree,
To turn again a sea-worn stone in the hand,
Because these things exist outside of me.

O far from the quiet room my spirit fills
The familiar valleys, is folded deep in the hills.

RUTH DALLAS, 'DEEP IN THE HILLS'

.

Sophia Geography

Preface

THIS IS THE STORY of many explorations into Spirituality, Landscape and Archetypes. It is as well just one personal, rather idiosyncratic journey of ideas, discovery and self-discovery. Like many travellers journeying through foreign lands in different physical and cultural landscapes, I have wondered how one's landscape affects one's sense of 'self'. Nor am I alone in this wondering – the relationship between 'spirituality' and 'landscape' has been felt and mused upon by travellers, geographers, mountaineers, poets, children, primal peoples, philosophers, religious thinkers, writers and artists since time immemorial – often with more questions than answers and a greater sense of the mystery than conclusion.

As a child in New Zealand brought up in the paddocks, a great dry riverbed, except in flash-flood, to the fore, and beyond that to the west the Southern Alps – my landscape was my given. *My landscape was myself. My landscape was alive.* The old wind-deformed pine trees, which protected our house and garden from the hot, dry Nor'Westerlies, were *my* pine trees and *my* friends. Mt Grey (Maungatere to the Maori, the origin of the shark tooth Nor'West Wind), the large blue-grey massif to the southwest, was *my mountain.* The paddocks, the trees and the atmosphere above the paddocks at dusk, were en-spirited with aura, God. My religion was animism. When I went to board in a country town, the landscape was alien and not alive. I felt less myself and, like countless other children boarding away from home, I was homesick for *my* landscape. I felt what the old Maori distant ancestors of the land must have felt when wrenched from their landscapes, their mountains and their rivers. Again, as a 17 year old, struggling for self-identity and living in the city, I wondered whether one's 'self' was determined by one's life point and place along history's continuum – or whether one could somehow transcend historical determinism and causality. I set myself the experiment of staying in a remote one room mountain hut, outside communication, for a week (water was by bucket from an icy stream down the mountain, the toilet through the bush to a long-drop, the fire by my chopping wood, and light by a kerosene lamp) where I would try and forget who I was (in other words my family, my history, my city landscape) in order to discover my *essence,* the '*real*' me. I found I could not do it – the beech forest became intrusively alive, not necessarily friendly, the possum eyes in the trees glowed and stared like searching torch lights in the dark. I had to resort to memories of my family, my city landscape and history, for comfort and security.

In 1987 as a traveller in China and Tibet I wondered why the Han Chinese and the Tibetans were so different. To some extent they looked similar but their character and spirituality was vastly different. Could their very different landscapes – one hugely over-populated, communist, materialist, Confucian, de-sacralised, 'civilised' and anthropocentric; the other sparsely populated, wild, rugged and mountainous – the home of Bon magic and Buddhist meditation – have something to do with this? Again, in Queensland I met with white, 'sophisticated', well-educated Australians, living on Aboriginal sacred land, who were becoming like their native Aborigine visitors, increasingly Aborigine in their values and spirituality. (For example, they lived tolerantly alongside 'dangerous' spiders and snakes in the house and garden. Spiders in the house were pointed out and not to be disturbed – one had to duck to avoid the spiders' webs in the kitchen). Obviously the landscape, and the Aborigines' perceptions of landscape, was changing them. I wondered about the early European Christian colonizers to Australia several centuries earlier and how their landscape perceptions would have been immeasurably different from the indigenous Aborigines' spiritual landscapes – same land *apparently*, but different landscapes. In another thousand years would this same harshly beautiful, colourful land co-create the emergence of yet another landscape in the minds of its inhabitants?

Which brings us to the questions; "*What/who are our landscapes* and how do they define what/who we are?" and "*Who are we and how do we define our landscapes?*" This book is the map of one writer's quest. It can be yours too, although you may choose divergent trails and reach different destinations.

Introduction

"TELL ME YOUR LANDSCAPE and I will tell you who you are." We are defined by our landscapes, as the Spanish philosopher Ortega y Gasset said. Yet this book shows that it is the archetypes which are behind our landscapes, which permeate our values and inform our spirituality. These form our inner landscapes.

Sophia Geography approaches the spiritual inherent in landscapes from a secular point of view. *Spirituality*, *landscape* and *archetypes* are ideas which can be explored historically, analytically and descriptively, or phenomenologically.

When I was about eleven or twelve, I tried to read the American evangelist Billy Graham's book *World Aflame*[1]. It was picked at random from my Mother's bookshelf, which also contained environmentalist Rachel Carson's *Silent Spring*[2]. *World Aflame* made me feel sick. It was a gut reaction which I did not understand at the time. I later came to realize it was a visceral reaction to a world view which was at violent variance with my own natural world view – a landscape which I perceived to be inherently spiritual, beautiful and good. This was my God, *a Spirit in everything*, and I unknowingly was a young Pagan. However Billy Graham did have a point to make. All was *not* good and beautiful with the *human* world. Rachel Carson would have agreed! And today we have a world of "clashing religious fundamentalisms", as has been described by Tariq Ali[3] – which is increasingly being countered by a wave of implacable and brilliant atheists arguing *The God Delusion*.[4] Have you gleefully surfed this atheistic wave with the religious skeptics, who rightfully and righteously dump on religious bigotry? Or do you wonder if something has been missed and lost, some essence which could have been salvaged from the sullied great religions? Do you feel confused, as if you and your values have been hit by a wave and dumped upon from a great height? Well maybe and maybe not... However do you seek refuge and salvation in the alternate realities of cyberspace? And do you sometimes wonder - while playing at the secular 'card table', within the 'genius' man-made world of technology, commerce, and consumerism – whether we are not after all going to 'hell in a handbasket'? Do you seek solace in the landscapes of the natural world? If so, this book is for you.

Sophia Geography is an exploration. It is an academic quest for clarification and enlightenment on ideas about spirituality, landscapes, archetypes – and finally it comes to a realization and explores the forgotten and hidden Sophia. This is not a dogmatic book, but rather it is a phenomenological exploration. Everything is up for discussion and disagreement. Setting out, this writer did not know the destination. The conclusion, like a lost continent emerging out of the mist, was a rediscovery. Whether it is *real*, is up to you.

IN THE FIRST PART of the book, **Chapters 1 to 4**, I explore the concepts of spirituality, landscape and archetypes.

Heraclitus said "You could not discover the limits of the soul, even if you travelled every road to do so; such is the depth of its meaning".[5] But perhaps you feel that spirituality makes no sense in our scientific and materialist age? If so, I hope **Chapter 1** will change your mind. I hope to persuade you that although spirituality has been undermined by twentieth century modernists and positivists, it is, nevertheless, a legitimate and credible concept which has changed over history. It was Carl Jung, on the trail of the ancient Gnostics, who reintroduced the idea that all religious experience is psychic in nature. Archetypal and Depth psychology has established this tradition once more in the twentieth century. Hence spirituality is inherent to the psyche (soul) and *all* the Gods are archetypes inherent within the psyche. *Individuation* is an inner spiritual quest or process towards the fullest possible realization of the self and the *imago dei* (the God-image) within the psyche or soul. Not only is this an ancient Gnostic idea of an *inner* spirituality – but increasingly spirituality is seen as a contemporary postmodern issue, in terms of creativity, inner experience and process.

Geography is above all the study of landscape. Geographers have argued that "Although the land exists, 'the scape is a projection of human consciousness, an image received' (Erlich 1987). Mentally or physically, we frame the view, and our apperception depends on our frame of mind".[6] **Chapter 2** explores landscape. Landscape is more than what is found in the viewfinder of a camera. It has a connection with one's self. We often have a fondness for a particular landscape, perhaps a childhood landscape – some even talk about "my landscape" as if it is interchangeable with "myself". Artists, poets, philosophers and travellers have pondered this question, as have geographers. Like spirituality, landscape has been a mobile and changing concept. From the objectivity, positivism and literalism of modernism to the inward subjective focus of humanistic, existential and postmodern geography, landscape would seem to be, like spirituality, an inner concept originating in the psyche. It is argued by this writer that landscape is a *'focus of perception'* and it is relational rather than objective.

For Belden C. Lane, "Landscape is a connector of the soul with being".[7] The Arctic explorer and environmentalist Barry Lopez argues "Our perceptions are colored by preconception and desire…the landscapes in which history unfolds are both real, that is, profound in their physical effects on mankind, and not real, but mere projections, artifacts of human perception".[8] Geographers have long recognized a link between mind, imagination and landscape. In **Chapter 3** it is shown that landscapes are both imaginal and visionary. They derive from personal and collective imagination. Imagination in creating landscape is inherent in postmodern geography and it becomes most apparent in a consideration of spiritual or religious landscapes.

In the West there have been discernable historical changes in spiritual imaginal-visionary landscapes – hence this writer describes 1) the primal, sacred, *Nature/Earth Landscape*; 2) the Judeo-Christian revelatory *Anthropocentric Landscape*; 3) the modernist, 'secular' *Technological/Materialist Landscape*; and 4) the *Postmodern Ecological Landscape* which points to an *Inner Landscape*

"All landscapes are *symbolic*, they express 'a persistent desire to make the earth over in the image of some heaven', and they undergo *change* because they are expressions of society itself, making history through time",[9] geographer Denis Cosgrove writes. **Chapter 4** is the pivotal chapter which threshes out the case for symbolic and mythological archetypes within landscapes. In order to give credence to the idea that there are archetypes behind and within our landscapes **Chapter 4** takes us on a journey towards an archetypal analysis of landscapes. Postmodernism sets the climate for an archetypal analysis. We explore what is meant by postmodernism in philosophy, science, religion and spirituality. Postmodern geographers have already recognized that there are connections and similarities between the knowledge perspective, or epistemology, of postmodernism and depth archetypal psychology.

We explore the evidence for Jung's theory of archetypes. This is controversial and fascinating stuff. Jung regarded himself as a scientist using scientific method. However Jung and his theory have been viciously attacked from some academic and religious quarters, surprising as it may seem to those outside the ivory towers and the religious establishments. The stakes, apparently, are high. However the author wades in unflinchingly, in support of Jung's challenge to orthodoxy. The evidence to support Jung and his theory of archetypes is strong. It comes from philosophers and scientists – in the form of similar or associative evidence from other disciplines and scientific evidence, evaluated by philosophical analysis, and orthodox science itself. However, ironically, having made this case, Jung's ideas were also a challenge to orthodox science. They were on the growing fringe of science where theoretical quantum physicists liked to play. Hence Jung's life-long collaboration on the theory of archetypes with Wolfgang Pauli, the winner of the 1945 Nobel Prize in Physics. Both Jung and Pauli saw complementary aspects in physics and the psyche and fundamental dynamical patterns which were both mental and physical. Archetypes in matter and mind account for synchronistic phenomena, in other words these abstract patterns could determine behaviour of matter in a noncausal way.

If you accept that archetypes exist, the rest of this chapter describes the *essence* of archetypes. The conclusion is that an *archetypal analysis of landscape* will involve: 1) looking for images which are universal, trans-historical, profound, numinous, generative, highly intentional and necessary; 2) looking for images which are 'a way of seeing', a locus of imagining and 'a way of seeing with the heart' (insight); 3) Looking for images which are inherently feelings, have an emotional possessive effect and that bedazzle consciousness; 4) looking for appropriate components of the psyche, Gods and myths; 5) looking for root metaphors.

THE SECOND PART of the book **Chapters 5 to 9** uses an archetypal analysis to explore the four imaginal –visionary landscapes described in **Chapter 3**.

Cultural historian Theodore Roszak has argued that "Mother Earth is as universal a symbol as our race possesses, at home even in those societies that have moved on to more civilized ways".[10] In **Chapter 5** it is shown that the Mother Earth Archetype is behind and imbues the nurturing values and spirituality of the *Nature/Earth Landscape*. An archetypal analysis is given which includes the shadowside of Mother Earth – destruction, chaos, death and annihilation of the ego. She is found in the ancient and terrible Goddess Kali, as well as in the warnings of twentieth and twenty-first century environmental and Gaian scientists.

Ecotheologian and Catholic priest Thomas Berry has famously made the observation, along with many feminists and environmentalists, that "The biblical tradition begins with the creation narrative wherein the Earth Mother of the Eastern Mediterranean is abandoned in favour of the transcendent Heaven Father…The natural world is no longer the locus for the meeting of the divine and the human. A subtle aversion develops toward the natural world, a feeling that humans in the depth of their beings do not really belong to the earthly community of life, but to a heavenly community".[11]

Chapter 6 makes the case that the transcendence of the monotheistic Heavenly God-Father Archetype over the universal Mother Earth Archetype amounted to a clash of archetypes in history and the repercussions continue today. A new *Anthropocentric Landscape*, with man as the central *'focus of perception'*, was brought forth and the *Nature/Earth Landscape* and Mother Earth were de-divinized, objectified and made ready for exploitation. Pagan religions, polytheism and in particular Goddesses and feminine power were driven underground by this jealous male Heavenly God-Father of monotheism. However this *separation* from Mother Earth and the *Nature/Earth Landscape* was necessary for the development of the Ego and Hero and individual identity. The shadowside of this archetype is scapegoating and warmongering against the 'othered ' and 'not chosen'.

For Erik Davis "Technology is neither devil nor angel. But neither is it simply a "tool" a neutral extension of some rock-solid human nature. Technology is a trickster…[The Trickster] Hermes became *agoraios*, "he of the agora," the patron saint of merchants, middlemen, and the service industry, while the god's epithet "tricky" came to mean "good for securing profit".[12] In **Chapter 7** it is shown that phenomenologically, the Trickster Archetype (and allied developing Ego and Hero) imbue the *Technological/Materialist Landscape* 'focus of perception'. The Trickster Hermes in mythology has had a long association with the marketplace, commerce, the deal, cross-roads, boundaries, trickery, magic, trade surplus, profit, transformation, technology and communications. The *Heavenly God-Father* is now 'dead' and the new usurper Trickster God is Man, Hero, Ego, Player, the Measurer and the Creator. Trickster's 'morality' is an amorality and a supra-morality. Trickster's shadowside is the world of *I-It*. Without care and love, the *'I'* uses that rendered objectified or *'It'* as a possession, play-thing, tool, 'means to an end', gratification. The *I-It* world of the Trickster is objective, casual, cool and impersonal.

Who is Sophia? **Chapter 8** is a rediscovery and an exploration of Sophia, the Wisdom Archetype, found both in the ancient world and today. The Sophia Wisdom Archetype (*Anima Mundi/World Soul*) values and spirituality are inherent in the *Postmodern Ecological Landscape* 'focus of perception'. Sophia's return has been forecast by a number of philosophers and psychologists, as well as predicted in ancient religious texts. Physician, psychoanalyst and writer Edward C. Whitmont wrote "The Goddess is now returning. Denied and suppressed for thousands of years of masculine domination, she also comes at a time of dire need… Mother Earth herself has been pressed to the limits of her endurance".[13] It is shown that Sophia Wisdom (*Anima Mundi /World Soul*) is both premodern and postmodern and is found in quantum physics, archetypal psychology and ecopsychology. Sophianic Wisdom, like Deep Ecology, involves the asking of deeper questions and the apperception of deeper realities.

Have you ever wondered how your *inner* Self connects with your outer landscapes?

Explored in **Chapter 9** is the *Postmodern Ecological Landscape* and the Sophianic *Inner Landscape (Mundus Imaginalis)* – together with *Sophianic Harmonic Archetypal Perception (Ta'wil)* and the *Visionary Geography of the Soul*. The role of the inner landscapes in the formation of outer landscapes is illustrated in the arguments of postmodern ecologists such as Barry Lopez; quantum physicists such as Wolfgang Pauli, David Bohm and F. David Peat; as well as that of philosophers Gilbert Durand and Henry Corbin. They point to the power of the imagination, inter-worlds, parallel worlds – the necessity of recognizing and rediscovering psycho-spiritual structures in order to perceive and meditate the Earth – hence *ta'wil*, harmonic perception, holographic perception, archetypal perception. Henry Corbin wrote "…ultimately what we call physics and physical is but a reflection of the world of the Soul; there is no pure physics, but always the physics of some definite psychic activity" and "The earth then is a vision, and geography a visionary geography…the categories of the sacredness "which possess the soul" can be recognized in the landscape with which it surrounds itself and in which it shapes its habitat…"[14] Thus in the end to perceive the Sophianic Soul of the Earth is to perceive one's own Soul. The psyche and the landscape have become one.

Note: For the academically inclined reader, the ***Appendix Notes*** are a reference which gives an overview, summarization, backgrounding and rationale for some of the current issues and on-going academic debates touched on in the chapters.

ONE

Spirituality Comes of Age

You could not discover the limits of the
soul, even if you travelled every road to do
so; such is the depth of its meaning.
– Heraclitus

Spirituality is Inner

FOR A LONG TIME IN THE WEST, spirituality belonged to religion. A person was either religious and spiritual or an atheist and non-spiritual. In particular, spirituality was synonymous with the monotheism – the belief or doctrine that there is only one male God – of Judaism, Christianity and Islam. This meant that when religion was degraded by the worst excesses of fundamentalism – arrogant authoritarianism, sexism, homophobia, bigotry, racism and war-mongering – spirituality was degraded by association. In very recent years a resurgence of atheism has become the popular counter to fundamentalism. One leader of the new atheist movement is that master counter-fundamentalist, conceptual swordsman Richard Dawkins. Dawkins, an Oxford University evolutionary scientist, has received a "rock-star welcome" from audiences around the world. In Christchurch he filled the local town hall of 2,500[1]– a capacity audience, in a remote country. This would surely be to the envy of any fundamentalist.

However spirituality is far deeper and more complex than fundamentalist movements, religious dogma or an association with orthodox monotheistic religions. In fact, in recent times spirituality is increasingly seen as distinct from external religion. Spirituality which is *inner* has come of age in a secular postmodern world. One can be a deeply spiritual non-believer. For example, for many scientists the idea of a pantheistic spiritual force in the universe and within the natural world is congenial. As Richard Dawkins has pointed out, this "is light years away from the interventionist,

9

miracle-wreaking, thought-reading, sin-punishing, prayer-answering God of the Bible, of priests, mullahs and rabbis, and of ordinary language."[2]

Spirituality is a philosophically mobile idea which has undergone historical change over the centuries. Despite modernist, and in particular, twentieth century attacks on it by logical positivism and pervasive undermining by scientific scepticism, it is nonetheless a legitimate and credible concept. As will be shown, what spirituality refers to is to be found *within* the psyche. The relationship between *spirituality* and *landscape* will be explored in subsequent chapters, in particular with respect to archetypes which are embedded in our landscapes.

Briefly, Western Spirituality

IN THE WEST spirituality is both a very ancient and a very recent subject of inquiry. It would appear to have many different meanings.[3] It has been described as a "notoriously vague term", and subject matter labelled 'spiritual' may seem to be ill-suited to rational inquiry.[4] However, toward the end of the twentieth century and the beginning of the twenty-first, spirituality has returned as a subject for academic study.[5] It sits shakily astride a twentieth century dominated by logical positivism, empirical science, Darwinian evolutionary theory and a scepticism of anything which smacks of religion or metaphysics. Until very recently one was either spiritual and religious, or secular – the latter meaning atheist and without spiritual or religious belief. Only in the past twenty or so years has the notion of '*secular spirituality*' come to be widely referred to and it has become acceptable to ascribe a spiritual dimension to people and activities not ostensibly religious; for example artists, scientists, ecological activists, holistic health practitioners.[6] What follows is a brief overview of how Western philosophical concepts of spirituality have changed over relatively recent centuries and in particular in the twentieth century.

Greek Spirit Words

FOR SIMPLICITY'S SAKE we begin with the ancient Greeks, bearing in mind that for even earlier, pre-monotheistic, religions – otherwise known as the Pagans, Canaanites, animistic, matriarchal and primal religions – the *spiritual* imbued everything in the natural and physical world. More will be said on this later.

For the ancient Greeks, all humans were spiritual beings. There were four important spirit words – *pneuma, nous, psyche* and *thumos.* "Humans were enfolded and sustained by cosmic *pneuma*; ruled by the universally operative faculty of rational cognition *nous*; vivified by an individual *psyche*; and had an emotional attraction to the right, the noble, and the good *thumos*".[7] In ancient Greek philosophy 'spirituality' had cosmic, intellectual, psychological and moral components and implications. This is a *holistic view* of spirituality which found favour once again in the late twentieth century.[8]

"Thou Shalt Have No Other God But Me"

SPIRITUALITY WAS CAPTURED by orthodox monotheistic religion. After the many Gods, or polytheistic, believing ancient Greeks – this multi-faceted view of spirituality was driven underground. The "Thou shalt have no other God but me" patriarchal monotheistic religions of Judaism, Christianity and the Church took over the concept of spirituality. Hence spirituality in the West was for many centuries equated with 'religion' – the 'spiritual teachings', the 'spiritual life', the 'devout life', the 'interior life' or the 'piety' within a particular religious faith. Spirituality was further equated with particular dogmatic and spiritual referents – Judaic spirituality, Christian spirituality, Islamic spirituality, Catholic spirituality, Protestant spirituality. Christianity brought about new norms for all thinking in the West – and part of its impact was a distinctive conception of the spiritual reflected in a new use of the word pneuma.[9] Indeed, both Christians and Jews saw divine pneuma as a benefit available to them by virtue of their membership in religious communities. The writings of St Paul, for example, show the 'pneuma' of the faithful must be distinguished from the unholy 'spirits' (of the pagans).[10] For Paul, 'spiritual reality' is imperishable and is separated from worldly reality.[11]

Following the work of the Early Church Fathers – philosophers such as Descartes, Kant, Hegel, Kierkegaard, Feuerbach, Marcel, Ebner and Buber, have further added to the discourse on spirituality. While less tied to the Christian and Jewish religious doctrines and orthodoxy of their times, they were nevertheless still influenced by them. They also introduced new elements into the dialogue, for example a *relational view* of spirituality, which remain with us today.

Spirit-Matter Separation

THE DUALIST VIEW is exemplified by French philosopher Rene Descartes (1596-1650), who laid down the philosophical foundations for the 'modern scientific age'. This happened some twelve hundred years after Augustine (354-430), the philosophical founder of the Western church, who in spite of his hostility to paganism, was nevertheless influenced by Greek Platonism and equated the 'spiritual' with God substance, subjectivity and soul. Ironically Descartes was to conceive of 'spiritual substance' in much the same way as St Paul. While Descartes was a physicist committed to mechanistic scientific explanation – and a spirit-matter dualism was an embarrassment, as causal relations between spiritual and material are difficult to explain – Descartes nevertheless reinforced the distinction between spiritual and material for religious reasons.[12]

Spirituality Rejected

IN THE *EMPIRICIST VIEW*, spirituality is rejected entirely. Perhaps the most important European philosopher of modern times, Prussian Immanuel Kant (1724-1804) was decisive on the issue of spirituality. Kant almost entirely ignored the German word for spirit – *Geist*. A forerunner of the scientist sceptics of today, Kant rejected epistemological claims of metaphysical supernaturalism – this meant questions as to the existence of God, soul and in fact anything which can not be resolved by an appeal to possible experience. Kant maintained they lacked any true cognitive foundation. Instead he was much more interested in illuminating *objectivity* and was concerned with objectively valid principles in scientific and moral judgement.[13]

Unfolding Spirituality

THE *IDEALIST VIEW* expounded by Hegel (1770-1831) was meant to overcome all dualisms. A major Western philosopher and a formidable critic of his predecessor Immanuel Kant, Hegel argued that spirit unfolds itself in nature and history. For Hegel, spirit moves the world as a formal and final cause. Spirit is the true meaning of things, their true nature and the end for which they will be realised. Take out any reference to God and this is a strikingly postmodern secular view of spirituality.

The Dane Soren Kierkegaard's (1813-1855) definition of spirit is similar to Hegel's. Kierkegaard was however, one of Hegel's more devastating critics. Widely credited with providing the tools for modern existentialism Kierkegaard gives a theological take. Spirit-words continue to be regarded as the property of Christianity. There is a distinction between divine and human spirit. "The individual must synthesize soul and body, the eternal-universal and the temporal-particular into a unity, a self – and this accomplished relation *when* it is accomplished, is called "spirit."[14] For Kierkegaard human individuals can only with great difficulty actualize themselves as spiritual beings.

Matter the Parent of Spirit

WITH HIS *MATERIALIST VIEW* of spirituality, German philosopher Ludwig Feuerbach (1804-1872) turned both Keirkegaard and Hegel on their heads. Rather than 'spirit' being the parent of matter, *matter is the parent of spirit*. Starting from physical matter he went on to explain the rise of human consciousness, ideas, culture and what is the nature of human spirituality. While Hegel expounded an idealist philosophy, Feuerbach expounded a materialist philosophy. This was to become the prevailing philosophy of the modern world in the twentieth century.

Spirituality in I-and-You

HOWEVER, FEUERBACH also had a *relational view* of spirituality. He asserted that "spirituality resides in the I-and-You sociality of mortal, sensuous beings".[15]

In fact Feuerbach maintained that the personality of God is none other than the projection of the personhood we find in humankind. We make God in our own image. Because the human spirit is creaturely it must relate itself to an Other. These connections and the relational aspects of Feuerbach's theory are developed further in the thought of Gabriel Marcel, Ferdinand Ebner and Martin Buber.[16]

Spirituality as Relational Dialogue

FRENCH PHILOSOPHER Gabriel Marcel (1889-1975) maintained that the spiritual life is a dynamic relationship between the mind and something outside it – "all spiritual life is essentially a dialogue" and uses for the first time, one of the words of real dialogue by referring to God as a "you".[17]

Ferdinand Ebner (1882-1931) an Austrian philosopher who developed a religiously informed philosophy of language, argued that the spiritual essentially belongs to the I-You relationship. For Ebner the human spirit "is essentially determined by its being fundamentally intended for a relation to something spiritual *outside* it, *through* which and *in* which it exists" – that is, God.[18]

This line of thought was developed further by Martin Buber, the Austrian Jewish philosopher (1878-1965) in his now famous formulated philosophy of spiritual dialogue. Buber's *I and Thou*, published shortly after Ebner's book, contains a formula for the Ebnerian idea "Spirit is not in the I but between I and You. It is not like the blood that circulates in you but like the air in which you breath".[19] Indeed, 'I and Thou' were words taken over from Feuerbach who had maintained that the "true dialectic is not a monologue of a solitary thinker with himself; it is a dialogue between I and Thou."[20] For Buber the spirit is wherever "encounter" occurs, whether it be with a human being, a cat, or a tree. As New Zealand theologian Lloyd Geering points out:

> Buber came to feel that spiritual power exists in the personal relations which draw people together in reciprocity. It led him to emphasise the value of true dialogue, and to suggest a fresh understanding of God as the Eternal thou present in all deep human relationships of the I-Thou variety.[21]

"Airy Impotence"

MODERN SCEPTICISM OF SPIRITUALITY dominated the twentieth century. James Lapsley has argued that "By the early twentieth century the word spirit had come to connote a vague sense of airy impotence, almost to the point of meaninglessness, in western theology".[22] The modern theologians who did consider the issue of spirituality in the twentieth century, showed a much closer affinity with biblical ideas than had most of their more recent predecessors.[23]

Reinhold Niebuhr's (1949) *The Nature and Destiny of Man*, posited nature and spirit as basic constituents of human beings. Although, significantly, he later abandoned 'spirit' for the secular concept of 'self' to refer to human beings. Paul Tillich (1963), Teilhard de Chardin (1959), and Wolfhart Pannenberg (1985) also used spirit as a major category. Tillich took the position that the spirit of human beings is a distinctive created spirit, whereas Teilhard and Pannenberg both argued for an identity between divine and created spirit which is thought to characterize *all* of life.[24]

A 'Nonsense Concept'

WHILE MANY WESTERN THEOLOGIANS during the twentieth century had become uncomfortable with the concept of spirit and spirituality, Western theology was itself under increasing philosophical attack and siege. Spirituality, metaphysics and theology became 'nonsense concepts' with the advent of logical positivism, the philosophical school based on linguistic analysis in the 1920s and 1930s. Logical positivism rejected metaphysical speculation and held that the only meaningful statements are those that are analytic or can be tested empirically. Based on linguistic analysis (to clarify the meanings of statements and questions) and on demands for criteria and procedures of empirical verification (for establishing at least in-principle truth or falsity of statements, by observation or experiment), logical positivism was essentially a systematic attack on metaphysics by demanding observations for conferring meaning. Metaphysics was rejected as nonsense.

In the modern world of the twentieth century it often seemed that 'spirituality' was on very tenuous ground as regards meaning. Evans (1993) has argued that the skeptical contemporary world-view regarding spirituality is to some extent in all of us: "It is part of the largely unconscious mind-set of our culture".[25]

'Secular' Postmodern Spirituality

HOWEVER, UNEXPECTEDLY spirituality has returned in a 'secular' postmodern age. While 'spirituality' cannot be proved as such, the concepts of 'spiritual' and 'spirituality' have not been disproved, nor have they been successfully rendered *nonsense* concepts.

In the postmodern era, the positivists and the sceptics brandishing scientism, have themselves come in for criticism. The Enlightenment model and modernist science with its off-shoot, technology, has been discredited as contributing to the degradation of the environment and threatening the planet. There is a new scepticism which questions whether scientism and its philosophical axioms are the best epistemological route forward, let alone the planet's saviour. The public is increasingly turning against a purist science and technology without debate on values, for example unease over biogenetic engineering. In the late twentieth and the early twenty-first century, positivism and scientism have been found wanting by many.

One can not live by positivism and scientism – at best they are tools for clarifying meaning, but are not the meaning itself. Spirituality, it would seem, has escaped and we are still searching for meaning. New Zealand botanist and ecologist, Philip Simpson illustrates this with James Lovelock's Gaia hypothesis, which he argues:

> ...provides an ethical or spiritual dimension to human life that is ecocentric rather than egocentric. Some see the living Earth concept in mystical terms. There is no doubt that a competitive model of Earth is damaging to our relationship to nature, and science is strangely lacking in providing meaning.[26]

Spiritual reality is being recognised, despite a lack of proof; while science is found to be lacking in meaning, even by some scientists. However the question of what 'spirituality' is, or how one defines it, remains.

One thing is certain however, 'spirituality' has become secularised. Jon Alexander maintains that the trend to use the word spirituality in an experiential and generic sense appeals to our irenic age but it also presents some theological difficulties: "Today we encounter the word spirituality so frequently in our reading and conversation that it is surprising to learn that its use is a recent phenomenon."[27]

John Elias argues that the 1960s began with the announcement that God was dead and it seemed that the United States had finally become a secular society – but by the 1970s some scholars were already talking about the return of the sacred and others were maintaining that the sacred had never left, except among certain social scientists. Elias maintains certain words are now heard that had virtually passed from usage, even in religious circles:

> While the word *religious* remained in use, the words *spiritual* and
> *spirituality* were rarely uttered during the decades when the focus was
> on the secularization of society and its institutions. Today these words
> are used without apology in both religious and non-religious circles.
> Social scientists use the term spiritual or sacred as a category to explain
> understandings of selfhood and human striving. Religionists use the
> words to highlight the highly personal elements of one's religious life.[28]

Whereas in earlier centuries spirituality had been equated with religion, now as Walter Principe points out, there were many aspects of religion which were less related to the spiritual ideal and some which were even opposed to it.[29] Van Ness argues that while Nietzsche was perhaps the most explicit in charting an irreligious spiritual path, spirituality born of radical scepticism is also found in the naturalistic and nondogmatic views of some Oriental sages.

A SPIRITUAL LIFE in a "world come of age" was notably also the argument of Dietrich Bonhoeffer, the German theologian executed by the Nazis for his part in a conspiracy to kill Hitler. Bonhoeffer was very impressed by his non-religious co-conspirators who were also executed and while he "characteristically identified spiritual life in theological terms, as life shaped by the indwelling of the Holy Spirit, his last writings place an emphasis on wholeness and vitality", which are the "hallmarks of a more general rendering of the spiritual dimension of human existence."[30]

Van Ness states that in Bonhoeffer's last writings "The positive evaluation of the secular world begun in the Ethics was even more firmly stated in the idiom of "the world come of age". Bonhoeffer argued that "God is increasingly being pushed out of a world that has come of age, out of the spheres of our knowledge and life, and that since Kant he has been relegated to a realm beyond the world of experience."[31]

If God was increasingly being pushed out of a world come of age as Bonhoeffer argued – Bonhoeffer's relation to the philosophy of Nietzsche is complex. However in his prison theological deliberations he seemed to move beyond Barth's dialectical appreciation of Nietzsche to a "closer embrace of a religionless or secular spirituality such as was championed by the author of Thus Spake Zarathustra".[32] Van Ness states that from "Nietzsche, and Kierkegaard and Barth also, Bonhoeffer learned that religion, including the Christian religion, was part of what an authentically spiritual life must criticize and move beyond."[33]

Given the many compromises of historical Christianity, some measure of worldliness and freedom to criticise was indispensable to a profound spiritual life. Both Nietzsche and Bonhoeffer opposed tyranny in both its secular and religious forms and both recognised the importance of spiritual discipline – for Nietzsche it was *solitude* and for Bonhoeffer it was *silence*. Both have a simplicity which confounds them being classified as specifically religious or irreligious.[34] Thus, the authentic spiritual life had to move beyond the dogma of monotheistic and often fundamentalist patriarchal religions in the West.

Spiritual Revolutionaries

THE FEMINIST REVOLUTION in the latter half of the twentieth century has embraced the new wave of secular spirituality. This has involved a challenge to, and a rebellion against, traditional patriarchal religions and of necessity a re-definition of what is essential in religion for women – a reconsideration of spirituality.

The roll-call perhaps begins with the coolly observant French academic and writer Simone de Beauvoir who, although not professing to be a feminist at the time of writing *The Second Sex* in the 1940s, has had a pioneering role in the challenge by feminist philosophy to the prevailing patriarchal ideologies of the twentieth century[35]. Then there was Merlin Stone who examined and dissected the archaeological evidence for the Goddess and the patriarchal Judeo-Christian cultures' suppression of women and their matriarchal religions[36]. Stone was closely followed by Naomi Goldenberg, a psychologist of religion and feminist theologian who maintained that "When feminists succeed in changing the position of women in Christianity and Judaism, they will shake these religions at their roots." [37]

American academic Mary Daly is perhaps the most damning, challenging, radical and creative of the recent feminist theologians and philosophers. A former nun and a Professor of Theology at Boston College, her critique of the detrimental effects of patriarchal religion is chilling[38]. More recently Muslim feminists, for example Irshad Manji (2003), have risked their lives by taking on fundamentalist patriarchal Islam.[39]

Feminist philosophers and theologians have confronted the authority of the dominant patriarchal monotheistic Western religious traditions and establishments head-on. They have realised that women's spirituality and dignity have been plundered and defiled along with the natural world. Based on this they have searched out and created alternatives. For example, the association of postmodern theology with process theology, the ecological movement and the feminization of the divine, is pivotal in the work of ecofeminist theologian Carol P. Christ[40] Postmodernist arguments are frequently used by feminists. For example, Ellen Leonard argues that no theology can claim universality and all theologies are political:

> Traditional Western theology is now seen as determined by dominant
> world powers and groups. The critique of this theology comes from the
> "new theologies" which argue that Western theology is culture-bound,
> church-centred, male-dominated, age-dominated, procapitalist,
> anticommunist, nonrevolutionary and overly theoretical.[41]

These feminist revolutionaries reject dualistic and hierarchical thinking which devalues women, body and nature.[42] They demand a *re-visioning* of the divine and a new theology in the light of contemporary experience – especially woman's experience.

For religious archetypes, icons and myths, feminists have harkened back to a pre-patriarchial era when the Goddess or Goddesses and polytheistic Gods were worshipped.[43] Feminist theologians have gone inwards *into the imagination* to focus on the *symbolic meaning* of the Goddess, Goddesses and other Gods, allowing them to explore new patterns of spirituality.[44]

Like their foremothers of the matriarchial 'pagan' religions, feminist theologians have turned to *Mother Earth* and tried to formulate a spiritual search which is nature and earth-centred. Ecofeminists are at the forefront of the ecology and ecospirituality movements. They have challenged traditional philosophy and theology by advocating a holistic understanding and epistemology with recognition of the spiritual interconnectedness of all of creation and co-responsibility for our world.[45] Ecofeminists have combined a critique of the destructiveness of patriarchal attitudes to nature and women, with an affirmation of a spiritual search which is nature-earth centred rather than anthropocentric. Ecotheologian and Catholic Priest, Thomas Berry argues that:

> The greatest support for the feminist, anti-patriarchal movement can
> be found in the ecological movement…What has become progressively
> clear is the association of the feminine issue with the ecological issue.[46]

Ariel Salleh maintains that:

> Ecofeminism confronts not only social institutions and practices, but
> the language and logics by which Western patriarchy constructs its
> relation to nature. In doing so, it has already travelled a long way down
> the very same road that deep ecological opponents of
> anthropocentricism are looking for.[47]

Ecospirituality

ECOSPIRITUALITY HAS BEEN ARGUED to be more important as a movement than any one of the great world religions. Ecospirituality is the experience of the *Divine Presence* or *Divine Reality* in the natural world.

This yearning for and returning to humankind's first religious awakening is a recent re-recognition of a timeless truth – and on these terms it is a recent development in the history of spirituality. *Ecospirituality, Gaia spirituality, Nature-earth spirituality* or *Nature-mysticism* are all new terms for this recent development.

Wayne Teasdale is one who maintains that ecospirituality and the Green Movement have emerged out of the negative results of modern industrial society. The destruction of the natural world has reawakened a passion for wilderness consciousness and nature-mysticism which is really a sort of spiritual or inner illumination. "It is the ability to perceive the Presence of the Divine immanent in the natural world"; and this is, as Evelyn Underhill tells us, "an overpowering apprehension".[48]

Teasdale concludes that ecospirituality is the most important development of the twentieth century, ranking it in significance to the discovery of the printing press and the Copernican Revolution. It brings a shift in paradigm, which brings with it a revolution in human consciousness. Teasdale maintains:

> Eco-spirituality is singularly more significant, as a movement, than any
> one of the great world religions, when regarded from the larger
> perspective of the earth process.[49]

A Sea-Change In Science

NEW EMERGENCE AND COMPLEXITY SCIENCE (Postmodern Science) also recognizes spirituality. Indeed, there has been a sea-change in science, for while spirituality has made a return in 'secular' society, science itself has become less materialist, reductionist, mechanistic and deterministic. For example theoretical biologist and complexity theory pioneer Stuart Kauffman notes that the "process of reinventing the sacred requires a fresh understanding of science that takes into account complexity theory and the idea of emergence. It will require a shift from reductionism, the way of thinking that still dominates our scientific world view."[50]

James Lovelock, Lynn Margulis, Humberto Maturana and Francisco Varela, Rupert Sheldrake, David Bohm, Roger Sperry and John Hitchcock are just a few of the more notable scientists who have challenged the traditional axioms of science, revolutionising perception of the world in such a way that the spiritual and the immaterial are allowed a foot in the door. The blurring of mind and matter, or spirit and matter, challenges the materialist and reductionist, mechanistic science of the modern era – advocates of which have separated off and marginalised the concept of 'spirit', often relegating it to the realm of formal, traditional and archaic religion.

The modernist view of an objective science which discovers Truth by examining what is 'out there' – hence the material and empirical world – has been further undermined by questions from biologists about the independent nature of cognition. Biologists and neurophysiologists Maturana and Varela argue that the act of cognition does not simply mirror objective reality "out there". Cognition is an active process, rooted in our biological structure, by which we actually create our world of experience through our coexistence. In arguing thus, they walk on the razor's edge, eschewing the extremes of representationalism (objectivism) and solipsism (idealism).[51] This new view of the world is relational and holistic.

Arguably, a new postmodern science is called for with new tools required for the description of this reality. Indeed, quantum physicist David Bohm, argued in 1988 for a "Postmodern Science and a Postmodern World".[52] For Bohm, a postmodern science would not separate matter and consciousness; meaning and value are as much integral aspects of the world as they are of us.[53] Elsewhere Bohm has proposed that the workings of the subatomic world only make sense if we assume the existence of other more complex non-local levels of reality beyond the quantum.[54] The level in which we live, where the particles appear to be separate, he called the 'explicate order' – but behind this is a deeper reality, in which separateness dissolves; and he called this the 'implicate order'

Roger Sperry summed up the changes in science in the latter part of the twentieth century and maintained that the prospects for uniting science and religion are brightened by recently changed views of consciousness and mind-body interaction.[55] In essence, Sperry's argument is that when the molecules and atoms of our world are seen to be moved by higher level forces that are not reducible in principle to the fundamental forces of physics – then mental, vital and spiritual forces, long excluded and denounced by materialist philosophy, are reinstated in non-mystical form.

Sperry's concepts of spirituality and theology are broad and not equated with traditional religious institutions. Sperry concludes:

> ...a naturalistic, scientific, or pantheistic theology is seen to yield a moral framework and outlook that has new credibility, satisfying spiritual and esthetic appeal and at the same time promotes values that would appear to be of the type needed to counter current global trends toward worsening world conditions.[56]

A broad concept of spirituality, unconfined to conventional religions is also held by quantum physicist John Hitchcock. In (1991) *The Web of the Universe: Jung, the "new physics" and human spirituality,* Hitchcock states that scientists can no longer ignore spirituality because spirit is inherently within matter; "...our "models" evolve toward greater and greater depth and subtlety. The case, as we now understand it, amounts to a *spiritual imperative*, even for physics itself."[57] Hitchcock also argues that:

> With the new visibility of the dimension of spirit in the atom, we can now see that from the point of view of physics, the physicist cannot avoid dealing with spirit, but must take account of the spirit aspect of spirit-matter, its patterning and dynamism. We don't any longer have the *intellectual luxury* of cutting spirit off from "matter" *if* we are part of the natural realm. A physicist will avoid doing anything intentionally mysterious with "spirit," but we also recognise that our "models" evolve toward greater and greater depth and subtlety. The case, as we now understand it, amounts to a *spiritual imperative*, even for physics itself.[58]

A new postmodern science has opened up the concept of spirit within matter and behind matter.

Inner Spirituality

WHILE TWENTIETH CENTURY behavioural psychology denies the existence of spirituality, soul and even consciousness, in line with scientific positivism,[59] there is a long historical tradition of locating spirituality or 'God' within the individual, in both psychology and religion – hence Jungian depth and archetypal psychology, world mythology, Gnosticism, Buddhism, Western and Eastern mysticism and the ancient primal and polytheistic religions of the world.

Depth and archetypal psychology maintain the idea of spirituality as being inner, inherent in the mind, or intrinsic to the psyche or soul. The Swiss psychiatrist Carl Jung (1875-1961), one of the greatest explorers of the human mind and a life-long student of world religions, both historical and cultural – is more than any other Western thinker in recent times associated with the search for *inner spirituality*. His thinking spans both modernism and postmodernism. English writer and broadcaster J.B Priestly (1894-1984), wrote of Jung in the *Sunday Telegraph*:

> He was on a giant scale...he was a master physician of the soul in his insights, a profound sage in his conclusions. He is also one of Western

Man's great liberators.[60]

Perceiving 'spirituality as intrinsic to the psyche' is both a recent phenomenon as well as having its roots in antiquity. However it has never been a mainstream focus of religion in the monotheistic West – and it is outside the orthodox religious establishments that it is again being seriously considered. Donald Broadribb argues that 'God' is increasingly being seen in terms of inner experience and process.

> In line with the more introverted religious philosophies of the East to
> which many Westerners are turning, "God" has come to be understood
> more and more as an inner experience and less and less as an
> identifiable "object" existing apart from the individual.[61]

Both Jung and the Gnostics of the early Christian period saw spirituality as an intrinsic property of the psyche. Self-exploration at the deepest levels, both believed, leads to spiritual wakening. In fact, "a true spiritual experience may be one of the most basic drives in the psyche, and may even be an essential psychological need."[62] Curtis Smith summarises Jung's view that "the human position is supreme, with the psyche and its realization serving as the basis of religious meaning."[63] To realise the psyche is to realise one's interconnectedness with all things:

> At the farthest reaches of the self-realization process the boundary
> between psyche and world blurs to the point of extinction, so that
> rather than an impenetrable wall separating psyche and world, psyche
> and world appear as points on a continuum, forming an indivisible
> whole. For Jung, therefore human existence is simultaneously universal
> and particular... to realize the self is to realize one's interconnectedness
> with all things.[64]

For Jung *all* religious experience is psychic in origin. While he is arguably the twentieth century's greatest thinker on religion and spirituality as grounded in the psyche, and hence of depth or imaginative psychology, he is not the only thinker to link spirituality with the psyche. Even Freud (1856-1939), who made a devastating critique of religion on the "manifest" level as illusion, was on the "latent" level preoccupied with religion as mystery deep within the psyche.[65]

THE INTERIOR JOURNEY into the depths of the psyche in search for the ground of all being, is inherent to both mysticism and depth psychology. Even within the Western monotheistic religions of Judaism, Christianity and Islam, which were not originally mystical, there are schools of thought and prominent individuals who have emphasised the subjective experience. 'God' and the Pleroma (representing a map of the soul) were not external realities 'out there' but were to be found within. Karen Armstrong, for example, points out that the Gnostics "showed that many of the new converts to Christianity were not satisfied with the traditional idea of God which they had inherited from Judaism."[66] Hippolytus in the *Heresies* admonishes:

> Abandon the search for God and the creation and other matters of a
> similar sort. Look for him by taking yourself as the starting point.
> Learn who it is within you makes everything his own and says, My
> God, my mind, my thought, my soul, my body. Learn the sources of
> sorrow, joy, love, hate. Learn how it happens that one watches without
> willing, loves without willing. If you carefully investigate these matters,
> you will find him in yourself.[67]

By concentrating on the divine energy within, rather than the nature of an external God outside, the mystic was better able to 'untie the knots' within the psyche and take ownership of personal 'evil', or the unrealised shadowside which conflicts with the ego, as Jung defined it. This was rather similar to the psychoanalytic attempt to unlock complexes which impede mental health and fulfilled living. Karen Armstrong, theologian and a former nun, argues:

> One of the problems of ethical monotheism is that it isolates evil. Because
> we cannot accept the idea that there is evil in our God, there is a danger that
> we will not be able to endure it within ourselves. It can then be pushed
> away and made monstrous and inhuman. The terrifying image of Satan in
> Western Christendom was such a distorted projection.[68]

It is not hard to see that the mystic was often at odds with the certainties of mainstream and more dogmatic forms of religion. Since each individual had "had a unique experience of God, it followed that no one religion could express the whole of the divine mystery".[69] Donald Broadribb makes the point that:

> Judaism, Christianity and Islam in their main streams have at times
> during their history persecuted union mystics as heretics who deny the
> essential division between humanity and God, reserving the possible
> full union of human and divine for only one person (Jesus, in
> Christianity) or denying it altogether (as in Judaism and Islam).[70]

MYTHOLOGY which is a feature of primal religions, the pagan and the early matriarchal religions, has often been an attempt to explain the inner world of the psyche. However as Armstrong points out, the Gods and Goddesses of the myths were regarded as heathen, inferior and a challenge to the supremacy of the monotheistic God of the prophets of Israel:

> The prophets had declared war on mythology: their God was active in
> history and in current political events rather than in the primordial
> sacred time of myth.[71]

Mythology was reasserted however when some monotheists turned to mysticism. Inadvertantly or not, the mystics reissued the challenge to the supremacy of a monotheistic God idealised in dogmatic and politically orientated religious traditions. The mystical experience of "God" has characteristics common to all faiths and hence it tends to pull down the barriers separating religions. Armstrong further describes the mystical experience as being subjective, involving an interior journey.

> [It is] not a perception of an objective fact outside the self: it is
> undertaken through the image-making part of the mind – often called
> the imagination – rather than through the more cerebral, logical
> faculty. Finally, it is something that the mystic creates in himself or
> herself deliberately: certain physical or mental exercises yield the final
> vision; it does not always come upon them unawares.[72]

Both Freud and Jung turned to the myths of the ancients to explain the inner world of the psyche and the unconscious.

The American Joseph Campbell's (1904-1987) work in the study of world comparative mythology and comparative religion, also has strong affinities with Jung and depth psychology. As Armstrong points out, the current enthusiasm for psychoanalysis in the West can be seen as a desire for some kind of mysticism because there are arresting similarities between the two disciplines.[73]

Psyche or Soul?

DEPTH PSYCHOLOGY, the modern field whose interest is in the unconscious levels of the psyche – that is, the deeper meanings of the soul – is itself no modern term. According to James Hillman, Jung is:

> ...the immediate ancestor in a long line that stretches back through
> Freud, Dilthy, Coleridge, Schelling, Vico, Ficino, Plotinus, and Plato to
> Heraclitus – and with even more branches which have yet to be traced.
> Heraclitus lies near the roots of this ancestral tree of thought, since he
> was the earliest to take psyche as his ancestral first principle, to imagine
> the soul in terms of flux and to speak of its depth without measure.[74]

Depth psychology is fundamentally an archetypal psychology of image. The Imagination is crucial to the psyche or soul. Hillman argues that in working towards a psychology of soul that is based in a psychology of image, suggests "both a poetic basis of mind and a psychology that starts neither in the physiology of the brain, the structure of language, the organisation of society, nor the analysis of behaviour, but in the processes of the imagination."[75] Ever since Heraclitus said "You could not discover the limits of the soul (psyche), even if you travelled every road to do so; such is the depth (bathun) of its meaning (logos)"[76] – the dimension of soul has been depth, not breadth or height. Soul is not on the surface or in superficialities but reaches down into hidden depths. For Hillman:

> The terms psyche and soul can be used interchangeably, although there is
> a tendency to escape the ambiguity of the word soul by recourse to the
> more biological, more modern psyche. Psyche is used more as a natural
> concomitant to physical life, perhaps reducible to it. Soul, on the other
> hand, has metaphysical and romantic overtones. It shares frontiers with
> religion.[77]

Hillman has a preference for 'soul' over 'psyche'; however Jung, after wavering between describing the object of psychology as 'seele' (soul) and 'psyche', eventually after 1933 settled for 'psyche'.[78] If it is accepted that there is an equivalence between 'psyche' and 'soul', the problem of how to define such a limitless concept remains. Hillman concludes that it resists all definition, as do all ultimate symbols, root metaphors for systems of human thought.[79] Jung himself never claimed to know what the psyche is. This was despite the fact that he "traced the origin of all religious traditions to the extraordinary creativity found in the human psyche".[80]

While it may not be possible to define 'psyche', an attempt can be made at a descriptive model. Jung proposed a model of the psyche based upon clinical psychiatric evidence and his very extensive study of cultures past and present. His model is that of a three-tiered structure correlated to different life-stages or ages – (1) an individual conscious ego (younger than our physical age); (2) a personal unconscious (going back to birth and prenatal experiences); (3) a collective unconscious (continuing the whole spiritual heritage of humankind's evolution born anew in the brain structure of every individual). Unlike the personal unconscious, which is made up of memories, the collective unconscious is made up of propensities or originating patterns which Jung called archetypes.

Archetypes

ARCHETYPES SUPPLY THE MOTIFS with which to structure the chaos of experience and they also structure the developing psyche itself. At this juncture it is important to briefly try and consider the nature of archetypes and, in particular, certain component archetypes of the psyche – for example the ego, persona, self, psychoid and God-image (Imago Dei) – which, as we shall see later, figure prominently in certain conceptions of landscape. Carl Jung argued that:

> the archetypes are as it were the hidden foundations of the conscious
> mind, or, to use another comparison, the roots which the psyche has
> sunk, not only in the earth in the narrower sense but in the world in
> general. Archetypes are systems of readiness for action, and at the same
> time images and emotions.[81]

However Jung's definitions of the 'collective unconscious' and 'archetypes' are fluid. Heisig claims that Jung "invokes for the archetypes at least three different theoretical functions: (1) as models for classifying psychological data, such archetypes are used as offering evidence helping to suggest the hypothesis of a collective unconscious (2) as specific innate patterns of psychic behaviour, they function as the formal causes of the psychic phenomena that constitute the data (3) as the primordial structures behind specific fantasy-images, they are said to embody the meaning of the processes of collective unconscious"[82] Whatever the precise and definitive definition of Jung's concepts of the 'collective unconscious' and 'archetypes', there is no doubt that he was the first immediate father of archetypal psychology. It is from Jung, for example, that comes the idea that:

the basic and universal structures of the psyche, the formal patterns of its relational modes, are archetypal patterns. These are like psychic organs, congenitally given with the psyche itself (yet not necessarily genetically inherited), even if somewhat modified by historical and geographic factors. These patterns or archai appear in the arts, religions, dreams, and social customs of all peoples, and they manifest spontaneously in mental disorders. For Jung they are anthropological and cultural, and also spiritual in that they transcend the empirical world of time and place.[83]

Hillman, who takes a rather postmodern line, emphasises the cultural, mythical, metaphorical and imaginal aspects of archetypes: "archetypal psychology's first links are with culture and imagination rather than with medical and empirical psychologies, which tend to confine psychology to the positivistic manifestations of the nineteenth-century condition of the soul".[84] For Hillman the irreducible language of archetypes is found in the "metaphorical discourse of myths", thus:

> To study human nature at its most basic level, one must turn to culture (mythology, religion, art, architecture, epic, drama, ritual) where these patterns are portrayed. The full implication of this move away from bio-chemical, socio-historical, and personal-behavioristic bases for human nature and toward the imaginative has been articulated by Hillman as "the poetic basis of mind". Support for the archetypal and psychological significance of myth, besides the work of Jung, comes from Ernest Cassirer, Karl Kerenyi, Erich Neumann, Heinrich Zimmer, Gilbert Durand, Joseph Campbell, and David Miller.[85]

The second immediate father of archetypal psychology is Henry Corbin (1903-1978), the French scholar, philosopher, mystic and translator/interpreter of early Islamic and pre-Islamic mystical thought.[86] And, as Hillman points out, the predecessors of Jung and Corbin go back to:

> …the Neoplatonic tradition via Vico and the Renaissance (Ficino), through Proclus and Plotinus, to Plato (Phaedo, Phaedrus, Meno, Symposium, Timaeus), and most recently to Heraclitus (Corbin's works on Avicenna, Ibn'Arabi, and Sohrawardi belong also to this tradition as does the work of Kathleen Raine on William Blake [1758-1835] and on Thomas Taylor, the English translator of the main writings of Plato and the Neoplatonists.[87]

The Psychoid Archetype

AT A DEEP LEVEL the human psyche or soul merges with the outer world. In this Jungian depth psychology accords with deep ecology in recognising that nature is a part of 'the self.[88] It was Jung who coined the term 'psychoid unconscious' to account for the unitary nature of psyche and world.[89] It is rooted in the unconscious, rather than being unified by an external metaphysical being or reality. More precisely:

the "psychoid unconscious" can be considered a further gradation of the unconscious where self and world meet, and where all opposites are reconciled. In the final analysis, then, the individual becomes the linchpin between the micro- and macrocosm.[90]

Jung himself argues that the psyche, "which we have a tendency to take for a subjective fact, is really a fact that extends outside of us, outside of time, outside of space like children's dreams which are a summary of what will be their life's problem... Our psyche can function as though space did not exist. The psyche can thus be independent of space, of time and of causality... The archetype is outside of me as well as in me. The psychoid archetype only resembles the psyche: animals, plants, the wind behave like us."[91]

"A Process and a Goal"

WHEN SPIRITUALITY IS INTRINSIC to the psyche from the point of view of Jung and other theorists, for example the physicist John Hitchcock – the realisation of the self, or individuation, becomes paramount and spirituality is both a process and a goal. Spirituality is a distillation and a refinement of spirit-matter. Jung argues that the origins of religious experience are in the human psyche itself.[92]

Heisig argues that Jung did not at any time claim that he could "prove" or "disprove" the existence of a transcendent God and in fact his personal views on a transcendent God are largely a matter for speculation. Those who call him an atheist or a pantheist have some justification and support. "On the whole it seems that he saw God as an ultimately unknowable and uncontrollable power at work within, yet not coextensive with, the collective unconscious in its widest sense".[93]

Dourley puts it more strongly: for Jung a conception of God as "wholly other" than humanity is "wholly inconceivable" and "one of the major pathologizing features of the Western religious tradition. For it removes from the fabric of life itself the psychic energies which fund life, "or it projects the source of these energies beyond life into transcendent deities whose ability to lend energy to life is greatly impaired by the projection itself ".[94] God can not be seen as discontinuous or wholly transcendent to human consciousness. "Jung's psychology locates the origins of human historical religions and their symbolic content in the interplay between human consciousness and its unconscious generator and precedent."[95]

THIS HAS BEEN ATTACKED as undermining religion. It challenges the foundations of an external creation and redemption found in Judaism and Christianity and so Jung's dialogue with various representatives of orthodox and transcendentalist positions both Christian and non-Christian was not always happy.[96] For Jung the deepest spiritual insights cannot be defined or proved, only experienced.[97] The God image, or Imago Dei, comes from within the psyche. It is an archetype.

> The idea of God is an absolutely necessary psychological function of an irrational nature, which has nothing whatever to do with the question of God's existence. The human intellect can never answer this question, still less give any proof of God. Moreover, such proof is superfluous, for the

idea of an all-powerful divine Being is present everywhere, unconsciously if not consciously, because it is an archetype.[98]

THE GOD-IMAGE ARCHETYPE displays the struggle of the psyche for self-realisation; [99] self-realisation is the spiritual goal for both the individual and all of humanity. It is an inner imperative. The realization of the self is more than a neutral therapeutic goal; it is the religious goal of Jung's psychotherapeutic system. Individuation is both a process and a goal.[100]

Curtis Smith argues that for Jung "the ultimate authority in life is not an external one – be it church or state – but an internal one. In this light the realization of the self is more than a pentultimate issue; rather, for Jung it is raised to the level of a religious concern for all of humanity".[101]

Again, the idea of 'spirituality' or 'the divine' within, is an ancient one. Jung held a very similar, if not identical, theory to the ancient Gnostics. As John Pennachio points out:

> Gnosis is defined as an intuitive process of knowing oneself. It is a
> series of secret mysteries and higher teachings maintaining that self-
> discovery at the deepest level is identical to knowing human destiny
> and God. Gnosticism took issue with institutionalized Christian dogma
> about the nature of the divine. For these reasons it was regarded as a
> Christian heresy and was systematically destroyed by the orthodox
> church in the early years of Christianity.[102]

WHAT THE CHRISTIANS regard as literal, the Gnostics regard as symbolic. Both Jung and the Gnostics held that ultimate knowing or truth only emerges as a result of an inner journey: "As is true for Jung, crucifixion, suffering and resurrection are interpreted as symbolic milestones on the way to spiritual enlightenment."[103]

For the Gnostics and Jung the inner journey and search for the centre is a religious quest and a search for the divine. Thus Pennachio concludes that "for Jung and the Gnostics spirituality is an intrinsic property of the psyche".[104]

This view that spirituality is inherent in the psyche, hence God or Gods are archetypes inherent within our psyche, constitutes an enormous challenge to monotheism.[105] Both the foundational and factual historicity and the external objectivity of monotheistic patriarchal religion is challenged by the primacy of the view that spirituality is inherent in the psyche.

ULTIMATELY, SPIRITUALITY is sourced in the psyche and is intrinsic to the psyche. The idea of spirituality as within, or 'intrinsic to the psyche (soul)' and its archetypes, is both a recent and a very ancient conception, which has always posed a serious challenge to monotheistic religions and theology.

In the second half of the book it will be shown that spirituality manifests in our landscapes phenomenologically via our Gods and archetypes. First, however, what is landscape? It is to an exploration of the 'landscapes' of the geographers that we now turn.

TWO

Landscapes of Geography

Although the land exists, 'the scape is a projection of human consciousness, an image received'.

– Erlich

Mentally or physically, we frame the view, and our appreciation depends on our frame of mind.

– J. Douglas Porteous

Landscape is not merely the world we see, it is a construction, a composition of the world. Landscape is a way of seeing the world.

– Denis Cosgrove

GEOGRAPHY IS ABOVE ALL the study of landscape. For geographers, the idea of landscape has undergone change and this is especially so from the mid-twentieth century onwards. Landscape has developed from a purely positivist and modernist, empiricist based concept, towards a cultural, humanist, existential, perceptual and postmodernist exploration. Landscape is now recognised by geographers as an *inner* perceptual conception.

The case here is that landscape is a *'focus of perception'* . By *'focus of perception'* is meant a focus in *seeing, feeling, being* and *relating* - and as such it is intrinsic to the psyche. The literary, the existential, the phenomenal and the *imaginal*, in the archetypal depths of the psyche, are all recognised by postmodern geographers as relevant. The academic study of 'geography of religion' has become a geography of landscape spirituality.

Geographers' Landscapes

IN THE FIRST HALF of the twentieth century geographers sought to establish universal laws such as those found in physics or chemistry in their science. Environmentalism was earlier rejected because it was regarded as insufficiently scientific.[1]

Eminent geographer Denis Cosgrove points out that early geographers and teachers like Freidrich Ratzel (1844-1904), William Morris Davis (1850-1934) and Andrew John Herbertson (1865-1915), as well as methodologists who followed them such as Alfred Hettner (1859-1941), Richard Hartshorne (1899-1992) and Carl Sauer (1889-1975), all regarded geography primarily as a *positive science.*[2]

Landscape as Object of Scientific Enquiry

IN 1925 CARL SAUER advanced the idea of landscape as a "static, determinate object of scientific enquiry".[3] However, eventually even those geographers keen to develop landscape as a "strictly scientific term" found it necessary "to recognize the subjective meaning implied by artistic and poetic usage of landscape".[4]

Cultural geography was an attempt to recognise the affective dimension of landscape. However some geographers argued that this was insufficient because it ignored the symbolic dimensions of landscape.[5]

"Ideologically-Charged"

COSGROVE ARGUED that landscape was an ideological concept; indeed, with respect to 'landscape, "we are dealing with an ideologically-charged and very complex cultural product".[6]

During the 1970s several geographers began to reorient the subject away from the social sciences and towards the humanities.[7] Humanistic geography examined the philosophical premises of geographical inquiry "at a time when the discipline was still preoccupied with technique and method" rather than with more fundamental questions of meaning, or epistemology.[8] There was also a focus on *landscape,* on *ideas of Nature* and on *human consciousness* itself within the longer tradition of human inquiry.

Humanist Geography Flowered

AS J. DOUGLAS PORTEOUS puts it "Humanistic geography, as the movement became known, lurked underground, to flower in the late 1970s".[9]

At the same time, the prevailing positivism was criticised for suppressing subjectivity, overlooking intentionality, and emphasising human passivity. Theoretical constructs associated with positivist modes of research were criticised for avoiding discussion of experiential relationships with the environment.

Geographers such as Yi-Fu Tuan argued that mainstream geography neglected human consciousness and the internal sensations and perceptions that contribute to experience and by which a person makes sense of their environment.[10] However humanist geographers saw their approach as complementary to the mainstream of geography. They did not deny the values of positivist approaches but sought to go further. Porteous put it this way:

> One of the approaches of humanistic geography involves the critical assessment of imaginative literature for its insights into the relationship between inner and outer landscapes. This approach is of vital importance to our understanding of ourselves, for while much literature seems particularist and place-specific ... it almost always, on perusal, comes to reveal the universal within the particular. The test of validity, always, is the question: Is this true for me?[11]

This pointed to other developments, as we shall see – hence to an existential approach to landscape and a move from the modernist, positivist view of landscape to a postmodern orientation.[12] Inherent to postmodern geography and postmodern landscape conception is the exploration of perception. Perceptual geography is now recognized as an important disciplinary trend within geography and landscape conception.[13]

A 'Way of Seeing'

PETER JACKSON concluded in 1989, that within the landscape tradition the emphasis is now on the idea of landscape as a social construction or a 'way of seeing', rather than being reducible to a series of physical traits.[14] He cited Cosgrove's definition of landscape and argued that there are potentially as many ways of seeing as there are eyes to see: "A reconstituted cultural geography must therefore be prepared to examine the multiplicity of landscapes that these plural conceptions of culture inform".[15]

As a case in point, Barry Lopez describes the mobile and changing nature of landscapes in a nation's history as follows:

> [T]he narrative direction that a nation's history takes is amenable to revision; and the landscapes in which history unfolds are both real, that is, profound in their physical effects on mankind, and not real, but mere projections, artifacts of human perception.[16]

TO ILLUSTRATE from a New Zealand perspective – the traditional Maori view of the landscape as being 'alive', and as a defining matrix of personal identity, was quite different from the view of the first European New Zealanders. Some prominent first Europeans to New Zealand were notable for viewing the landscape as something objective – 'out there' to be tamed, civilised, cultivated in order to fit a European ideal and so exploited, not only for a personal living, but for amassing wealth and profit. Several generations later, when Europeans became Pakeha New Zealanders, some regret was felt at the early colonialist exploitation of the indigenous landscape and the destruction of forests. The natural New Zealand landscape was cherished and sought out for spiritual sustenance. In particular, this 'way of seeing' was expressed by the writers and poets of the 1930s and 1940s; mountaineers, trampers and skiers have for the most part continued their long tradition of revering the natural landscape.

Today there are conflicting perceptions of the New Zealand landscape. Commercial interests with multi-national backing and government departments including the Department of Conservation and both Pakeha and Maori, have financial interests in the commodification of natural landscape and nature experience – hence the tourist dollar, mining, native timber-felling, real estate development, power generation, thirsty dairying in inappropriate areas of dry grassland, leading to depletion and pollution of rivers and waterways, and financially motivated immigration consultancies. The natural landscape, including National Parks, is not infrequently seen in primarily objective terms, as a resourse to be utilised to maximise corporate and government profit.

In opposition to all this are many New Zealanders – Maori, Pakeha and new immigrants – who have lived deeply in and felt intensely for this land, sometimes for generations and sometimes not. They feel a spiritual affinity and identity with the indigenous, pristine landscape and wish to conserve and restore what remains. In particular these New Zealanders wish to keep our National Parks unspoiled: unexploited commercially, aesthetically and environmentally unpolluted, and in the spirit in which they were originally gifted and conceived by our Maori and British colonial ancestors – as loved landscapes with old and humble huts of unique value in and of themselves; spiritual reservoirs (not to be paid for but our birthright), to be approached with reverence and care by all New Zealanders and visitors regardless of race. These New Zealanders wish to safe-guard and care-take the intrinsic values of mountains, flowing rivers, the pristine waterways, lakes, wetlands and the quality of the soils, flora and fauna in their natural landscapes. In this landscape they perceive their soul as New Zealanders.[17]

Perceptual Geography

TODAY, WITHIN THE GEOGRAPHER'S profession, the concept of landscape is recognized as a changing and mobile one. Moreover, amongst geographers landscape is increasingly regarded as a perceptual concept and a multiplicity of landscapes are recognised. The idea of landscape as a 'way of seeing' has overtaken the positivist idea of landscape as reducible to a series of objective physical traits. As Cosgrove has remarked:

> Landscape is not merely the world we see, it is a construction, a
> composition of the world. Landscape is a way of seeing the world.[18]

And Yi-Fu Tuan notes whereas "in the early 1960s a new way of doing human-cultural geography emerged… it now goes generally by the name of perceptual".[19]

In the 1960s perceptual geography came of age. David Lowenthal, for example, argued that :

> Essential perception of the world , in short, embraces every way of
> looking at it, conscious and unconscious, blurred and distinct,
> objective and subjective, inadvertent and deliberate, literal and
> schematic. Perception itself is never unalloyed: sensing, thinking,
> feeling, and believing are simultaneous independent processes.[20]

Landscape – a 'Focus of Perception'

LANDSCAPE IS a *'focus of perception'* and by this is meant a *focus in seeing, feeling, being* and *relating*. Landscape as a 'focus of perception' is a manifestation of personal and collective creativity and imagination, which originates in the psyche.

Denis Cosgrove comes close to describing landscape as a 'focus of perception' when he concludes that:

> landscape is a social and cultural product, a way of seeing projected on
> to the land and having its own techniques and compositional forms; a
> restrictive way of seeing that diminishes alternative modes of
> experiencing our relations with nature.[21]

A 'focus of perception' excludes to some extent other ways of seeing and experiencing the landscape which are not in focus. Like horse blinkers one sees, feels, has being in, and relates to what is focused upon and ignores what is out of intentional focus.

A 'focus of perception' is relational rather than objective, originates in and is mediated by the inner psyche of the individual, and is a manifestation of personal and collective creativity and imagination.

Pre-verbal, Universal, Landscape Perception

GIVEN THAT LANGUAGE is inextricably tied up with our perception of landscape, at this point one could ask, along with the deconstructionists, whether it is language which ultimately creates our perception of landscape and our 'being' in landscape. Or is the landscape - in which we have 'being' – based on something more fundamental than language?

It was philosopher Martin Heidegger (1889-1976) who referred to language as "the house of being".[22] In support of Heidegger, Saroj Chawla suggests there is "a close relationship between language, philosophy, and our handling of the natural environment".[23] For example, in comparison with Amerindian languages, English language habits are not very conducive to a holistic and careful attitude towards the natural environment. English as the 'language of technology', is now being adopted by other cultures and becoming a world language. If any change is to come about in our attitudes to the natural environment "it will have to be at the level of perception, and at the linguistic level, such perception is reflected in language".[24]

Sallie King, however, goes further. She suggests the reality of a non-verbal cognition and unmediated perception, which is independent of a verbal-cultural tradition:

> The sensorial experience of listening to music, as of drinking coffee,
> illustrates that there is something even in mundane experience that
> eludes the grasp of language: our ordinary lives are full of qualities
> beyond the denotative reach of our words... In coffee and music we
> have seen the reality of non-verbal cognition, we have seen the
> impossibility of the verbal-cultural tradition producing the
> experience.[25]

King suggests that we need to examine further the way in which "reflective consciousness inspects non-verbal knowledge and issues its report".[26] She also suggests that phenomenological data for such inquiry can be found in both mystical and secular experiences. Furthermore, the universality of pre-verbal landscape perception is shown in our ability to imagine and enter into others' perceptions of landscape, even that of animals. As Lopez points out:

> In recent years the writing of people like Joseph Campbell and Claude Levi-Strauss has illuminated the great panorama of human perceptual experience, pointing up not only the different approaches we take to the background that contains us (the landscape) but the similarities we seem to share.[27]

We can apprehend, understand, and imagine other human and even animal perceptions of the landscape, even those which diverge markedly from our predominant 'focus of perception'. Lopez makes a plea for tolerance for perceptions of landscape other than our own:

> It seemed clear to me that we need tolerance in our lives for the worth of different sorts of perception, of which the contrasting *Umwelten* of the animals on the island are a reminder. And we need a tolerance for the unmanipulated and unpossessed landscape. But what I came to see, too, was that we need to understand the relationship between tolerance and different sorts of wealth, how a tolerance for the unconverted things of the earth is intertwined with the substance of a truly rich life.[28]

While, as Takeshi Yamagishi has pointed out, the individual's existential landscape may be a 'primary landscape'[29], our ability to understand, imagine and enter into other's perceptions of landscape is universal.

Direct, primal, feeling and mystical perception of the "unmanipulated and unpossessed landscape" is, as Lopez argues, the substance of a truly rich life.

TO SUMMARISE, landscape is not something totally objective 'out there', independent of us and our 'being-in-the-world'. We generally bring a cultural, experiential and linguistic component to our 'focus of perception' and *our being* in landscape. However, it can be argued that there are some direct primal, feeling and mystical experience aspects to perception and perception of landscape, which are unmediated by language and prior to the subject-object split. This is not to deny that such experience can not be described later, however inadequately, and moulded to fit in with our existing epistemology and cultural perception of landscape. The implication of all this is that landscape perception can be at a deep level, unmediated, potentially universal and therefore not totally culturally determined. As we shall see, this type of perception is archetypal.

A Focus in Seeing

COSGROVE FAMOUSLY ARGUED that landscape is 'a way of seeing' and the way people see their world is a vital clue to the way they understand that world and their relationships with it.[30] Landscape denotes the external world mediated through the personal subjective experience. Landscape is not merely the world we see, it is also a construction and composition of that world. Landscape is both object and subject. Cosgrove maintains that:

> it is in the origins of landscape as a way of seeing the world that we discover its links to broader historical structures and processes and are able to locate landscape study within a progressive debate about society and culture.[31]

Porteous reaches a similar conclusion:

> We frame the view…(for)when we consider landscape, we are almost always concerned with a visual construct. Landscape is something we look at or imagine as a visual metaphor… Although the land exists, 'the scape is a projection of human consciousness, an image received' (Erlich 1987). Mentally or physically, we frame the view, and our appreciation depends on our frame of mind.[32]

However this 'focus in seeing' or apprehending the landscape is an inexact and imperfect science at best – if indeed it can be called a science at all. It is more of a mystery and a creative dialogue. As Lopez states:

> Our perceptions are colored by preconception and desire. The physical landscape is an unstructured abode of space and time and is not entirely fathomable; but this does not necessarily put us at a disadvantage in seeking to know it… believing landscapes to be mysterious aggregations, it becomes easier to approach them.[33]

A Focus in Feeling

LANDCAPE IS a *focus in feeling*. For environmental psychologist Roger Ulrich, environmental perception is not restricted to vision but is multimodal and *feeling, or affect,* is central:

> Affect is central to conscious experience and behavior in any environment, whether natural or built, crowded or unpopulated. … because virtually no meaningful thoughts, actions, or environmental encounters occur without affect … an affective state is an important indicator of the nature and significance of a person's ongoing interaction with an environment.[34]

Moreover there is no evidence that feelings are preceded by cognitive processes. Ulrich argues that there is mounting empirical support for the view that "many affects are essentially precognitive and constitute the initial level of response to environment."[35] Ulrich maintains that while culture is an important and significant variable influencing aesthetic reactions, it has perhaps been overstated.[36] He argues that "there is no evidence that fundamental perceptual and cognitive processes vary between cultures" and further that "emotions are universal and have the same qualities across different cultures".[37]

Ulrich's conclusion that "feelings, not thoughts, come first in environmental encounters, and the observer's initial feeling reaction shapes subsequent cognitive events"[38] has been supported by the research of others.[39] Cross-cultural, universal, pre-verbal, precognitive emotive perception is inherent to archetypes. This is significant because as we shall see, it points the way forward to an archetypal analysis of landscape.

A Focus in Being – Existential Landscapes

THE IDEA THAT LANDSCAPE is a personal 'focus of being' - rather than simply existing statically and objectively out there - finds a philosophical home in existentialism.[40]

The geographer Yi-Fu Tuan puts it this way: under "existentialism" the geographer seeks meaning in the landscape as he would in literature, because it is a repository of human striving:[41]

> The landscape itself can hold no deep meaning for us unless we can
> discern in it traces of "fate" and "destiny", that is, unless we can see in it
> the effects of deterministic and probabilistic laws; or unless the landscape
> is – like an old letter – revelatory of the people who "wrote" it.[42]

Tuan concludes that in searching the landscape for meaning, this is the existentialist realm and the method most appropriate is phenomenological.[43] Like the phenomenologist, the geographer's quest – broadly conceived – is the understanding of "man-in-the-world".[44]

Geographer Lowenthal signals a profound difference between the external, individual observer and the insider-participant.[45] The integrity of the existential insider's experience is at risk of being denied if subjected to classification and analysis of rigorous scientific enquiry.

On the importance of 'being' in perception and epistemology, philosopher Mark Johnson argues for "embodied understanding" in that we "are never separated from our bodies and from forces and energies acting upon us to give rise to our understanding (as our "being-in-the-world")".[46]

TAKESHI YAMAGISHI DESCRIBES the insider existentialist view of landscape well:

> Human beings are not merely inside landscapes; they are living within
> landscapes. Not only do our life histories include various landscapes, but
> our bodies and personalities have also internalized these landscapes....
> A person who does not have a landscape that is remembered, retained in

the mind, and recalled, is a person who has almost lost his self and his life history.[47]

A drastic change in landscape can lead to a sense that we have lost our home. An individual's life history is greatly influenced by the social experience and landscape experience and these form an integral part of his or her identity.

Landscape is an essential referent in the understanding of the life history of an individual. In this regard Yamagishi argues for a "primary landscape", meaning "a landscape that forms the center of one's foundation, perspective, and orientation; such a landscape is the primary landscape"; thus the "primary landscape is the landscape that offers us a valid point of view and perspective when we attempt to understand a particular region or place, the daily lives of the local people and their life histories".[48]

Furthermore he notes the propensity to speak "about 'my' landscape as inseparable from 'my' viewpoint, 'my' body, 'my' everyday experience, as if landscape were *myself*, nothing more, nothing less".[49]

Yamagishi concludes that landscape is our basis of being; in our life histories, our dreams, our dramas there is no better book, no better mirror, than the landscape itself.[50]

A Focus in Relating – Saint-Exupery's Geography Lesson

GEOGRAPHERS HAVE LONG maintained that landscape involves relationship and interaction. However this constitutes a challenge for the epistemology, or theory of knowledge and meaning, of *modernism*, *objectivism* and *scientism*.

Inherent in *relating to* and *interacting with* the landscape are questions concerning certain traditional dualisms, which have been of ongoing concern to geographers.

The pioneering aviator, poet and award winning French writer Saint-Exupery (1900-1944) had a passionate if short life. His engagement with landscape is used by geographer Edmunds V. Bunkse as an illustration for criticism of traditional empiricist-based geography that otherwise ignores the personal and subjective relationship with landscape.

> Saint-Exupery's geography lesson... is seen in the context of the dehumanization of landscapes and lives by Cartesian-inspired science... (He) has purposely juxtaposed individual sensory, pragmatic, and poetic encounters with landscapes against the generalities and abstractions of geographers, which he clearly finds meaningless and insignificant.[51]

Bunkse argues that it illustrates a problem which still concerns geographers, namely "the seemingly unbridgeable dualism of the general, the abstract, the aggregate, the nomothetic, versus the specific, concrete, individual, idiosyncratic, and poetic".[52]

Bunkse makes an appeal for reaching into the *imagination* to seek out the spirit of landscapes.[53] This emphasis on the imagination is essentially a new postmodern epistemological perspective. This is shown by Saint-Exupery's geography lesson which is an "alarmed concern for the rapid dehumanization of modern lives and landscapes," and the loss of spirituality, particularly in mechanistic landscapes.[54]

While Saint-Exupery loved the airplanes he flew and saw the airplane as representing the best results of a technology based on Cartesian science that was transforming the world, the rapid mechanization of human life appalled him:

> Many human-oriented values were being lost in the wave of increasing mechanization. The greatest loss by far was that of spirituality – not spirituality in the context of formal religions but in the general sense of the ineffable and mysterious, of transcendence attached to things and events.[55]

For Saint-Exupery, "spirituality develops through the quest of being above and beyond materials" and "spiritual meaning is found in seizing the particular from the general"; as when his car broke down in North Africa during the war and he was forced to travel by cart:

> Those olive trees were no longer just so many trees along the road, whizzing past at 130 kilometers an hour. I now saw them in their natural rhythm, slowly making olives. The sheep no longer merely served to reduce one's speed, they came alive. They ate and gave wool and the grass once again had meaning, since they grazed on it.[56]

SAINT-EXUPERY'S PLEA FOR SPIRITUALITY and morality in human life and landscape came during World War II and his fight against Nazism. However he was less concerned with the immediate enemy than with what would happen after the war was won.

Bunkse says of Saint-Exupery that he "wanted to make certain that human life and landscape be framed as much by the poetics of arts-and-letters humanism as by Cartesian science. And that is indeed his geography lesson for geographers".[57]

Saint-Exupery had a dynamic model of civilisation that he thought he was fighting for during the Second World War. It was developed in an unmailed letter to General X, shortly before Saint-Exupery's last mission over France:

> I don't care if I am killed in the war. But what will remain of what I have loved?…What is valuable is a certain ordering of things. Civilization is an invisible tie, because it has to do not with things but with the invisible ties that join one thing to another in a particular way.[58]

When Saint-Exupery talks of 'invisible ties', similarities can be seen with Martin Buber's 'world of relation' and the two primary modes of relating, *I-Thou* and *I-It*.

Bunkse asks "How does the modern milieu, its landscape, and technocracy affect human beings in the short run, and by implication, in the long run of human evolution?"[59] It is to this question we return later when we consider archetypal landscapes and in particular the technological/materialist landscape.

ARCTIC EXPLORER Barry Lopez, who has lived and hunted with Eskimos, has noted differences in the way in which our modern technological/materialist culture relates to the Arctic landscape - *objectively as a landscape for exploitation* of resources - and the relationship that the native Eskimo hunters have with their landscape. He describes his experience hunting with the Eskimo and the 'focus in relating' as follows:

> To hunt means to have the land around you like clothing. To engage in a wordless dialogue with it, one so absorbing that you cease to talk with your human companions. It means to release yourself from rational images of what something "means" and to be concerned only that it "is." And then to recognize that things exist only insofar as they can be related to other things. These relationships – fresh drops of moisture on tops of rocks at a river crossing and a raven's distant voice – become patterns. The patterns are always in motion.[60]

By contrast, Lopez argues, Western culture has tended to turn all elements of the natural world into objects.

> We have turned all animals and elements of the natural world into objects. We manipulate them to serve the complicated ends of our destiny. Eskimos do not grasp this separation easily, and have difficulty imagining themselves entirely removed from the world of animals. For many of them, to make this separation is analogous to cutting oneself off from light or water. It is hard to imagine how to do it.[61]

Lopez concludes that the depersonalization of relationships is a most confusing aspect of Western culture for the Eskimo to grasp.

ENVIRONMENTAL PSYCHOLOGIST Cindy Katz and geographer Andrew Kirby also address the issue of *relating* in environment and landscape perception.

They argue that the "externalisation of nature is built into our concepts of science";[62] that the perspective based on natural rationality "has insinuated itself into our lives, and has withdrawn from us the comprehension of nature within everyday life".[63]

Western science excludes and marginalises alternative epistemologies. Science's tenability and applications in dominant social practice are based on the assumption that "this world view evolves in isolation, that science is 'pure'... (however, in reality) ... science walks hand in hand with other representatives of domination".[64]

In point of fact, ever since the Enlightenment, "the narratives of science have been embedded in the social relations of capitalism within which projects are constructed in particular ways, unmistakably tied to the manipulation of nature".[65]   Within the ideology of Western advanced capitalism, Katz and Kirby conclude, it is attractive to construct nature as very different from ourselves. By encoding ourselves as a civil society *apart* we then "engage in the collective repression of universal nature and of ourselves as part of nature".[66]

Participatory, Poetic Landscapes

HUMANISTIC, EXISTENTIAL and postmodern geographers, who have questioned viewing the world through an objectivist epistemology, or theory of meaning – are supported by some Western philosophers, biologists, neurophysiologists, environmentalists; and East Asian philosophy, particularly Taoism and Buddhism. Here very briefly, are the arguments of some others who advocate meaning or an epistemology based on an active and *relational* process of perception and cognition.

OBJECTIVISM AS A 'GODS-EYE-VIEW' of reality independent of human understanding is opposed by philosophers Mark Johnson and Hilary Putnam. According to the Objectivist orientation, which is rooted deeply in the Western philosophical and cultural tradition, the world consists of objects that have properties which stand in relationships independent of human understanding. Human beings can have no significant bearing on the nature of meaning and rationality.[67] Johnson, like Putnam, argues for realism based on our mediated understanding of our experience. They argue that experience is an "organism-environment interaction". The organism and its environment are not independent and unrelated entities.[68] Johnson concludes that objectivity "does not require taking up God's perspective, which is impossible; rather, it requires taking up appropriately shared human perspectives that are tied to reality through our embodied imaginative understanding".[69]

Biologists Humberto Maturana and Francisco Varela reach very similar conclusions to Mark Johnson's "embodied understanding" by "offering a scientific study of cognition as a biological phenomenon" wherein "the extremes of representationalism (objectivism) and solipsism (idealism)" are eschewed.[70] The act of cognition does not simply mirror an objective reality "out there" – rather it is rooted in our biological structure and is an active process in which we actually create our world of experience through the process of living itself. We are "continuously immersed in a network of interactions, the results of which depend on history".[71]

Steve Odin observes that "the primacy accorded to relational 'field' over that of the 'substantial objects' implicit in the ecological world view is also at the heart of the organismic paradigm of nature in East Asian philosophy, especially Taoism and Buddhism".[72]

Aldo Leopold (1887-1948), environmentalist, scientist, ecologist, forester and writer of the classic 'A Sand Country Almanac' (1949) is widely regarded as establishing environmental ethics as a distinct branch of philosophy. His ethics arise from a "metaphysical presupposition that things in nature are not separate, independent, or substantial objects, but relational fields... the land is a single living organism wherein each part affects every other part".[73]

J. Baird Callicott an American philosopher of environment and ethics, follows the insights of Leopold and argues that "object-ontology is inappropriate to an ecological description of the natural environment. Living natural objects should be regarded as ontologically subordinate to "events" and/or "flow patterns" and/or "field patterns".[74]

THE *RELATIONAL FIELD* idea of environment or landscape, has been promoted by ecologists and some significant philosophers, East and West. In the Western philosophic tradition, English philosopher and mathematician, Alfred North Whitehead (1861-1947) was seminal with this view.

Modernism and hence objectivism was systematically challenged by Alfred North Whitehead. Regarded as one of the earliest postmodernists, Whitehead whose contribution to philosophy, mathematics and logic as well as metaphysics is "considered by many to be one of the great intellectual achievements of all time"[75] is known in particular for his *relational field view of reality*. A.N. Whitehead gave the field concept of nature implied by ecology its fullest systematic expression in his *process metaphysics* and *philosophy of organism*.

As Odin points out, Whitehead "elaborates a panpsychic vision of nature as a creative and aesthetic continuum of living field events arising through their causal relations to every other event in the continuum".[76] Odin argues that nature, in terms of the Gaia hypothesis, is "a synergistic ecosystem of symbiotic relationships" and this is the relational view of reality of many ecologists as well as much philosophy of East Asia based on Taoism and Buddhism.[77]

Polish philosopher Henryk Skolimowski is another one who argues for a new epistemology based on a "participatory concept of truth" wherein 'objectivity' "has become a myth which is pernicious and which we need to transcend".[78] He holds that there is "a close and inevitable relationship between the view of the cosmos of a given people (cosmology) and the system of knowledge of a given people (epistemology). One recapitulates the other, and is in the image of the other. Thus *the outer walls of the cosmos are the inner walls of the mind.*"[79] In other words, there is a close and inevitable relationship between the landscape 'focus of perception' of a given people and the system of meaning or knowledge (epistemology) of a given people.

For example, Lopez argues that the rational, scientific approach to land loses something profound; *rather the land is like poetry*. For instance:

> A Lakota woman named Elaine Jahner once wrote that what lies at the heart of the religion of hunting peoples is the notion that a spiritual landscape exists within the physical landscape. To put it another way, occasionally one sees something fleeting in the land, a moment when line, color, and movement intensify and something sacred is revealed, leading one to believe that there is another realm of reality corresponding to the physical one but different.
> In the face of a rational, scientific approach to the land, which is more widely sanctioned, esoteric insights and speculations are frequently overshadowed, and what is lost is profound. The land is like poetry: it is inexplicably coherent, it is transcendent in its meaning, and it has the

power to elevate a consideration of human life.[80]

The Quality of Relation

THE QUALITY OF RELATION, explored by the Jewish religious thinker Martin Buber, in the now classic *I and Thou*,[81] is relevant and to a large extent encapsulates the dualism which has for so long fascinated and preoccupied geographers – between subject and object, observer and phenomena observed, art and science, lifeworld (being-in-the-world), and the world of knowledge. The quality of relation is inherent in landscape 'focus of perception'.

MARTIN BUBER BEGINS his magisterial work thus: "The world is twofold for man in accordance with his twofold attitude. The attitude of man is twofold in accordance with the basic words he can speak".[82] There are two basic words (word pairs) or modes of existence, *I-Thou* (or *I-You*) and *I-It*. *I-Thou* can only be spoken with one's whole being; whereas *I-It* can never be spoken with one's whole being.[83] The quality of the *I-Thou* attitude or mode of existence is a very different quality of relation than that of *I-It*. In fact while *I-Thou* is described as the primary word of relation; *I-It* is better described as the primary word of experiencing and using.[84]

> While *I-Thou* is characterised by "mutuality, directness, presentness, intensity, and ineffability", *I-It* lacks mutuality. "It is always mediate and indirect and hence is comprehensible and orderable, significant only in connection and not in itself." The *Thou* of *I-Thou* and the *It* of *I-It* may equally well be a person or persons, an animal, a tree, objects of nature, a spirit or even God without a change in the primary word.[85]

What is important is the quality of relation, not the object. The quality of the *I-Thou* relation is reciprocity; there is a two-way attraction, mutuality of response, an encounter one with the other in genuine meeting and it "involves the whole of whatever is at each end of the poles of the encounter".[86] Geering observes that, for Buber:

> I responds to his or her Thou with emotions as well as with intellect – with body, mind and soul. The I responds, as we may be inclined to say, in a *fully personal* way. But in the I-It mode of existence the I does not respond with his or her whole. In particular it is the personal self which is not given. The I *uses* the It, treats It as his or her possession or as a tool. Where the I-Thou is personal, the I-It is impersonal. The I who says 'I-Thou' is not the I who says 'I-It'.[87]

But the quality of relation is not static. *I-Thou* can become *I-It* and *I-It* can turn into *I-Thou*: "The individual You must become an It when the event of relation has run its course. The individual It can become a You by entering into the event of relation".[88] *I-Thou* and *I-It* must alternate. There is nothing inherently evil in the *It-world* which has brought great benefits to humankind and without it the modern world of science and technology would never have emerged. In this Buber is a realist.[89] However, evil for

Buber is the predominance of *I-It* to the exclusion of relation.[90]

TO RECAP; Saint-Exupery's plea in the first half of the twentieth century for spirituality and morality in human life and landscape, is very much a plea for *I-Thou*, and the *world of relation*. His "alarmed concern for the rapid dehumanization of modern lives and landscape" is an abhorrence for the *world of It*.[91] When Saint-Exupery wrote shortly before his last mission over France that he didn't care if he was killed in the war, only for what would remain of what he had loved – he is describing the *world of relation*. What matters are certain orderings of things and invisible ties.[92]

When Katz and Kirby make a critique which argues that the "externalisation of nature is built into our concepts of science", and that "Western Science excludes and marginalizes alternative epistemologies"; and further that the "exploitation of nature is coincident with its constitution as something apart and 'other'," they are drawing attention to *the world of It*.[93]

As we have seen, landscape as a '*focus of perception*' involves a *focus in relating*. The quality or type of the relating is determined by the individual, who lives within a cultural milieu, as well as the landscape in focus. Unlike the *world of It*, the *I-Thou relation* is reciprocal, lyrical and outside time and space.

This *I-Thou* quality of relation between individual and landscape in focus is described by Lopez:

> Whatever evaluation we finally make of a stretch of land… no matter
> how profound or accurate, we will find it inadequate. The land retains
> an identity of its own, still deeper and more subtle than we can know.
> Our obligation toward it then becomes very simple: to approach with
> an uncalculating mind, with an attitude of regard. To try to sense the
> range and variety of its expression – its weather, and colors and
> animals. To intend from the beginning to preserve some of the mystery
> within it as a kind of wisdom to be experienced, not questioned. And to
> be alert for its openings, for that moment when something sacred
> reveals itself within the mundane, and you know the land knows you
> are there.[94]

Geography of Religion

GEOGRAPHERS HAVE ALWAYS RECOGNISED a relationship between religion and landscape. However, what this relationship is and whether there is, or has been, a real field which can be called '*geography of religion*' has been debated.[95] In 1967, geographer C.J Glacken, recognising the relationship, commented:

> In ancient and modern times alike, theology and geography have often
> been closely related studies because they meet at crucial points of
> human curiosity. If we seek after the nature of man and the earth, and
> if we look at the earth, questions of divine purpose in its creation and
> of the role of mankind on it inevitably arise.[96]

Almost ten years later, Yi-Fu Tuan would pronounce in 1976 that the geography of religion is a field "in disarray".[97]

THE PROCESS OF WORLDWIDE secularization begun in the 1960s led to Buttner in 1980 calling for "the incorporation of this widespread process of secularization into the geography of religion to prevent it from becoming a 'geography of relics', restricted to the study of those ever-shrinking areas in which religion still has a formative effect on the environment".[98]

In 1981 David E. Sopher asked whether there was, indeed, a 'Geography of Religion'.[99] Sopher asked to what extent should the geographer, as social scientist, defer to the scholar of religions? Should the geographer become a scholar of religions if, as Erich Isaac[100] in 1962 thinks, the key to the geography of religion is the study of religion itself?

Sopher concluded that geographic work that deals with religion is likely to remain diffuse. In fact, questions about the validity and viability of geography of religion as a separate subfield are not important. Rather, one could look forward to the withering away of geography of religion as a subfield, as the discipline of geography as a whole matured, "to the extent that geography is prepared and able to take man seriously, to accept as data his symbols, rites, beliefs and hopes in all their cultural actuality, religion broadly conceived must become a central object of the discipline's best endeavours".[101]

In fact 'Geography of Religion' was not withering away so much as broadening and metamorphising into a geography of spirituality. It's establishment as a field within geography was not at issue in 1990 when Lily Kong presented a broad historical and contemporary perspective on religio-geographical literature.[102]

Kong concluded that "the geography of religion may develop into a 'geography of spiritual attitudes' instead".[103]

Kong asked "How does the spiritual come to be expressed and conveyed, particularly in an area of human life where words are presumably an inadequate way of expressing feeling?"[104]

Towards a Geography of Landscape Spirituality

BY THE EARLY 1990s, *reciprocity* was becoming important when thinking about landscape. "The reciprocity of meaning between place, landscape and religious experience is receiving increased attention among geographers of religion"[105] wrote geographer A. Cooper in 'New directions in the geography of religion' in 1992.

It was as if he was addressing J. Kay who two years earlier had expressed frustration with the ways in which religio-geographical analysis had failed to engage with the interaction between individual's interpretations of place and landscape and their religious experience.[106] S. Bhardwaj, 1990, also recognised the need to engage in interaction and emphasised the active role of human *individuality, imagination* and *emotion.*[107]

Religious experience perceived as being passive and consensual was being rejected. Emphasis was now on *interaction, symbolism, imagination, emotion, reciprocity –*

particularly with the natural environment – and *experience which is active and individual* rather than passive and consensual. These are all defining characteristics of spirituality and a postmodern landscape meaning.

Emphasis on *spiritual meaning* within landscape was *this-worldly* and of the inner psyche rather than *other-worldly* and authoritarian, as in the traditional monotheistic religions. In reflecting on the ways in which geographers of religion were beginning to regard reciprocity between geographical and religious experience, one of Cooper's conclusions was that:

> the ways in which places, landscapes and religious experience are being conceived are not isolated from other aspects of social and material relations. That is, religio-geographical reciprocity is located within the contested, negotiated and dilemmatic context of other forms of cultural and ideological meaning, and social and material relations.[108]

THE ARCHETYPAL-IMAGINAL methodological approach of geographer Peter Bishop continues in this radically different postmodern spiritual direction. In 1989 Bishop explored the complex relationship between geography, imagination and spirituality in the encounter between travellers and Tibet.[109] He aimed to "examine the phenomenology of a sacred place in the process of its creation, fulfillment and subsequent decline", and he was especially concerned with "the relationship between interior phenomenology of a sacred place and the wider context outside its boundaries. It is therefore less of a historical narrative than an in-depth analysis of inner meanings".[110] Travel texts are seen as psychological documents. They reveal significant aspects of the "fantasy-making process of a culture and of its unconscious", thus:

> While the study is methodologically based in archetypal psychology, it also draws widely from such disciplines as humanistic geography and French deconstructionism… It is therefore an attempt to develop an imaginal approach to cultural analysis, one that traces the movement and transformation of images whilst simultaneously leading them back to their root- metaphors.[111]

The idea of sacred landscapes in which the mythic or archetypal have been stressed, are part of a tradition, as Bishop acknowledges.[112]

THE MYTHIC AND THE ARCHETYPAL are inherent in the writings of French philosopher, theologian and translator, Henry Corbin (1903-1978); French philosopher, sociologist and anthropologist Gilbert Durand (1921-2012); Romanian born historian and philosopher of religion Mircea Eliade (1907-1986); psychiatrist and philosopher of religion Carl Jung (1875-1961); archetypal psychologist and philosopher James Hillman (1926-2011); philosopher of phenomenology, landscape, place and space, Edward Casey; and anthropologist and psychologist John Willoughby Layard (1891-1974).

In particular, phenomenology, perception and experience of landscape and place have also been investigated by German philosopher Martin Heidegger (1889-1976); French philosopher Gaston Bachelard (1884-1962) and American geographers Yi-Fu Tuan, Edward Relph and David Lowenthal. The social context of sacred landscape and the social context of the perceptions of landscape have been studied by many of these authors.

Valuable insights for this approach have also been drawn from extensive studies by anthropologists studying primal spirituality; for example Australian Aboriginal sacred sites and sacred journeys.

AN ARCHETYPAL-IMAGINAL ANALYSIS must be distinguished clearly from a philosophical analysis. Bishop has argued "The former is less concerned with logical or epistemological differences ... than with their archetypal and metaphorical relationships. A theoretical consistency is less important than an imaginal one".[113] In this view the underlining image or metaphor is fundamental. The aim is not to achieve a theoretical reconciliation but to open up a field of ideas that has both the width and the capacity to endure contradictions. Bishop suggests that:

> imaginal analysis must bear in mind the dominant root-metaphors of
> any theory that it uses to craft the imaginal material. A polytheistic
> approach does not exclude any perspective on the grounds of
> theoretical incompatibility, but instead tries to relate theories through
> their common grounding in imaginal reality.[114]

LISTENING TO THE ROOT-METAPHORS of theories relieves them of their literalness; it "allows space for the material; the textual images to speak pluralistically" and so analysis then becomes a matter of image-work, a crafting of images.[115] The theories do not stand in a privileged position above the primary material, but take their place as imaginal texts alongside the travel accounts and other historical documents.

For Bishop, 'geography of religion' becomes a 'geography of spirituality or soul'. He sees his study as a contribution towards "the return of the soul to the world, to an *anima mundi* psychology. The world presents itself in its images".[116]

The idea of the individual soul or psyche, and hence spirituality, as enmeshed in the outer world is not a new idea, as was shown when we probed the concept of spirituality in Chapter 1. For example, Jung's concept of the psychoid archetype is explicit in linking the personal and collective unconscious with the outer world. The world as metaphor and the archetypal approach to spiritual landscapes, which has been touched on in this chapter, is examined in detail in later chapters and particularly in the writings of Henry Corbin.

In this chapter it has been shown that, like spirituality, landscape is a mobile and inner conception. Landscape is a 'focus of perception' and as such originates in the human psyche. Geography of religion has become a geography of landscape spirituality. It is to an exploration of Western spiritual *Imaginal-Visionary Landscapes* that we now turn.

THREE

Imaginal-Visionary Landscapes

Landscape is a connector of the soul
with Being.

— **Belden C. Lane**

Our perceptions are colored by
preconception and desire... the landscapes
in which history unfolds are both real,
that is, profound in their physical effects
on mankind, and not real, but mere
projections, artifacts of human perception.

— **Barry Lopez**

L ANDSCAPES ARE *imaginal* and they are visionary.[1] They are both timeless and they are time-bound, hence particular spiritual imaginal-visionary landscapes predominate in particular historical epochs.

GEOGRAPHERS HAVE FOR A LONG TIME understood the idea that our landscapes spring forth from personal and collective imagination.

However it is the postmodern geographers who place most importance on the role of the imagination in creating landscape. In part this is due to their understanding and receptivity to depth, analytical and archetypal psychology, where there has been a revival of interest in the image, the imagination and the *imaginal*. It is an old way of finding meaning and it is a theory of knowledge which has had a relatively recent revival in the twentieth century.

Seminal in the revival of this epistemology, or imaginal theory of knowledge and meaning in recent times are such thinkers as Jung and his theory of the *collective unconscious*; Bachelard, Professor of Philosophy of Science at the Sorbonne, who raised *poetic imagination* to a level equal in importance to scientific knowledge; Claude Levi-Strauss (1908-2009) anthropologist and ethnologist, regarded as the "father of modern anthropology", who spoke of cultures which did not neglect the *feminine guide of the imagination, the creative Sophia*; Henry Corbin, with his translations of the ancient Persian pre-Islamic Mystics and the Mazdean, Shi'ite and Sufi mystics (thirteen centuries in which the *imaginal* has been the focal point); as well as the romantics, the surrealists and most recently postmodernists.

Gilbert Durand concludes that imagination gives "the possibility of experiencing the noumenal... the imaginal is the New World that allows the revival of this gnosis".[2]

It is however in the consideration of sacred landscapes and sacred places that the role of the imagination becomes most apparent.

Postmodern Geographers and Imaginal Landscapes

THE LINK BETWEEN mind, imagination and landscape has been celebrated by some eminent geographers. As geographer historian John Kirtland Wright (1891-1969) once commented; "The most fascinating *terrae incognitae* of all are those that lie within the minds and hearts of men".[3]

David Lowenthal is another geographer who has made a strong advocacy for personal and collective cultural imagination and creativity as underlying our images and ideas of the world and the earth.

> Every image and idea about the world is compounded, then, of
> personal experience, learning, imagination, and memory... The surface
> of the earth is shaped for each person by refraction through cultural
> and personal lenses of custom and fancy... We are all artists and
> landscape architects, creating order and organizing space, time, and
> causality in accordance with our apperceptions and predilections...
> The geography of the world is unified only by human logic and optics,
> by the light and color of artifice, by decorative arrangement, and by
> ideas of the good, the true, and the beautiful.[4]

Placing this within a temporal and historical perspective, Lowenthal emphasizes the importance of image:

> The lineaments of the world we live in are both seen and shaped in
> accordance, or by contrast, with images we hold of other worlds, past
> worlds, future worlds. We constantly compare the reality with the fancy.
> Indeed, without the one we could neither visualize nor conceptualize the
> other.[5]

In 1971 geographer Yi-Fu Tuan maintained a deep identity between man and world: how we think about the world is revelatory of the inner man. Thus geography "reveals man... knowledge of the world elucidates the world of man: the root meaning of "world" (wer) is in fact man: to know the world is to know oneself... Geography mirrors man".[6]

For geographer Denis Cosgrove "all landscapes are *symbolic*" and are "expressions of cultural values, a code by which collective meaning can be read"; they express in the words of geographer Donald Meinig 'a persistent desire to make the earth over in the image of some heaven' and they "undergo change because they are expressions of society, itself making history through time".[7]

In 1991 geographer H.K. Yoon coined the term *'geomentality'* which, he maintained, is "the foundation of and key to understanding geography of mind".[8] A geomentality can be held by an individual or a group of people about a particular environment. It is "an established and lasting frame (state) of mind regarding the environment".[9]

Coinciding with and stimulated by the advent of postmodernism, geographers have had a renewed revival of interest in metaphor, image and imagination in the creation of landscape. For example, D. Matless, 1992, argued that geographers exploring landscape:

> have sought to develop a form of analysis in which transcendent,
> ahistorical, biological or spiritual categories are explored to investigate
> human responses to landscape. Cosgrove in particular phrases this
> approach in postmodern terms, and in doing so raises key issues
> regarding the status of image and metaphor…Whether or not they
> conceive of their endeavor as 'postmodern'… there would appear to be
> a search underway for an elevated, transcendent base.[10]

Denis Cosgrove, 1990, pronouncing the status of *image* and *metaphor* and depicting his approach to geography and landscape in *postmodern* terms, puts the case as follows:

> My argument is that both in the later sixteenth century – immediately
> preceding the Scientific Revolution, and in the closing decades of the
> twentieth century – following the scientific and intellectual
> contributions of relativity and psychoanalysis, there have been serious
> attempts to collapse Modernist distinctions between spirit and matter,
> humans and nature, subject and object, *poesis* and *techne*. In both cases
> understanding is constituted neither in solely operational, nor entirely
> speculative terms, but rather through the construction of metaphor
> and image by individuals actively embracing the materiality of the
> world, recognizing the necessity of mechanical intervention in
> transforming nature, but refusing to be ruled by the materialist and
> mechanical vision of Modernism. Metaphor and image are conceived
> not as surface representations of a deeper truth but as a creative
> intervention in making truth.[11]

For Cosgrove people "seek to create meaning and do so through metaphor" and that rather than being grasped by empirical observation or measurement this meaning is "apprehended phenomenologically, below the intellectual level of formal science".[12] Further, meaning is "increasingly constructed through images".[13] Postmodernism has promoted in some respects an "evocative sense of metaphor as that which lies between fact and idea. The metaphor may thus picture or *represent* an understanding which must otherwise remain unarticulated."[14] In the words of K. Harries: "What metaphor names may transcend human understanding so that our language cannot capture it".[15]

Radically for a geography which has traditionally been entrenched in scientific empiricism, Cosgrove argues that "Scientific discourse has always been metaphorical in the Aristotelian sense, but has proclaimed a privileged 'truth' for its metaphors or models in representing reality". However, with the shift from metaphors of science to those of the arts and the "rejection of foundationalism in post-modern writings" there is an implied "relativity in which the competing claims of different representations can not be evaluated".[16] If pure perspectivalism is accepted it "opens the door, at least in thought, to transcendence of its own limits, to metaphysics and thus to the collapse of clear distinctions between science and poetics".[17] Cosgrove concludes:

> We need to locate the history of our discipline within a broader
> historiography of constant metaphorical and imaginative
> reconstruction of nature and our place within it, not seeking ultimate
> foundations for spatial and environmental metaphors and images but
> rather respecting them as 'more or less adequate and fragmentary
> repetition of that speech which nature, or perhaps God, addresses us.[18]

In the postmodern camp and tracking a new way forward, Peter Bishop explores links between landscape geography, archetypal psychology and postmodern epistemological ways of knowledge and meaning. Bishop maintains that the attitude towards rhetoric, metaphor and imagery is central to the definition of postmodernism and postmodern scholarship – "that questions about the relationship between archetypal psychology and geography mirrors the wider postmodern phenomenon of comparative knowledges".[19]

THE EMPHASIS ON METAPHOR, symbolism, transcendence and imagistic reconstruction are characteristic of both postmodernism and an archetypal analysis. As we have seen, the role of the imagination in the creation of landscape is of increasing interest to geographers. However it is in the consideration of *spiritual landscapes* and *sacred places* that landscape as a manifestation of personal and collective imagination becomes most apparent. And so we now turn to a consideration of *historical changes in spiritual imaginal-visionary landscapes.*

Four Imaginal-Visionary Landscapes and Historical Changes

POETS, MYSTICS, DEEP ECOLOGISTS, mythologists and religious savants have always shared and cherished the role of imagination within landscape. For children, mystics and primal peoples, the immersion of imagination in the sacred *Nature/Earth Landscape* can also be an existential way of being.

Paradoxically, it would seem that spiritual and imaginal-visionary landscapes are simultaneously both *timeless* and have undergone *historical change*. There is a timelessness or historical transcendence in our understanding of and our potentiality to participate in different spiritual imaginal-visionary landscapes which could be called archetypal. This archetypal aspect of landscape, which is historically transcendent or centred in the individual's psyche, will be considered in the next chapter.

At the collective level, particularly in the West, there have been discernable historical changes in spiritual imaginal-visionary landscapes. The collective historical change in sacred landscape imagination has been noted by a number of geographers and cultural historians.[20]

IN THE WEST the progressive delineation of four major historical changes in imaginal-visionary landscapes is proposed, namely: from (1) the primal, sacred *Nature/Earth Landscape*; to (2) the Judaic-Christian *Anthropocentric Landscape*; to (3) the modernist 'secular' *Technological/Materialist Landscape*; then to (4) the *Postmodern Ecological Landscape* and a consideration of an *Inner Landscape*.

With the *Postmodern Ecological Landscape* we seem to have created a full circle return to the sacred *Nature/Earth Landscape* imagination and vision. However, it is a self-conscious return and it often comes with an awareness of the role of the imagination and the inner mind (or psyche/soul) in creating and choosing landscape. We can by virtue of will change the way we imagine and visualise the landscape and hence our 'focus of perception'.

THE FOLLOWING POINTS can be made with regard to the four spiritual imaginal-visionary landscapes as noted above: (1) Each of these landscapes is a major 'focus of perception' – hence a major focus in seeing, feeling, being and relating. These landscapes are not necessarily a totality (2) They are inherent to Western culture and history but there may be other landscapes and good arguments for other landscapes. (3) The four landscapes are *not* mutually exclusive.

While each of the landscapes has been predominant at particular times in Western history, at the individual level they are not mutually exclusive. An example of this is that there can be no *Nature/Earth Landscape* without an *Anthropocentric Landscape* for humans at least. This is because people are brought up as social animals and cannot survive apart from other people from birth. The *Nature/Earth Landscape* even for primal peoples and cultures will always be peopled and infused with an anthropocentric culture.[21]

The Primal, Sacred 'Nature/Earth Landscape'

MIRCEA ELIADE, the historian of religion, once noted that:

> It was the prophets, the apostles, and their successors the missionaries who convinced the western world that a rock (which certain people have considered to be sacred) was only a rock, that the planets and stars were only cosmic objects – that is to say, that they were not (and could not be) either gods or angels or demons.[22]

Earth worship persisted up to about 500 CE in Europe and is thought to have originated in Mesopotamia and spread throughout the Near and Middle East, Europe, Africa and Asia. Earth worship corresponds to animism – the belief that everything is endowed with soul/spirit. Indeed, the concept of animism "extended to plants and animals because of the spiritual power (mana) they were perceived to have as children of the Earth Mother".[23]

Earth worship persists today among certain 'native' and aboriginal tribes who choose to retain their primal knowledge and traditions, with a relationship of kinship between human beings and all of creation – vegetation, animals, the elements and other planets.[24] It is an holistic approach to life, with strong emphasis on the *I-Thou* relationship.[25]

THE TRADITIONAL MAORI LANDSCAPE exemplifies the primal and sacred *Nature/Earth Landscape*. In the Maori cosmology all living things are descendents of Rangi (the Sky Father) and Papa (the Earth Mother) and thus are related. The ancient Maori regard for their land was such that "at times it seems doubtful whether it is the tribe who owns the mountain or river or whether the latter own the tribe".[26]

For traditional Maori, separation from one's landscape was a spiritual as well as a physical dislocation. The alienation of Maori land to Europeans was sometimes referred to as the death of the land.[27] The intense and mysterious ties with the land were such that before being executed one Maori prisoner asked his captors to allow him to view his tribal territory once more and drink from his river.[28]

The *Nature/Earth Landscape* 'focus of perception' was to change with the advent first of Judaism and then Christianity, where a monotheistic patriarchal God held dominion over nature and conferred human dominion over nature to 'the chosen' and 'the righteous'. With the domination by missionary Christianity over primal peoples and their spirituality, the power balance shifted and the primal, sacred *Nature/Earth Landscape* was challenged and superseded by a new revelatory *Anthropocentric Landscape*.

Geographer of religion Erich Isaac (1960) drew the landscape distinction between primal "magical-cosmic religions" where "everything is potentially sacred, but only in a few chosen places is the potential realised" on the one hand, and the "great religions of revelation" where God is "in no way confined by space" and the divine is removed from the landscape, on the other.[29]

For Isaac, religions of revelation "contrast with the magical-cosmic religions in that the divine is outside of nature and man, and no site is intrinsically holier than any other. Sites are hallowed by God's choice of them at a particular historical moment. The tendency of religions of revelation is thus to remove the divine from the landscape".[30]

Paradoxically, "while God is conceived as in no way confined by space", God is at the same time "confined in so far as He (sic) is regarded as peculiarly attached to certain specific localities" or holy sites.[31]

The man-made city in monotheistic religions came to symbolize the heavenly order. As Yi-Fu Tuan points out "The city symbolized heavenly order. Within its walls one found just rules and discriminations; beyond them lay chaos and arbitrariness. The most heart-felt eschatological longings drew on city imagery in utterance".[32] This reinforced the alienation felt for the *Nature/Earth Landscape* outside the city walls.

Jerusalem was the Holy City – the prime City of God. According to the Genesis myth of creation, "the earth was without form and void, darkness hovered over the face of the abyss and a mighty wind swept over the face of the waters" although, in the end, there is perfect order.

> St. John saw a new heaven and a new earth on which there no longer
> existed any sea or darkness for the glory of God gave light. In the
> beginning was confusion. In the end St. John beheld the holy city of
> Jerusalem, which had the crystalline structure and radiance of some
> priceless jewel (Revelation xxi).[33]

While God may be found in his Holy City Jerusalem, on the other hand it is argued by Belden C. Lane that for the Judeo-Christian tradition, a "God made proximate in place may be no God at all".[34] The call to abandon the security of place is a persistent theme throughout Western religious thought. Samuel Terrien maintains that the theme of God's *elusive* presence forms the heart and soul of biblical theology in both the Old and New Testaments.[35]

The Father-God is distanced from the *Nature/Earth Landscape* and in consequence it is de-sacralised. God is above nature. As Belden C. Lane points out, the German sociologist Max Weber (1864-1920) "spoke of this insistent rejection of pagan animism to have resulted in a 'disenchantment' of the world within the western mind, a freeing of nature from its intense religious associations".[36]

THE GOD OF THE OLD TESTAMENT, while distanced from nature, nevertheless establishes *dominance over nature and confers the privilege of domination to the 'chosen'* – the righteous and the faithful. God has the power to use nature to punish transgressors with natural disasters.

Thus geographer Jeanne Kay, writing in *The Annals of the Association of American Geographers*, 1989, maintains that human dominion over nature is inherent in the Hebrew Bible (or Old Testament within the Christian Bible):

> the Bible's most persistent environmental message is that God confers
> human dominion over nature to righteous or faithful people, whereas
> God punishes transgressors with natural disasters... The themes of a
> beneficent environment as God's rewards for good human behavior
> and a deteriorating environment as God's punishment for evil resound
> throughout the Bible and were favorite themes of the prophets.[37]

Christianity had followed in the Hebraic tradition of domination over nature. Yi-Fu Tuan points out that for early Christianity an express purpose was to "loosen man's earthly bonds so that he might more easily enter the heavenly kingdom".[38]

A CHANGE IN LANDSCAPE FOCUS AND IMAGINATION occurred, from one of perceiving the sacred in nature and the earth to an anthropocentric focus of perceiving the sacred to be in a heavenly 'other world' and in man's soul - as distinct from his 'profane' physicality which linked him with other animals and the natural world.

This is well illustrated in the recounted experience of Petrarch, the fourteenth-century Renaissance humanist, poet and scholar. Taking a day off from his work on letters Petrarch decided to climb Mount Ventoux in southern France. From the summit of some 6,000 feet he took delight in the views of the distant chateau country of Avignon and the feeling of being "free and alone, among the mountains and forests".[39] But as he stood in wonder he felt the urge to open Augustine's *Confessions*, which he had brought along in his pocket, and there he read to his chagrin the Bishop of Hippo's accusing words: "Men go gape at mountain peaks, at the boundless tides of the sea, the broad sweep of rivers, the encircling ocean, and the motions of the stars: And yet they leave *themselves* unnoticed; they do not marvel at themselves".[40] Petrarch later wrote that "I was abashed and I closed the book, angry with myself that I should still be admiring earthly things who might long ago have learned....that nothing is wonderful but the soul".[41] He left the mountain hurriedly, reflecting on how easily the world's beauty can divert men and women from their proper concerns.

The Revelatory 'Anthropocentric Landscape'

BY STANDING HIMSELF in spiritual opposition to the *Nature/Earth Landscape* and hence separating himself away from this landscape, Judaic and Christian man was enabled to objectify and secularize it.

The Canaanite and pagan pervasive *I-Thou* relationship with a polytheistic sacred *Nature/Earth Landscape* was driven underground by the powerful, transcendent, patriarchal, monotheistic religions and their adherents who perceived the spirituality and religions of these peoples as a threat to their hegemony.

The relationship with the natural landscape was to become increasingly *I-It* and de-sacrilised. The new focus was now on man and his salvation in an *Anthropocentric Landscape*, separated from the *Nature/Earth Landscape,* which had become perceived as profane. This in turn would open up the way for scientific study and the technological and materialist, manipulated, landscape of the modern era. It was to be the landscape of I-It relations par excellence. Belden C. Lane describes the new state of affairs, or rather the new landscape focus:

> In much of Jewish and Christian theology the freedom of a
> transcendent God of history has regularly been contrasted with the
> false and earthbound deities of fertility and soil. God has been removed
> from the particularity of place, extracted from the natural
> environment. Hence, the tendency in western civilization has been
> toward the triumph of history over nature, time over space, male
> dominance over female dependence, and technological mastery of the
> land over a gentle reverence for life... The result has been a rampant
> secularization of nature and activism of spirit in western life, leaving us
> exhausted in our mastery of a world stripped of magic and mystery.[42]

Geographer Yi-Fu Tuan argues, it is now generally agreed that the "intense attachment to land based on the belief that the sacred soil is the abode of the gods waned as man acquired increasing control over nature and as Christianity spread to dominate the Western World".[43]

FROM AN AOTEAROA NEW ZEALAND PERSPECTIVE, ecologist Geoff Park recounts the relationship of Maori to the land prior to the advent of missionary Christianity:

> Before contact with the missionaries of the 19th century, Maori believed their physical health and wellbeing were achieved in two principle ways. One was by maintaining the mauri of their places – the life force by which their natural elements cohere. The other was by lifelong observance of the laws of tapu. Rites and rituals broke down the barriers between people and other species, allowed people to flow spiritually into nature and for nature's rhythms to permeate their own being. A host of daily tasks depended on conscious connection, both to benefit nature and limit human excesses.[44]

In contrast, the early European explorers, scientists and colonialists were outsiders who found the landscape harsh and despite using Maori guides and experts, they were sometimes patronising and critical of the Maori relationship with the landscape.

The new colonizers brought with them a new vision of the landscape. The New Zealand landscape – as exemplified by the vision of Edward Gibbon Wakefield (1796-1862), the British politician and driving force behind the early colonisation of New Zealand, via the direction of The New Zealand Company – had exploitative and monetary value.

The new colonialists also desired to populate and tame the New Zealand landscape. One could term these landscape perspectives as anthropocentric and materialist. Generally the colonialist and the missionary view from London was that the Maori *Nature/Earth Landscape* perspective and hence Maori spirituality was primitive, backward and in need of salvation:

> Clearing the land was equated with Christianising the country.
> Converting the Maori to Christianity was seen as one's duty
> inextricably bound up with another, that of "civilizing" the landscape.
> The firm assumption was that both duties would inevitably bring
> improvement. By the time the twentieth century arrived the landscape
> was regarded as an adversary against which the settlers pitted
> themselves.[45]

An example of an early missionary's attitude to the Maori *Nature/Earth Landscape* perspective and spirituality is given in a sermon by the young German missionary Cort Schnackenberg at one of the Wesleyan West Coast mission stations in 1844. Schnackenberg admonishes Maori to:

> ...apply the same rule to the cultivation of your hearts – the light from
> Heaven is shining upon you – look at yourself in that light and if you

> find your mind, your heart to be a wilderness, cultivate it in the same
> manner as you do your fields, cut down the bush, great and small –
> spare no sin… dig your hearts by deep repentance that it may become
> soft and fit to receive the seed of God's word – if it strikes root within
> you. Watch it carefully and weed your hearts ever afterwards until the
> harvest – in times past the preaching of God's work produced no fruit
> in this place, because it fell on strong ground, or was choked in the
> bush.[46]

Park notes that while Schnackenberg and his wife were told by European visitors that
they were living in the finest place in New Zealand, this:

> representative of religion committed to getting away from nature could
> only see what he called 'The Tapu of Mokau' cruelly infusing the lives
> of the river people. [Maori] were intelligent enough, even 'touched
> occasionally by nobility', but their primitive union with nature had
> empowered 'the works of the devil' – pagan spirits, cruelty and
> superstition – to operate unchecked.[47]

However, as is often the case, there is another side. This writer's own nineteenth
century northern Irish ancestors who settled in Canterbury opined in letters sent home
after six months in New Zealand:

> I feel as happy as a king. I have not been to church, mass or meeting
> but twice since I left home and that was in Australia. There is not a
> house of worship within 25 miles of me. I used to have some queer
> notions about religion and you need not be surprised if they are queer
> still (such as no personal Devil yet Devils many). I have nature in her
> truest form and revelation for my guide and with God for friend and
> Father I may be little worse than many who like the parson's horses
> find their way to the church gate but there they leave their religion
> behind and if far from church be near grace. I am far enough from
> church but I sincerely believe New Zealand is as near heaven as any
> country. But for the people I can not say… there are times when the
> more lonesome the place and the wilder the scene, I take the most
> delight."[48]

It must be admitted that other early Europeans, or the new Pakeha, also saw the
landscape as inherently beautiful because it *was* God's handiwork.[49]

By contrast, Lynn White, JR writing in *Science*, 1967, is explicitly damning of Judeo-
Christianity's impact on the *Nature/Earth Landscape*.[50] He argues in his now famous
paper 'The Historical Roots of our Ecological Crisis', that modern science and
technology have grown out of Judeo-Christian values of man's transcendence of and
mastery over nature, which has caused an ecological crisis:

> The victory of Christianity over paganism was the greatest psychic
> revolution in the history of our culture… Our daily habits of action …

> are dominated by an implicit faith in perpetual progress which was
> unknown either to Greco-Roman antiquity or to the Orient. It is
> rooted in, and is indefensible apart from, Judeo-Christian teleology...
> We continue to live, as we have lived for about 1700 years, very largely
> in a context of Christian axioms... By destroying pagan animism,
> Christianity made it possible to exploit nature in a mood of
> indifference to the feelings of natural objects.[51]

From the thirteenth century until the late eighteenth century – when the hypothesis of God became unnecessary to many scientists – every major scientist up to and including Leibniz and Newton explained his motivations in religious terms. Thus modern science "is an extrapolation of natural theology" and modern technology can be at least partly explained by the "Christian dogma of man's transcendence of, and rightful mastery over, nature" because:

> Over a century ago science and technology – hitherto quite separate
> activities – joined to give mankind powers which, to judge by many of
> the ecological effects, are out of control. If so, Christianity bears a huge
> burden of guilt... Our science and technology have grown out of
> Christian attitudes towards man's relation to nature which are almost
> universally held not only by Christians and neo-Christians but also by
> those who fondly regard themselves as post-Christians. Despite
> Darwin, we are *not*, in our hearts, part of the natural process. We are
> superior to nature, contemptuous of it, willing to use it for our slightest
> whim.[52]

The fact that most people do not think of these attitudes as Christian – that is "that nature has no reason for existence save to serve man" – is irrelevant; because no new set of basic values has been accepted by our society. Both "our present science and our present technology are so tinctured with orthodox Christian arrogance toward nature that no solution for our ecological crisis can be expected from them alone. Since the roots of our trouble are so largely religious, whether we call it that or not. We must rethink and refeel our nature and destiny".[53]

Here again a qualification should be added. Different spiritual imaginal-visionary landscapes can be held and interwoven at the same time – either by individuals or by different sectors of the same society.

In this regard Peter Bishop points out, in a note to this author, that care should be taken that the view of non-western religions in terms of environmentalism should not be too idealized nor should be the "historical suddenness and definitiveness of a shift to a modernist, secular landscape". In particular, Bishop argues:

> There have been numerous counter-trends. For example, the bulk of
> Europe's population in the 18th and even 19th century were peasants and
> farm labourers. Their relationship to nature sustained continuity with
> much earlier beliefs. Much of the European Romantic tradition valued
> nature in terms of its spirituality. Nature writing, especially in North

America was a major influence throughout the 19th century and into the 20th.[54]

A LANDSCAPE 'FOCUS OF PERCEPTION' is not necessarily a totality of landscape perceptions in a particular historical period nor is it mutually exclusive, although it can be a major trend. Hence an analysis of landscape should not be reductive – rather it requires an attitude of circumspection and awareness of complexity while still taking cognisance of predominant phenomenology.

In other words, what we are talking about here is a *predominant* spiritual imaginal-visionary landscape 'focus of perception' – in this case the revelatory *Anthropocentric Landscape.* If White's and the other theorists' arguments are accepted, there will still be exceptions and counter-trends.

The Modernist, Secular 'Technological/Materialist Landscape'

THE SACRED IS ALMOST completely leached from the *Nature/Earth Landscape* and replaced by a sceptical secularism. This is the imaginative construct and 'focus of perception' of the scientific, realist and objectivist mind. In the new modernist, 'secular' *Technological/Materialist Landscape,* it could be argued that 'religious' enthusiasm is now for the idea of man and man-made progress in scientific discoveries and technological and materialist creations - as opposed to an omnipotent, transcendent God Father revealed through the Bible (His 'Holy Word') and in His holy places: temples, cities and churches.

The *Nature/Earth Landscape* where all natural phenomena are intrinsically sacred has been left far behind and is no longer regarded as a threat. It is derogated as 'primitive' or 'romantic sentimentality' or 'new age nonsense' by the positivist sceptic and materialist alike.

IN THE EARLY 1960s, Erich Isaac described this situation in geography of religion, where in a modern, secular culture, religion's impact on landscape is minimal. He argued that geography of religion had become in practice "an essentially ethnological and historical study... religion as a great basic power in transforming the landscape has virtually ceased to operate".[55]

Isaac drew a distinction between 'religion' and the 'religious impulse', which could be imputed to 'secular ideologies'. He argued that humanity has become the new object of worship and man's secular ideologies have important parallels to religion:

> It is not accurate to say that the religious impulse as a transforming
> power in the landscape has virtually disappeared in the 20th Century.
> What has actually happened is that this impulse has been translated
> into another form. ... This ... has made it possible for secular
> ideologies to develop, bearing certain important parallels to religion.
> The important ideologies of the 19th and 20th centuries postulate a
> world order which must be brought into being.[56]

One can think of a number of ideologies that would fit Isaac's description of the religious impulse - in particular Marxism and Capitalism, both of which are based on salvation through material progress, although Marxism in theory is more concerned with social equality and justice. It is arguable that the underlying ideology of the twentieth century is that of *human progress as salvation, here on earth, based on a technological/materialism*. Indeed, Isaac concluded that for those studying the religious motive in cultural landscape the study of the role of ideology in landscape transformation is essential:

> Problematic though it be, the study of transformations of the landscape
> made upon ideological principles constitutes the major material for
> one who would study the religious motive at work in the cultural
> landscape of the present day.[57]

Geographer Yi-Fu Tuan, 1978, also noted the decline of the sacred and transcendental and questioned whether in fact there is now a secular church – a church which "is increasingly a social and service center". In contrast, the medieval church "however much it catered to secular activities, was primarily sacred space: it radiated power".[58] Wistfully he concluded that contemporary life has lost its sense of the sacred, whether it be in the forests and streams or the sacred space of the church:

> Today the gods no longer dwell in forests and streams. If we abuse nature
> we shall pay for our wantonness in the long run and ecologists can tell us
> just how this will happen with the help of systems analysis and
> computers. But such rational and longwinded argument cannot chill our
> spine as can the belief that if we polluted a sacred spring our limbs would
> at once wither. …our pretense to scientific understanding and power has
> also corroded our feeling for profound mysteries. The world seems
> transparent. Contemporary space, however colorful and varied, lacks
> polarized tension as between the numinous and the quotidian.
> Contemporary life, however pleasant and exciting, moves on one plane –
> the plane encompassed by rational and humanist vision. Ecstasy and
> dread, the heights and the depths, the awesome and the transcendent
> rarely intrude on our lives and on our landscapes except under the
> influence of chemical stimulus… A sense of holiness and of worldly
> splendor has dimmed in modern times, and some people feel the loss.[59]

Belden Lane also expresses a sense of the loss of the sacred and the mysterious for modern humanity: "As much as we might be tempted, amid the spiritual poverty of our contemporary life, to reach back to a renewed sense of paleolithic wonder, it is no longer possible or perhaps even desirable. The oracle is dumb. All shrines are defunct".[60] His description of modern life exemplifies the loss of and the longing for both the *Nature/Earth Landscape* and the revelatory *Anthropocentric Landscape* of patriarchal monotheism:

> The rootless character of American life, the Neo-Platonic impulse
> within the history of western spirituality, radical monotheism's

> stubborn resistance to circumscribing the holy – all these would seem
> to minimise the significance of the phenomena [sacred space] being
> considered here. They are joined, finally, by the extraordinary impact
> of modern, critical thought in desacrilizing the world of nature, driving
> all mystery from it.[61]

He agues that, since Descartes and the Enlightenment:

> we no longer attribute numinous power to the landscape. The world is
> not for us the clear window of access to God that it might once have
> been… Yet human beings have never more longed for an awareness of
> God's presence than today. Seldom have they been so divorced from a
> sense of place and the experience of meaningful dwelling that it can
> provide. Modern men and women, no less than their forebears, still
> hunger for the power of myth and place.[62]

Perhaps anticipating the imaginal *Postmodern Ecological Landscape*, Lane concludes:

> If there is hope for a rediscovery of the spirit, it will not be found in
> looking back to an innocence once lost, a simplistic return to the
> paradise of Eden. It will demand a reaching through and beyond the
> harshest criticisms leveled by the whole of western spiritual tradition. It
> will require a *metanoia*, a turning away from all efforts to manage the
> mystery of God. Only then may it be possible to encounter, by grace, a
> second naivete – a renewed sense of wonder glimpsed within the
> myriad landscapes of the holy.[63]

Lane places emphasis on the imagination, the experience of meeting and the mystery of grace and wonder which reveals the spiritual multiplicity of landscapes. This points to a description of the *Postmodern Ecological Landscape* to which we now turn.

The Inner, Imaginal 'Postmodern Ecological Landscape'

FACED WITH AN ECOLOGICAL CRISIS, the landscape which now confronts us is postmodern and ecological in focus. The *Technological/Materialist Landscape* is now frequently being questioned and even rejected for what could be termed a new, inner and imaginal *Postmodern Ecological Landscape*.

This *Postmodern Ecological Landscape* is concurrent with a revision in epistemology. As has been shown, the modernist domination, objectification and externalisation of nature, built into concepts of science and modernist epistemology, has been increasingly criticised.[64]

With the *Postmodern Ecological Landscape* we seem to have returned to the primal animist sacred *Nature/Earth Landscape* imagination and vision. The difference is that perhaps we are more self-consciously and deliberately aware of the imagination in creating landscapes.

It could be argued that it is the inner archetypal landscapes of the psyche, from which the imagination springs, that creates the outer landscapes of our being in the world. Indeed, as shall be shown in the final chapter, this is what was argued by Henry Corbin in his translations and interpretations of the writings of the ancient Persian pre-Islamic mystics and the Shi'ite, Mazdean and Sufi mystics in respect to their 'visionary geography'.

If this *inner landscape* of the psyche – or as cultural historian William Irwin Thompson terms it, "imaginary landscape of the "middle way of the mind", in which "we humans come to know our world"[65] – is accepted, then we would seem to have arrived at, or spiraled into, old understandings, feelings and rememberings of our spiritual embeddedness in the natural world.

American environmentalist and academic Lynn Ross-Bryant argues that Barry Lopez is one of a number of contemporary writers of ecological literature who offers a postmodern and holistic view of humans, nature and spirit. Most of these writers share a sense that "in allowing the mysterious otherness of nature to present itself, the ultimate dimension of life, the sacred, is revealed".[66]

For Lopez, imagination is the key to the relations and interactions between the natural world and human beings. These relations are mediated by the imagination and creations of the imagination. Thus Lopez asks: "How do people imagine the landscapes they find themselves in? How does the land shape the imaginations of the people who dwell in it? How does desire itself, the desire to comprehend, shape itself, the desire to comprehend, shape knowledge?"[67]

Lopez argues that we must approach the land with an "uncalculating mind" and with an attitude of regard, because whatever evaluation we finally make will be inadequate: "To intend from the beginning to preserve some of the mystery within it as a kind of wisdom to be experienced, not questioned. And to be alert for its openings, for that moment when something sacred reveals itself within the mundane, and you know that the land knows you are there".[68]

Imagination, mystery, wisdom, the sacred within the mundane and the reciprocity of I-Thou relation are all characteristics of the *Postmodern Ecological Landscape*. Lopez speaks of a relationship with the arctic landscape which is *mystical, emotional, lyrical* and *reverent*:

> I came to believe that people's desires and aspirations were as much a part of the land as the wind, solitary animals, and the bright fields of stone and tundra. And, too, that the land itself existed quite apart from these.[69]

This is a very different imagination and 'focus of perception' from the secular *I-It world* of the modernist *Technological/Materialist Landscape*, in which the sacred has been critically and rationally excised from the landscape.

Oil workers in the arctic told Lopez "the Arctic was really a great wasteland 'with a few stupid birds', too vast to be hurt. Whatever strong men could accomplish against the elements in such a place, they insisted was inherently right." A drilling supervisor said "Technology is inevitable. People just got to get that through their heads".[70]

Lopez like other recent writers of ecological literature, who could be described as postmodernist, share not only an extensive knowledge of the land but also an unabashed *I-Thou relation* with the *Nature/Earth Landscape*. They are not restricted by the *I-It* objectivist epistemology of science, technology and materialism. Rather they are willing and unafraid to use poetic language and acknowledge imagination and metaphor as a means of exploring and describing other ways of knowing. There is an emphasis on wholeness and relationship with the natural world. In Lynn Ross-Bryant's words:

> Their intent is to know humans better by knowing them as part of the natural order, and, insofar as possible, through metaphor and imagination, to know the land better as well. Through this use of the imagination they come to an awareness of the whole process of which humans are an interrelated part which leads them to a double emphasis, first on human responsibility to the whole and all its parts and second on human spirituality as it is rooted in this experience of the whole.[71]

Unlike The Judaic-Christian *Anthropocentric Landscape* where the sacred is transcendent, and the *Technological/Materialist Landscape* where the sacred is leached from the landscape and men would objectify and manipulate the land to their own materialist 'progressive' ends, there is a revisioning in landscape perception by these environmentalist writers towards a *Postmodern Ecological Landscape*.

These writers "share a love for and extensive knowledge of the land emphasizing nature as nature rather than nature as a springboard to transcendent reflections on humans".[72] Ross-Bryant argues that for Lopez there is an interaction between humans and nature:

> imagination and desire encounter the landscape and the living things in it: knowledge is gained – not simply of one's imagination, nor purely of the land, but of the mysterious process in which land and humans – all living things – are involved.[73]

This is in essence a description of the mystical *I-Thou relation*.

Lopez wants to change the way we imagine the world. He shows the different ways in which Eskimos, explorers, painters and oil workers have *imagined* the arctic landscape and the *consequences of their imagination*. Ross-Bryant says of Lopez's spirituality and what he identifies as *sacred* is an encounter with wholeness and mystery in the encounter with the earth:

> The experience of wholeness and mystery that he everywhere encounters in the things and people of the earth is the heart of his spirituality and his connection with what he identifies as the sacred.[74]

THE IMAGINATION HAS A ROLE IN EVOLUTION and one might add a spiritual revolution. Lopez states "The continuous work of the imagination...(is)...to bring what is actual together with what is dreamed is an expression of human evolution".[75]

It could also be argued that it is the continuous work of the imagination to bring what is actual together with what is dreamed of, that is reflected at the collective level in historical changes in landscape 'focus of perception'. In this regard, it is worth noting Bishop's argument that:

> Postmodernism marks not so much the *end* of history, as the *end* of history as concrete reality … Indeed, it marks the beginning of history (the past memory) as a *metaphorical* reality. By identifying the possible *plurality* of histories, HISTORY can be deliteralised. Like all the old literal power-words – Progress, Duty, Heritage, God – 'History' now becomes an *imagistic* truth.[76]

For cultural historian William Thompson the orthodox religion of our era is "scientific materialism,"[77] but at the same time "Gaia [the Earth] is a new landscape" and the new mentality is a "planetary culture" or "postmodernism".[78] While he uses different terms, Thompson's arguments accord with the perspective of the postmodern ecological landscape.

Thompson critiques modernism and argues for the return of the imagination as a mode of participatory perception – a way of being in the world and knowing.

> [T]he value of the imagination returns to challenge the reductionist mentality of modernism that ruled during the period of the mechanization of the world picture.[79]

Thompson points out that in the straightforward linear world that Whitehead called "scientific materialism", "it is precisely simile and metaphor that the materialist is trying to eliminate in reductionism" and that:

> this naïve philosophy, cultural constructs like "space" and "objects" are taken to be independent of the mind that frames them through its own threshold of possible perceptions, and by a strange inversion that amounts to a perversion, "mind" and "culture" are reduced to accidental collisions of these imaginary "real" objects in "real" space.[80]

We are at one of "those exciting times when the creative imagination of an entire civilization is undergoing a transformation of its basic mentality".[81] The dynamic mentality of modernism, the mentality of Galileo, Newton and Descartes with its linear equations is moving into a postmodernist science of which Chaos Dynamics is one important expression.[82]

The Gaia hypothesis has stimulated a new way of knowing the planet and it is "as large and imaginatively provocative for our era as Darwinian evolution was for our great-grand parents time".[83] It gives "a new way of appreciating how the part participates in the whole".[84]

Again there is great emphasis on the imagination. Thompson maintains that the imagistic mode that we call the Imagination is an ancient faculty which seems to involve a prelinguistic form of mind in which "thought is developed through correspondences, homologies, and participations of identity".[85]

The imagination "is like a transformer" and metaphors are by their very nature transformers.[86] Thompson argues that it is the "metaphorical process through which the Imagination takes in knowledge and steps it down into the conventional imagery of the sensory world with which we are all familiar... the Imagination is an intermediate realm, the realm of the artist, scientist, or prophet who renders the Intelligible into the Sensible".[87] The fundamentalist is not able to follow the symbolic utterance and takes image literally.[88] Thompson concludes that:

> Between the heights of the macrocosm of the Gaian atmosphere and
> the elemental depths of the microcosm of the bacterial earth lies the
> middle way of the Mind and it is in this imaginary landscape of the
> middle way, whether we call it the Madhyamika of Buddhism or the
> Christ of Steiner or the *Da'at* of the Kabbalah, that we humans take our
> life and come to know our world as the dark horizon that illuminates
> our hidden center.[89]

In Thompson's view, landscape is inextricably tied to the interior mind and the imagination; and this is a postmodern view of landscape.

LANDSCAPES ARE BOTH IMAGINAL AND VISIONARY. In this chapter it has been shown that landscapes are sourced in the personal and collective imagination of the psyche. That our landscapes derive from personal and collective imagination has long been recognized by geographers wrestling with the concept of landscape. The prime role of the imagination in creating landscape is inherent in postmodern geography. It is however in the consideration of spiritual landscapes that the role of the imagination becomes most apparent.

At the collective level, particularly in the West, there have been discernable historical changes in spiritual imaginal-visionary landscapes: the primal sacred *Nature/Earth Landscape*; the Judeao-Christian revelatory *Anthropocentric Landscape*; the modernist 'secular' *Technological/Materialist Landscape*; and the imaginal *Postmodern Ecological Landscape* which allows for an *Inner Landscape* from which our outer landscapes are a manifestation and materialization.

With the *Postmodern Ecological Landscape* we seem to have created a full circle return to the animist, sacred, *Nature/Earth Landscape* imagination and vision. The difference is that we are more consciously and deliberately aware of the imagination in creating landscape.

Paradoxically, it would seem that spiritual and imaginal-visionary landscapes have simultaneously undergone historical change and are timeless. There is a timelessness or historical transcendence in our understanding of and our potentiality to participate in different spiritual, imaginal-visionary landscapes, which could be called archetypal. This archetypal aspect of landscape, which is historically transcendent and centred in the individual's psyche, is the subject for the next chapter.

FOUR

Towards Archetypal Landscapes

> All landscapes are *symbolic,* they express
> 'a persistent desire to make the earth
> over in the image of some heaven', and
> they undergo *change* because they are
> expressions of society itself, making
> history through time.
>
> **– Denis Cosgrove**

> In one sense, natural landscape does
> not exist. We inescapably shape the
> world, even if only with our minds and
> not our hands.
>
> **– Peter Bishop**

Setting the Climate

POSTMODERNISM SETS THE SCENE for an archetypal analysis of landscape. For this reason it is worth looking briefly at postmodernism and postmodern theology.

David Harvey defined postmodernity as the situation in which the world finds itself after the breakdown of the Enlightenment project. Modernity lasted from the latter part of the eighteenth century until well into the twentieth and it was aimed at getting all the world's diverse peoples to see things the same way, that is, the rational way.[1]

Other writers on postmodernism have expressed similar views to Harvey. Kevin Vanhoozer, for example, notes that postmodernists reject the epistemological foundationalism of reason: "They do not reject 'reason' but 'Reason'. They deny the notion of a universal rationality; reason is rather a contextual and relative affair. What counts as rational is relative to the prevailing narrative in a society or institution".[2]

Postmodernism calls into question 'foundationalism' and 'methodology'. It is the result of the repeated failure of modernity to establish a secure foundation and a secure method built on this foundation.[3] "Classical foundationalism" and "rigorous method" are characterized by "objectivism"; which as Richard Bernstein argues, "is the basic conviction that there is or must be some permanent ahistorical matrix or framework to which we can ultimately appeal in determining the nature of rationality, knowledge, truth, reality, goodness, or rightness".[4]

The theory of the philosopher Friedrich Nietzsche (1844-1900) is regarded as an important precursor of postmodernism. Nietzsche:

> announces the death of modernity's god. In doing this his work
> expresses both the final working out of modernity's project and a
> postmodernism that will gather pace to become, finally, a culturally
> dominant force... With the death of God Nietzsche announces the
> overcoming of metaphysics, for he announces that there is no
> foundation, no ground, no origin that ultimately is not governed by a
> perspective, i.e., we, as human beings, desire and require it.[5]

Similarly, the ideology of modernism was systematically challenged by philosopher Alfred North Whitehead (1861-1947), a seminal, if not the earliest, advocate of postmodernism – "Although the term 'postmodern' was not used by Whitehead himself, the notion is implicit in his 1925 book *Science and the Modern World*".[6]

Postmodern Quantum Physics

QUANTUM PHYSICS AND POSTMODERNISM are inextricably linked as many philosophers since Whitehead have recognised. Both pose revolutionary challenges to traditional epistemologies, whether they be cultural, religious or scientific. The implications of quantum physics have given impetus to postmodern challenges to modernist epistemologies.[7]

For physicist David Bohm a "postmodern world" and a "postmodern science" are not only feasible and logically consistent but amount to a revolution in world view and an imperative for survival.[8] This is not to negate the successes and positive advances made by the modernist world view. As Bohm points out, the mechanistic reductionist program still provides the motivation of most scientific enterprise and has been very successful in certain areas, for example genetic engineering in medicine; but it is not the *whole* picture and, in fact, mechanistic reductionism has been "so successful that it threatens our very existence as well as to produce all sorts of other dangers".[9]

Theologian David Ray Griffin reinforces this view of constructive *post*modernism as not being an *anti*-modernism: "The term *postmodern*, however, by contrast with *premodern*, emphasizes that the modern world has produced unparalleled advances that must not be lost in a general revulsion against its negative features".[10] And postmodern science, according to Bohm "should not separate matter and consciousness and should therefore not separate facts, meaning and value".[11] Postmodern epistemology is situational, contextual, perception bound and composed of multiple realities. Postmodernism is inherently pluralistic. As Walter Anderson states:

> Seeing truth as made, not found – seeing reality as socially constructed – doesn't mean deciding there is nothing "out there". It means understanding that all our stories about what's out there – all our scientific facts, our religious teachings, our society's beliefs, even our personal perceptions – are the products of a highly creative interaction between human minds and the cosmos.[12]

Revolutionising Religion

POSTMODERNISM HAS IMPACTED on religion. While modernist concerns with falsifiability have undermined, some would say fatally, orthodox religions; the impact of the postmodern pluralist spirituality challenge to fundamentalism is particularly devastating.

Vanhoozer distinguishes 'modern theology' from 'postmodern theology' and describes the situation of theology within postmodernism. Modern theology is situated within the Enlightenment critical and scientific narrative, while postmodernity marks both the end of theology and new beginnings. Postmodernity lets the particulars speak for themselves without having to conform to prevailing ideology or political system.[13]

Arguably the most appropriate methodologies for postmodern discourse are *phenomenology, existentialism* and *hermeneutics.*

For example, Dan Stiver talking about theological method in particular, emphasizes hermeneutics in postmodern theology; the "intertextual" and "intratextual nature of postmodern theology; the pluralistic spirit and the *situated nature* of the theologian. Contrary to those who would deny a distinction between modernist theology and postmodern theology, Stiver argues that theology in modernity relied largely on a foundationalist paradigm. The basis for theology had to be "nailed down" first.[14] However, it was largely on the defensive because theology could hardly measure up to public standards for rigorous certainty and unchallengeable methods.

Postmodern Spirituality

THE RENAISSANCE OF 'SPIRITUALITY' has been associated with postmodernism.

"Postmodernity as spiritual condition" is argued by Vanhoozer. The condition of postmodernity "is neither simply philosophical nor simply socio-political, but *spiritual,* a condition in which belief and behavior come together in the shape of an embodied spirit".[15]

Ecofeminist, postmodern theologian Carol P. Christ argues that together with "many spiritual feminists, ecofeminists, ecologists, antinuclear activists, and others" she shares "the conviction that the crisis that threatens the destruction of the earth is not only social, political, economic, and technological, but is at root spiritual".[16]

Frederick Mark Gedlicks argues that for "religious pluralism to flourish in a postmodern era, the predominant expression of belief must be spiritual, rather than fundamentalist".[17] He distinguishes fundamentalism, metanarratives, discrimination and government power from postmodernism, religious liberty, nondiscrimination, government absence and spirituality. That the concepts of 'spirituality' and 'postmodernism' have both been linked in *De Paul Law Review* (2005), a secular law journal dealing with the laws of state and society, would indicate perhaps that both concepts have now 'come of age'.

GORDON D. KAUFMAN (1925-2011), the renowned American liberal theologian whose research, writing and teachings had a profound influence on constructive and systematic theology - gives an early working example of postmodern spiritual theology. He places an emphasis on *mystery, imagination,* and *imaginal construction.* Kaufman maintains theology is, and always has been, an activity of "imaginative construction" by persons attempting to put together as comprehensive and coherent a picture as they could of humanity in the world under God.[18]

For Kaufman theology as "imaginative construction" contrasts with the conventional conceptions of theology whereby the work of theologians is "understood to consist largely in exposition of religious doctrine or dogma (derived from the Bible and other authoritative sources)".[19] Rather than concentrating on traditional doctrines, dogmas and their systematic presentation in a new historical situation, Kaufman places emphasis on imaginative construction and the powers of the human imagination: 'symbolic perspective' and plurality.

Hence Christianity is just one of a plurality of world views. He stresses de-emphasizing traditional doctrines in new historical situations, and the de-emphasis of the importance of literal historicity. All this exemplifies a postmodernist theological perspective.[20]

Postmodernist Geographers and Archetypal Perspective

THE IMPORTANCE OF IMAGE, metaphor, symbol, imaginative reconstruction, plurality and a de-emphasis on the importance of philosophic and scientific reduction and historical literalism, can be seen in the writings of a number of postmodern geographers. In particular, the postmodern connections and similarities with depth psychology are drawn by Denis Cosgrove and Peter Bishop.[21]

Bishop is the geographer most explicit in drawing links between postmodernism, geography and archetypal psychology. He points out that "Archetypal psychology is less a system of ideas, or a new psychological school, than *a way of* metaphorising" and further that in "archetypal psychology the poetic basis of consciousness and knowledge, one that is expressed metaphorically in images, is stressed", indeed:

> By not giving a view of fragmentation and contradiction as
> pathological problems, archetypal psychology parallels some important
> ideas in postmodern geography... the focus of archetypal psychology
> intersects with the geographer's re-examination of historiography of
> geography. ... In an archetypal approach, following Jung's lead, there is
> an attempt to let the images speak for themselves, to be a study in

imagination rather than just a study *of* the imagination.[22]

Bishop points out that the importance of Jung and post-Jungians in postmodern studies should not be ignored: "Jung's insistence on the validity of *poesis* and the importance of deferring to poetics finds ready support among many geographers who have themselves turned their attention to literature as a source of knowledge".[23] Jung was fascinated with the language of the imagination and dedicated to articulating and promoting it. He distinguished on the one hand "thinking in words", "thinking with directed attention" and on the other hand the *fantasy-thinking* in which "image piles on image, feeling on feeling". Jung asked: "How are fantasies made and what is their nature? From the poets we learn much, from the scientists little".[24]

Prior to Bishop, Denis Cosgrove also described similarities between Jung's thinking and postmodernism:

> Jung's argument brings us close to some of the ideas being advanced in contemporary post-modernism. The underlying contentions are that the foundationalist philosophical position derived from Descartes, Locke and Kant is exhausted, the Enlightenment belief in reason no longer philosophically tenable. The key distinctions of object and subject, appearance and reality, being and becoming, upon which modern philosophy was erected have collapsed in the face of insights from Nietzsche, Husserl, Heidegger and others, and we have witnessed the limitations of linear discourse.[25]

Importance of Image

IN ESSENCE, in postmodernism meaning is increasingly being seen to be constructed through images. Archetypes are inherently images.

Philosopher Edward S. Casey argues that while Jung is at first glance apparently pre-modern with his emphasis on images; his root premise that "image is psyche" and his suspicion of metaphysical language puts him in league with Heidegger and Derrida.[26] This is very characteristic of the postmodernist enterprise. Images and words come together at the level of the human being and are grounded in the psyche – a collective basis which modernists failed to acknowledge. Jung and Saussure were joined by thinkers as diverse as Levy-Bruhl and Chomsky, who also asserted "the transpersonal foundation of the imagination and language, whether in the guise of collective representations or universally shared rules of generative grammar".[27] By contrast, "the modernist conception renders the self incapable of the symbolic activity of the psyche in its cosmic and collective dimensions".[28]

The writings of postmodern geographers and Jungians equally demonstrate that image, symbol and metaphor form the language of both postmodernism and archetypes.

Archetypal Theory and Carl Jung

BECAUSE BOTH JUNG and archetypal theory have come under attack in recent years, it is worthwhile to briefly clarify the epistemological parameters, controversial issues, and answers to challenges. In essence, archetypal theory is associated with the life-long thought, work and research of Carl Jung. As James Hillman argues, it was Jung "who reintroduced the ancient idea of archetype into modern psychology".[29]

THE EVIDENCE given for archetypes in this chapter is largely based within the parameters of Jung's archetypal theory – 'archetypes of the unconscious'. This is not to say that Jung is the only archetypal theorist. Henry Corbin, James Hillman and others, throughout history, are also important. Corbin is particularly seminal in regard to archetypal landscapes, as we shall see in the last chapter. Hillman is an important contemporary archetypal philosopher and theorist, who "offers a way into Jung – and a way out of Jung, especially his theology. For to stay wholly with this one thinker is to remain a Jungian, which as Jung himself said is possible only for Jung".[30]

By calling on Jung to begin with, Hillman states he is acknowledging the fundamental debt archetypal psychology owes to Jung. Jung is the immediate ancestor in a long line that stretches back through to Plato and to Heraclitus, with even more branches yet to be traced. But Hillman also acknowledges "the second immediate father of archetypal psychology", namely Henry Corbin (1903-1978).[31] Hillman argues that for Corbin the fundamental nature of the archetype is accessible to imagination first and presents itself as an image; hence the entire procedure for archetypal psychology as a method is imaginative.[32]

Jung's Challenge

JUNG'S THINKING SPANS both modernism and postmodernism. Jung is now recognized as an important postmodernist. Of course, Jung and his theory of archetypes are controversial in some quarters. Perhaps this is not surprising. Jung implicitly challenged the patriarchy and the ideologies behind patriarchal hegemony. He challenged Freud, the undisputed 'Father of Psychoanalysis'. Jung wanted to go beyond Freud's foundationalist theories of sexuality – for example the 'Oedipus complex' and 'penis envy' – to an exploration of spirituality.

Jung was a life-long student of world religions, both historical and cultural. He challenged head on Western monotheistic cultures with the concept of an *inner spirituality* within the archetypes of the collective unconscious. This spirituality was pluralistic and had many potential 'Gods'. In this, it was more akin to Paganism, alchemy, Gnosticism, the hermetic traditions and the mystical and esoteric wisdom streams. Jung challenged the monotheistic 'God/Father' concept. This was just one archetype among many; hence Jung challenged the hegemony of the traditional religious institutions and their foundational disciplines. In particular, he challenged fundamentalism and modernist theology. For Jung the God image, or *Imago Dei*, comes from within the psyche. It is an archetype. It displays the struggle of the psyche for self-realisation; which is the spiritual goal of the individual and all of humanity.

THE SOUL AS THE FEMININE PRINCIPLE or anima archetype within the human being, was emphasized by Jung. It is perhaps because of this that he was well regarded by educated and independent women, both in his time and after his death.

As well, the anima archetype within is congenial to openly gay men, and those heterosexual men secure enough in their personhood and masculinity to be happy to enjoy and acknowledge their feminine side. This recognition of the archetypal power of the *anima,* redeemed the feminine, long derogated within traditional patriarchal monotheism. For example Jung argued that the "whole nature of man presupposes woman, both physically and spiritually." [33]

Attack and Defence

PERHAPS THE MOST VIRULENT attack in recent years against Jung and archetypal theory has come from Richard Noll. [34] But Anthony Stevens, archetypal theorist and research psychiatrist, has decisively refuted Noll's attack. In particular, Stevens has argued there is a biological component to archetypal theory. [35]

Jung's theory of archetypes is compatible with evolutionary psychology and evolutionary psychiatry and these two new disciplines do not "contradict or supersede Jung's original insights into the nature and influence of archetypes which make up the human collective unconscious", rather "they corroborate and amplify them":

> They confirm that human experience and human behaviour are
> complex products of environmental and hereditary forces. The
> environment activates the archetype which mediates the experience
> and behaviour. Archetypes are intermediate between genes and
> experience: they are the organizing schemata by which the innate
> becomes personal. [36]

Although Stevens argues that Jung's theory of archetypes has scientific credibility insofar as it is closely related to the nascent, science-based or scientifically respectable, evolutionary psychology and evolutionary psychiatry - Stevens also recognizes that he walks a fine line between the Jungian postmodernists (who emphasize the cultural, *content*, imaginal and free-will, non-reductionist aspects of archetypes) and the 'genetic determinists', or material reductionists (who emphasize the biologically and materially determined *form* of archetypes). The latter sometimes seek to reduce culture and the content of archetypes to one and the same.

To complicate things further, the scientific validity of the theories of evolutionary psychology and evolutionary psychiatry are increasingly controversial among scientists themselves - for example evolutionary biologists, and neurobiologists such as Steven Rose. Theories of evolutionary psychology and psychiatry are also questioned on moral and political grounds by other philosophers, sociologists, psychologists and law makers. [37]

Jung rises above the controversy. Stevens concurs with Jung who drew a distinction between the *form* of an archetype and the *content* of an archetype:

> Jung specifically distanced himself from the position which critics have
> accused him of adopting: 'Again and again', he wrote, 'I encounter the

mistaken notion that an archetype is determined in regard to its content, in other words that it is a kind of unconscious idea (if such an expression be permissible). It is necessary to point out once more that archetypes are not determined as to their content, but only as regards their form, and then only to a very limited degree. A primordial image is determined as to its content only when it has become conscious and is therefore filled out with the material of conscious experience'.[38]

Stevens argues that "One of the most congenial attributes of Jung was his Janus head which enabled him to look at and comprehend both the imaginal life of the spirit and the organic processes of biology and thus transcend the Cartesian divide".[39]

Recently 'Emergence Theory' has provided another challenge to the reductionist theory of human nature, culture and scientific thinking.[40] This comes not only from reductionism's proven inadequacy, but the search for an alternative and a successor in a more complex theory. Emergence theory has implications not just for reductionism but for evolutionary theory and epistemology:

The greatest impact would surely be in the field of consciousness studies, where the mind-body problem could be solved by appealing to mental causation as a legitimate category augmenting, but not reducible to, physical causation. This would enable scientists to take consciousness seriously as a fundamental property of the universe, and not as an irrelevant and incidental epiphenomenon.[41]

'Emergence theory' would enable – if not endorse – Jung's 'theory of archetypes', hence the primacy of the psyche and synchronicity.

JUNG WAS PRO-SCIENCE, but he was *not* a physical or biological *reductionist*, which is a very narrow view of scientific validity, one which postmodernism challenges.

As Stevens points out, "Jung's vision was to develop such breadth as to embrace those arch-antagonists science and religion, conceiving man's spiritual life not as a denial of evolutionary origins but as an expression of them".[42] However, where Jung's methods differed was in "observational emphasis". While other disciplines, such as ethology (the study of animal behaviour in their natural environment) concerned themselves with "behaviour which is objective, 'outer' and public; analytical psychology deals with behaviour which is subjective, inner and private"; indeed, these "two disciplines ... may be regarded as antinomies, in the sense that they are complementary attempts to comprehend the same universally occurring phenomena".[43] Thus Stevens concludes:

So, just as Darwin found homologues in anatomy, and the ethologists have demonstrated homologues in patterns of behaviour, so Jung traced homologues in symbols. It was this insight which caused him to formulate the theory of archetypes, which attributed the universal occurrence of homologous symbols and myths to the existence of universal structures within the human mind.[44]

Evidence For Archetypes

EVIDENCE FOR ARCHETYPES can be divided into several different categories: (1) *'associative evidence'*, similar or associative theory which overtly supports archetypes or bears a resemblance to archetypal theory; (2) *'scientific evidence'*, where it is argued Jung's method which is descriptive and phenomenological is not unscientific, and 'archetypes' are given theoretical support from the theory of other scientists; (3) *'evidence from quantum physics'*, which is support from the theory of quantum physicists.

Complicating the issue of evidence for archetypes is that *acceptable* evidence is dependent on how archetypes are defined. Different theorists have defined archetypes in different ways. For example, while the leading Romanian and latterly American academic historian and philosopher of religion Mircea Eliade (1907-1986) and James Hillman define archetypes in similar ways to Jung, there are also differences. Jung, a self-described empiricist, wanted a naturalistic theory of archetypes which had scientific credibility. Hillman would abandon the scientific approach to archetypes altogether and advocate instead that we see science from the viewpoint of archetypes. For Hillman, science itself is a sort of myth and fantasy of the soul.

Even within the archetypal theory of one thinker, most notably Jung, there can be many strains of thought which can appear contradictory. Jung, however, is acknowledged as the pre-eminent thinker on archetypes in the twentieth century – and it is precisely because his theory encompasses both modernist scientific perspectives and evidence from quantum science and postmodern and mystical perspectives that his thought is so compelling, evocative and complex.

Walter A. Shelburne philosophy professor and founding member of the Applied Philosophy Institute, California, has studied and examined the scientific and logical evidential parameters of Jung's theory of archetypes in depth. He concludes:

> even though there are these many strains of Jung's thought – a philosophical emphasis, a mythos emphasis, as well as a scientific emphasis – this is not to say that everything Jung said has to be evaluated from the critical standpoint of any one particular point of view. For...in spite of the confusion that Jung creates by working over his material from these methodologically divergent perspectives, a legitimately scientific perspective can nonetheless be reconstructed from his thought.[45]

Archetypes and Platonic Forms

'ARCHETYPE' IS GREEK in origin and dates from classical times.[46] Jung's first use of the term archetype was in 1919 and Jung makes the point strongly that 'archetype' was synonymous with 'Idea' in Platonic usage. He consistently states that the term has precisely that pre-existent, *a priori* meaning that it had for Augustine and Plato.[47] In particular Jung acknowledged his debt to Plato, describing archetypes as "active living dispositions, ideas in the Platonic sense, that preform and continually influence our thoughts and feelings and actions".[48]

ARCHETYPES ARE TIMELESS, for Jung, as for Mircea Eliade. Eliade, like Jung, compares archetypes to the Platonic "forms that exist "on supraterrestrial planes".[49] But while there are striking similarities in Jung's and Eliade's understanding of archetype, there are also sharp divergences.

The whole thrust of Eliade's ontology is towards *escaping* the profane time of history and maximising our consciousness of sacred mythic time of eternal archetypes. As Dudley points out: "The archetype has an exclusively positive and redemptive role in Eliade's scheme of things. With Jung however, the case is different. For him the archetype can be both positive and negative, redemptive and destructive".[50]

To become *subsumed* into the collective unconscious where archetypes reign, for Jung, is to lose oneself. The goal is a balance and connectedness between ego and archetypes, hence individuation which can occur through a dialectic between the individual ego and archetypes.[51]

Despite their differences, Jung and Eliade's understanding of archetypes is strikingly close. They staked their life's works on the existence and understanding of archetypes. Both believed that humankind's survival depends on developing consciousness of the archetypes.[52]

Like archetypes themselves, the theory of archetypes, as Stevens points out, recurs in different guises at different times and places; indeed:

> the theory has been rediscovered and propounded in different
> terminologies by the ethologists (Lorenz's innate releasing
> mechanisms), Gestalt psychologists (Wolfgang Kohler's isomorphs),
> developmental psychologists (John Bowlby's behavioral systems),
> biologists (Ernst Mayr's open programs), anthropologists (Fox's
> biogrammar), and psycholinguists (Naom Chomsky's language
> acquisition device).[53]

THE ARCHETYPE POSSESSES A FUNDAMENTAL DUALITY: it is both psychic and nonpsychic. What is passed on from generation to generation is a structure – a *characteristic* patterning of matter and it is this 'physic' pattern which forms the replicable archetype of the species. As Stevens describes it, the archetypal hypothesis proposes we possess innate neuropsychic centres which orchestrate the common behavioural characteristics and experiences of all human beings regardless of culture, race or creed. This is akin to Jean Piaget's mental developmental stages, Fox's idea of inbuilt programmes for learning, and H.F and M.K. Harlow's theory that "social development depends on the motivation of a sequence of affectional systems".[54] Other theorists whose thinking has an affinity with the archetypal hypothesis and hence provide associative evidence include Kepler, Kant, Lorenz and Pauli. They have emphasized "inner ideas" or *images* which correspond with external events perceived through the senses.[55]

Scientific Evidence?

UNLIKE HILLMAN, who would subsume science into an archetypal perspective and hence rejects scientific standards as a measure of archetypal validity, Walter A. Shelburne argues that Jung was open to the scientific perspective.[56] Jung stated that:

> Psychic events are observable facts and can be dealt with in a 'scientific' way... I do make the claim of being 'scientific' because I do exactly what you describe as the 'scientific method'. I observe, I classify, I establish relations and sequences between the observed data, and I even show the possibility of prediction.[57]

The phenomenological method was recommended by Jung for the study of archetypes and by this he meant the theoretically unbiased observation of phenomena. The scientific method employed by Jung did *not* however employ the experimental technique. He argued he had to investigate the phenomena as it appeared in his patients *without controls or manipulations.*[58] Jung gathered his evidence from his observations of patients' dreams and visualisations in his clinical psychiatric practice. He supplemented these findings with the study of myths, symbols and religions from around the world.

THE "UNIVERSAL OCCURRENCE of homologous symbols and mythologems" caused Jung to postulate the existence of universal structures of the human mind, hence archetypes of the collective unconscious.[59] Stevens states that in contemplating the apparently infinite multiformity of symbolisms, richly complicated but ingeniously diverse, Jung realized that there were universally recurrent themes. By tracing the homologues in symbols, Jung was able to formulate his theory of archetypes. The evidence Jung found for the universal occurrence of homologous symbols and mythologems pointed to universal structures of the human mind, archetypes.[60]

Joseph Campbell (1904-1987), the comparative mythologist, reached the same conclusions as Jung from his cross-cultural studies and observations which supported universally occurring myths and symbols.[61]

Archetype Falsifiability and Predictability

RATHER THAN ATTEMPTING to show a similarity with paradigmatic models of 'hard' science such as physics and chemistry, Walter A. Shelburne attempts to establish that Jung's theory of archetypes is not unscientific. He looks at archetypes from the point of falsifiability – what counts as observational evidence for the presence of an archetype.[62]

The validity of the theory can be evaluated by a non-Jungian, for while understanding how the theory works involves specialised knowledge, it can be "checked independently of a detailed knowledge of the manifestations of individual archetypes".[63] Shelburne shows that examples can be given to indicate what sort of evidence would count against the theory and hence what is incompatible with it. A plausible test for falsifiability is essential to any theory claiming the status of scientific validity.

However, as Jung recognized, one chief problem with archetypal theory is that it does not seem possible in principle to *predict* when an archetype will be manifested, nor what its appearance will be like, except in broad outlines.[64] Shelburne argues that, in this regard, *archetypal theory is more like evolution theory* than Newtonian mechanics.[65]

While evolution is subject to unforseeable environmental factors, the appearance of archetypes depends on interrelation with the existing cultural matrix. With the individual, predicting the appearance of archetypes is possibly even more complex. In Shelburne's opinion, "in order to be able to separate the variables at work in determining how environment conditions the appearance of archetypes in the individual, we would need to perform an isolation experiment on a human being lasting several years".[66]

Given the problems of predictability, Shelburne concludes that archetypal theory is an immature theory from a scientific viewpoint but "this is not to say that the theory is not scientifically defensible or that its methods are inadequate for what they attempt to accomplish".[67]

Archetype Nature versus Nurture

THE ARCHETYPAL IMAGE is the end result of interaction between the innate archetype and the environment. If Shelburne is correct, the problem then arises as to how the *innate nature* of the archetype can be established, as opposed to being *acquired*.

Jung maintained that his clinical evidence was that the persons involved had no previous exposure to the motifs that appeared in their visions and dreams. As a human subject cannot be isolated from cultural influences, the question remains as to whether the subject could have learned of the motif, or been mistaken or deceptive in their descriptions. There is also the possibility of suggestion from the investigator.[68] While Jung maintained he could easily multiply his examples, the problem of a limited number of these individual cases remains nevertheless:

> Establishing such facts not only requires lengthy and wearisome
> researches, but is also an ungrateful subject for demonstration. As the
> symbols must not be torn out of their context, one has to launch forth
> into exhaustive descriptions, personal as well as symbological, and this
> is practically impossible in the framework of a lecture.[69]

At the cross-cultural level it is even more difficult to establish the innate origin of symbolic motifs. Shelburne states that "anthropologists tend either to accept the theory and interpret their data from a Jungian perspective or reject the theory from an unknowledgeable standpoint".[70]

Experiments designed to induce altered states of consciousness have been used to see whether anything similar to descriptions of archetypal motifs were reported. R.E.L. Masters and Jean Housten conducted 206 drug sessions with LSD-25 and peyote over a period of more than 15 years and discovered mythological and religious symbolic imagery was often encountered.[71] Psychiatrist Stanislav Grof whose work also involved LSD research in Prague, obtained results supporting Master's and Houston's research.[72]

Shelburne concludes that despite the influence of Jung's work and the problem of suggestion, these results seem to constitute convincing evidence for the archetypal theory.

Archetype Evidence from Operational Science

AT THE LEVEL OF PRACTICAL operational science, Charles R. Card argues that the concept of archetype is at the forefront of scientific thinking.[73] This is particularly the case in biology and sociology. However "in many areas of science there are emerging phenomena and concepts used to explain them which have associations and correspondences to the Jungian concept of archetype, although the conceptual link often goes unrecognized.[74] An example is within computer science where an attempt is being made to develop an archetypal approach to computer programming in order to "unify sequential, parallel, and distributed approaches to computing".[75]

Of special interest is the archetypal behaviour in the dynamics of non-linear systems. Within *chaotic dynamics*, an area of nonlinear dynamics claimed by some to constitute a new science, 'chaotic' or 'strange' attractors share some of the important characteristics attributed to Jung's conception of archetypes.[76]

However Card concludes that to equate archetypes with strange attractors and vice versa "would lead to a reductive collapse of the mental and physical realms, when in fact a more profound understanding of the basis by which these two realms are somehow distinguishable is urgently needed".[77]

Jung's Challenge to Orthodox Science

IRONICALLY, WHILE Anthony Stevens, Walter A. Shelburne and more recent theorists such as Charles R. Card have made a good case for Jung's theory of archetypes from the perspective of orthodox science this whole endeavour is somewhat paradoxical.

As Shelburne admits "Jung's science already incorporates a brave new vision of what it means to be scientific which owes a great deal to the inspiration of relativity and quantum physics".[78]

Jung's "science" never did "fit neatly into the ideal of what science should be, if this ideal is taken from the natural sciences as a model".[79] Shelburne warns that one should also be wary of falling into the trap of trying to make a psychology such as Jung's theory of archetypes scientific by modelling it on an already outmoded concept of science.

While behavioural psychologists have emulated classical Newtonion physics – Jung's scientific method is descriptive and phenomenological. It is an attempt to legitimate alternative ways of scientific investigation "in the face of prohibitive difficulties of employing experimental methods with regard to archetypal phenomena".[80]

Jung's ideas were on the growing fringe of science. As Shelburne points out:

a critic might argue that reconstructing Jung's idea of archetypes from the standpoint of a scientific outlook, *we* are in effect cutting out of the theory the progressive aspects of it where Jung was beginning to grope toward a new vision of reality transcending the limiting scope of scientific method.[81]

The theory of archetypes fits better into the realm of quantum physics and emergence theory.

Archetypes, Quantum Physics, Consciousness

CARL JUNG'S MEETING with quantum physicist Wolfgang Pauli (1900-1958), winner of the 1945 Nobel Prize in Physics, was one of the most significant intellectual engagements of the twentieth century in this regard. Their collaboration would lead to the development and elaboration of Jung's archetypal hypothesis and the theory of synchronicity.[82] As a result of perceiving parallel developments in depth psychology and quantum physics Jung and Pauli eventually developed the following propositions:

(1) Physics and psyche represent complementary aspects of the same transcendent unitary reality, the unus mundus.
(2) Archetypes act as fundamental dynamical patterns whose various representations characterise all processes whether mental or physical.
(3) Archetypes acting simultaneously in both the realms of matter and mind account for synchronistic phenomena.[83]

That consciousness and the quantum world are fundamentally linked, or share similarities, is an argument made in various ways more recently by other philosophers. For example philosopher Christian de Quincey points out that quantum physics and consciousness share characteristics and metaphors:

Classical physics could shed no light on the nature of consciousness – because, unlike matter, mind could not fit the criteria and methodology of standard science: measurement, separate-identity, determinism, reductionism, objectivity. But quantum physics challenges each of these criteria. The quantum possesses many characteristics reminiscent of consciousness.[84]

Archetypes and Synchronicity

PAULI SHOWED THAT BENEATH MATTER, abstract pattern determines the behaviour of matter in a noncausal way.[85]

The 'theory of synchronicity' originally grew out of Jung's psychotherapeutic experiences and his theory of archetypal symbols, as well as meanings in alchemy. While Jung had talked about "synchronicism' as early as 1929, in particular with regard to Eastern philosophy and the *I-Ching*, it was thanks to the new quantum physics, particularly Heisenberg's 'principle of uncertainty' and Pauli's 'exclusion principle' that the theory could be expanded further with new scientific plausibility.[86]

In collaboration with Pauli, Jung explored the question of hidden symmetry within the universe from the perspectives of both physics and psychology and published his ideas on synchronicity.[87]

SYNCHRONICITY IS DESCRIBED variously as "the coincidence in time of two or more causally unrelated events which have the same or similar meaning" and "acausal parallelisms".[88] As with archetypes, essential to synchronicity is *meaning*.

Jung's position was that while causal explanations of natural events, inherited from the modern scientific view, are valid for explaining much of what occurs in nature and experience, they are insufficient to explain all.[89] Phenomena exist which "cannot be explained causally unless one permits oneself the most fantastic ad hoc hypotheses".[90] As Cosgrove states:

> Jung's position would find some agreement from scientific 'realists' and critics like Paul Feyerabend. Relativity theory indicates that space and time may be reduced to zero under certain conditions where, logically, linear causality becomes impossible. It collapses distinctions between being and becoming. Only an enduring unity, or an inexplicable discontinuity make sense under these conditions, description becomes purely contextual. To accept this unity may render us silent. But characteristically humans seek to create meaning and do so through metaphor. The metaphors of synchronicity are those of harmony and correspondence… This principle of meaning cannot be grasped through empirical observation or measurement, but rather apprehended phenomenologically, below the intellectual level of formal science.[91]

Charles Card has argued that if quantum mechanics led to a revolution in physics, it is a revolution not yet completed. There is the *mystery of non-locality* at its heart – in other words the phenomenon where measurements made at the microscopic level refute local realism and are independent of our description of how nature operates. This may entail deeper and more fundamental changes to our scientific *weltbild*, world view, than those already taken place. Card concludes that quantum non-locality "is the most dramatic indication of the possibility of archetypal order in quantum phenomena".[92]

Archetypal Holographic Universe

THE 'HOLOGRAPHIC UNIVERSE' idea, or holographic model, has also been suggested as a mechanism for explaining the existence of archetypes.[93]   Theoretical physicist David Bohm argues that behind the quantum lies an even deeper reality which he called the *implicate order*, which causes apparently random quantum processes to unfold as they do. The implicate order is "enfolded" in the *explicate order* or *manifest reality* detectable at the quantum level and the level of everyday experiences. Interestingly, de Quincey draws links between the theory of Bohm and Jung:

> Like Bohm, Carl Jung proposed that below the conscious mind lies the

unconscious psyche, and that below causal matter lies the realm of indeterminate quantum events. Deeper still, below both the level of unconscious psyche and quantum events, lies the realm of a-causal archetypes. Jung called it the "unus mundus," an indivisible continuum of "psychoid" events. ("Psychoid" means of the nature of both psyche and matter). The archetypes can never be known directly; they can only be inferred from their effects on the conscious psyche (eg. in dreams via the unconscious) and on material objects (eg. patterning of physical processes via quantum events).[94]

Evidence from psychiatrist Stanislav Grof indicates that archetypal images can be modelled by the holographic idea; that holography's success at modeling many different aspects of the archetypal experience suggests that there is a deep link between holographic processes and the way archetypes are produced; and that evidence of a hidden, holographic order surfaces virtually every time one experiences a nonordinary state of consciousness.[95]

Holist physicist, philosopher and author F. David Peat, states that Pauli was fascinated with the idea that just as Jung had identified the *objective* element within the collective psyche, physics would have to come to terms with the *subjective* aspects of matter, which he termed "the irrational".[96] Pauli found this dualism between objective and subjective especially significant and indicative that there was a much deeper connection between mind and matter:

> Below the everyday appearances of matter, in which the scientist acts as an impartial observer, are encountered quantum processes in which observer and observed are intimately linked. Below this level, Heisenberg and others have hinted, there may no longer exist a fundamental ground of matter but, rather, fundamental symmetries and ordering principles.[97]

At their deepest, the subjective layers of matter and the objective layers of the mind are hidden from direct perception. Their existence can only be inferred from their impacts at higher levels. It is possible that below quantum phenomena there is a new, nonmaterial level of symmetry. Could it be, asks Peat, that below the collective unconsciousness there is something beyond mind; "a fundamental dynamic ordering perhaps? ... (whereby) ... At such a level the division between mind and matter would no longer apply and the domain of creative ordering and objective intelligence would have their ground".[98]

Recent support for Jung's theory of archetypes has come from Christopher Isham, a theoretical physicist at Imperial College London, whose main research interests are quantum gravity and foundational studies in quantum theory. He has linked space and time and the development in quantum theory of the space-time continuum with progress in philosophical and psychological thought from Plato to Kant to Jung.[99]

'Emergence Theory' which involves the shift away from materialist, mechanistic reductionism that has dominated the modernist scientific world view, towards mental causation which is not reducible to physical causation, also gives further support for archetypal theory.[100] Also, Christopher Hauke argues that while the writing of Jung and post-Jungians has been ignored as "anachronistic", "archaic" and "mystic", it is more relevant now than ever before. Not only is it a response to modernity, it offers a critique of modernity and Enlightenment values which brings it into line with postmodernism.[101] As has been shown, postmodernism is inherent to both quantum physics and archetypal epistemology

Essence of Archetypes

IN ORDER TO CLARIFY what is meant by *an archetypal analysis of landscape*, a consideration must be made as to what is the *essence* of an archetype or archetypes. On the face of it this is not easy. Much has been said about the theory and form of archetypes and much less about their essence. In his essay 'Mind and Earth', Jung wrote:

> …[T]he archetypes are as it were the hidden foundations of the
> conscious mind or, to use another comparison, the roots which the
> psyche has sunk not only in the earth in the narrower sense but in the
> world in general. Archetypes are systems of readiness for action and at
> the same time images and emotions.[102]

Despite devoting over fifty years to the study of archetypes, Jung concluded that they must defeat all attempts to grasp them academically. He argued that an archetype's "very nature makes it incapable of precise definition".[103] Jung states of archetypes that:

> [I]t is essential to insist that they are not mere names, or even
> philosophical concepts. They are pieces of life itself – images that are
> integrally connected to the living individual by the bridge of emotions.
> That is why it is impossible to give an arbitrary (or universal)
> interpretation of any archetype.[104]

ARCHETYPES ARE INTIMATE, emotional, experiential images. According to Jung archetypes "gain life and meaning only when you try to take into account their numinosity – ie., their relationship to the living individual".[105] Anthony Stevens concludes that, in the end, "you cannot define an archetype, any more than you can define meaning. You can only experience it".[106]

ARCHETYPES ARE EXPERIENTIAL and have 'feeling tone'. Jung states "Those who do not realize the special feeling tone of the archetype end with nothing more than a jumble of mythological concepts, which can be strung together to show that everything means anything – or nothing at all".[107] Thus a further characteristic of archetypes is delineated – their special 'feeling tone'.

ARCHETYPES ARE 'METAPHORS', 'images' and entail an 'imaginative style of discourse'. Hillman has argued that the "curious difficulty of explaining just what archetypes are suggests something specific to them":

> That is, they tend to be metaphors rather than things. We find
> ourselves less able to say what an archetype is literally and more
> inclined to describe them in images. We can't seem to touch one or
> point to one, and rather speak of what they are like. Archetypes throw
> us into an imaginative style of discourse.[108]

Hillman points out that it is as *metaphors* that Jung writes of archetypes, while yet insisting on their indefinability. To take an archetypal perspective, is to approach basic questions of soul and psychology first of all by means of the imagination.[109]

ARCHETYPES ARE AXIOMATIC, universally accepted, self-evident images of psyche or soul. They are not just any image. As Hillman states, they are "the *deepest patterns of psychic functioning*, the roots of the soul governing the perspectives we have of ourselves and the world. They are the axiomatic, self-evident images to which psychic life and our theories about it ever return".[110]

ARCHETYPES ARE IMAGISTIC UNIVERSALS, trans-historical, profound, generative, highly intentional and necessary. Hillman states that any "image termed 'archetypal' is immediately valued as universal, trans-historical, basically profound, generative, highly intentional, and necessary".[111]

ARCHETYPES ARE 'A WAY OF SEEING'. Edward Casey has argued that "an image is not what one sees but the way in which one sees. An image is given by the imagining perspective and can only be perceived by an act of imagining".[112] This is reminiscent of Cosgrove's definition of landscape as "a way of seeing"; for landscape "is not merely the world we see, it is a construction, a composition of that world. Landscape is a way of seeing the world".[113]

ARCHETYPES ARE A LOCUS OF IMAGINING. This involves a 'seeing-with- the-heart', *in-*sight; seeing-through, hearing-into. While images come and go as in dreams, with their own rhythm and in their own fields of relations; images are also fundamentals which make psychodynamics possible and they therefore claim authority, objectivity and certainty. Hillman argues, that in the end, "the mind is in the imagination rather than the imagination in the mind. The noetic and the imaginal no longer oppose each other".[114] The archetypal image is not merely something seen, but *'a way of seeing'*; and moreover a *'way of seeing with the heart'*. It is *in*sight. "We do not literally see images or hear metaphors; we perform an operation of insight which is a seeing-through or hearing into".[115]

ARCHETYPES BRING FORTH all knowledge and experience. The archetypal image is the means by which the world is imagined, the modes by which all knowledge and experiences become possible. Hillman argues:

> [The archetypal image] operates like the original meaning of idea
> (from Greek *eidos* and *eidolon*): not only 'that which' one sees but also
> that 'by means of which' one sees. The demonstration of archetypal
> images is therefore as much an act of seeing as in the object seen, since
> the archetypal image appears in consciousness itself as the governing
> fantasy by means of which consciousness is possible to begin with.[116]

ARCHETYPES ARE VALUES and feelings. The feeling aspect of the archetypal image points to value. The archetypal image is at once animated, emotionalized and placed in the realm of value. The feelings inherent in the image make the image felt as a specific value. Feelings are inherent in archetypal images. Feelings accompany, qualify and energize images. Feelings belong to the reality of the image, hence they are universal and not merely personal. Feelings elaborate on the image's complexity. They are as complex as the image that contains them. Hillman thus argues that the implication is that the archetypal image is at once animated, emotionalized and placed in the realm of value. "The word 'archetypal' ... rather than pointing *at* something archetypal points *to* something, and this is *value*".[117]

ARCHETYPES HAVE EMOTIONAL, POSSESSIVE effect. As Hillman observes, "one thing is absolutely essential to the notion of archetypes; their emotional possessive effect, their bedazzlement of consciousness so that it becomes blind to its own stance".[118]

Writing on Jung's theory on archetypes, Dudley notes that whenever "a situation occurs which corresponds to a given archetype, that archetype becomes activated and a compulsiveness appears, which, like an instinctual drive, gains its way against all reason and will.[119] Dudley points out that this is what Jung calls the "absorptive power" of the archetype. It explains not only its widespread occurrence, but also the "passionate intensity with which it seizes upon the individual".[120]

An archetype can be compared with a God.[121] Because the archetype has this emotional possessive effect, the power to bedazzle consciousness and it sets up a style of consciousness and a universe which holds everything in its sway. An example is the hero archetype:

> The archetype of the hero, for example, appears first in *behavior*, the
> drive to activity, outward exploration, response to challenge, seizing and
> grasping and extending. It appears second in the *images* of Hercules,
> Archilles, Samson (or their cinema counterparts) doing their specific
> tasks; and third, in a style of *consciousness,* in feelings of independence,
> strength, and achievement, in ideas of decisive action, coping, planning,
> virtue, conquest (over animality), and in psychopathologies of battle,
> overpowering masculinity, and single-mindedness.[122]

ARCHETYPAL GODS ARE IMAGINED. God and Gods are polytheistic. They are cosmic perspectives in which the soul participates. They are not believed in literally or theologically, rather they are *imagined*. They involve places and the phenomenol world. The Gods are discovered in recognising the orientation of one's perspective (one could say one's 'focus of perception'); or as Hillman puts it "one's psychological sensitivity to the configurations that dominate one's styles of thought and life".[123] For Hillman:

> Archetypal psychology does not attempt to correct the Judeo-Christian
> religion as illusion (Freud) or transform it as one-sided (Jung). It shifts
> the ground of the entire question to a polytheistic position. In this
> single stroke, it carries out Freud's and Jung's critiques to their ultimate
> consequent – the death of God as a monotheistic fantasy, while at the
> same time restoring the fullness of the Gods in all things.[124]

ARCHETYPES RESTORE THE SPIRITUAL within the material. In other words, archetypes and the Gods restore spirituality to the world. The Gods are places, and myths make place for psychic events. Thus:

> Gods are imagined as the formal intelligibility of the phenomenal
> world, allowing each thing to be discerned for its inherent intelligiblity
> and for its specific place of belonging to this or that *kosmos* (ordered
> pattern or arrangement). The Gods are *places,* and myths make place
> for psychic events... By offering shelter and alter, the Gods can order
> and make intelligible the entire phenomenal world of nature and
> human consciousness... We discover what belongs where by means of
> likeness, the analogy of events with mythical configurations.[125]

ARCHETYPES STRUCTURE THE PSYCHE. The archetypal nature, images and events can be discerned in structural components of the psyche, or personality, in Jungian practice – for example, *Shadow, Ego, Self, Anima.*

Archetypal psychology emphasises and extends Jung's personified naming of the components of the personality. These basic structures are imagined to be partial personalities. They can be termed 'archetypal persons' – for example, *Trickster, Old Wise Man, Great Mother, Hero.* "As Jung refined his insight into these complex persons, the persons of our complexes, he discovered that their autonomy and intentionality derives from deeper figures of far wider significance. These are the archetypes, the persons to whom we ultimately owe our personality".[126]

In other words, the personified Archetypes can be regarded as, in effect, Gods. Indeed, Hillman asks the question: "Archetypes or Gods" and argues that by considering the personified archetypes *as* Gods they become more than constitutional propensities, instinctual behaviour patterns and ordering structures of the psyche. They now become recognisable 'persons' with individual styles of consciousness, or, in Jung's words "typical modes of apprehension".[127]

Hillman argues that the personified archetypes – Gods, persons – each with "typical modes of apprehension":

> present themselves each as a guiding spirit (*spiritus rector*) with ethical
> positions, instinctual reactions, modes of thought and speech, and
> claims upon feeling. These persons by governing my complexes,
> govern my life. My life is a diversity of relationships with them. As
> *persons* they do not differ from the Gods, heroes and daemons; only as
> *concepts* in the abstractions of a science can we distinguish them from

the figures of myth and cult.[128]

Our psychic conditions are derived from these figures, or archetypes, and not vice versa. Or as Jung puts it: "The psyche creates reality every day".[129] So Hillman argues that, in this view, personality is seen less in terms of stages in life, typologies of character and functioning, and energy towards social and individual goals. Thus "personality is imaginatively conceived as a living and peopled drama in which the subject 'I' takes part but is neither the sole author, nor dictator, nor always the main character".[130]

ARCHETYPES ARE ROOT-METAPHORS, IDEAS, MYTHS, MOTIFS. Archetypes are primarily metaphors. As Hillman notes, archetypes tend to be metaphors rather than things. We are less likely to describe them literally and are more likely to describe them in images. They throw us into an imaginative style of discourse. "All ways of speaking of archetypes are translations from one metaphor to another".[131]

Even the language of science and logic with its sober operational definitions is ultimately metaphorical. In fact, Hillman argues that it is no less metaphorical than the "image which presents the archetype as root ideas, psychic organs, figures of myth, typical styles of existence, or dominant fantasies that govern consciousness".[132] Archetypes "direct all fantasy activity and images into its appointed paths", and these paths are mythological. Thus:

> we see that fantasy flows into particular motifs (mythologems) and constellations of persons in actions (mythemes). These patternings appear in myths the world over, and in literature, art, scientific theories, and theological doctrines; also in dreams, even the dreams of children, and in the delusional systems of the insane – wherever imagination manifests itself in the products of the mind. Within these fantasy-images are the archetypal persons of myths.[133]

Peter Bishop has argued that:

> an imaginal analysis must bear in mind the dominant root-metaphors of any theory that it uses to craft the imaginal material. A polytheistic approach does not exclude any perspective on the grounds of theoretical incompatibility but instead tries to relate theories through their common grounding in imaginal reality.[134]

Listening to the root-metaphors relieves them of their literalness and allows images to speak pluralistically. Analysis "becomes a matter of image-work, a crafting of images":[135]

> An archetypal analysis is less concerned with logical or epistemological differences between disciplines or theories than with their metaphorical even aesthetical relationship… Questions of 'who?' and 'where?' are preferred to those of 'how?' and 'why?'; 'who?' not in the sense of personal subjectivity, but in identifying the personages speaking from within the imagination… An ability to assess imagistic

resonances, rather than philosophical compatibilities, becomes important. Leaping associations, fortuitous, synchronicitic, or serendipitous encounters between images become valued.[136]

Archetypal Analysis of Landscapes

WE CAN NOW ASK AND ANSWER, with justification, the question: How does one attempt an archetypal analysis of landscape? It will involve: (1) looking for images which are universal, trans-historical, profound, numinous, generative, highly intentional and necessary; (2) looking for images which are 'a way of seeing', a 'locus of imagining' and 'a way of seeing with the heart' (insight); (3) looking for images which are inherently feelings, have an emotional possessive effect and that bedazzle consciousness; (4) looking for appropriate components of the psyche, Gods and myths; (5) looking for root metaphors.

It is to an archetypal analysis of the *Nature/Earth Landscape*, the *Anthropocentric Landscape*, the *Technological/Materialist Landscape* and the *Postmodern Ecological Landscape* – the *Inner Landscape*, that we now turn.

FIVE

Mother Earth

Mother Earth is as universal a symbol as
our race possesses, at home even in those
societies that have moved on to more
civilized ways.

– Theodore Roszak

Our Global Eternal Mother

IN OLD EUROPEAN-BASED SOCIETIES the Mother Earth Archetype was found
in pre-Hellenic Greece, influenced by Crete, ancient Anatolia and the Near East.
She was part of the Celtic tradition which extended in a broad sweep from
Northern Ireland to Central Europe; Northern Italy and as far east as Central Anatolia,
the Galaticia highlands of Turkey; and south to the Iberian Peninsula - Spain ,
northwest Galicia, and Portugal. Mother Earth worship persisted up to 500 CE in
Europe and persists today in primal indigenous peoples who choose to remain in their
own traditions:

> [T]he Primal Ancestress, the Old One or mother figure of the
> Paleolithic Age (25,000–15,000 BCE) which by the Neolithic Age
> (8,000–3,000 BCE) became identified as Mother Earth, the creative
> power of the universe. Being born of Mother Earth, everything that
> existed was perceived as partaking of her spirit and there developed a
> relationship of kinship between human beings and all of creation –
> vegetation, animals, the elements, and other plants. This holistic
> approach to life is thought to have originated in Mesopotamia
> spreading throughout the Near and Middle East, Europe, Africa and
> Asia. The creation stories of Native Americans throughout the
> continent make it clear that this relationship was universal.[1]

Recently feminists, ecologists and postmodern neo-pagans have also taken up Earth worship. The Mother Earth image is again in fashion; but the roots of archetypes are always deeper than fashion – indeed the"very words for nature in European languages are feminine". For example:

> *phusis* in Greek, *natura* in Latin, *la nature* in French, *die Natur* in German. The Latin word *natura* literally meant 'birth'. The Greek word *phusis* came from the root *phu* – whose primary meaning was also connected with birth. Thus our words 'physics' and 'physical', like 'nature' and 'natural', have their origins in the mothering process.[2]

In the mythologies of antiquity *Mother Earth* was an aspect of the Great Mother Goddess. The Great Mother was frequently the source of the universe, its laws, the ruler of fate, time, eternity, truth, wisdom, justice, love, birth and death:

> She was Mother Earth, Gaia, and also the goddess of the heavens, the mother of the sun, the moon and of all heavenly bodies – like Nut, the Egyptian sky-goddess; or Astarte, the goddess of heaven, queen of the stars. She was Natura, the goddess of Nature. She was the world soul of Platonic cosmology; and she had many other names and images as the mother and matrix and sustaining force of all things.[3]

Papatuanuku and the Gaia Hypothesis – Maori Mythology Meets Science

FOR THE OLD NEW ZEALAND MAORI, *Papatuanuku* was a personification of the Earth. Like the Greek 'Ge' or 'Gaia', *Papatuanuku* is *Mother Earth*, the archetype.

Tohunga and theologian, Maori Marsden (1924-1993) argues that "Papatuanuku – 'Land from beyond the veil', or originating from the realm beyond the world of sense-perception, was the personified form of 'whenua' – the natural earth".[4]

Papatuanuku is an organic Mother, like the Earth Mother of Old Europe.[5] "Papatuanuku is our Mother and deserves our love and respect. She is a living organism with her own biological systems and functions creating and supplying a web of support systems for all her children whether man, animal, bird, tree or grass".[6]

Papatuanuku, Mother Earth, understood as a living organism and revered by the Maori of antiquity, strikingly resembles James Lovelock's *Gaia* hypothesis – the recent scientifically based and described Gaia, also regarded as a living organism.

Up until seventeenth century Europe the root metaphor binding self, society and the cosmos was that of organism and the idea of nature as a living organism and a nurturing Mother. This had philosophical antecedents in ancient systems of thought. Indeed, "Central to the organic theory was the identification of nature, especially the earth, with a nurturing mother: a kindly beneficent female who provided for the needs of mankind in an ordered, planned universe".[7]

For the Roman Stoics from the third century BCE to the first century CE, the world was an intelligent organism and God and Mother were synonymous.

In a theory which is strikingly similar to Lovelock's Gaia Hypothesis – which showed that the Earth, its rocks, oceans, and atmosphere, and all living things are part of one great organism evolving over the vast span of geological time – the Roman Stoic, Lucias Seneca (4B CE – 65 CE) argued that the earth's breath nourished both plant life and the heavens.[8] Analogies were drawn between the human body and the body of Mother Earth.[9]

For old primal religions, the Mother Earth Archetype remains the supreme underlying holistic force within their landscape. Harold Turner argues that there is "a profound sense in many primal societies that man is akin to nature, a child of Mother Earth and brother to the plants and animals which have their own spiritual existence and place in the universe".[10]

That the Earth is a living, conscious being that must be treated with respect and loving care, is also a very central belief to Native American cultures where the "Earth may be referred to as Mother, or Grandmother, and these are quite literal terms, for the Earth is the source, the mother of all living beings, including human beings".[11]

Black Elk, a Lakota, asked: "Is not the sky a father and the earth a mother and are not all living things with feet and wings or roots their children?"[12] Black Elk spoke resentfully of white pressures on the Sioux to sell their land: "only crazy or very foolish men would sell their Mother Earth".[13]

By the 1960s the Native American had became a symbol in the ecology movement's search for alternatives to Western exploitative attitudes:

> The Indian animistic belief-system and reverence for the earth as
> mother were contrasted with the Judeo-Christian heritage of dominion
> over nature with capitalistic practices resulting in the "tragedy of the
> commons" (exploitation of resources available for any person's or
> nation's use).[14]

The relevance of the Mother Earth Archetype today can be seen in the modern ecology movement, Lovelock's Gaia hypothesis, and the ecofeminist movement which has reasserted the association between women and nature.

David Suzuki and Peter Knudtson argue that modern ecology is a continuation of the age old human quest for a deeper understanding of the *relationships* which mysteriously and invisibly connect living things to each other and the earth: "Today's infant science of nature's patterns and relations has scarcely begun to unveil the tangles of bonds that exist between the species, forces, and materials of the natural world".[15] However, what is being increasingly revealed is a central biological truth, that the "earth's fragile, enveloping film of life and life-supporting air, water, and soil is a single ecological whole or biosphere".[16]

Biochemist Rupert Sheldrake concludes that despite the fact that in the last few centuries an educated minority in the West has believed the scientific mechanistic myth that the Earth is dead, throughout history practically all humanity has believed it to be alive.[17] While most scientists use the vernacular of their profession and tend to view the earth's "exquisite self-regulating tendencies as merely a manifestation of the system's many machinelike feedback mechanisms, referred to collectively as homeostasis"[18] other scientists have viewed it increasingly in a more *poetic* light.

Former NASA scientist and formulator of the Gaia hypothesis, James Lovelock, openly expresses his awe and reverence in like fashion to Native elders the world over, who continue to address the same earth – or any of the transcendent or spiritual dimensions they perceive with it – with undisguised love, respect and awe. For many primal peoples the earth is their living, nurturing, reciprocally affectionate *Mother Earth.* Lovelock has christened this "wonderous lifelike biosphere system *Gaia, this total planetary being,* in honour of the earth goddess of Greek myth":[19]

> The idea that the Earth is alive is at the outer bounds of scientific
> credibility. I started to think and then write about it in my early
> fifties… My contemporary and fellow villager, the novelist William
> Golding, suggested that anything alive deserves a name – what better
> for a living Planet than Gaia, the name the Greeks used for the Earth
> Goddess?[20]

Ecofeminism is a driving spiritual and philosophical force behind the ideology of the ecology movement. Indeed, Carolyn Merchant argues that "Women and nature have an age-old association – an affiliation that has persisted throughout culture, language, and history":[21]

> The ancient identity of nature as a nurturing mother links women's
> history with the history of the environment and ecological change. The
> female earth was central to the organic cosmology that was undermined
> by the Scientific Revolution and the rise of a market-orientated Europe.
> The ecology movement has reawakened interest in the values and
> concepts associated historically with the premodern organic world.[22]

Mother Earth is a timeless archetype which continues to move modern technologically sophisticated man, albeit unexpectedly.

The Bulgarian cosmonaut Aleksandr Aleksandrov, awed by the vision of Earth from the perspective of outer space, described his feelings this way: "And then it struck me that we are all children of our Earth. It does not matter what country you look at. We are all Earth's children, and we should treat her as our Mother".[23]

The Great Nurturer

SANDRA LEE, NEW ZEALAND MINISTER OF CONSERVATION, 1999-2002, and a Maori, once said, in reference to the earth: "It is Mother, Papatuanuku; we shouldn't strive to have power over her, but rather acknowledge that she is the essence which nurtures us and enables us to be".[24]

Intrinsic to the Mother Earth Archetype and the *Nature/Earth Landscape* is *nurturing*. This is characteristic of old European and near Eastern spirituality as well as old Maori mythology, lore and proverbs. It is also true of Native American Indian spirituality and that of other primal peoples. Nurturing is a universal feeling and root metaphor inherent in the Mother Earth Archetype and the *Nature/Earth Landscape*. Nurturing and mothering are components of the individual personality and the collective psyche.

THE OLD MAORI SAW THE EARTH as their Mother. Papatuanuku, Mother Earth, is "someone who nurtures us and to whom we in turn owe important duties of care".[25] In Maori mythology the elemental gods of the natural world are children of Mother Earth and stay close to their nursing Mother.[26] In Maori mythology it is the Earth Mother who is ultimately responsible for all the foods which sustain us – especially crops such as the kumera (sweet potato) which grow directly within her body. The seasons which relate to *Papatuanuku* and the growing and harvesting of her foods are found in many ancient Maori proverbs.[27] *Papatuanuku's* children live and function in a symbiotic relationship:

> From unicellular through to more complex multi-cellular organisms
> each species depends upon other species as well as its own, to provide
> the basic biological needs for existence. The different species contribute
> to the welfare of other species and together they help to sustain the
> biological functions of their primeval mother, herself a living organism.
> They also facilitate the processes of ingestion, digestion and waste
> disposal... they cover her and clothe her to protect her from the
> ravages of her fierce son, Tawhiri the storm-bringer. She nourishes
> them and they nourish her.[28]

Nurturing by and of Papatuanuku, Mother Earth, is not just a symbiotic physical relationship, it is also a spiritual nurturing. Maori Marsden points out that *Papatuanuku* belongs to an older primeval order. Her sustenance derives not only from the *mauri* – the life force immanent in all creation which generates, regenerates and upholds creation – active within her, but is supported by other members of that order.[29] Marsden defines the *mauri* as "the bonding element that knits all the diverse elements within the Universal 'Procession' giving creation its unity in diversity. It is the bonding element that holds the fabric of the universe together".[30] *Mauri* is a force or energy mediated by *Hauora* – the Breath of the Spirit of Life. "Mauri-ora was the life-force (mauri) transformed into life-principle by the infusion of life itself".[31] This view was not unique to the New Zealand Maori.

In old European mythology, "Mother Earth was seen to be very active. She was thought to exhale the breath of life, which nourished living organisms on her surface".[32]

Anthony Stevens, on the Mother Archetype, notes that:

> It is necessary to repeat that when Jungians speak of a mother
> archetype, they are not referring to an innate image but to an inner

dynamic in the phylogenetic psyche. The 'artefacts' of this dynamic –
its symbolic residues – are to be found in the myths and artistic
creations of mankind. The 'symbolic canon' of the mother archetype is
very extensive… However some expressions are so universally
encountered that they can be mentioned here: as Mother Nature and
Earth Mother she is goddess of fertility and dispenser of nourishment;
as water or sea she represents the origins of all life as well as a symbol
of the unconscious, the fount of all psychic creativity; as Moon
Goddess she exemplifies the essential periodicity of womanhood. She
also takes the form of divine animals: the bear (jealous guardian of her
children), the celestial cow, who nourishes the earth with milky rain.[33]

Jung speaks of the qualities associated with the *Mother Archetype* as "maternal
solicitude and sympathy…all that is benign, all that cherishes and sustains, that fosters
growth and fertility".[34] The nurturing Mother Earth Archetype, while a component of
the inner psyche, also extends to the outer world and is found in symbols:

> The archetype is often associated with things and places standing for
> fertility and fruitfulness: the cornucopia, a ploughed field, a garden. It
> can be attached to a rock, a cave, a tree, a spring, a deep well, or to
> various vessels such as the baptismal font, or to vessel-shaped flowers
> like the rose or the lotus. Because of the protection it implies, the magic
> circle or mandala can be a form of mother archetype.[35]

The nurturing Mother Earth Archetype, while associated with *particular* cultures, is to
be found in *all* cultures and mythologies.

Erich Neumann points out that Mother Goddess cultures and their mythologies are
intrinsically connected with fertility, growth and agriculture in particular – hence with
the sphere of food, the material and bodily sphere.[36] As the good mother:

> she is fullness and abundance; the dispenser of life and happiness; the
> nutrient earth, the cornucopia of the fruitful womb. She is mankind's
> instinctive experience of the world's depth and beauty, of the goodness
> and graciousness of Mother Nature who daily fulfills the promise of
> redemption and resurrection, of new life and new birth.[37]

Rupert Sheldrake, biochemist, argues there "is something to be found 'in nature' which
many of us feel we need… Nature is calm, kindly and nurturing, like an ideal wife".[38]

> Nature was traditionally idealized as benevolent Mother in images of
> the Golden Age. All was peaceful and fertile; nature gave freely of her
> bounty; animals grazed contentedly; birds sang pure melodies; flowers
> were everywhere, and trees bore fruit abundantly. Men and women
> lived in harmony.[39]

In old Europe with the development of agriculture Mother Earth gave way to a more
restricted notion of the Great Goddess of vegetation and harvesting.   For example, in

Greece Gaia was replaced by Demeter – but women were still closely associated with agriculture and soil fertility. Of course, metaphors connecting women with the ploughed earth and fertility exist all over the world. For example, in an ancient Hindu text it is written: "This woman is come as a living soil: sow seed in her, ye men!" and in the Koran: "your wives are to you as field".[40] As Sheldrake points out, the "same metaphor is implicit in our word semen, the Latin word for seed".[41] The *Mother Earth Archetype* invites feelings of a return to the protection of the maternal nourishing womb.

Morality Based in Belonging

MOTHER EARTH ENGENDERS a feeling of belonging, a longing to belong, an envelopment of belonging. The archetype also engenders feelings of reciprocity and the *I-Thou* relation.

Speaking from a Maori perspective, as Maori Marsden has said; "the sense of interrelatedness between people and nature creates a sense of belonging to nature, rather than being ascendant to it, as humans are born from 'mother earth' and return to her on their death".[42] All elements of the natural world are related through *whakapapa* (genealogy) in the Maori worldview. While people tested the boundaries of their relationship with the environment, a complex set of concepts and rules grounded in the spiritual world ensured that they did not push this relationship too far.[43] Even when one is destroyed by evil personified (*whiro*) or bad luck (*maiki*) one can find belonging, repose and rest within Mother Earth:

> Their loveliest Mother Earth
> Enshrines the fallen brave;
> In her sweet lap who gave them birth
> They find their tranquil grave.[44]

This Mother-love that outlasts all races and all creeds is expressed by Maori in the aphorism, "*He aroha whaereere, he potiki piri poho*".[45] *The realm of the sacred is within the natural world.* This means that feelings of belonging, reciprocity, awe, love, oneness and wholeness are enhanced. In other words the *I-Thou relation* is sanctified and inherent to the Mother Earth Archetype and the Nature/Earth Landscape.

From an Indian perspective, as noted anthropologist and scholar of his own Native Indian Tewa Pueblo tribe, Alfonso Ortiz puts it: "Indian tribes put nothing above nature. Their gods are part of nature, on the level of nature, not supra anything. Conversely, there's nothing that is religious versus something that is secular. Native American religion pervades, informs all of life".[46]

Like the spirituality of the old Maori, the spiritual (*mauri*) is within – not exterior and divided into the sacred and the profane. For example, a well brought up Pueblo Indian will sing while working among the corn, because if you have good thoughts and heart while you work, you will have a good harvest. In the dances one is renewed if one has heart and spirit in the dance.

The gods are not supernatural. They are experienced rather than revealed. The *I-*

Thou relation of the Indians and primal peoples towards Mother Earth may be contrasted with the *I-It relation* of the religious views of their colonialists:

> The overall ideals of the American Indians were conservational, in
> contrast to the Judeo-Christian view expressed in the Bible (Genesis
> 1:36) where God says that man is to have dominion over fish, birds,
> cattle, and the earth, and is to fill the earth and subdue it. But what was
> piety to the Christians was in this case impiety to the Indians. Each side
> seemed crazy, impious and depraved to the other.[47]

For the Native American Indian, kinship extended to include the animal world. Even in the killing of the prey, the *I-Thou relation* of reverence was evident. Irving Hallowell, showed how different tribes' kin terms for animals such as beavers, moose, deer, elk, eagles function as analogues of human relationships. Indeed, not just the human but the entire biotic community is related.[48]

THE NATIVE AMERICAN KINSHIP with all beings, based on the belief that all are *'Thous'* rather than *'Its'* and each having their own kind of *orenda* or spirit which is as sacred as one's own, though of a different kind, led to harmonious, co-operative and reciprocal relations.

The buffalo were regarded as a people who voluntarily sacrificed some of their members to human needs in a form of brotherhood – hence the buffalo people are deserving of respect, conservation and preservation of the species.[49]

Alfonso Ortiz points out that if you perceive things about creatures you can honour them, for example the butterfly embodies elusiveness and hence before going on a war party or raid warriors paint themselves with butterfly symbols to invoke this power of elusiveness.

In the desert country the Hopi celebrate a little beetle that obliterates its tracks as it moves through the sand – because for warriors this ability is important.[50] The beaver also has things to teach if only we can perceive them. As Ortiz states:

> We are talking about new ways of perceiving relationships among
> human beings – a troublesome species – and the earth. Those ways are
> already there in Indian teachings, as is the idea of sharing the earth
> with other life forms and developing new forms of respect in order to
> develop new relationships with them.[51]

To trust the judgement of beavers and to look to beetles and bugs and butterflies for lessons, or perceive the qualities that native people have always perceived in their kin and natural environment, is to be imbued in the *I-Thou relation* and the Mother Earth Archetype:

> "You don't ask, How can I use it? Most peoples believe they may use
> anything of the earth for their own benefit. In Native American
> religions, kinship with nature is the postulate".[52]

As early as 1946, H. and H.A. Frankfort, John A. Wilson, Thorkild Jacobsen and William A. Irwin were claiming that the "fundamental difference between the attitudes of modern and ancient man as regards the surrounding world is this: for modern, scientific man the phenomenal world is primarily an 'It'; for ancient – and also for primitive – man it is a 'Thou'.[53]

Broadribb describes the *I-It* perspective baldly: "In the Western religions it is assumed that everything in 'nature' was created by God for humans to exploit".[54] This believed God-given right over nature is very much an anthropocentric as opposed to the eco-centric, nature-centred environmentalist view of morality as inherent in the Mother Earth Archetype. "The Western tradition pictures nature as material, mechanical, and devoid of spirit (reserving that exclusively for humans), while the American Indian tradition pictures nature throughout as an *extended* family or society of living, ensouled beings".[55]

The sacred *I-Thou relation* to Mother Earth is given in the anecdote of a traditional American-Indian who is asked "How much of the earth is sacred space?" to which the answer is unhesitating: "All". As one Chief put it: "Every part of this soil is sacred in the estimation of my people".[56] As environmentalists Donald Hughes and Jim Swan note, when "tribal elders speak of Mother Earth, they are not using a metaphor. They perceive the earth as a living being, sacred in all her parts".[57]

The moral code inherent to *Mother Earth* requires a proper *spiritual balance* between humans and non-humans. For everything that is taken something must be offered in return. The permanent loss of a species tears at the balance of the world. Humankind depends on Mother Earth for life and her other children depend on humankind to maintain a proper balance.[58]

Lame Deer, a Lakota medicine man, spoke of *understanding with the heart*, holism, symbols and images, where the spiritual and commonplace are one. In this he exemplifies the sense of belonging to Mother Earth and reciprocity (*I-Thou* relation):

> I am an Indian. I think about ordinary, common things like this pot.
> The bubbling water comes from the rain cloud. It represents the sky.
> The fire comes from the sun which warms us all – men, animals, trees.
> The meat stands for the four-legged creatures, our animal brothers,
> who gave of themselves so that we should live. The steam is living
> breath. It was water; now it goes up to the sky, becomes a cloud again.
> These things are sacred… We Indians live in a world of symbols and
> images where the spiritual and the commonplace are one. To you
> symbols are just words, spoken or written in a book. To us they are part
> of nature, part of ourselves – the earth, the sun, the wind and the rain,
> stones, trees, animals, even the little insects like ants and grasshoppers.
> We try to understand them not with the head but with the heart, and
> we need no more than a hint to give us the meaning.[59]

The ability to "see with the heart" and be a part of the Mother Earth Archetype is not something unique to indigenous peoples. In fact it is argued that most everyone "has or can acquire such openness if he or she is receptive and willing to try to understand with the heart".[60]

For example, anthropologist Richard Nelson went to the Alaskan Koyukon tribe pursuing a traditional anthropological study, but what he took away was a new perception and a new and deeper understanding of reality:

> Where I came from, the raven is just a bird – an interesting and
> beautiful one perhaps, even an intelligent one – but it is a bird, and that
> is all. But where I am now, the raven is many other things first, its form
> and existence as a bird almost the least significant of its qualities. It is a
> person and a power, God in a clown's suit, incarnation of a once-
> omnipotent spirit. The raven sees, hears, understands, reveals...
> determines. What is the raven? Bird-watchers and biologists know. But
> those like me, who have heard and accepted both, are left to watch and
> wonder.[61]

THE SPIRITUALITY OF ANIMISM, Mother Earth worship, is described by Andree Collard and Joyce Contrucci:

> Earth worship corresponds to what textbooks call animism, namely,
> the belief that everything that lives is endowed with soul/spirit.
> Animism is always labelled primitive, and 'primitive' carries a host of
> negative connotations only because the reference point used is our so-
> called advanced stage of civilisation. Animism extended to plants and
> animals because of the spiritual power (mana) they were perceived to
> have as children of the Earth Mother.[62]

Within the belonging, reciprocity and sense of sacredness of those imbued with the Mother Earth Archetype there is nothing that is sacred versus something that is secular. The Gods are a part of nature. They are not supra anything. There is no supernatural monotheistic one and only God, nor is there a supernatural externalised Satan, Devil or Hell. Everything that lives is imbued with soul and spirit and is therefore sacred. Ethical values and morality are based in feelings of belonging, kinship, reciprocity and the I-Thou reverential relationship with the Earth Mother and the Nature/Earth Landscape.[63]

Timelessness, Mythology, Being

IDENTITY AND SPIRITUALITY within the Mother Earth Archetype are found in 'timeless mythology' and 'being'. This is more important than 'becoming' and historical development. Ones sense of landscape 'place and space' has more value and importance than linear 'historicity'.

In Maori tribal belonging, for example, lore and mythology was identified with and written over the tribes' mountains, hills and valleys, its rivers, streams and lakes, and upon its cliffs and shores. Hunting, gathering and cultivation, together with their lore and mythology, were seasonal and hence time was bound within mythology, circular and never-ending. The old Maori dwelt and had 'being' predominantly within the non-linear timeless, mythological landscape. *Whakapapa* (descent) and kinship were not so much historical as inextricably tied to the mythology of the land. Tribal identity and personal identity were tied with mythology and genealogy, connected with the land and landscape. Te Maire Tau points out:

> [F]or Maori the boundaries of time and space are irrelevant. This does not mean Maori do not have a sense of time and location. There is enough evidence to show that events were ordered, albeit by an imprecise system of genealogy. However, precision in the ordering of time was not central to the Maori view of the world. Consequently, time was not the primary principle in any attempt to recollect the past. ...Virtually the only realm of 'meaningfulness' to Maori is that of 'mana'.[64]

Furthermore, *mana* "is one's spiritual, personal and ancestral prestige and authority that is determined by personal actions and descent lines from gods and ancestors".[65]

For the old American Indian, spirituality is *experienced* rather than revealed. It depends on direct experience for credibility and perpetuation. Alfonso Ortiz states:

> You're not expected to believe in something that happened two thousand years ago in the Near East for the credibility of the religion. Rather, the religion is based on where the people live, the creation or emergence from the earth, and the migrations that took place close by. Often these migrations are retraced in pilgrimages. These are religions of place rather than history.[66]

Such religions are not easily transported. They do not proselytize or attempt to convert, nor do they make universalist claims. "Native American religions are set more in place and space than in time. Native cultures also live more in place than time. Western cultures are driven by history; a sense of linear, irreversible time. They're driven by unique events, piled on by competing ideologies".[67]

However, it is true to say that today the old Indian culture has been undermined economically by the predominant cash economy of the United States and the same could be said of other primal cultures which have been transmuted into corporate cultures, with all the corporate and profit-making values which this universal culture entails. More will be said on this later when we explore the Trickster Archetype and the *Technological/Materialist Landscape*.

"No Such Thing as Emptiness"

LANDSCAPE PLACE AND SPACE IS METAPHYSICAL. For old primal, indigenous inhabitants of the land, there was 'no such thing as emptiness' and no such thing as 'being alone' or in 'complete solitude' in the landscape.

For the Australian Aborigine, for example, the idea of quitting the tribal landscape in order to seek solitude was entirely alien.[68] The Aborigine had a complex metaphysical relationship with the landscape. One's Dreaming Country conditioned all one's actions. Tribal place and space meant a close proximity to one's ancestors, Dreaming cult-heroes and totemic birth place. Even when physically alone the Aborigine lives in and is sustained by a metaphysical community.

For the Native American Indians there was "No such thing as emptiness" - the land, place and space, was a "bountiful community of living beings of whom the humans were only one part ... (the landscape) was a place of great sacredness in which the workings of the Great Spirit, or Great Mystery, could always be felt".[69] In the Mother Earth Archetype, place and space have pre-eminent importance; because *place and space are where the heart is.* Identity and spirituality is with the landscape: '*We are the land*'.

Terrible Mother's Shadowside

A CHILLING DESCRIPTION of the shadowside of Mother Earth is given by James Lovelock:

> Gaia, as I see her, is no doting mother tolerant of misdemeanors, nor is she some fragile and delicate damsel in danger from brutal mankind. She is stern and tough, always keeping the world warm and comfortable for those who obey the rules, but ruthless in her destruction of those who transgress. Her unconscious goal is a planet fit for life. If humans stand in the way of this, we shall be eliminated with as little pity as would be shown by the micro-brain of an intercontinental ballistic nuclear missile in full flight to its target.[70]

Like all archetypes, the Mother Earth Archetype possesses both positive and negative attributes; an ageless union of opposites within the same archetype.

The immense creativity of nature is awesome and potentially catastrophic. This is an awareness which 'modern man' with his focus on the *Technological/ Materialist Landscape* often forgets – until nature unleashes a natural apocalypse like the 2004 Boxing Day Tsunami on the coasts of Asia.

Awe always involves a component of fear and this is especially so for those who live closest to nature – the old primal peoples whose lives were focused on the *Nature/Earth Landscape* and who dwelt within the spirituality of the Mother Earth Archetype. The rituals and mythology of primal peoples centred around propitiation to an Earth Mother who can be both *all* nurturing and life giving, yet terrible in her annihilation. Theodore Roszak describes it this way:

> The Earth does go so powerfully and competently about her work, bringing forth the crop, ushering in the seasons, nurturing the many species that find their home in her vast body. She can, of course, also be a menacing giant; that too is remembered in myth and folklore. Many

of the oldest rituals are acts of propitiation offered to a sometimes
fierce and punishing divinity, and Earth who can be an angry mother
as well as a bountiful one.[71]

Mother Earth was an important aspect of the Great Mother Goddess. Anthony Stevens, research psychiatrist, describes the shadowside of the Mother Archetype in general:

> where the Good Mother's symbols are the flowing breast, the abundant
> cornucopia, the fruitful womb, the Terrible Mother is the bloodstained
> goddess of death and destruction; she is Kali dancing on the hapless
> form of Shiva… she is 'dark all-devouring time, the bone-wreathed
> lady of the place of skulls', the Mayan goddess Ixchel, with deadly
> snake on head, animal claws, and crossed bones on her mantle – the
> emblem of death… She is Rangda who steals children… and the
> Gorgon with writhing snakes around her head (at whom men have
> merely to glance to be instantly turned to stone). The animal forms
> which she most characteristically adopts are the dragon and the
> devouring sea serpent, with whom the heroes of countless mythologies
> have grappled down the eons of man-made time. Universally, the
> negative aspects of the mother has been personified in monsters,
> gorgons, witches, ghouls, who have murdered the sleep of children
> (and adults) since the dawning of mankind. Both 'Good' and 'Terrible'
> aspects of the mother archetype condition the behaviour of mother and
> child at a predominantly unconscious level of psychic activity.[72]

Jung wrote of the negative side of the Mother Earth Archetype that it "may connote anything secret, hidden, dark; the abyss, the world of the dead, anything that devours, seduces, and poisons, that is terrifying and inescapable like fate".[73]

WE ARE ALL CHILDREN within the Mother Earth Archetype and hence vulnerable. Rupert Sheldrake argues "Like human mothers, nature has always evoked ambivalent emotions. She is beautiful, fertile, nurturing, benevolent and generous. But she is also wild, destructive, disorderly, chaotic, smothering, death-dealing – the Mother in her terrifying form, like Nemesis, or Hecate, or Kali".[74]

The shadowside of the Mother Earth Archetype is all too real *outside* the comforts and relative security of man-made 'civilization' and technology, especially in the towns and cities. However the power of wild untamed nature – hurricane strength storms, mountainous seas, life-strangling droughts, life shrivelling, desiccating cold fronts, fatal diseases, wild ravenous animals and the lurking imagined dangers of the unknown in the darkness, remains an ancestral memory.

Even today, within the comparative safety and speed of international transport, the reassurance and comforts of modern medicine, city lights, national electricity power grids and space umbrella satellite communication systems – there is the threat of solar storms (coronal mass ejections), mutating viruses, antibiotic resistant bacteria. Increasingly there is also man induced global catastrophes: catastrophic climate effects with frequent 'super storms', intense heat waves becoming commonplace, 'ice storms', arctic ice melts, widespread releases of the methane greenhouse gas, water contamination and scarcity, ocean acidification and ozone depletion.

The Desire to Subdue

OUR "FEAR OF WILD, UNTAMED nature feeds the desire to subdue her, a desire at least as old as civilisation".[75] Sheldrake concludes that Man likes to be safely in control. The shadowside of the Terrible Mother is associated with the horror of uncontrolled death and destruction – the annihilation of man's individual and collective ego. As Erich Neumann describes:

> Behind the archetype of the terrible Earth Mother looms the experience
> of death, when the earth takes back her progeny as the dead, divides
> and dissolves them in order to make herself fruitful. This experience
> has been preserved in the rites of the Terrible Mother, who, in her
> earth projection, becomes the flesh center and finally the sarcophagus –
> the last vestige of man's age-old and long-practiced fertility cults.[76]

THE "STRONGER MASCULINE EGO consciousness becomes, the more it is aware of the emasculating, bewitching, deadly, and stupefying nature of the Great Goddess".[77] Neumann concludes, that in the end, the "conquest of the mother archetype has its proper place in the myth of the hero".[78]

It is to these matters we turn in the next chapter, when we consider the Heavenly God-Father, Ego and Hero Archetypes imbuing the *Anthropocentric Landscape*.

SIX

Heavenly God-Father

The biblical tradition begins with the
creation narrative wherein the Earth
Mother of the Eastern Mediterranean is
abandoned in favor of the transcendent
Heaven Father.

– **Thomas Berry**

The God of the Jews, Christians and
Muslims is a transcendent God: a God out
there, apart from nature, dominant and
masculine. He made man in his own
image. So man, too, is set apart from
nature; indeed he is explicitly invited to
people the earth and rule over it.

– **Walter Schwarz**

God-Father Clash

T HE TRANSCENDENCE OF the Western monotheistic Heavenly-God-Father
Archetype over the universal *Mother Earth Archetype* was a clash of
archetypes in history and it is a clash of archetypes which continues to this
day.[1] This clash brought forth a new Anthropocentric Landscape.

It also brought forth a new concept of man (made in the image of the God-Father
and a new development in man's psyche with his separation from the Mother Earth and
the ascendance of the Ego and Hero components of the personality.

The clash between the transcendent God-Father and Mother Earth is seen in the anguish of indigenous peoples, in the subjugation of women and the exploitation of nature

It is evidenced in the conflicted psyches of individuals and in the historical warring of religious fundamentalist cultures and factions dominated by the archetype of a monotheistic God-Father who is exclusivist, jealous and warlike and who bestows his favours on 'the chosen'.

Supplanting Mother

NO ONE KNOWS FOR SURE when men started to challenge the power of the Goddess and set about a long history of subjugation of women, desecration of temples, and destruction of those animals that had been sacred to her. The recorded appearance of god-worshipping males – variously called Indo-Europeans, Indo-Aryans, and Aryans – in the Middle East some 6,000 years ago suggests older beginnings since they are said to have come from north of the Caucasus.[2]

Lithuanian-American archaeologist, Marija Gimbutas (1921-1994) suggests that it was the Indo-European incursion of warlike nomadic tribes, worshippers of the masculine sky gods, that replaced the matracentric cultures of Old Europe with an "autocratic warrior" society. They claimed for themselves the virtues of "civilization". However prior to their conquest there had been a "civilization of the goddess" marked by peace and high art and under the spell of the original version of Gaia.[3] The clash of archetypes is illustrated in epic myths, for example, Marduk, the great male deity, who ousts Ti' amat from power and tears her body to shreds in order to construct a new world of warlords and patriarchal masters more to his liking:

> In the Book of Genesis (first millenium BC), a document that codifies
> in writing many strands of older oral traditions, the intent to suppress
> the Great Mother (Ishtar, Inanna, Ti'amat etc.) is very clear. Some
> practices of her cult are openly condemned as they clash with the
> monotheistic, male tradition of the Hebrews. Mostly they are omitted.
> An earlier version of the Genesis creation myth attributes a spirit of
> rebellion to the first woman, Lilith. In the later version, which we all
> know, Lilith is replaced by Eve (Gen. 1:26)... born of Adam's rib and
> made submissive to him in another (Gen. 2:23) ... (Thus) ... Genesis
> presents the view that God created everything and gave it to man to
> dominate. The degrees of his domination range from benevolent
> stewardship, to conquest (Gen.1:28) and outright oppression.[4]

Transcendence

"IMPLICIT IN MONOTHEISM is a movement toward transcendence. In Israel's monotheism it was inevitable. A God such as envisaged by Israel must be exalted in divine quality far above puny man, above this earth, and above all that is of the earth and earthy".[5] As theologian, Lloyd Geering states:

> When the Israelite prophets laid the foundation of (mono)theism they

unfortunately left behind the gender complementarity which had
existed hitherto among the deities of the ancient religions. Previously
the divine figures had been conceived as gods and goddesses, who even
entered into romantic and procreative relationships with each other.
The Sky-Father had been complemented by the Earth-Mother; and in
many primitive myths of origin it was by their copulation that these
two completed the creation process. The Israelite prophets were so
successful in their rejection of the goddesses as a class that no word for
goddess is found in the Hebrew Bible and even the name of the
Canaanite fertility goddess, Ashtoreth, appears in an adulterated form,
having had the vowels of the Hebrew word meaning 'shame' inserted in
it![6]

Mother Earth and the other Goddesses were eliminated by the prophets, which left all
super-human power to the monotheistic Heavenly God-Father. Geering concludes that:

> The elimination of the chief feminine deity, followed by the affirmation
> of the male deity as supreme and unique, had the long-term effect of
> devaluing the feminine gender and all virtues associated with it.[7]

Women and Mother Earth De-Sacrilised

WHEREAS PREVIOUSLY WOMEN had been associated with the Mother Earth
Archetype and hence shared in her sacredness, in Judaism and later Christianity women
were de-sacrilised and thought to desecrate holy places. "In both Jewish and Christian
traditions the natural physiological functions of the female body were thought to have
the capacity to desecrate holy places and this meant that women had to be kept at a
distance from 'the holy of holies'."[8] Those peoples who continued to dwell in and owe
their allegiance to the Mother Earth Goddess Archetype and the *Nature/Earth
Landscape* were persecuted. The Heavenly-God-Father of the Jews was a jealous God:

> I am the Lord thy God…Thou shalt have no other Gods before me.
> Thou shalt not make unto thee any craven image, or any likeness of
> anything that is in the heaven above or that is in the earth beneath or
> that is in the water under the earth. Thou shalt not bow down thyself to
> them nor serve them, for I thy God am a jealous God.
> (Exod. 20:2-5)

The Hebrews (and later the Christians and the Muslims) conducted a long struggle
with the archetypal Mother-Earth worshipping religions of the surrounding peoples
who worshipped in the sacred groves and high places: God commanded the destruction
of those places.[9] Pagan nature worship was considered depraved:

> The religions of Canaan, ornate as they were with divine symbols in
> public worship and privates shrines, were in large measure
> characterized by features of so-called nature worship… Canaanite
> worship of the forces of life meant public immorality as a sacred rite
> and commonly of disgusting depravity.[10]

Hence the following quote from the Bible: "Upon every high hill and under every green tree thou didst bow thyself playing harlot" (Jer. 2:20). As the Frankforts conclude: "All was gathered up in Israel's theological uniqueness and in her consciousness of that uniqueness. The righteousness and holiness of God imposed upon the Israelite an exacting standard of action and thought and, in turn, revealed the depravity of pagan religion".[11]

"Attack On Their Soul"

IN NEW ZEALAND, the Gods of nature and the Mother Earth Archetype Papatuanuku were replaced by the transcendent monotheistic Heavenly God-Father Archetype of the Christian colonizers. Moana Jackson has spoken movingly of the devastating combined effects of colonization and spiritual conquest on the old Maori soul:

> Reduced to a minority in the place of their ancestors, Maori then became susceptible to attacks on their institutions and the land base upon which they grew... the need to civilize and save the natives justified the imposition of a religion and a God whose worship would provide a better existence after death... In fulfilling that role (the agents of colonization) had to teach the Maori to fear God, to respect Pakeha law, and to acknowledge the validity of Pakeha values and institutions... The soul of a people, the essence of their being, exists within the warmth of their philosophy; it is nurtured and sheltered by the wisdom of their beginning word. To oppress a people, to set in place the bloody success of colonization, it is necessary to destroy the soul. For the Maori, the attack on their soul was so terrible it led to a weakening of faith in all the things which had nourished it. The demeaning of the values which cherished it, the language which gave it voice, the law which gave it order, and the religion which was its strength, was an ongoing process which ultimately affected the belief of Maori in themselves... Maori began to develop an internalized state of alienation in which they rejected themselves because the meanings which their philosophy gave to their existence were being removed. In their place an alien philosophy was being erected ... That awful cost was paid, and that belief developed, because colonization demands not only the physical acquisition of power and resources, but the spiritual denial of the indigenous word.[12]

The Heavenly God-Father was supreme and above nature; nothing was sacred except the God-Father and what He decreed.

Usurping Sacred Space

BY WAY OF COMPARISON, Donald Hughes and Jim Swan state that while, in the traditional American Indian view, all of nature is sacred and the universe is "a sacred continuum that contains foci of power", this is not the concept of sacred space which entered the medieval and modern mind.

This view was transformed by the Hebrews, who while they had their sacred places (for example Sinai where God gave Moses the commandments; Bethel where Jacob wrestled with the angel; Mount Zion), "the dominant view in Judaism held that God the Creator is not to be identified with His creation, even though it might serve as a marvelous sign of his power and benevolence".[13] In other words, since God is transcendent he cannot be said to dwell in any spot on earth in an ontological sense.[14]

While Mount Zion was a sacred place, the Judaic view was that it was sanctified by God's people at his command and not because of any inherent sacredness.

For the Hebrews "Temple space" was sacred.[15] Ultimately nothing of the Earth is sacred, apart from that which the God-Father consecrates: "Nothing is sacred, on this tradition, except God and what, like Sinai, is specifically dedicated to God. 'The Lord is in his holy temple; the Lord's throne is in heaven'."[16]

Despite some passages in the Old Testament which show the Hebrew's love of inanimate nature, "God, for Israel, was supreme above nature and employed it for his purposes. However intimately related to natural phenomena, God was more than, and distinct from, them".[17] Indeed, the entirety of "nature was the work of the Lord and visible evidence of his reality, of his power, and of his immediate participation in affairs of the world".[18]

"A Subtle Aversion"

CATHOLIC PRIEST, cultural historian and ecotheologian, Thomas Berry (1914-2009) writes:

> [T]he relationship between the human and divine is constituted in terms of a covenant between a chosen people and a personal transcendent creative Father deity. This becomes the context in which human-divine affairs are worked out over the succeeding centuries. The natural world is no longer the locus for the meeting of the divine and the human. A subtle aversion develops toward the natural world, a feeling that humans in the depth of their beings do not really belong to the earthly community of life, but to a heavenly community.[19]

Collard and Contrucci note that:

> since God creates nature, nature is everything in the universe that existed before the appearance of human beings. By the same token, it is everything that man cannot create. Envy of Mother Earth is expressed by projecting upon God the ability to create life. The solution is to erase the Goddess. Before 'the beginning' to which Genesis refers, 'the earth was a formless void' (Gen. 1:1-2). A few thousand years later, the writers of the Gospels gathered what suited Christianity from the Old Testament. They kept nature and women in a position of subordination to man… God is given the power of language as he pulls creation out of nothingness and names it. 'In the beginning' clearly refers to the beginning of God worship and cancels everything that came before (goddess worship) by not mentioning it.[20]

Objectification of Nature

IN THE HEBREW SCRIPTURES can be found the beginnings of the objectification of the *Nature/Earth Landscape*. This is where the sacred Mother Earth is rendered to the perceptual world of '*I-It*'. Robert Faricy points to the transcendence of God and consequent de-divinization and de-personalisation of the world in these scriptures, for :

> God is understood as absolutely transcendent and the world as non-
> divine. This de-divinization of nature is a basic premise, or prime
> requisite, for technology and political and social progress. However,
> de-divinization, as such, tends to lead to de-personalization. When
> nature is de-divinized, 'there is the tendency to de-personalize it'.[21]

The *I-Thou relation* reserved for a personal Heavenly God-Father and for human nature, in particular "the chosen – and taken away from the natural world, which is de-divinised, de-personalised and rendered objectified *I-It*, is a characteristic of the *Anthropocentric Landscape*. That which is rendered *I-It* or the *Other* (the world of the non "chosen") – hence the "idolators", the Pagans, those faithful to the 'old religion' of the sacred earth – is devalued, persecuted and scapegoated. As Charlene Spretnak points out:

> The Other as an individual or group less worthy than the inflated "I" or
> "we", was frequently subjected to armed aggression. For both the Jews
> in Canaan and later the Muslims in Arabia, the neighboring "idolators"
> they attempted to exterminate were the faithful of the "old religion" of
> the sacred earth, people who still worshipped in sacred groves and at
> sacred springs. The oldest of their deities were manifestations of the
> Goddess... The Christian conquerors in the New World treated the
> Indian nations and their nature-based spirituality in a similar way. It is
> clear from the first commandment in both the Judeo-Christian and
> Islamic traditions that expanding allegiance to "the one god" by forced
> conversion of "idolators" was considered an imperative in claiming
> religious and political turf during the formative periods... Another
> common thread running through all three Semitic traditions is their
> effort to cast women in decidedly inferior roles to those of men. This
> bias, which was present from the beginning, has proven to be an
> obsessive campaign over the centuries.[22]

The allegiance of mankind was swung from the Mother Earth-Goddess Archetype to the transcendent Heavenly God-Father. Religious history and mythology was re-written so that not only did the God-Father supplant Mother Earth, he *created* her. "The earth is the Lord's, and everything in it." (Ps. 24: 1. NIV). The attempt was made to eliminate the Mother-Earth-Goddess Archetype. She was defiled, erased and re-created, as we shall see.

'The Chosen'

ARGUABLY, THE WESTERN PSYCHE is rooted in the myth which, in effect, equates man with God.[23] It is also centred on the concept of '*the chosen*' for, as Jaffe notes, in broad terms, the:

[F]irst or Jewish dispensation was centered on the Law and on collectivity, that is, the Israelites, a chosen people, the first-born of God and the sacrificed of God. The second or Christian dispensation was centered on faith and on a single individual conceived of as divine, Jesus Christ the chosen one, the first-born of God and the sacrificed of God. The third, the new or Psychological dispensation, is centered in personal experience and on each individual considered as partaking of the divine, and on each of us the chosen one, the first-born of God and the sacrificed of God.[24]

In other words, consecrated to God, beloved of God and heir to his kingdom, the Israelites, Christ and Christians are 'the chosen'. The writer of Psalm 8 expresses the staggering generosity of God in placing the human in charge of all creation:

Yet you have made him little less than a god;
You make him master over all that you have made, putting everything in subjection under his feet. (vv.3.5,6.REB)

"THE CHOSEN are made in the God-Father's image and are given dominion over the earth: "Then God said, 'Let us make man in our image, after our likeness; let them have dominion over the fish of the sea, over the birds of the air, and over the cattle, over all the earth and over every creeping thing that creeps on the earth'." (Gen. 1.26).

This has been the perspective not only of Jews but also Christians and Muslims as intimating the charter which grants the right to subdue the earth and all its inhabitants. The 'Heavenly Father' according to Genesis also issued the impositional fructifying mandate to mankind: "Be fruitful and multiply; fill the earth and subdue it" (Gen. 1:28).

Australian philosopher and historian of ideas, John Passmore (1914-2004) points out God added two significant riders. It is clear from the first that the human should not expect to subdue the earth by either love or natural authority, rather by force: "And the fear of you and the dread of you shall be upon every beast of the earth, and upon every fowl of the air, upon all that moveth upon the earth and upon all the fishes of the sea: into your hand they are delivered" (Gen. 9:2-3). The second rider – "every moving thing that liveth shall be meat for you" – permitted the eating of the flesh of animals. Whereas in the Garden of Eden, Adam, along with the beasts, had been a vegetarian now all living things were handed over by God to Adam and his descendants as their food.[25]

Anthropocentric Focus

A MAN-CENTRED PERSPECTIVE is the basis on which nature is viewed and judged. This leads on to an *Anthropocentric Landscape*. Walter Gulick observes of the Torah[26], that nature "is viewed and judged from a highly anthropocentric perspective. It is to be managed either by God or by God's representatives on earth: human beings".[27]

Nature becomes an instrument of the God-Father's divine justice. The prophets state that humans have no mastery over nature when their evil provokes God to anger.

Christianity, derived from Judaism, continues this tradition of the primacy of anthropocentrism and the dominion, subjugation, conquering and trampling by the God-Father and his 'chosen' over Mother Earth.

John Biggs makes a linguistic analysis and argues that the second part of the directive given to humankind at creation, namely "subdue the earth and... have dominion over... every living thing" (Gen. 1.28) means that Christianity is often accused of interpreting this verse in terms of unrestrained domination:

> Whatever translation is used, words like 'subdue', 'rule over', or 'have
> dominion' need careful attention. It is not that they should be
> explained away: they carry a forcefulness which cannot be ducked. The
> Hebrew word *kabash* from which 'subdue' is derived, suggests a
> treading down, or conquering, and the term *radah* which gives us 'rule'
> resembles the verb to trample.[28]

The Christian theologian Thomas Aquinas continued in this tradition. For Aquinas there was a hierarchy within creation: plants for the benefit of animals and both for the benefit of mankind. The life of animals and plants were not to be preserved for themselves but for the use of humankind. Biggs concludes that this "historical viewpoint is seen as being worked out with wanton exploitation as man subjects nature for his own selfish purposes".[29]

Edward C. Whitmont (1912-1998), Jungian psychoanalyst, points out how Christianity forged a vast gulf between humanity and nature.[30] He describes the anthropocentrism of Christian theology in which nature does not have intrinsic value, but value only in-so-far as it contributes to human welfare. The ecological crisis is a direct result of these attitudes.

Whitmont's views are preceded by Nietzsche, Lynn White Jr. (1967) and British historian Arnold Toybnee (1889-1975), to mention just a few of the more prominent thinkers.[31] For example, Ian McHarg argues that the value system which has created Western man's environmental ills is sourced in "the Judeo-Christian-Humanist view which is so unknowing of nature and of man, which has bred and sustained his simple-minded anthropocentrism".[32] Toybnee states:

> Some of the major maladies of the present day world – in particular the
> reckless extravagant consumption of nature's irreplaceable treasures,
> and the pollution of those of them that man has not already devoured –
> can be traced back to a religious cause, and this cause is the rise of
> monotheism... monotheism, as enunciated in the book of Genesis, has
> removed the age-old restraint that was once placed on man's greed by
> his awe. Man's greedy impulse to exploit nature used to be held in
> check by his pious worship of nature.[33]

Lynn White Jr., as already discussed, maintains that traditional Western Christianity has been both *anthropocentric* and arrogant towards nature. Mainstream Christianity is neither ecologically oriented nor environmentally concerned. Exploitation of nature is allowed by Christianity:

> By destroying pagan animism, Christianity made it possible to exploit
> nature in a mood of indifference to the feelings of natural objects… The
> spirits in natural objects, which formerly had protected nature from man,
> evaporated. Man's effective monopoly on spirit in this world was
> confirmed, and the old inhibitions to the exploitation of nature
> crumbled.[34]

Friedrich Nietzsche (1844-1900), the seminal German philosopher, shared crucial concerns with contemporary environmentalist writers, especially deep ecologists.[35] Nietzsche's thinking here closely parallels that of Lynn White Jr.

Nietzsche criticized Western philosophical and religious thinking for being rather too "otherworldly", "anti-natural" and "anthropocentric". He rejected the humanity-nature dichotomy and recognizing the importance of environmental factors suggested the interrelatedness of all living things. He called for a "return to nature" and a dispossession of anti-natural tendencies in traditional Western thinking.

IN SUMMARY; exploitation of Mother Earth by the 'chosen' is given sanction by the Heavenly God-Father. This perspective imbues a predominantly *Anthropocentric Landscape* focus of perception, where Mother Earth is de-divinised, objectified and ready for exploitation. Robert Faricy puts it this way:

> The world has no magical power to save us or to destroy us; the power
> belongs to God. A fearful and awe-filled attitude towards the world has
> been replaced by a matter-of-factness about the world, and magic has
> been replaced by prayer. Thus we are freed from nature and nature is
> itself freed for our use. Both we and nature are de-divinized and freed
> for progress. This matter-of-factness about both us and nature is the
> pre-condition for the development of science, for technology and for
> social, political and economic progress.[36]

Collard and Contrucci conclude "Woman had perceived herself as being like unto nature; man named himself as distinct from nature".[37]

For Max O. Hallman the "Christian dichotomy between humanity and nature has often served as the foundation for unabashed anthropocentrism, or to use Nietzsche's words, for 'an insane self-elevation of man above the world'."[38]

And Lynn White Jr. concludes that "Especially in its Western form, Christianity is the most anthropocentric religion the world has seen".[39]

Ego and Hero Separation

THE "MYTH OF PATRIARCHAL KINGSHIP" argues Edward C. Whitmont "engendered that particular form of ego consciousness we have come in our time to consider consciousness *tout court*. It is centered in a rationalizing, abstracting, and controlling *I*, ego."[40] In other words, the *Nature/Earth Landscape* was objectified and rendered an '*It*' and the '*I*' of the ego became pivotal to the *Anthropocentric Landscape* focus of perception.

Whitmont argues that, while we now condemn this separation of Western humanity from its instinctive side, there was nevertheless a psychological need to tear loose from the Great Mother Goddess of Nature:

> For the sake of an independent sense of personality one had to heed the command of the one and only patriarchal "I am that I am", and forget the powers of the encompassing unitary reality. These powers were the gods who are also *animals, plants, stones, places* and *times.* These were henceforth to be considered reasonless dumb creatures and inanimate, even dead matter. Humanity had to subdue the earth and make it serve the *I.*[41]

Jane Roberts (1929-1984), American writer and channeler of "Seth", puts it this way "The ego ... needed to feel its dominance and control, and so it imagined a dominant god apart from nature".[42] Concepts of God went hand-in-hand with the development of consciousness.[43] The ancient Mother-Goddess concept would become "unconscious".[44]

> God the Father would be recognized and the Earth Goddess forgotten. There would be feudal lords, therefore, not seeresses. Period. Man would believe he did indeed have dominion over the earth as a separate species, for God the Father had given it to him.[45]

This growth of ego consciousness set up both challenges and limitations.[46] Roberts suggests that it would only be much later that the ego could expand, once sure of itself, and realize these limitations and become aware of realities it had earlier ignored.[47]

The hero myth and hero archetypal image has long been associated with the struggle of ego separation from the Mother Archetype and the natural world, as Carl Jung, philosopher psychologist Erich Neumann (1905-1960), and others have pointed out at length. Neumann argues that "through the masculinization and emancipation of ego consciousness the ego becomes the 'hero':[48]

> With the hero myth we enter upon a new phase of stadial development. A radical shift in the center of gravity has occurred. In all creation myths the dominant feature was the cosmic quality of the myth, its universality; but now the myth focuses attention upon the world as the center of the universe, the spot upon which man stands. This means, in terms of stadial development, not only that man's ego consciousness has achieved independence, but that his total personality has detached itself from the natural context of the surrounding world and the unconscious... Thus the hero is the archetypal forerunner of mankind in general.[49]

On the negative side, the hero is often associated with war. Whitmont describes the patriarchal ego as heroic. It can be seen in present and past wars. It is both the glory and the Achilles' heel of the male ego and male national identity:

> The patriarchal ego is heroic. Its idealized achievement is conquest of
> self and world by sheer will and bravery. Personal feeling, desire, pain
> and pleasure are disregarded. Failure to do so is accounted weakness.
> The resulting psychological achievement is a sense of personal identity
> vested in a body-limited, separate self, answerable to the law of the
> group and God-king. Consciously, now it no longer feels organically
> contained in, or one with, group, world, or the divine. Unconsciously,
> however, it is still dominated by group values.[50]

The individuated ego of the individuated or higher self is the most advanced
development of ego as hero. This is to be distinguished from the nascent ego and hero,
which are engaged in separation and emancipation from the Mother and Mother Earth
Archetype and which characterise the *Anthropocentric Landscape*.

Interestingly, analogies have been drawn with the Christ story as a paradigm of the
individuated ego and hero and the Heavenly God-Father as a superego. Archetypal
theorist Edward F. Edinger (1922-1998) has argued that the image of Christ gives a
picture of the individuated ego which is conscious of being directed by the higher Self.
He states:

> The Christian myth applies to a much higher level of ego development.
> Christ is both man and God. As man he goes to the cross with anguish
> but willingly, as part of his destiny. As God he willingly sacrifices
> himself for the benefit of mankind. Psychologically this means that the
> ego and the Self are simultaneously crucified.[51]

Needless to say however, the 'Christ Hero' depiction should not be confused with
Christians and their actions in the name of Christianity; and while Christ has been
argued to personify the individuated ego or hero, it is argued by theologian and analyst
Donald Broadribb (1933-2012) that the moral function of the monotheistic Heavenly
God-Father is best described as *superego*.

Superego Morality

IT IS TO THE SUPEREGO MORALITY of the Heavenly God-Father archetype and the
Anthropocentric Landscape that we now turn. Donald Broadribb argues that the:

> superego – which essentially is each person's internalization of society's
> *dos* and *don'ts* – does fit reasonably well with the picture of God
> presented in the Old Testament, if we allow for a bit of artistic license.
> It is certainly not out of the question that Yahweh (the Old Testament
> Hebrew name of God) and God the Father in the New Testament and
> Christian doctrine really are faltering attempts to express the partly
> unconscious experience of the superego in each of us, commanding
> what we should and should not do or think.[52]

The connections between the Father Archetype and the Father-in-Heaven as Lawgiver,
voice of collective authority, defender of Faith, guardian of the status quo and bastion

against all enemies, are drawn by Anthony Stevens:

> In myth, legend and dreams, the father archetype personifies as the Elder,
> the King, the Father in Heaven. As Lawgiver he speaks with the voice of
> collective authority and is the living embodiment of the *Logos* principle:
> his word is law. As Defender of the Faith and of the Realm he is guardian
> of the status quo and bastion against all enemies. His attributes are
> activity and penetration, differentiation and judgment, fecundity and
> destruction.[53]

The God-Father Archetype's characteristics of penetration, differentiation, judgment
and destruction have been seen in the speeches of warring fundamentalist politicians.
The fact that this rhetoric largely cloaks imperialist strategic economic ambitions is
beside the point; the rhetoric bolsters the moral imperative of this archetype.
Whitmont points out that on the stage of history the establishment of God's kingdom
globally is to be accomplished by the "chosen ones":

> The infidels are to be converted to the only true belief through political
> and/or military conquest. If the standards, beliefs, and laws of the
> chosen people or nation are the only true ones, arrived at through
> religious revelation, then those of other peoples must be mere
> superstition or morally wrong.[54]

Law, tradition, civilization, culture, ego, consciousness and will, are regarded as
inherently masculine. As Erich Neumann argues, this is the man's world, representing
"heaven" – as opposed to the feminine and the unconscious, as well as the often
invisible share of women in this culture:

> The man's world, representing "heaven", stands for law and tradition,
> for the gods of aforetime, so far as they were masculine gods. It is no
> accident that all human culture, and not Western civilization alone, is
> masculine in character, from Greece and the Judeo-Christian sphere of
> culture to Islam and India. Although woman's share in this culture is
> invisible and largely unconscious, we should not underestimate its
> significance and scope.[55]

The anthropocentric male who is ego-centred and the God-Father superego-centred
'morality', inherent in the Heavenly God-Father Archetype, overrules the 'morality of
belonging' of the Mother Earth Archetype:

> The male collective is the source of all the taboos, laws and institutions
> that are destined to break the dominance of the uroboros and Great
> Mother. Heaven, the father, and the spirit go hand in hand with
> masculinity and represent the victory of the patriarchate over the
> matriarchate. This is not to say that the matriarchate knows no law; but
> the law by which it is informed is the law of instinct, of unconscious,
> natural functioning, and this law subserves the propagation,
> preservation and evolution of the species rather than the development

of the single individual.[56]

The underlying conflict in the moral basis of the two archetypes is underscored by Collard and Contrucci. 'Man' by naming himself by an act of separation from nature, animals, woman and demanding power over and ownership of them becomes lord (*dominus*) meaning domination and domestication. Thus:

> nature is no longer treated as a complex of self-regulated organisms
> under a 'law' of communal kinship but is brought under *the law* of one
> king, the single rulers of monarchy and monotheism. Responsibility
> (ability to respond) gives way to obligation as ethics become arbitrary –
> functions of will rather than principles arising from reality. Thus good
> and bad give way to standards of right and wrong to which it is
> politically dangerous not to conform.[57]

Alienation

THE RULERSHIP OF the Heavenly God-Father not only creates a morality which is anthropocentric but, according to its critics, is to a large extent alienating – of the male human being from nature, women, animals, and from himself and his own conscience.

Moral authority comes from *without* and from *above* rather than from *within*. Adherence to the moral imperatives of Mother Earth – feelings of belonging, reciprocity I-Thou, love – is replaced by adherence to the moral imperatives of the Nation, law, authority, judgement, obedience, defence, protection and war:

> Father-rule tears morality out of the fabric of social conscience which
> had given mother-rule its cohesiveness and turns it into a political
> category dictated and policed from the outside, from above. In other
> words, father-rule destroys the moral relationship with nature
> characteristic of mother-rule by changing the concept of *nature* into
> one of *nation* which, like man's holdings (family), needs defense and
> protection.[58]

Gulick points to the anthropocentric/legalistic and judgmental morality of the Torah where Nature is viewed as peripheral and something to be managed either by God or his representatives.[59]

Ecologists, ecofeminists and ecotheologians have long been critical of anthropocentrism and the moral value system which over-rides ethics of the co-operative symbiosis of people with their environment.

Thomas Berry argues that in the biblical tradition wherein the creation narrative abandons the Earth Mother in favour of the transcendent Sky Father, not only does a subtle aversion develop towards the natural world but woman becomes the instrument of the entry of *evil* into the world:

In the biblical narrative, woman becomes the instrument of the entry of evil into the world and for the breakdown in human-divine relations. Only in a derivative sense, through their association with men, do women function in the public life of the sacred community... The rulership of men in the church, by divine determination, assured the relegation of women to subordinate status in the religious community, the denial of integral participation in religious ritual, the identification of women with seduction and evil.[60]

War

THE JUSTIFICATION OF WAR is inherent to the morality and values system of the Heavenly God-Father Archetype. Thus:

[The] need for war is built into the concept of nation. Unlike nature, which provides a common identity to all that is born of Mother Earth, a nation identifies individuals as isolates by separating them from the group. Individuals are then recombined in unstable aggregates held together by a shared hostility against 'outsiders'... The need for communal identity lives on in the human mind but is no longer nourished from inside the organism of the group. Instead, like the new ethics, it is arbitrarily chosen – people rally behind unstable symbols like flags and leaders, ideas and heroes.[61]

It is not surprising that the autocracy, legalism, dogmatism and punishment inherent in archetypal God-Father morality leads to war and its justification. Whitmont states:

The God-King and supreme law giver is good and just by definition. Any doubt of his goodness and justness or any infraction of his laws evokes a most catastrophical outbreak of his jealous rage. Whatever customs happen to be at variance with his law are heretical and deserve the severest punishment. The result is a rigid legalistic system, a codification of acts, actions, and attitudes purporting to represent standards of goodness in absolute terms. Thereby culture-bound customs become identified with absolute and eternal values. Morality becomes petrified in legalism. Variant opinions, in respect to what in any case is humanly unknowable, are heresies punishable by death or exclusion from the community. "Sin is the transgression of the law".[62]

As Whitmont points out, goodness becomes synonymous with obedience to communal law and is accomplished by an act of will and self-denial, compliance and social adaptation. Whatever has been established by the God-King can only be good and just: "Evil, then, is disobedience and nonconformity, freely willed, preventable and punishable".[63]

It is an autocratic, authoritarian, arguably fascist form of morality, which leaves no room for individual principled or autonomous moral thinking. As Markley and Harman observe:

The Semitic God was seen as a male Being "out there", an image that closes the inward way of mysticism, since what is to be found within oneself is not divinity (as in India and the Far East) but only one's "soul", which may or may not be found in a proper relationship to God. A proper relationship can be achieved only by obedience to God's commandments and membership in God's favored tribe. Not as a free individual, but only as a member of the High God's "chosen" race (or church, in later versions) is one effectively in God's care. In this view the human was seen as a servant, created to serve the One God by having dominion over all other forms of earthly creation.[64]

Guilt

ALMOST FROM THE BEGINNING, Christianity saw guilt and death as collective and as punishment from God, so Donald Broadribb argues:

> The whole of humanity is ridden with guilt. Humanity (which is the literal meaning of the word Adam) has disobeyed God from the start and, consequently, has been sentenced to death, as told in the story of the Garden of Eden at the start of the Bible. For this reason death is universal. Humanity by its own innate nature is disobedient to God; humanity is sinful.[65]

Disobedience to God's laws; sin, guilt and death, are all tied together. Freedom from guilt and death can only come about by carefully obeying God's laws, which in turn are sourced in the Jewish sacred writings as well as inspiration claimed by the early Apostles.

However some of the most influential early Christians, in particular the Apostle Paul, continued to feel guilt and death, despite strictly adhering to God's Laws. This led to the view that it is not possible to free oneself from humanity's collective guilt and hence the doctrine of 'Original Sin'.

Broadribb concludes that this was an agonised response to perfectionalism demanded by many Christian teachers and also said to have been demanded by Jesus.[66] Thus 'man' was so far from the perfection of the God-Father that the highest human attainments – even the best aspirations – are acceptable only by divine grace.

For the Old Testament Hebrew thinkers, sin was primarily rebellion, either wilful and deliberate, or unconscious through forgetting God and absorption in other interests.[67] Whitmont powerfully describes the God-Father superego and morality:

> The effects of shame and guilt, of "Thou shalt" and "Thou shalt not" are a training of judgement and self control. The law states what is right and wrong, good and bad. The will carries out the dictates of law and judgment. It enforces their demands upon the resisting natural and instinctual urges. Spirit is set against nature in a heroic effort to subdue man's animal nature... The patriarchal superego conditioned ego is, as a result, conquest orientated. Its sense of identity rests upon its power

> to enforce order and upon its capacity to conquer, possess, and
> assimilate resisting objects and opponents. Failure of any of these
> capacities engenders a sense of inadequacy and inferiority. Inferiority
> feelings, the power drive, anxiety, possessiveness, envy, jealousy, and
> the compulsion to subdue and conquer are the mainsprings of the
> patriarchal ego… External collective authority and internalized
> superego shame and guilt are, then, inescapable and necessary phases
> of patriarchal ego development … They have placed their mark on
> cultural standards. It is through the theophany of Israel, the Decalogue,
> and its subsequent Christian legalism that this decisive internalization
> of ethical standards has occurred.[68]

Broadribb asks how we can reconcile the traditionally gentle and forgiving nature of Jesus, who restored people to life, with the image of "a furious God who brings death upon every living thing because of universal guilt"?[69] It can be argued that the Jesus tradition is best aligned with the Sophianic, Gnostic, inner-wisdom tradition and archetype, rather than the God-Father archetype.

Active Social Concern

ON THE OTHER HAND, argues H. and H.A. Frankfort, while monotheism may be no more than despotism in religion, the great achievement of Israel was not primarily that the oneness of the world and God was asserted, but rather the righteous character of the God so affirmed: "Israel's monotheism was an ethical monotheism".[70]

Spretnak also gives a positive rather than critical view and so recognises the *imperative of active social concern* in the Semitic religious traditions, hence in Judaism, Christianity and Islam:

> Two related elements in Judaism – prophetic anger and social
> legislation – have deeply influenced the responses in Western
> civilization to suffering, cruelty, and oppression. The prophets of
> Hebrew scriptures vigorously denounce acts of inhumanity, including
> causing suffering without deliberation. Their vigilance is an example of
> naming and condemning oppressive practices. In addition, a large
> portion of the law of the Torah (the first five books of the Bible)
> prohibits injustice and inhumanity as violations of the community's
> relationship with God. The manifestation of the divine in Hebrew
> scriptures responds especially to the poor and disadvantaged – the
> sojourner (outsider), the fatherless, the widowed. (Such concern is
> especially strong in the book of Deuteronomy.) Hence in the evolution
> of Judaism, as well as those religions that grew from its foundation,
> Christianity and Islam, active social concern is an imperative linked
> with the quality of one's spiritual practice.[71]

This monotheistic imperative of active social concern is certainly inherent in the Archetypal God-Father morality and the *Anthropocentric Landscape*. However, whether or not this imperative is considered to have been overwhelmingly successful – when balanced against the results of abuse of the Earth, environmental destruction, religious and nationalist wars and the persecution of the heretics and dissenters (the non "chosen") over the centuries – is debatable.

Becoming and History

'BECOMING' AND 'HISTORICAL DEVELOPMENT', which give identity and spirituality, are the main focus of consciousness within the Heavenly God-Father Archetype and the *Anthropocentric Landscape.*

This is more important than 'place and space', mythology, 'timelessness and being', which are so important in the Mother Earth Archetype and the *Nature/Earth Landscape.* The Mother Earth Archetype, if she is associated with time at all, is associated with *mythical* and *cyclical time.*

The God-Father Archetype – being differentiated from the uroborus (the womb), the unconscious and the undifferentiated embrace of the Mother Earth – is associated with *ego* and *hero* development and the conquering of death, therefore the preoccupation with historicity and becoming:

> The Goddess represented life as it was; the God represented life as man
> wanted it to be, celebrating only what he fashioned with his own hands,
> from his own will. She had appeared in her triple aspect, renewing herself
> in the perpetual life-death cycle; he appeared alone, fixed for ever in
> ageless vigour. She had accepted death as part of life; he was immortal.[72]

Hero in the Anthropocentric Landscape

THE INDEPENDENCE OF the Ego from nature, dividing the world into subject and object, frees it to contemplate its immortality untrammelled from cyclical time and the Hero is born.[73] It is the Hero who, through his feats in real and mythological history, conquers death and becomes immortal. Historicity and becoming are all-important.

The *Anthropocentric Landscape* is the place where we can all become heroes. Against the forces and the odds, we try to determine our personal and collective futures.

Ironically, we have become so caught up in our heroic personal endeavours that the timelessness of the land – the importance of place and space – and the importance of being, dwelling within this timelessness, is often a fleeting and treasured experience. It is treasured because it is the exception rather than the rule. It is a peak experience which points to meaning beyond the humdrum of everyday striving, the banality of much of man's material status and political ambitions.

Nature "fades into the background"

THE PREDOMINANCE OF HISTORICITY over nature, place and space, is embedded in the Bible. Gulick is succinct:

> To reflect upon the integrity of the land apart from human use would
> require an abstract quality of thought not characteristic of the biblical
> worldview. In sum, nature in the Bible is generally either regarded as a

> resource, or it fades into the background while in the foreground, the
> significant drama of history is played out.[74]

The significant drama of history in the Bible is the eschatological expectation of an immanent end to the world, which had its origins in Judaism. It was associated with the hope and expectation of the coming of the Messiah, or Davidic ruler, who would make the world for the Jews, in particular, a more joyful place to live:

> When the first Christians came to affirm that Jesus of Nazareth was in
> fact the Messiah, it served only to intensify their expectations that the old
> age would very soon, and in a cataclysmic way, be replaced by a new
> world. The writer of Revelation had a vision of it taking place: "I saw a
> new heaven and a new earth, for the first heaven and the first earth had
> passed away."[75]

Messianic Hero in Linear History

THE DRAMA OF HISTORY and salvation to come, was all-important within orthodox Christian monotheism. Jesus, the Messiah or Christ, was the archetypal hero who vanquished death, not only through his own resurrection, but for all Christian believers through his perfection and his sacrifice.

At first it was thought that the resurrection of Jesus heralded a new age just around the corner. However, as time passed and there was no dramatic change in world conditions, Christians increasingly looked to 'the Second Coming' of Christ before a New Age could be realised. This had the advantage of not coming into conflict with the Judaic belief in their own Messiah, who had yet to come.

Christians turned their expectations from the earthly salvation to salvation in the next, unseen, higher, spiritual world where after 'death' their souls would become immortal.

There is a very close relationship between time and religious questions, as Lloyd Geering points out. The Bible begins with a reference to time: 'In the beginning…'

While the concept of God can be conceived of as timeless in the Augustinian sense, the biblical view of time and the predominant Western anthropocentric view of time has been linear. "The Biblical view of time superimposed the linear view over the Pagan cyclical view (sometimes now called the spiralling view). This is reflected in the Biblical story of creation in a seven-day week".[76]

THE LINEAR VIEW OF TIME eventually became the dominant view in the three main God-Father archetypal monotheistic religions of the Middle East, which looked back to creation in the past and to the future for fulfillment, salvation and eternal life. This linear view of time is inherent in the *Anthropocentric Landscape* and predominates in the West.

Scapegoating and Warmongering

THE SHADOWSIDE of the Heavenly God-Father is scapegoating and warmongering against 'the other' or the *not* 'chosen'. In particular, it is the scapegoating of the feminine:

In the patriarchal world, propitiation of aggression through the sacrificial
rite had to come under the rule of ethics. It had to be justified by
principles of right and wrong. We find the mythical expression of this
fact in the Jewish scapegoat ceremony. It's later elaboration is Christ's
offering. The principle common to both of them guilt and atonement for
guilt – are still the basis of ethics and of justified aggression in the
modern world. Aggression is turned against the guilty self or against
another person into whom we project the guilt.[77]

Whitmont maintains that the scapegoat motif is reinterpreted from the older
matriarchal and mythical view in which the Dionysian god and his substitute victim
die in order to be reborn and so express renewal; hence the Great Round, the maternal
cycles of ebb and flow.[78]

In Christianity, Christ, the son of the Heavenly God-Father, dies in order to atone for
those who have "sinned through ignorance" (Lev.4:2). Christ is the 'Lamb of God that
carries the sins of the World'; Christ embodies the scapegoat motif central to
Christianity. However, he is a willing and knowing scapegoat, and by transcending the
Ego and defeating death he is thereby also a Hero. This could perhaps be called the
positive scapegoat.

Scapegoating and the Self

FOR MANY, THE CHRIST example is an unattainable ideal at best and an empty
presumption at worst. Whitmont states:

> Sin, guilt, and ethical condemnation of human nature are basic to later
> Christian theology and to medieval and postmedieval Western culture.
> As man is now declared a sinner before God, we all have become
> scapegoats. We are all weighed down with guilt and self-rejection, not
> only for what we do, but also for what we are, for our "bad" desires and
> instinctual urges, for the foibles of human nature. We cannot accept the
> facts of our authentic natural being – our desires and instinctual needs,
> our aggressive, destructive, and power urges. But what we deny we
> cannot discipline either. Wanting to be seen and seeing ourselves as good
> only, we reason away our antisocial and selfish urges but are quick to see
> them in the other fellow.[79]

That Old Devil Projection

THE NEGATIVE AND shadowside of scapegoating is where those aspects of our
personal nature which we cannot accept are projected onto other people, who are
sometimes then persecuted.

Only the God of the Law is deemed good, therefore all evil must come from "natural
man", "the other", the *not* "chosen. That which is culturally unacceptable (and therefore
evil) cannot be the domain of the All Good God who originated the Law. It is therefore
projected onto Satan or the Devil. Fundamentalists, those who adhere most strictly and

literally to '*the Law*' and 'the Truth' of the 'One True God', are often those most rigorous in their scapegoating of others:

> In the form of righteous zeal, repressed violence becomes fanatical do-gooding, intolerant destructiveness toward the unreformed and unreformable self, or toward the wrongdoing others. Based on the current dictates of the cultural superego the ego arrogates to itself the authority of being able to decide what is good or bad for itself, for others, and for the world at large. Learning by trial and error is excluded. The result is the godlike inflation of modern people, the intolerance of creeds and convictions other than one's own.[80]

Spretnak has already pointed out the unfortunate fact that the Semitic traditions, from their inception and despite their active social concern, "have demonstrated a rather harshly limited sense of divine community": the "Other", individual or group, deemed less worthy and inferior than the inflated "I" or "we", was subjected to aggression and extermination.[81]

From the social point of view, Christian ideology has had little place for universal equality and freedom when it comes to slavery and the subjection of women. The church never condemned the practice of slavery, even in modern times and, ironically, while male slaves were allowed positions of authority in the Church, free women were not admitted to such positions. This was despite the fact that from its beginnings women played a very supportive role in the Christian movement. Donald Broadribb argues:

> [T]he elaboration of religious doctrine was, and continues to be, kept firmly in the hands of men. This seems paradoxical in the light of the fact that usually 80 percent or more of the people present at a Christian religious meeting are female ... organization and doctrine are prescribed by men while active participation is by tradition allocated to women.[82]

Hidden Clergy Sexual Abuse

AUSTRALIAN JOURNALIST Muriel Porter, a prominent layperson within the Anglican Church, has asked what the outsiders have long asked: Why have church leaders failed to deal with sexual abuse of women and children by male clergy? Why have the churches failed to come to terms with their ancient suspicion of both women and their sexuality? [83] Sexual abuse and victimisation of women and children is, of course, not confined to the orthodox Christian Church; it is found in both orthodox Judaism and orthodox Islam, as well as in other patriarchal religious traditions.

It is not a question which would have been asked until recently. Abuse of women and children was hidden, particularly in religious institutions, and if it was exposed at all, the victim was usually blamed, if not wholly then at least partially, for in some way tempting the sin.[84]

Redress has come from the *secular courts* and secular society *outside* religious institutions – just as the movements for justice and equality for women, gays, slaves, African Americans and Native Americans have come from *outside* the churches, synagogues and mosques.

Canadian Muslim feminist Irshad Manji has put her life on the line by challenging fundamentalism and arguing for reformation in which Muslim women are empowered and lead the way forward to reason and reinterpretation of the Koran. She wants women to have the freedom to express themselves without fear of being maimed, tortured, raped or murdered at the hands of the Islamic State.[85]

The Holocausts

WINSTON CHURCHILL DESCRIBED the first "Holocaust" of the twentieth century to be that of the killing of 1.5 million Christian Armenians by the Ottoman Turks during the First World War. In what was a precursor to the Second World War murder of six million Jews by the Nazis – Armenian men, women and children, including children were stuffed , sometimes 90 people per wagon, into cattle trucks for deportation.

As Robert Fisk states, it was "Ottoman Turkey's attempt to exterminate an entire Christian race in the Middle East" and significantly "One authority on extermination who did recognise the Armenian genocide was Adolf Hitler. In a 1939 speech, in which he ordered the killing, "mercilessly and without compassion", of Polish men, women and children, he concluded: "Who, after all, speaks today of the annihilation of the Armenians?"[86]

The most extreme example of scapegoating in the twentieth century was the Holocaust with its systematic and technologically efficient extermination of six million Jews. *And let us not forget* - an estimated half a million Rom Gypsies (almost the entire Eastern European Gypsy population), 5,000 to 15,000 gays, three million Polish men and women of non-Jewish, Christian ancestry; Communists, Atheists, non-mainstream Christians like the Jehovah Witnesses; and resisters from Russia, Eastern Europe, Holland, France and Germany were also incarcerated in concentration camps and killed. Then there were the handicapped, disabled and those deemed 'useless', 'ethnically tainted' or 'immoral' who were put to death "like dogs and cats". It is estimated eleven million were killed during this Holocaust.

What is not widely recognised is the influence of Catholicism on Adolf Hitler and Nazism.[87] Hitler was born into a Catholic family and many who knew him well argued he remained a Catholic all his life. Certainly there is much anecdotal evidence to support this view. As well, his anti-Semitic, anti-gay, conservative views on the family and women's roles in society, anti-Communism and anti-atheism, had parallels with monotheistic orthodox Catholicism. [88]

Witch Hunts

SEVERAL CENTURIES EARLIER another example of scapegoating on a systematic mass scale was the great European witch hunts. Anthony Stevens states:

> [T]he persecution of witches was a particularly nasty example of
> religious scapegoating. The witch was much more than a
> personification of the Terrible Mother: she was a victim of
> displacement of the xenophobic reaction normally reserved for
> members of the out-group. As the 'enemy within' society, the Mistress
> of Satan came to afflict the Righteous; she was a cancer that had to be
> burnt out of the body politic if God's will was to prevail and all godly
> souls be preserved. As scapegoat, the witch carried the collective guilt
> of the population, and as a focus of group hatred she permitted all
> 'decent' people to remain peacefully unconscious of their own evil
> propensities. Her sacrifice at the stake promoted the cohesion of the
> Christian community by enabling its members (the godly in-group) to
> reaffirm their allegiance to the ordinances of God.[89]

While the estimated number of witches brought before trial and those executed varies widely from several hundred thousand to nine million – there is no doubt that most of those accused were women, approximately 75 to 80 percent.[90]

The myths of persecution need to be understood , concludes Martha Reineke, if we are to break the persecutory structure at its roots.[91]

This is particularly relevant today as fundamentalist Christians and Jews seek to demonise Muslims as terrorists and vice versa; and as all of these monotheistic God-Father archetypal religions have 'othered', objectified, rendered non-chosen and sometimes demonised and persecuted women and gays (males often regarded as feminine and not 'real' men).[92]

Back to the Future

FEMINIST THEOLOGIANS like academic philosopher and theologian Mary Daly (1928-2010) have challenged the God-Father scapegoating myths, particularly as they relate to women and the environment.[93]   As Lloyd Geering points out, it was only to be expected that:

> [O]ne of the strongest challenges to traditional theism has been
> mounted by the modern feminist movement. For women to become
> truly liberated they must be free not only from male domination but
> also from a dominating male deity. The two go hand in hand, for as
> Mary Daly said, "Where God is male, then the male is God."[94]

Most recently ecofeminists – and male feminists like historian Theodore Roszak (1933-2011) who recognise that environmental issues are also feminist issues – have led the environmental movement by challenging the denigration of the natural world by an anthropocentrism imbued with and informed by the Heavenly God-Father archetype and the patriarchal myth of man's inherent right to domination, subjugation and exploitation.[95]

Never-the-less, the Heavenly God-Father and the *Anthropocentric Landscape* had prepared the way for the *Technological/Materialist Landscape* and the Trickster. It is to these matters we now turn.

SEVEN

Trickster

Technology is neither devil nor an angel.
But neither is it simply a "tool" a neutral
extension of some rock-solid human
nature. Technology is a trickster...

[The Trickster] Hermes became agoraios,
"he of the agora," the patron saint of
merchants, middlemen, and the service
industry, while the god's epithet "tricky"
came to mean "good for securing profit".

– **Erik Davis**

Freely developing technology has
always been an historical wild card and a
potentially destabilizing element. Free
markets and technologies do not
necessarily produce a stable, predictable
social order, but they do promote
individual liberty.

– **Frederich R. Lynch**

"Trickster God is Universal"

THE TRICKSTER ARCHETYPE – or Trickster God, otherwise known in the West as the Greek God Hermes – *is universal*. Trickster is found in the mythologies of many peoples. Like Hecate – whose cult probably spread from Anatolia into Greece and who is associated with Hermes – Trickster is the quintessential master of boundaries and transitions. He brings both good luck and bad, both profit and loss. He is the patron of both travellers and thieves. Like Hecate, Trickster is the guide of souls to the underworld and the messenger of the gods. He surprises mundane reality with the unexpected and miraculous. In traditional primal cultures, Trickster emerges under the dominance of the Earth Mother.[1] Combs and Holland point out:

> The trickster god is universal. He is known to the Native American
> peoples as Ictinike, Coyote, Rabbit and others; he is Maui to the
> Polynesian Islanders; Loki to the old Germanic tribes of Europe; and
> Krishna in the sacred mythology of India. Best known to most of us in
> the West is the Greek god Hermes, who represents the most
> comprehensive and sophisticated manifestation of the Trickster.[2]

However, the Trickster God is not confined just to traditional primal cultures - today he is well and truly at home in the *Technological/Materialist Landscape*.

Trickster is at Home Today

AS JUNG STATES, the Trickster appears par excellence in modern man:

> He is a forerunner of the saviour, and like him, God, man, and animal
> at once. He is both subhuman and superhuman, a bestial and divine
> beingwhose chief and most alarming characteristic is his unconscious.[3]

While Hermes the Greek God is not reducible to the Trickster; in the West, the Trickster is frequently associated with Hermes – for example 'Trickster Hermes' and 'Hermes the Trickster'. Combs and Holland argue that the Trickster God is universal:

> Best known to us in the West is the Greek God Hermes, who represents
> the most comprehensive and sophisticated manifestation of the
> Trickster.[4]

The Trickster, like Hermes and Hecate, is also specifically associated with liminality[5] – thresholds, or the point beyond which a sensation becomes too faint to be experienced.

Above all the Trickster is fun. In the *Technological/Materialist Landscape* we are all imbued with the Trickster and 'his' exploits – both angelic and devilish. We partake in his exuberance, ambitions, boundary exploration, trickery, games, sleights-of-hand, personas, commercial success, communications expertise, technological genius, liminality and in his shadow-side – if not in actuality then in fantasy. We both applaud him and are appalled by him. We live vicariously through the Trickster and his shadow via entertainment – films, video games and the mass communications of television, internet, texting, smart phones, magazines and books.

Today we are imbued with the Trickster. For those whose *'focus of perception'* is primarily the *Technological/Materialist Landscape*, the symbolic correspondence between the individual's *inner life* and the *outer world* has many of the characteristics inherent in the Trickster Archetype. When "an individual's inner life corresponds in a symbolic way to the outer objective world, the two are connected by meaning".[6] In other words the *inner life* connected by *symbolic meaning* to the *outer world* is an indication of the governance of an archetype. As Combes and Holland state:

> The themes carried by archetypes are universal: they are neither wholly internal nor wholly external but are woven into the deepest fabric of the cosmos. This notion is supported by Jung's idea that archetypes have their origins in the *unus mundus*, or "one world", which is at the foundation of the psyche and the objective, physical world. Bohm's concept of the holographic universe offers similar possibilities. It follows, then, that myths as expressions of archetypes might be expected to portray certain aspects of the object world as well as depicting psychological realities. Indeed many of the Greek Gods represent aspects of reality that overarch both the inner worlds of human experience and the external worlds of nature and society.[7]

Trickster Hero

THE HERO AND EGO are more developed in the Trickster than in the *Anthropocentric Landscape* of the Heavenly God-Father Archetype.

While the hero myths vary enormously in detail, structurally they are very similar. There is a universal pattern even although the myths were developed by groups or individuals without direct cultural contact.

The special function of the hero myth is the development of the individual's ego consciousness and his exploration and coming to awareness of his own strengths and weaknesses, which equips him for later challenges of life.[8] Joseph L. Henderson argues:

> Over and over again one hears a tale describing a hero's miraculous but humble birth, his early proof of superhuman strength, his rapid rise to prominence or power, his triumphant struggle with the forces of evil, his fallibility to the sin of pride (*hybris*), and his fall through betrayal or a "heroic" sacrifice that ends in his death.[9]

Erich Neumann states "The hero is always a light-bringer and emissary of light ... The hero's victory brings with it a new spiritual status, a new knowledge, and an alteration of consciousness": the heroic age is characterised as the "predominance of individual personality".[10] All are characteristics of the Trickster Hero.

The heroic culminates in the *Technological/Materialist Landscape* in the development of science and the world as object:[11]

> The activity of masculine consciousness is heroic in so far as it voluntarily takes upon itself the archetypal struggle with the dragon of

the unconscious and carries it to successful conclusion... The
correlation of consciousness with masculinity culminates in the
development of science, as an attempt by the masculine spirit to
emancipate itself from the power of the unconscious. Wherever science
appears it breaks up the original character of the world, which was
filled with unconscious projections. Thus, stripped of projection, the
world becomes objective, a scientific construction of the mind.[12]

THE TRICKSTER HERO PITS HIMSELF AGAINST THE OLD GOD. Neumann
maintains that in the modern world the disintegration of the old system of values is in
full swing.[13] In the modern world the hero with his human ego pits himself against the
old deity. Thus:

the hero ceases to be instrument of the gods and begins to play his own
independent part as a human being; and when he finally becomes, in
modern man a battleground for suprapersonal forces, where the
human ego pits itself against the deity. As breaker of the old law, man
becomes the opponent of the old system and the bringer of the new,
which he confers upon mankind against the will of the old deity.[14]

"Professional Boundary-Crosser"

TRICKSTER HERMES HAS had a long historical association with the marketplace,
commerce, merchants, cross-roads, boundaries, trickery, the con-artist, theft, gift-
givers, the magus, magic, craft, trade-as-equitable-exchange, surplus, profit,
middlemen, connections, mediation, invention, goods, possessions, transformation,
information.

The earliest markets, as Dudley Young points out, were set up in reserved areas of
boundaries to minimize the risks of violence, raiding and war; thus merchants were
"professional boundary-crossers."

Men also crossed the bounds for wives, seduction and marriage.[15] In other words,
Hermes the Trickster God is the embodiment of all that goes on in the materialist
landscape. For example, "Hermes' ability to reach through the cracks of ordinary
reality and make connections between the known and unknown arises in part,
surprisingly, from his ancient role as patron of commerce".[16]

In primitive Greek villages marketplaces lay on the borders, between settlements and
these luminal zones were ever believed to be imbued with magic: Norman O. Brown
argues "Primitive trade on the boundary was deeply impregnated with magical
notions".[17] The mystery of exchange between a village and its unknown, often feared
neighbours, was frequently overseen on the boundaries and crossroads by Hermes the
Trickster God.

They were magical communications often in places sacred to Hermes and often the
traders conducted their business in silence, never actually meeting, but leaving an
object and later finding it exchanged for other goods. Thus "Hermes' place in ancient

commerce illustrates his role in connecting the known with the unknown across borders".[18]

In fact Hermes the Trickster can appear at any boundary, individually set, conscious or unconscious, or those set by culture.

The Greeks marked crossroads, borders of villages and doorways to their homes with the *herm*, a pillar of rectangular shape surmounted with the head of Hermes (and graced as well with a healthy phallus).

Erik Davis describes the ambiguity, excitement, magic and liminality of the crossroads; where the gift, the barter, meetings, communication, as well as theft and trickery are part and parcel of market trade and commerce:

> Crossroads are extremely charged spaces. Here choices are made, fears and facts overlap, and the alien first shows its face: strange people, foreign tongues, exotic and delightful goods and information. Crossroads create what the anthropologist Victor Turner calls "liminal zones": ambiguous but potent spaces of transformation and threat that lie at the edge of cultural maps... In archaic times, the exchange of goods often took place at crossroads and village borders; these swaps were fraught with ambiguity, for they blurred the distinction between gift, barter, magic, and theft. As the commercial networks of the Greek city-states developed, the economic border zone eventually shifted from the wild edges of the village into the more organized markets at the heart of the new urban centers. The outside was swallowed within. Hermes became *agoraios*, " he of the agora," the patron saint of merchants, middlemen, and the service industry, while the gods' epithet "tricky" came to mean "good for securing profit."[19]

As his wand and flying sandals suggest, Hermes is the most magical of the Greek Gods. He is the shaman and the Trickster:

> The Greek word for tricky is *dolios*, and this, together with the thieving words built on *klept*, were major epithets of Hermes. The third one of importance was *kerdoos*, and though all three in Homeric usage involved the tricky, the skillful, and the magical (all of these meanings survive in our word "crafty"), only the last added the further notion of "gainful." Thus the one who is skilled in magical practices, and the crafting technologies that obviously supersede them, will use these skills for the manipulation and appropriation of objects that will augment our prosperity; and thus Hermes was the god not only of thieves and craftsman, but also of merchants and gift-givers.[20]

Market Magician - Money, Magic, Shit, Surplus

FASCINATION IN THE *Technological/Materialist Landscape* with possessions and money lies in their ability to possess and transform – hence they are magical in effect. Dudley Young states:

> To seize or be seized is to be transformed, to have one's identity, even
> the contours of one's body changed. The moment I seize an object, take
> it unto myself and call it mine, my being is altered instantaneously, and
> the passive voice used in the legal formulation points to the sense in
> which one is possessed and altered by one's possessions.[21]

Money is hermetical in that it originates and thrives in the marketplace, but "it is also
magical, secretive, elusive, fast-moving, and deceitful … notably swarmlike in its
tendency to consume what it touches, fascinate and repel with its potent nothingness,
and accumulate in amorphous heaps that give the distinct impression of breeding".[22]

Money, abundance, surplus and superfluous are all descriptors of the materialist
market landscape. Money and abundance draws us irresistibly to the question of shit and
surplus – as well as magic, paradox and the Trickster. As Dudley Young describes it:

> The first connotation of shit is surplus; and since surplus,
> superfluousness, and abundance are hallmarks of divinity, shit will be
> perceived as magical from the start… This manifestly magical stuff, at
> once good and bad, from which we have drawn the most profound
> inferences about the human condition, is also just a load of shit,
> nothing at all. For comic relief from the appalling paradox we think of
> Trickster, whose frequently shitty exploits often issue unaccountably in
> gifts to mankind.[23]

THE CAPITALIST CORPORATE culture today has many of the Trickster's archetypal
characteristics. The corporation in the last 150 years has risen from relative obscurity
to become the world's dominant economic institution. Corporations are now in a
position to dictate the economic policies of governments. With the creation of the
World Trade Organisation (WTO) in 1993 and other trade pacts, deregulation and
globalization has strengthened. The economic sovereignty of nations has been
undermined.

Corporations - Bigger than the Church

THE CHURCH, in other times, has had its functions taken over by the modern
corporate. Joel Bakan argues:

> Today, corporations govern our lives. They determine what we eat,
> what we watch, what we wear, where we work, and what we do. We are
> inescapably surrounded by their culture, iconography, and ideology.
> And like the church and the monarchy in other times, they posture as
> infallible and omnipotent, glorifying themselves in imposing buildings
> and elaborate displays. Increasingly, corporations dictate the decisions
> of their supposed overseers in government and control domains of
> society once firmly embedded within the public sphere.[24]

While Trickster characteristics imbue the materialist market landscape, as we shall see,
Trickster is also inherent in the technological landscape which informs and

increasingly directs the materialist landscape. Technological innovations have profoundly enabled and enhanced the corporate world's mobility and portability through communications and transportation. Large jets, new shipping container techniques, integrated rail and track networks have increased speed and efficiency in the transportation of goods and services. Long-distance phone networks, fax, telex and internet mean that corporations can outsource and produce goods and services speedily at substantially lower costs.

Techno-Wizardary – the Tricksters' Playground

IRONICALLY, WHILE THE IMAGE of technology is secular, it rests on Christian myths, as Davis points out:

> [T]his secular image was framed all along by Christian myths: the biblical call to conquer nature, the Protestant work ethic, and, in particular, the millennialist vision of a New Jerusalem, the earthly paradise that the Book of Revelation claims will crown the course of history. Despite a century of Hiroshimas, Bhopals, and Chernobyls, this myth of an engineered utopia still propels the ideology of technological progress, with its perennial promises of freedom, prosperity, and release from disease and want.[25]

The old image of technology for well over a century was industrial. Lewis Mumford called it the "myth of the Machine" and, as Davis points out, it rested on "the authority of technical and scientific elites, and in the intrinsic value of efficiency, control, unrestrained technological development, and economic expansion".[26]

The new image of technology is less mechanised and described in the mythology of information, electronic mindscloud computing, infinite databases, computerized forecasting, hypertext libraries, virtual realities, micro-chip engineering, artificial intelligence, bio-engineering, and global internet and telecommunication networking. Hence:

> Boundaries dissolve, and we drift into the no-man's zones between synthetic and organic life, between actual and virtual environments, between local communities and global flows of goods, information, labor, and capital. With pills modifying personality, machines modifying bodies, and synthetic pleasures and net-worked minds engineering a more fluid and invented sense of self, the boundaries of our identities are mutating as well. The horizon melts into a limitless question mark, and like the cartographers of old, we glimpse yawning monstrosities and mind-forged utopias beyond the edges of our paltry and provisional maps.[27]

The playground of the Trickster is new technology. Erik Davis argues:

> Of all the godforms that haunt the Greek mind, Hermes is the one who would feel most at home in our wired world. Indeed, with his

mischievous combination of speed, trickery, and profitable mediation, he can almost be seen as the archaic mascot of the information age... He flies "as fleet as thought", an image of the daylight mind, with its plans and synaptic leaps, its chatter and overload. Hermes shows that these minds are not islands, but nodes in an immense electric tangle of words, images, songs, and signals. Hermes rules the transtemporal world of information exchange.[28]

"A Host of Guises"

TRICKSTER IS MASTER of the persona and masks. His ego is fluid. He is both hero and anti-hero. Davis states:

> More than mere delivery boy, Hermes wears a host of guises; con artist, herald, inventor, merchant, magus, thief... Lord of the lucky find, Hermes crafts opportunity like those brash start-up companies that fill a market niche by creating it in the first place".[29]

The Greeks were quite clear about it – Hermes is a thief. However the Trickster's banditry is not based on raw power. He is no mugger or thug. Hermes is the hacker, the spy and the mastermind. He is executor of the slickest legal contracts.[30]

Lives On the Edge

THE TRICKSTER LIVES on the edge. The Trickster demands freedom and individual liberty – which are not necessarily compatible with predictability and stability. He is at home with 'chaos theory' and an unpredictable world. Unlike Apollo who can be considered the god of science in its ideal pure form:

> Hermes insists that there are always cracks and gaps in such perfect architectures; intelligence moves forward by keeping on its crafty toes, ever opening into a world that is messy, unpredictable, and far from equilibrium. The supreme symbol for the fecund space of possibility and innovation that Hermes exploits is the crossroads – a fit image as well for our contemporary world, with its data nets and seemingly infinite choices.[31]

"Mercurial Networks"

THE TRICKSTER EMBODIES the mythos of the information age:

> Hermes would approve of the Internet, a mercurial network of far-flung messages that functions as a marketplace of ideas and commodities... the Net opens up a technological liminal zone that swamps the self with new paths of possibility. Indeed, the mythic attraction of the Net turns on some of the very same qualities associated with the youthful trickster: speed, profit, innovative interconnection, the overturning of established orders.[32]

Technology,"Trickiness"

ON THE NEGATIVE SIDE, like the internet, the Trickster traffics in deception. He lies and steals. The dark side of the net is in the hidden machinations of new corporate media powers, a social and psychological life which is atomised and bedeviled with confusing amoral personas, a widening gap between those that can afford the new technology and the poor – the players and the played, or preyed upon. The Trickster and technology are intimately connected. The Trickster is mastermind of techne or the art of craft. In the language of Homer, the word for "trickiness" is identical to the word for "technical skill." Technology is a trickster. In the words of Erik Davis:

> Hermes thus unveils an image of technology, not only as useful
> handmaiden, but as trickster. For all its everyday efficacy, technology
> stands on shifting ground, giving us at once more and less than its
> spectacular powers first suggest. ... Hermes' trickery is not merely a
> rational device, but an expression of magical power. The god's magic is
> ambiguous, because we cannot clearly distinguish the clever ruse from
> the savvy manipulation of some unseen natural fact. With such
> Hermetic ambiguity in mind, we might say that technology too is a
> spell and a trick, a device that crafts the real by exploiting the hidden
> laws of nature and human perception alike.[33]

In other words, both the Trickster and technology have the power to spellbind. They have the magical power of the magus, the magician and a God.

'God is Dead'

THE HEAVENLY GOD-FATHER has largely been rendered redundant or made existentially irrelevant in the *Technological/Materialist Landscape*.

The new God is 'Man'. Humanism has replaced Deism. 'Man' is the hero, the measure, the creator, the player and the new Trickster God. 'Man' is the magus, the magician and the techno-wizard. The human being is the entrepreneur, the commodity creator, producer, trader, the money maker, the economic determiner and the market player. In December 1984 British philosopher and theologian Keith Ward, an ordained priest in the Church of England, noted:

> It is not that people know what God is, and have decided to reject him.
> It seems that very few people even know what the orthodox traditional
> idea of God, shared by Judaism, Islam and Christianity, is. They have
> not the slightest idea what is meant by the word God. It just has no
> sense or possible place in their lives. Instead they either invent some
> vague idea of a cosmic force with no practical implications at all; or
> they appeal to some half-forgotten picture of a bearded super-person
> constantly interfering with the mechanistic laws of Nature.[34]

That was 1984, in liberal Britain. Then followed a heavily politicised Christian Right revival in the United States and the God of the Old Testament was back as a force to be reckoned with. But many others did not like what they perceived God to be. By 2006, the attitudes of many towards the Heavenly God-Father Archetype had hardened into antipathy. In 2006 Richard Dawkins wrote:

> The God of the Old Testament is arguably the most unpleasant
> character in all fiction: jealous and proud of it; a petty, unjust,
> unforgiving control-freak; a vindictive, bloodthirsty ethnic cleanser; a
> misogynistic, homophobic, racist, infanticidal, genocidal, filicidal,
> pestilential, megalomaniacal, sadomasochistic, capriciously malevolent
> bully.[35]

Nor was Dawkins the only contemporary best-seller hostile to the Heavenly God-Father Archetype. The atheists of monotheism like Christopher Hitchens, Sam Harris and Daniel Dennett were coming out of the closet from all directions, with a vengeance.[36]

In fact there had been an increasing climate of skepticism about the God-Father Archetype throughout much of the twentieth century. In 1937 Carl Jung came to express the strange and mysterious phenomenon of the 'Death of God' as a psychic fact of our time. "I know – and here I am expressing what countless other people know – that the present time is the time of God's disappearance and death".[37] For years Jung had observed the Christian God-image fading in his patient's dreams – that is in the unconscious of modern man.[38] Anthony Stevens also recognised the 'Death of God' in our time, despite the fact that an archetype can never be killed off completely:

> That the God archetype nowadays leaves so many of us untouched by
> its numinosity is because we have grown up in a culture whose 'God is
> dead' and whose religion is decayed, and the archetype has not been
> actualized in us. Yet it slumbers on in the deeper recesses of the Self.[39]

Stevens saw the 'Death of God' as a rejection of the morality, values and spirituality which the God-Father represents. As a corollary, the morality, values and spirituality of the *Anthropocentric Landscape* was being replaced by the morality, values and spirituality of the *Technological/Materialist Landscape* and the Trickster:

> The contemporary decline in the position of the father has coincided
> with a most interesting cultural development: the emergence of an
> anti-authoritarian *Zeitgeist*, especially amongst the young, which
> manifests itself in a blanket hostility towards the traditional patriarchal
> values enshrined in Judeo-Christian civilization for millennia. This
> phenomena must engage our attention here because it affords an
> example of what may happen when a society of individuals collectively
> shares in the rejection or repression of integral components of an
> archetype. What have been rejected in this instance are those aspects of
> the Father and the archetypal Masculine which relate to the
> maintenance of law and order, discipline and self-control, morality and
> responsibility, courage and patriotism, loyalty and obligation, the
> exercise of authority and command, all of which have been under

attack throughout the last two decades as being inimical to freedom
and creativity.[40]

In 2004, atheism, agnosticism and humanism were being proposed as subjects for
religious education in schools in Britain. This radical syllabus reform was planned in
response to falling church numbers. It was argued by Ben Rogers, author of the report
for the *Institute for Public Policy Research* think tank that there are significant
"numbers of people who are atheists or whose families are atheists and who are coming
into a class where their family's view is not acknowledged" and further that it should be
possible "to have a conversation about ethics that doesn't collapse into a conversation
about religion".[41] While 19% of Britons attended weekly religious service in 1980, by
1999 this had fallen to seven percent.[42]

However, amongst academic theologians, philosophers, historians and those who cared
to think and read about the matter, there was a knowledge that the 'God is Dead' atheists
and sceptics had been around for several centuries at least. Theologian and historian,
Karen Armstrong makes the point that:

> By the beginning of the nineteenth century, atheism was definitely on the
> agenda. The advances in science and technology were creating a new
> spirit of autonomy and independence which led some to declare their
> independence of God... The idea of God which had been fostered for
> centuries in the Christian West now appeared disastrously inadequate
> and the age of reason seemed to have triumphed over centuries of
> superstition and bigotry... Some people tried to save God by evolving
> new theologies to free him from inhibiting systems of empirical thought
> but atheism had come to stay.[43]

It was Friedrich Nietzsche in 1882 who dramatically announced 'the death of God'.
Nietzsche argued that human beings would have to become gods themselves. In '*Thus
Spake Zarathustra*' (1883) he proclaimed that the 'Superman' would replace God. The
Christian God, Nietzsche argued, was pitiable, absurd and "a crime against life", in
which people were taught to fear their bodies, their passions and their sexuality.[44]
Nietzsche had correctly interpreted the signs of the times, but he was not the first to say
'God is Dead'.

During the nineteenth century one major philosopher after another challenged the
existence of God – at least in the traditional form of a God-Father supernatural deity
'out there', with an 'objective existence'.

For example, Ludwig Feuerbach (1804-1872) argued God was simply a human
projection; Karl Marx (1818-1885) saw religion as "the sign of the oppressed creature...
the opium of the people, which made his suffering bearable"[45]; Charles Darwin's *The
Origins of the Species* (1859) seemed to contradict the Biblical account of creation; and
Sigmund Freud (1856-1939) maintained that a personal God was nothing more than an
exalted father-figure, the result of infantile yearnings for a powerful, protective father and
the desire for justice, fairness and life which went on forever. Religion belonged to the
infancy of the human race, but people must outgrow God in their own good time. Freud,

as Karen Armstrong points out, was emphatic about his faith in science. Science was the new logos and would take God's place as humanity had come of age. [46]

Crisis in 'God-Talk'

THE 'DEATH OF GOD' was an indication of a crisis in 'God-talk'. A hundred years after Nietzsche, John Macquarrie could say:

> There was a time in Western Society when 'God' was an essential part of everyday vocabulary. The word was on everybody's lips… this kind of God-talk has virtually ceased… People once knew, or thought they knew, what they meant when they spoke of God, and they spoke of him often. Now the name of God seems to have retired from our everyday discourse.[47]

Dietrich Bonhoeffer (1906-1945), the German theologian who opposed Hitler and was executed by the Nazis, argued that people could no longer be religious in the traditional way and this led him to explore the outlines of what was later called 'secular Christianity'.

Paul Tillich (1868-1965), perhaps the most creative theologian of the twentieth century, was convinced that the personal God of traditional Western theism had to go. However, because he believed religion was necessary for humankind, he tried to resume 'God-talk' by speaking of God as 'being-itself' or 'ground of being'. In other words, God was becoming removed from a literal and personal concept and moved towards being a symbolic and metaphorical term.

Don Cupitt, Dean of Emmanuel College, Cambridge, went one step further by absolutely denying the objective reality of God. Dubbed 'the atheist priest', Cupitt took a 'non-realist' position. 'God-talk' was a symbolic language, originating in ancient mythology, which was useful to refer to the highest ideals, values and aspirations to which one gives allegiance. The theistic image of God as a personal divine Creator was dead. Cupitt was joined in this view by a number of other theologians, for example Ronald Gregor Smith who confessed it difficult to assign meaning to God and questioned whether a theistic worldview was essential for Christianity.

Taking "final leave of God"

IN THE 1960s, exactly eighty years after Nietzsche, a group of radical theologians solemnly announced the 'Death of God'; and in 2002 New Zealand theologian Lloyd Geering argued that Christianity must become non-theistic and 'take final leave of God'.[48] Geering argued this primarily for reasons of freedom and the ultimate salvation of humankind and life on the planet. He further argued that theism must be abandoned because of "the patriarchal and male-orientated character of the culture to which it led and which it continues to support".[49] As Armstrong points out:

> The idea of a personal God seems increasingly unacceptable at the present time for all kinds of reasons: moral, intellectual, scientific and

spiritual. Feminists are also repelled by a personal deity who, because of 'his' gender, has been male since his tribal, pagan days. Yet to talk about 'She' – other than in a dialectical way – can be just as limiting, since she confines the illimitable God to a purely human category. The old metaphysical notion of God as the Supreme Being, which has long been popular in the West, is also felt to be unsatisfactory. The God of the philosophers is the product of a now outdated rationalism, so the traditional 'proofs' of his existence no longer work. The widespread acceptance of the God of the philosophers by the Deists of the Enlightenment can be seen as the first step to the current atheism. Like the old Sky God, this deity is so remote from humanity and the mundane world that he easily becomes *Deus Otiosus* and fades from our consciousness.[50]

At the same time Armstrong noted that on the one hand "if the human idea of God no longer works for us in the empirical age, it will be discarded" yet, on the other, new symbols will be created "to act as a focus for spirituality".[51] It is to these new symbols we now turn.

Theism Rejected by Humanism

GEERING PUTS IT THIS WAY: theism is rejected by humanism, in which all our values, concepts and religions are human in origin, and so:

> [T]he final rejection of theism can be called humanism, although even this term also has a variety of shades of meaning. It is secular humanism which quite specifically denies reality to divine spiritual beings of any kind and as a consequence rejects 'acts of God', miracles, divine revelation, and all things supernatural. This humanism acknowledges that all of our values, concepts, and religions are of human origin.[52]

Man is Hero, if not now God, because he creates the concepts of God. Humanism supersedes theism and deism.

Man the Measure and Creator

SPIRITUAL SYMBOLISM IS swept away. Man becomes the measure and creator in the new science and physics.

Margaret Wertheim, science writer and physicist, shows how conceptions of space, the universe and religion have co-evolved:

> One of the major effects of the scientific revolution was…to write out of our vision of reality any conception of spiritual space, and along with that any concept of spirit or soul… the end result of this mechanism was a desanctified and purely physicalist vision of reality.[53]

Galileo with his razor-sharp reductionist mind, abstracted out of the world around him the essential features for a new physics. The new physicists sought to represent in a rigorous mathematical fashion, physical relationships between material bodies in Euclidean space. For these scientists Euclidean space was not just the background to reality, its very neutrality supposedly guaranteed that science itself would be neutral and objective.[54]

As well as being 'the measure' in the new philosophical world space of physical objects, physics and science – Man was also increasingly viewed as 'the *Creator*' in a new man made *Technological/Materialist Landscape.*

W hereas all previous history had been that of man living in a world that was *given,* now man was increasingly living in a world *created* by man. It was a world increasingly determined not by the gifts of nature and God but by the manufactures and materialist designs of man. Thus:

> Marx was deeply impressed by the way in which the split between
> money as means of exchange, and money as self-generating capital,
> seemed at the same time both to make possible and also to justify the
> technological exploitation of the planet on which the industrial
> societies of Western Europe had embarked. He argued that the result of
> this interpenetration of the monetary and technological revolutions
> was altering the very quality of human life. All previous history had
> been that of man living in a world that was *given.* But now men were
> learning what it was to live in a world that was to an ever increasing
> degree made *by* man, rather than given *to* man, in a world where
> conditions were determined not by the gifts of nature, but by the
> manufactures of man.[55]

By the mid-twentieth century in America at least, technology, the child of science was providing Americans with such convenience, comfort, speed, hygiene and abundance that there seemed no reason to look for any other sources of fulfillment or creativity, Neil Postman describes the new Trickster's Landscape:

> To every Old World belief, habit, or tradition, there was and still is a
> technological alternative. To prayer, the alternative is penicillin; to
> family roots, the alternative is mobility; to reading, the alternative is
> television; to restraint, the alternative is immediate gratification; to sin,
> the alternative is psychotherapy; to political ideology, the alternative is
> popular appeal established through scientific polling. There is even an
> alternative to the painful riddle of death, as Freud called it. The riddle
> may be postponed through longer life, and then perhaps solved
> altogether by cryogenics. At least, no one can easily think of a reason
> why not.[56]

The Player

RELIGION, LIKE EVERYTHING else, becomes simply presented as entertainment on television. Man the preacher and the presenter is the Hero who sidelines God. Postman states:

> Everything that makes religion an historic, profound and sacred
> human activity is stripped away; there is no ritual, no dogma, no
> tradition, no theology, and above all, no sense of spiritual
> transcendence. On these shows, the preacher is tops. God comes out as
> second banana.[57]

Most of the religion available on television is "fundamentalist", which Postman argues "explicitly disdains ritual and theology in favor of direct communication with the Bible itself, that is, with God", thus:

> on television, God is a vague and subordinate character. Though His
> name is invoked repeatedly, the concreteness and persistence of the
> image of the preacher carries the clear message that it is he, not He,
> who must be worshipped.[58]

If Hollywood and television evidence man as creator, director, string-puller, player and presenter, upstaging God Himself – cyberspace creates dreams of immortality, transcendence and omniscience, to challenge heaven and religion.

Dreams of Immortality

CYBERFICTION IS FULL of accounts of humans being downloaded, uploaded and off-loaded into cyberspace.

As Margaret Wertheim points out, rather like the medieval Christian Heaven, cyberspace becomes a place *outside* space and time, where the body can somehow be reconstructed in all its glory:

> What is extraordinary here is that while the concept of transcending
> bodily limitation was once seen as *theologically possible*, now it is
> increasingly conceived as *technologically feasible*.[59]

The fantasies of cyber-immortality are not just in the minds of science fiction writers. Much of the philosophy is emerging from science itself – cognitive science, robotics and information theory. "Immortality, transcendence, omniscience – these are dreams beginning to awaken the cyber-religious imagination".[60]

However, as Wertheim points out, fantasies of reincarnation, immortality and the soul's eternity entail no ethical demands or moral responsibilities in cyberspace.[61] Furthermore "unlike genuine religions that make ethical demands on their followers, cyber-religiosity has no moral precepts. Here... one gets the payoffs of a religion without getting bogged down in reciprocal responsibilities".[62]

This is very much a Trickster solution to religion. In fact, the existence of religion is somewhat ambiguous in the context of the *Technological/Materialist Landscape* Religion, or rather a spirituality of some sort, still lurks in the background. As Eric Davis remarks, while "technology has certainly hastened the horsemen of secular humanism and the rise of mechanistic ideology, it has also subliminally reawakened and fleshed out images and desire first cooked up in the alchemical beakers of hermetic mysticism".[63] Davis concludes:

> Regardless of how secular this ultra-modern condition appears, the velocity and mutability of the times invokes a certain supernatural quality that must be seen, at least in part, through the lenses of religious thought and the fantastic storehouse of the archetypal imagination.[64]

Man is the New Trickster God

MAN IS THE NEW TRICKSTER GOD and he plays at the edges of mind and matter, super-nature and the supernatural. Davis argues:

> The powerful aura that today's advanced technologies cast does not derive solely from their novelty or their mystifying complexity; it also derives from their literal realization of the virtual projects willed by the wizards and alchemists of an earlier age. Magic is technology's unconscious, its own arational spell. Our modern technological world is not nature, but augmented nature, super-nature, and the more intensely we probe its mutant edge of mind and matter, the more our disenchanted productions will find themselves wrestling with the rhetoric of the supernatural.[65]

Old phantasms and metaphysical longings have not simply disappeared. The New Jerusalem, the futuristic image of heaven on earth is the myth of progress – hence via reason, science and technology we can perfect ourselves and society. This is the "secular offspring of Christianity's millennialist drive".[66] As Davis notes "Technology is neither a devil nor an angel. But neither is it simply a 'tool', a neutral extension of some rock-solid human nature. Technology is a trickster".[67]

Thus is man the sorcerer, techno-wizard, magus and string-pulling master behind technology – with its images of soul, redemption, the demonic, the magical, the transcendent, the hypnotic and the alive. This is the new Trickster God.

Supramorality and Amorality

THE NEW 'MORALITY' in the *Technological/Materialist Landscape* is embodied by the Trickster Archetype. The *moral law* of the Heavenly God-Father Archetype in the *Anthropocentric Landscape* is superseded by a *supramorality* and an *amorality*. As Anthony Stevens has pointed out, traditional patriarchal values of law and order, discipline, self-control, responsibility, courage, patriotism, loyalty, obligation, authority and command are now seen as inimical to freedom and creativity.[68]

In this new landscape agonies are seldom felt for – obedience to the God-Father's law, perfectionism, sin, shame, guilt, divine and/or final judgment, entrance to heaven or hell.

In fact many would light-heartedly profess to prefer hell as more interesting than the traditional view of heaven. The conventional morality of monotheistic religion and the Heavenly God-Father's Church, Synagogue or Mosque is no longer unquestioned.

THE MATURE CORPORATE CULTURE exemplifies the pervasive Trickster Archetype, within the *Technological/Materialist Landscape* and the Trickster amorality and 'religion'. This is despite tricky public relations which would have us believe that corporations behave morally. The corporate executive is often frank, playful and sometimes gleeful, showing a full cognisance of his duplicity and Tricksterish amorality. Joel Bakan illustrates Trickster amorality and 'religion':

> "I'm sucking on Satan's pecker" is how Chris Hooper, a highly
> successful television ad director and voice-over artist, describes his
> work for the likes of McDonald's, Coca-Cola, and other major
> corporations. Hooper says his job is to create "images that are trying to
> sell products to people that they don't really need" which "encourage
> very sophomoric behavior, irresponsible, hedonistic, egotistical,
> narcissistic behavior."[69]

Steve Kline, a communications expert who specializes in children's culture states: "We are 'producing kids as consumers' ... and becoming less good at creating 'competent citizens...good, moral, and virtuous human beings'."[70] And Marc Barry, who has worked for a quarter of the Fortune 500 companies and is a corporate competitive intelligence expert, self-described as "Essentially I am a spy" – comments that "There's so much trickery and deception in my job that I don't really want it in my private life":

> At work, Barry says, he is a predator engaged in morally dubious tasks.
> Corporations hire him to get information from other corporations:
> trade secrets, marketing plans, or whatever else might be useful to
> them. In his work, he lies, deceives, exploits, and cheats... For Barry, a
> regular day at the office is filled with venal actions and moral
> turpitude.[71]

Anita Roddick, the late founder of the Body Shop, shares the view that the corporate world is amoral and a "religion of maximizing profits. However, Roddick fought it and regretted it:

> Roddick blames the "religion of maximizing profits" for business's
> amorality, for forcing otherwise decent people to do indecent things:
> "Because it has to maximize its profits... everything is legitimate in the
> pursuit of that goal, everything... So using child labor or sweatshop
> labor or despoiling the environment... is legitimate in the maximizing
> of profit.[72]

Robert Hare points out that executives acting as corporate operatives display many attitudes and actions which can be characterized as psychopathic.[73] It goes without saying that the psychopathic characteristics of the corporation and its executives are also the worst, amoral characteristics of the Trickster.

A pragmatic, human-based morality, rather than a purportedly 'divinely' inspired law, guides man and woman in the *Technological/Materialist Landscape*. Where individuals do operate on a principled, altruistic, selfless level of moral development, it is because they choose this level of operation, not because they are compelled to by an external religious authority decreeing it.

Thus is 'man' finally superman and his/her morality, for better or worse, is often a supramorality and an amorality founded on individual freedom and creativity.

Personas and Masks – "We are what we Consume"

SEEMING-OVER-BEING; personas, masks, play, simulation, stimulation, entertainment, consumption, sensation, power, manipulation, trickery and the *World of I-It* are all features of the Trickster Archetype and the *Technological/Materialist Landscape* and characterise a supramorality and an amorality.

As a case in point 'Seeming over being' is found in the phenomenon of marketing over talent. Marketing, advertising and consumption are characteristic of the corporate *Technological/Materialist Landscape*. They affect the individual's sense of self – and one could argue morality and spirituality – which becomes Trickster-like and fluid according to the products consumed. As Robert Sack notes:

> We consumers, and the commodities and places we consume, are
> major forces shaping modern landscape".[74]

Furthermore, as "places become 'consumed', they lose much of their former uniqueness. Commercialization makes them appear like other places".[75]

Sense of self is appealed to more and more through advertising, marketing and acts of consumption. People are presented with the power of the product to help them distinguish themselves from others. Advertisements segment the sense of self: "A multitude of products can represent the entire self or even its tiniest part".[76]

Advertising enables the individual, through their consumption of products, to create personas and masks: We are what we consume. Sack argues that consumption, as a symbolic system, is most like old fashioned magic and ritual. "Both advertising and magic/ritual impute powers to objects. Both claim these powers can be tapped by individuals if they are undertaking prescribed actions".[77] Magic and power is the realm of the Trickster, thus:

> Consumption undoes contexts to create contexts, undoes social
> relations to create social relations, and undoes meaning to create
> meaning. The segmentation of context and the isolation of self makes
> the complex and personal experiences and meanings of modern life
> difficult to share.[78]

The consumer becomes the consumed. The self is manipulated by the products consumed for stimulation, simulation, sensation and entertainment. Personas, masks, play, 'seeming over being' may be fun for a while but can lead to skepticism and are often curiously unsatisfying in the end. Superficiality, alienation and fragmentation of self are the downside.

Corporations use "branding" or personas "to create unique and attractive personalities for themselves".[79] They may even claim to have a 'soul'. Again, there is evidence with corporate life of 'magic', transformation, seeming, personifications or personas, artificial bonding and the scope for sleight of hand, manipulation of consumers, employees and regulators. These are all characteristics of the Trickster. As for advertising, Sack argues:

> Its rhetoric of indirection, its capacity for change, its brevity, its ability to make a pattern when absolutely none existed before, all help to make advertising applicable to anything, even to things such as conservation and gay liberation, that are not strictly items of the market place. But once it embraces these issues, advertising's structure transforms their meanings. They too become like commodities; they too become segmented and abstracted from context. As advertising works, it creates its own skepticism. Many know that the claims of ads are not really true.[80]

This underside crisis of meaning and loss of identity is not just a characteristic of the world of consumption, marketing and advertising, in short the materialist landscape; it is also a characteristic of the technological landscape. Michael Heim notes sadly:

> We begin as voyeurs and end by abandoning our identity to the fascinating systems we tend. The tasks beckoning us to the network make us forget our elemental loss in the process... So entrancing are these symbols that we forget ourselves, forget where we are. We forget ourselves as we evolve into our fabricated worlds.[81]

Trickster's Trump – Multiple Selves

HOWEVER, TRICKSTER-LIKE, multiple selves or persona need not imply a "loss of self" or a "crisis of meaning", but rather an *amplitude of self* and an *enrichment of meaning*. Here the Trickster does a turn and comes up trumps!

Not so long ago, stability, rigid gender, racial and social class roles, as well as repetitive labour and consistency were socially valued and culturally reinforced - but today these stable social worlds have broken down. Now, as Sherry Turkle points out, a multiplicity of selves, fluidity, adaptability and change are what are valued.[82] We are indeed living in the archetypal value system of the Trickster.

Personas, masks, play, simulation are descriptors of the internet in particular. The computer has become more than a tool and a mirror. Virtual worlds beckon to us beyond the looking glass. "Cyberspace", used to describe virtual worlds, grew out of science fiction but increasingly it is part of everyday life. Throughout cyberspace millions of internet users are engaging in networking, psychosocial experimentation and play. In new virtual communities one can have 'intimate' relationships with people never met. Sherry Turkle points out "Many insist that their lives contain a dimension that is *not* physically reducible. Embodied or not, 'cyber-selves' are real, and the space of their action, though immaterial, is nonetheless a genuine part of reality".[83]

> One parallel here is with masks. As actors and shamans attest, masks
> are powerfully transformative objects… In cyberspace, one may have
> any number of different, virtual alter egos operating in a variety of
> different MUDs, literally *acting out* different cyber-selves in each
> fantasy domain.[84]

People around the world can create digital alter egos and collectively "other worlds". As befits the Trickster:

> Multiple viewpoints call forth a new moral discourse. I have said that
> the culture of simulation may help us achieve a vision of a multiple but
> integrated identity whose flexibility, resilience, and capacity for joy
> comes from having access to our many selves. But if we have lost reality
> in the process, we shall have struck a poor bargain.[85]

Ambivalence – the "smiling face"

IT WAS THIS NEW moral discourse, or some would call it an amorality, that concerned the philosopher Martin Heidegger. Along with other thinkers he came to see technology as the root evil of the twentieth century. Yet despite this, as Heim points out, "his death in 1976 did permit him to see the century's most powerful technological revolution: the proliferation of the micro computer".[86]

Dominic Balestra also describes the new moral ambivalence underpinning the *Technological/Materialist Landscape*:

> Once we recognise that modern, scientific reason is a "power
> knowledge" whose concrete manifestation is technology, then it
> becomes quite clear that either technological or scientific progress will,
> at best, be ambivalent. For every advance in the power of manipulative
> control carries with it an increase in the potential threat to our human
> freedom.[87]

R. L. Thayer also hints at amorality: "Many of us would like to think that well-intentioned government, religion, ethics, and philosophy control our world, but evidence inherent in the landscape suggests that scientific-technologic-economic determinism is the key operator".[88]

Amorality and a culture of entertainment go hand in glove. Neil Postman writes of the ensemble of electronic techniques which are calling into being a new world – a *'peek-a-boo' world* – in which events pop into view for a moment and then vanish again. He describes this 'seeming' world: "It is a world without much coherence or sense; a world that does not ask us, indeed, does not permit us to do anything; a world that is, like a child's game of peek-a-boo, entirely self-contained. But like peek-a-boo, it is endlessly entertaining".[89]

Online multimedia, comprising computer and television entertainment on demand, is the command centre of this 'new epistemology'. Television, Postman argues, has become our culture. There is no subject of public interest – politics, news, education, religion, science, sports – that is not covered by television and public understanding of these subjects is shaped by television. Television is transforming our culture into one vast arena for show business.[90]

This amorality of the media is recognised by its creators, administrators and company directors. "No one", argues Bogart, "has made more scathing comments on the mass media than the talented people who come out of the industry itself. Media producers and entrepreneurs often express themselves as shocked by what they have to do to earn a living, and take pains to distinguish their own personal preferences from those of the public at large".[91]

Bogart concludes that the marketplace profit centered rules are not necessarily the only ones, or even the most appropriate ones, that should apply to institutions that shape national values and character. In other words, profit and marketplace values are shaping national values and character. This is code for amorality rules. Profit values, goal oriented on appeasing the insatiable appetites for distraction and entertainment, risk turning culture into a burlesque. This is the realm of the Trickster.

WHILE GEORGE ORWELL feared those who would ban books and an externally imposed oppression, Aldous Huxley's *Brave New World*, foresaw that people would come to love their oppression and the technologies that undo their capacities to think. Huxley feared we would be overcome by a trivial culture. In *Brave New World Revisited,* he argued that the civil libertarians and rationalists who are ever on the alert to oppose tyranny had "failed to take into account man's almost infinite appetite for distractions."[92] Culture was in danger of becoming a burlesque.

As Postman points out: "What Huxley teaches us is that in the age of advanced technology, spiritual devastation is more likely to come from a smiling face than from one whose countenance exudes suspicion and hate".[93]

Time, Place, Space – Playing at the Boundaries

PLAYING AT THE BOUNDARIES of time, place and space could be said to underlie and form the substrate of the Trickster's *Technological/Materialist Landscape.*

Historicity and linear time *appear* the norm. The materialist, production based and market focused, world economy is driven by linear timelines, deadlines and economic and market forecasting. Technology is also linear time and future driven towards progress and the mythology of some technologically engineered utopia – a New Jerusalem where there is perennial freedom, prosperity for all and a release from disease and want.

However there is a playing at the boundaries of time, place and space and all is not necessarily as it seems. Combs and Holland point to the affinity the Trickster seems to have with *synchronicity* or acausal highly meaningful coincidences. They argue that whenever human experience undergoes transitions, or breaks through frontiers to the unexpected, there we find the Trickster Archetype:

> Synchronistic coincidences are, from the Jungian perspective boundary events. They manifest, for instance, as transitions across the margin between psychological reality on the one hand and physical reality on the other.[94]

The symbolic correspondence between the deepest layers of the mind and the external world, in which final causes are at best a mystery, is a synchronistic event.

THE SYNCHRONISTIC GIFTS of the Trickster are most accessible to us when we are in or near boundaries, or experiencing transitional states. The Trickster Archetype is not bounded by the known – rather the totality of existence is encompassed in some way by this archetype: "The world of modern mechanistic science is a world bounded by the rigid constraints of causality. It is the Trickster's predilection to cross such boundaries, bringing the unexpected to the commonplace." [95]

The Trickster plays the devil with the traditional scientific myth of causality and linear time. As Combs and Holland put it: "Synchronicity represents a hostile other because it is acausal, and as such blasphemes against the mythos of the causality principle".[96] As astrophysicist Marcus Chown notes, the paradox is that we have a powerful sense that time 'flows' from the past, through the present to the future; and indeed this has survival value.[97] Where would we be without bedrock existential certainty in linear time and the causality principle? In fact:

> We live in a world in which, for the last fifty or sixty years, subatomic physics has described a universe founded at bottom on acausal connections, on paradoxical and seemingly illogical relationships and observations. Yet as a culture we still deny acausal, symbolic connections as part of our lives and the lives of our souls.[98]

The result is that the Trickster continues to play the devil with us. Our notion that everything is explicable in terms of cause and effect and everything can be understood by the rational faculty is continually being challenged, whether we acknowledge it or not.

The Trickster also plays the devil with our views of *fixed place* and *physical, static space*. Place seems fixed. However as Sack has pointed out, consumerism and advertising shape our sense of place and landscape. Place is no longer fixed and landscape is a moveable feast.[99] Again the Trickster archetype is in evidence. He plays with the boundaries of place and physical landscapes so that they are no longer what they originally seemed.

Space appears to be physical and static; yet cyberspace is more than the sum of its parts. Although cyberspace is a technological by-product of physics – silicon chips, optic fibres, liquid display screens, telecommunications satellites, electricity powering the internet – and could not exist without physics; yet neither can it be said to be a purely physicalist conception of the real. It is not reducible to the physicality from which it springs.

CYBERSPACE IS AN EMERGENT phenomenon. The Trickster is at hand – exposing the paradoxical edges. Wertheim argues that indeed the "advent of cyberspace returns us to a dualistic theater of reality. Once again we find ourselves with a materialistic realm described by science, and an immaterial realm that operates as a different plane of the real".[100]

Cyberspace, in some profound way, is another place. Although the body may remain in the chair, when one "goes into" cyberspace at least some aspect of the self is teleported into another arena, which has its own logic and geography. Cyberspace is a real place, despite its lack of physicality.

As Wertheim points out, even in our profoundly physicalist age, "space" describes far more than just the physical world – for example; chemists talk of 'molecular space' in the design of new drugs; biologists talk of 'evolutionary space' of potential organisms; mathematicians study 'topological space', 'algebraic space', 'metric space'; chaos theorists look at 'phase space' when studying weather, as do physicists when studying the motion of galaxies and quantum behaviour of atoms; 'viral space' has been posited by those studying infectious disease.[101]

After three hundred years of physicalism, 'cyberspace' helps make explicit nonphysical extensions of human beingness. "In short, there is a sense in which cyberspace has become a new realm for the mind. In particular it has become a new realm for imagination; and even, as many cyber-enthusiasts now claim, a new realm for the 'self'."[102]

In the Trickster *Technological/Materialist Landscape*, space can be turned from a physicalist, objective, phenomenon into an interior, subjective, non-physicalist phenomenon. With the Trickster Archetype, space can be both physical and non-physical.

Trickster's Shadowside – 'World of *I-It*'

ENHANCED BY THE WIZARDRY of technology and driven and sanctified by the materialist profit motive, the *'World of I-It'* comes into its own. Revelling in the *'World of I-It'*, is the Trickster and his shadow side - which is today at his most dangerous, subhuman and bestial. Carl Jung stated with a chilling certitude that:

> The so-called civilized man has forgotten the trickster. He remembers
> him only figuratively and metaphorically, when irritated by his own
> ineptitude, he speaks of fate playing tricks on him, of things being
> bewitched. He never suspects that his own hidden and apparently
> harmless shadow has qualities whose dangerousness exceeds his
> wildest dreams.[103]

The shadow side of the Trickster Archetype in the *Technological/Materialist Landscape* is the *'World of I-It.'* *'I-It'* is the primary word of experiencing and using. *'It'* lacks reciprocity and mutuality. *'It'* is without care and love. *'I'* uses the *'It'* as a possession or a tool and a 'means to an end' , which is often self-gratification. The *'I-It world'* is objective, causal and impersonal. Lloyd Geering describes the *'World of I-It'* succinctly:

> This is a world in which there is no reciprocity. It is a world where there are objects to be used by the I, observed by the I, experienced by the I. In this world the I stands unrelated to the It, as an observer, an onlooker or a user. The I remains detached, not being personally or subjectively involved. Buber often speaks of this as the It-world... The It-world is a man-made world in which the I reigns supreme.[104]

In the *'World of I-It'* we view ourselves, others and nature, not with care and reciprocity, as in the *'I-Thou relation'*, but from an emotional distance - as actors, objects, entertainments and commodities. The Trickster's shadow comes into play particularly in advertising and the entertainment media - there are no sanctions on bloated appetites, fantasies, desires – for food, sex, commodities, entertainment, perversions, killings and destruction.[105] In the *'World of I-It'* everything is emotionally distanced, objectified and is fair game. Every obscenity is given license.

Carl Jung argues that the Trickster "is both subhuman and superhuman, a bestial and divine being, whose chief and most alarming characteristic is his unconscious"[106] and "a collective shadow figure, a summation of all the inferior traits of character in individuals".[107]

"Externalities" and "Rogue Economics"

THE CORPORATE WORLD which drives modern capitalism exemplifies the *'World of I-It'*. Like the psychopathic personality it resembles, the corporation "is programmed to exploit others for profit. That is its only legitimate mandate".[108] As Joel Bakan points out, nothing in it's legal makeup limits its selfish pursuits. It often destroys lives, damages communities and endangers the planet as a whole:

> As a psychopathic creature, the corporation can neither recognize nor act upon moral reasons to refrain from harming others. Nothing in its legal makeup limits what it can do to others in pursuit of its selfish ends, and it is compelled to cause harm when the benefits of doing so outweigh the costs. Only pragmatic concern for its own interests and the laws of the land constrain the corporation's predatory instincts, and often that is not enough to stop it from destroying lives, damaging communities, and endangering the planet as a whole.[109]

'Externalities' is the coolly technical jargon of economics for, in the words of economist Milton Friedman "the effect of a transaction... on a third party who has not consented to or played any role in the carrying out of that transaction".[110] Corporations must always act in accordance with the legal rule to serve their own best interests, that is that maximize shareholder's wealth.[111]

The "externalizing" machinery of corporate economics and operations has been likened to that of "a shark" or "a killing machine".[112] Executive decisions are purely technical, emotionally distanced, objectified:

> Once the executive is at work, the aims of the….corporation must be taken as a given… tasks characteristically appear to him as merely technical. He has to calculate the most efficient, the most economical way of mobilizing the existing resources to produce the benefits…at the lowest costs. The weighing of costs against benefits is not just his business it is business.[113]

For the morally blind corporation, people and the environment are tools to generate as much profit as possible. Dehumanization is part of the system.[114] Commercial exploitation is the ethos and, as Bakan notes:

> [T]he idea that some areas of society and life are too precious, vulnerable, sacred, or important for the public interest to be subject to commercial exploitation seems to be losing its influence… Increasingly, we are told, commercial potential is the measure of all value, corporations should be free to exploit anything and everything for profit, and human beings are creatures of pure self-interest and materialistic desire. These are the elements of an emerging order that may prove to be as dangerous as any fundamentalism that history has produced. For in a world where anything or anyone can be owned, manipulated and exploited for profit, everything and everyone will eventually be.[115]

ROGUE ECONOMICS is capitalism's new reality.[116] So argued economist Loretta Napoleoni in 2008 as she predicted the looming 2008-2009 global recession. Described as "A devilishly enjoyable journey into the money veins of the new global order",[117] Napoleoni details a world reshaped by dark economic forces in which millions of ordinary people are made victims, their lives trapped in a fantasy consumerist world. For example, "What do Eastern Europe's booming sex trade, America's subprime mortgage lending scandal, China's fake goods industry and celebrity philanthropy in Africa have in common?" Napoleoni shows that international free trade, deregulated financial markets, political upheaval and the internet have created conditions in which unscrupulous entrepreneurs trade without restriction. While bio-pirates troll the blood industry and games like World of Warcraft spawn online sweatshops, rogue industries and corporations are being allowed to transmute into global empires.[118]

Here one can perceive behind her described *Technological/Materialist Landscape* the values of the archetypal Trickster's laughing and seductive, sinister shadow.

Voyeurism – Viewing *Ourselves* as Objects

IN 'REALITY TV' we become voyeurs, and we view ourselves as objects, actors, entertainment and commodities.[119] 'Reality TV' has become one of the hottest commodities in the industry. Reality shows are relatively cheap to produce and the financial returns can be significant. 'Reality', however, is manipulated to some considerable extent. The cameras presence changes the sense of everyday. Editing of segments also changes 'reality'. But the real problem is the potential for boredom; for example brushing teeth, watching television and sleeping. Reality show producers take measures to stop dullness occurring by manipulating the environments in which the 'actors' find themselves, or casting volatile and divergent personalities to provoke entertaining interactions.

This raises the question of at what point *'reality' becomes 'unreal'*, exploitative, bizarre, puerile, immoral, or simply obscene? The following examples illustrate the Tricksterish delight in extreme voyeurism and entertainment derived from viewing our fellow human beings as objects in reality television. Alison Hearn remarked on the makeover show 'The Swan':

> I watched the first installment ... with horror and disgust. The show takes 24 women, puts them through extreme physical and mental makeovers in order for them to compete in a beauty pageant at the end of the series... Where will this homogenizing, corporate colonization of real people and real experience end? .... Yes, my friends, it is indeed a trick mirror.[120]

George Will, commenting on the Fear Factor noted that the programme:

> [I]n its first episode ... attracted nearly 12 million voyeurs to watch simpletons confront their fears, for a fee. In that episode, confronters were covered by a swarm of biting rats. This week the program featured a willingness to eat worms and sit in a tub of them... Optimists concluded that NBC had underestimated the viewing public. The optimists were, as usual, wrong... So NBC sank to the challenge of thinking lower. But it had better not rest on its laurels because its competitors in the race to the bottom will not rest, and the bottom is not yet in sight.[121]

Shadows and Mirrors

ZIAUDDIN SARDAR TAKES A LOOK at the dark side of cyberspace. He argues that Europe's imperial past obsession with political and cultural conquest is revealed again in cyberspace, which is surrogate for the old colonies. The 'new continent' is artificially created to satisfy the insatiable desire for new wealth and riches.[122]

In what is a very good description of the Trickster Archetype, Sardar argues that there are two Janus-like faces of Western civilisation: one is the projected innocence, standard-bearer and enforcer of universal law and morals of civilisation and the other is the pathologically untamed, psychotic inner reality.

To look at the darker inner side of the West, which it projects on other cultural and mental landscapes, he argues, we must look at cyberspace, which is the West's latest conquest and colonial domain:

> The net, in fact, provides us with a grotesque soup of information: statistics, data and chatter from the military, academia, research

institutions, purveyors of pornography, addicts of Western pop music and culture, right-wing extremists, lunatics who go on about aliens, pedophiles and all those contemplating sex with a donkey. A great deal of this stuff is obscene; much of it is local; most of it is deafening noise. Our attention is constantly being attracted by someone trying to sell us something we don't want, some pervert exhibiting his perversion, groups of cyberfreaks giggling in the corner, while giant corporations trade gigabytes of information about money and death.[123]

Sardar goes on to point out that most people on the internet are white, upper and middle-class Americans and Europeans; and most are men. This is not surprising because cyberspace, like earthspace, has not really been designed with women in mind:

Most video games are designed with a very white, Western male view of what children find interesting: killing, shooting and blowing things up... The women in these games, if there are any, are either simply cyberbimbos, electronic renderings of Barbie dolls, or are as psychotic as the male characters.[124]

The '*I-It world*' of cyberspace sex and war games is similar in many regards to the 'amateur' videos taken by American soldiers with their Iraqi prisoners.

One has to wonder whether their reality is copying the 'illusions' made in cyberspace or whether the cyberspace creations are copying a reality already out there, independent of cyberspace – a warped inner reality of the mind. Unfortunately the sexual 'entertainments' of the '*I-It world*' of cyberspace is very little different from the videos made by the American soldiers with their captives at Bagdad's Abu Ghraib jail.[125]

There is a trickster multiple irony in the West's own digital cameras exposing its real inhumanity, immorality, amorality and depravity. Sardar concludes:

Manufacturing fantasies that provide escape from the injustices of the mundane world is so much easier than dealing directly with real people, with real lives, real histories and real emotions, living in their own non-programmed, real communities. Under colonialism these fantasies framed and controlled non-Western cultures of the world. In the new colony of cyberspace, they bounce right back to surround Western man in the darkness of his own projections. Cyberspace, with its techno-utopian ideology, is an instrument for distracting Western society from its increasing spiritual poverty, utter meaninglessness and grinding misery and inhumanity of everyday lives.[126]

This is indeed a description of the Trickster's shadows and mirrors world of 'I-It'.

Pornography's Shadow "Death of the Heart"

IF EVER THERE was an example of the shadowside of the Trickster Archetype and the *Technological/Materialist Landscape* then the worst shadowside of pornography has to have a top billing. Interestingly, Dudley Young notes that the Trickster has historical form in this general area:

> Perhaps best known in versions collected from American Indians, Trickster is an obscene figure who seems to be rising from the depths of unconscious and polymorphous desire toward the light of human clarity and adult separation. Somewhere between monster and child, this inchoate power is instinct with metamorphosis and hence has no determinate shape, but in the admirable version of the mid-Western Winnebago-Sioux, one can at least discern lengths of intestine wrapped around the body, and an equally long penis, similarly wrapped. Thus what we can see is a figure defined, encircled, and hence controlled by two bloated appetites, for food and for sex. The third one, which these two together call forth, is the appetite for killing and destruction, and this is symbolized to some extent by the penis as snake and as battering ram, but chiefly by the anus, home of the fart and the turd, located at the end of the intestine. Trickster is more than a little intrigued with this aperture, and tries to engage it in conversation. Despite such plain speaking, as it were, Trickster seeks to satisfy his desires by more or less elaborate deceits, which he practices by means of a protean power to alter his contours and assume any shape he likes. Utterly unprincipled and amoral, he seems to float upon the ever-changing tides of fantasy and desire, and his shape alters to suit the moment.[127]

Techno-wizardry has enabled pornography to flourish. High-tech quality photography, printing, video-making, virtual reality and the availability internationally of internet cyberspace has made pornography pervasive and ubiquitous.

Pornography is a multi-billion dollar international industry and market, which has been largely controlled by organised crime in the United States and the United Kingdom.[128] The United States, home to more than 60 percent of the reported internet sites, was followed by South Korea, Russia, Brazil, Italy and Spain. The Rome-based non-profit group Rainbow Phone reported in January 2004 that 17,016 websites featuring explicit child pornography were reported in 2003 to international and police groups. This was estimated to be a rise of over 70 percent compared with 2002 and it confirms a massive increase in online pedophilia on the internet, as well as a worrying lack of legislative measures.[129]

The trickster demands freedom and individual liberty but when it comes to pornography it is a very shady, ironic and sinister freedom and liberty indeed! One has to ask "Whose freedom?" and "Whose individual liberty?" The worst shadow-side of pornography – the objectification, commodification and abuse of primarily women and children – is the betrayal of the '*I-Thou*' ethos of respect, care, reciprocity and love.

Catherine Itzin describes the '*World of I-It*' – the objectification, abuse and torture of women and children – as condoned by a supposedly respected, reputable and moral British governmental committee, the Williams Committee on Obscenity and Film Censorship in the name of 'freedom' and 'liberty'.[130] This is the shadowside of the Trickster in operation. The Trickster arguments for 'freedom' and 'liberty' to objectify, abuse and torture women and children, are to be seen for what they are – 'tricked out' logic expressing the amoral, immoral '*I-It*' shadow-side of the Trickster Archetype. Griffin argues that pornography is "the death of the heart ... (for) ... this is the task of pornography – to chain and imprison the heart, to silence feeling".[131]

Yet it is also cruel to the souls of men: "In the pornographic mind, women represent a denied part of the self; in this mind a woman is a symbol for a man's hidden vulnerability. Here disguised in a woman's body are his own feelings, and his own heart".[132] This denial by men of their feelings and their own hearts is a point which Peter Baker also recognises:

> There is something very sad and desperate about men's use of
> pornography as a substitute for real human contact... pornography
> and the associated portrayal of women in advertisements, films and
> television serves to maintain the current system of economic and social
> organization by encouraging men to view human relationships in a
> limited, instrumental way. Pleasure is brief and is limited to the
> genitals. There is little kissing, cuddling, hugging, fondling, touching.
> Sexual activity without penetrative intercourse almost never occurs;
> people are never just pleased to be close, warm and affectionate.[133]

It is ironic that in the Trickster's giving man 'everything' – simulated supremacy, freedom, individual liberty, access to 'every' and 'all' simulated women (and children) objectified to use for pleasure, to dominate and to subordinate - man with his clever tricks has been tricked out of what matters most. The *I-Thou* relation is denied in pornography in favour of *I-It*. Because pornography is inherently *I-It*, it can only flourish in a world which is predominantly *I-It*, which is the *Technological/Materialist Landscape*. Susan Griffin takes the argument further by maintaining that pornography, by reducing a whole being with soul to mere matter, shows that nature and matter itself is despised:[134]

> The pornographic mind would separate culture from nature. It would
> desacralize matter. It would punish matter with image. Pornography's
> revenge against nature is precisely to deprive matter of spirit... it is the
> pornographic culture's goal to separate *itself* from nature. But this is a
> separation which requires a kind of mental acrobatics. For such a
> separation is a delusion. Consciousness and meaning are part of
> nature. All our metaphors, our very language, emanate from and
> imitate the physical... When bodily knowledge and language are
> separated, we ourselves experience a terrible separation which ranges
> all the way from grief to despair to madness.[135]

Pornography is thus related to the abuse of nature.

"Dissection of Nature" – Francis Bacon 'Father of Modern Technology'

IF DESCARTES CAN be called the 'Father of Modern Philosophy, and Galileo the 'Father of Modern Science', then Sir Francis Bacon (1561-1626) can be called the 'Father of Modern Technology'.[136] Carolyn Merchant argues that Francis Bacon was responsible for transforming the tendencies already extant in his society into a total program advocating the *control* of nature for human benefit:

> Disorderly, active nature was soon forced to submit to the questions
> and experimental techniques of the new science.[137]

In the latter half of the seventeenth century Bacon's followers realized, even more clearly than Bacon himself, the connections between mechanics, the trades, middle-class commercial interests, and the domination of nature".[138] This was the beginnings of a pervading *Technological/Materialist Landscape*. Seventeenth-century scientists reinforcing aggressive attitudes towards nature spoke out advocating "mastering" and "managing" the earth.[139] To 'be known', 'mastered', 'managed' and 'used', in the services of humans, are the words and language of the '*World of I-It'*. While Bacon "advocated the dissection of nature in order to force it to reveal its secrets," English philosopher Joseph Glanvill went further. For Glanvill anatomy was "most useful in human life" because it … "tend[ed] mightily to the eviscerating of nature, and disclosure of the springs of its motion".[140]

Nature is to be disemboweled, killed, in order to disclose what makes it work. Nature is to be gutted. The imagery is of death and turning nature into a lifeless, souless, machine or mechanism. The imagery is also very reminiscent of the worst of pornography. Susan Griffin and Carolyn Merchant would be in agreement on the language used to objectify both women, the feminine and nature. Merchant writes:

> The new image of nature as a female to be controlled and dissected
> through experiment legitimated the exploitation of natural resources.
> Although the image of the nurturing earth popular in the Renaissance
> did not vanish, it was superseded by new controlling imagery… From
> an active teacher and parent, she has become a mindless, submissive
> body. Not only did this new image function as a sanction, but the new
> conceptual framework of the Scientific Revolution – mechanism –
> carried with it norms quite different from the norms of organicism.
> The new mechanical order….and its associated values of power and
> control… would mandate the death of nature. [141]

The Baconian method which "advocated power over nature through manual manipulation, technology, and experiment", was also a conceptual power structure and tied in closely with philosophy. *Nature is perceived as a machine.*[142]

In the twentieth century Martin Heidegger would argue that Western philosophy since Descartes has been fundamentally concerned with power. In other words he was speaking of the '*World of I-It'*. Heidegger saw horrific dangers inhering in our ways of thinking which drive technology. The problem was not so much the existence of technology but our orientation to technology.

Against an orientation that investigates all aspects of the world and assumes that the world can be grasped and controlled through measurement and categorization; Heidegger argues that the world "needs" us to care for it, that humanity "is needed and used for the safekeeping of the essence of truth".[143] In other words an '*I-Thou relation*' is needed. Michael Heim argues that:

> No philosopher highlights the clash between technology and human
> values so sharply as Heidegger. Not only did he make technology
> central to metaphysics, but he came to see in it the root evil of the
> twentieth century, including the Nazi German catastrophe, which he
> described as "the confrontation of European humanity with global
> technology".[144]

The will to manipulate is a characteristic of the Trickster. The triumph of will towards manipulation, over *theoria,* or meditative thinking, characterises the Trickster as well as 'technological' thinking. This, argues Paul Crowley, has had an adverse effect on language, intelligence, culture and religious values.[145] Heim concludes that technology "is, in essence a mode of human existence".[146]

Alienation of the individual from Nature and Self is the price of what Heidegger called "the essence of technology". This is the '*I-It*' mode of thinking and existence. This is perhaps the '*problem of our times*' and recognised by many thinkers, although using different language and coming from different perspectives.[147] As an example of just one of these thinkers, Jung Hwa Yol argues that:

> Modern man as *homo oeconomicus* is driven to produce, fabricate and
> consume more and more things with the unbound aid of technology.
> As a matter of fact, the industrious ethos of *homo faber* coincides with
> that of technomorphic civilization whose *telos* is propelled by the
> modern idea of progress.[148]

Pointing out the difference between modern man in the *Technological/Materialist Landscape* and the Deep Ecologists' moral attitude to nature in postmodernity, Jung Hwa Yol continues:

> *Homo oeconomicus* too is the product of modernity, and he is no friend
> of "the earth first" or deep ecology. Rather, he is antithetical to the
> moral sense of nature. He is dictated and dominated by the rationality
> of industry and utility whereas respect or responsibility governs the
> rationality of a deep ecologist.[149]

In the twentieth century, 'rationality', 'industry', 'utility', 'produce', 'fabricate', 'consume' are all words indicative of the '*World of I-It*', the Trickster and the corporate *Technological/Materialist Landscape*. A profound alienation not only from Nature but also from Self is the end result of living in the '*World of I-It*'.

"Frankenstein Monsters" Corporate Psychopaths

THE CORPORATE IDEAL of human nature, rapaciously consumerist and psychopathic, inevitably becomes dominant, as the corporate *I-It world* dominates society through privatization and commercialization. This is a frightening prospect, as Joel Bakan points out in an interview with Noam Chomsky, because the corporation is designed to be a psychopath, purely self-interested, incapable of concern for others, amoral and without conscience.[150] Bakan points out that philosopher Mark Kingwell argues along similar lines:

> From the point of view of the corporation the ideal citizen is a kind of insanely rapacious consumer" driven by a "kind of psychopathic version of self-interest".[151]

As, corporations want to remove obstacles and regulations that limit their freedom to exploit people and the natural environment. Over recent years, through lobbying, political contributions and sophisticated public relations, they have turned much public opinion and the political system against regulation.[152]

Trickster-like, the monster we have created threatens to destroy us.[153] In 1933 Supreme Court Justice Louis Brandeis likened corporations to "Frankenstein monsters; once corporations exist, like the monster, they threaten to overpower their creators. Government regulatory systems were designed to keep the monster on a chain to stop it from causing harm.[154] Dominic Balestra has also likened technology to a "New Frankenstein with the:

> dreadful possibilities of a too successful technology already remaking the earth into an artificial environment... The New Frankenstein is an excellent Technology, so autonomous as to render the maker neither divine nor human and whose creation, unlike that of Frankenstein's, is too artificial to need or desire human care.[155]

THIS 'NEW FRANKENSTEIN' personifies the *'World of I-It'* – the Trickster's shadow-side which permeates the *Technological/Materialist Landscape*.[156] And Frank Fisher describes the alienation caused by the proliferation of mechanism in all aspects of life – so much so that our humanity has lost its interdependence with nature, thereby causing our loss of Self.[157]

The environmental crisis is a crisis of Self, living in the *'World of I-It'*, where even the games male children play are simulated *I-It* – a virtual reality smorgasbord of confrontation, violence, war and death – there is little room left in perceptions and psyches for mutuality between Self and Nature. The God-Father archetypal values, which would *'other'* nature and the feminine, fuels the Trickster's shadow *'World of I-It'* in the *Technological/Materialist Landscape*. Theodore Roszak explains and blames the objectification and negation of others, especially Nature, in terms of "The patriarchal ego, which has been found at work everywhere from the workshop of the warlike Father God of the Old Testament to the bellicose video games and movies that treat adolescent boys to the thrill of world-shattering violence".[158] Indeed:

> There is no question but that the way the world shapes the minds of its
> male children lies somewhere close to the root of our environmental
> dilemma... The bodies fly, the buildings explode, the vehicles collide,
> the blood gushes. All the kindest appeals and gentlest gestures on the
> part of ecofeminism and Feminist Spirituality pale before the virulent
> power of images like these that tempt but do not assuage the most
> violent appetites of the death instinct.[159]

"Tricked-out"and Homeless

POIGNANTLY, RONALD FLETCHER asks, despite our affluence and technological
skills and our "tricked-out appearance of being civilized", whether we have not in our
innermost hearts become homeless?:

> Behind the sophisticated façade of our society, beneath the surface of
> all its material and technical improvements, is there an underlying
> moral malaise at work? Under the continual play, from birth onward,
> of the media and advertising might it not be that appetite has displaced
> sentiment, that expediency – the way to success in the dominant ethos
> of "getting and spending" – has displaced morality, that sanctions no
> longer carry any disapproval that is at all disturbing? ... Might not the
> tragedy of our time lie just in this: despite all our plentitude of
> technological skills, our tricked-out appearance of being civilized, we
> have become in our innermost hearts, in the innermost depths of the
> human spirit, homeless?[160]

THERE CAN BE NO HOME within the Trickster's shadowside, the '*World of I-It*'.
There is no place where we can feel truly at ease – nurtured, nurturing, dwelling secure
in repose and mutuality – whether it be in society, nature or in self.

EIGHT

Sophia's Return

...the Sophianic form of Mazdean devotion to the Angel of the Earth ultimately tends to cause the opening up in consciousness of that archetypal Image which depth psychology calls Anima, and which is the secret presence of the Eternal feminine in men.

– Henri Corbin

The Goddess is now returning. Denied and suppressed for thousands of years of masculine domination, she comes at a time of dire need... Mother Earth herself has been pressed to the limits of her endurance.

– Edward C. Whitmont

The Philosopher's Angel

ISDOM IN IT'S many meanings and aspects is associated with the Sophia Archetype. Universally Sophia is found in many different religions and cultural traditions. The Sophia Wisdom Archetype is returning in the environmentalist political Green Movement, postmodern Ecospirituality and Ecofeminism.

Perhaps more than any other recent philosopher, Henry Corbin (1903-1978) has brought the Sophia archetype once more to our attention. Henry Corbin was the renowned French scholar, philosopher and mystic, principally known for his translations and interpretations of the Sophianic mystical philosophy of ancient Persia, from Mazdean Iran to Shi'ite Iran.[1]

IN IRANIAN SUFISM, Sophia is the philosopher's angel. Sophia is also the visionary organ of the soul. Sophia is the *World Soul/Anima Mundi*, the Divine Feminine and Perfect Nature. The word 'philosophy', which means 'love of wisdom', comes from the Greek word *philein* (brotherly love) and *Sophia*, meaning wisdom. Pythagoras (sixth century BCE), it is claimed, was the first to call himself, not 'wise' *per se*, but rather a "*lover of wisdom*", hence *philo-sophia*.[2] Prior to Pythagoras wise men called themselves sages, meaning "those who know". As historian and theologian Karen Armstrong points out:

> Wisdom (*Sophia*) was the highest of all the human virtues; it was
> expressed in contemplation (*theoria*) of philosophical truth which, as
> in Plato, makes us divine by initiating the activity of God himself.
> *Theoria* was not achieved by logic alone but was a disciplined intuition
> resulting in ecstatic self-transcendence. Very few people are capable of
> this wisdom, however, and most can achieve only *phronesis*, the
> exercise of foresight and intelligence in daily life.[3]

Opening up of Consciousness

SOPHIA IS ASSOCIATED with the *anima* and the *soul* – the opening up of consciousness and hence Wisdom.

The *anima*, independent from the uroboric dragon or the all engulfing- Mother, becomes a component of the Hero's personality. The *anima* in her highest form is Sophia, the sublime partner and helpmate of the Ego and the secret presence of the Eternal feminine in men.

Erich Neumann argues that the "*anima* is a symbolic and archetypal figure, being made up of magical, alluring and dangerously fascinating elements which bring madness as well as wisdom". Thus the anima stands at the frontiers of personality with "mixed archetypal and personal characteristics"; Shaman like, she :

> has human, animal, and divine features, and can assume corresponding
> shapes when enchanted or disenchanted... As the soul, she can no
> more be defined than man can define woman; yet, although exceeding
> the heights and depths of a man, she has finally entered the human
> sphere, a "you" with whom "I" can commune, and not a mere idol to
> be worshipped. ... the anima figure is broken down in the
> individuation process and becomes a function of relationship between
> the ego and the unconscious.[4]

Neumann goes on to describe the meeting between the masculine world of ego consciousness and the feminine world of soul which is creativity. Postmodernism also emphasizes process and creativity:

> Only by relating to the reality of soul – the freed captive – can we make

the link with the unconscious truly creative, for creativity in all its
forms is always the product of a meeting between the masculine world
of the ego consciousness and the feminine world of soul. ...When she
appears in her highest form, as Sophia, the anima clearly reveals this
basic function of hers as the sublime partner and helpmate of the ego.[5]

In the Beginning there was Sophia

SOPHIA AS SOUL is described by Henry Corbin, as preceding male and female
differentiation. Corbin also describes Sophia as anima, which is the imaginative
consciousness in the form of an archetypal feminine being:

> Eternally Feminine, preceding even terrestrial woman because
> preceding the differentiation of male and female in the terrestrial
> world, just as the supracelestial Earth rules over all the Earths, celestial
> and terrestrial, and exists before them. Fatima-Sophia is in fact the
> Soul: the Soul of creation, the Soul of each creature, that is, the
> constitutive part of the human being that appears essentially to the
> imaginative consciousness in the form of a feminine being, *Anima*. She
> is the eternally feminine in man, and that is why she is the archetype of
> the heavenly Earth; she is both paradise and intuition into it...[6]

As already described, the archetype Sophia, as anima, is responsible for the opening up
of consciousness. She is the secret presence of the Eternal Feminine in men. It is by
devotion to the spirituality of the Earth, the Spiritual Earth, that the Sophianic
archetypal image, anima, the secret presence of the Eternal Feminine in man, is opened
up.[7]

Both silent and veiled, the archetype Sophia is associated with the wisdom which
precedes speech. This is the wisdom of the mystics and the visionaries, the wisdom of
the heart and the wisdom within us all:

> Sophia is both silent and veiled, unlike her partner, the Logos, who
> goes forth speaking openly. But the silence of Wisdom precedes the
> speech of the Logos. It is for this reason that the deacon at the Eastern
> Orthodox liturgy cries out, "Wisdom, let us attend!" that we might
> listen to the wisdom of the heart.[8]

Archetypal Sophia is primal and hence she is often called the Black Goddess – although
this is not necessarily a blackness of skin. She is the keeper of both earthly and heavenly
wisdom; she is associated with the wisdom that transcends dualism:[9]

> In her pure numinosity, Sophia is forbidding... Because she is a guide
> who always leads [the gnostic] towards the beyond, preserving him
> from metaphysical idolatry, Sophia appears to him sometimes as
> compassionate and comforting, sometimes as severe and silent, because
> only Silence can "speak," can indicate transcendences.[10]

So in the beginning the Gnostic Sophia preceded male and female differentiation. And 'the word' was preceded with 'the silence' of transcendent wisdom, the wisdom of the Sophia of the mystics.

Universality of Sophia

FROM ANCIENT to modern times the Sophia Wisdom Archetype is evident universally, if often hidden in the wisdom of esoteric and mystical traditions, because Sophia's pre-eminence was driven underground by the patriarchal, monotheistic religions of the West.

SOPHIA IS SIMILAR to the Great Goddesses of the Near East – *Maat, Themis, Isis, Demeter-Persephone, Athena*.[11] Indeed:

> At one time, long before the priesthood inserted itself as indispensable for individual access to the sacred, the Great Goddess during the Neolithic era served the human psyche as an image of the Whole. Wisdom was one aspect of the Great Goddess. Various Goddesses personified wisdom centuries before Sophia entered the religious literature of Judaism: Nammu and Inanna in Sumeria, Maat and Isis in Egypt, and Athena and Demeter in Greece.[12]

Kathleen Granville Damiani describes the wisdom of Isis, who was identified with Sophia in ancient times. She is the wisdom behind the Gods and the creator God. She is the archetypal life force behind the individual personified god archetypes. In this sense she and her wisdom are pre-existent and pre-eminent.[13] And as has been shown by Corbin, Sophia is found in pre-Islamic Zoroastrian angelology of ancient Persia and in Sufism.

Sophia Mother of All Buddhas

BUDDHISM OF THE SAME ERA had Sophia correlates which are central to major developments in later Buddhism from *Madhyamiki* philosophy to *Vajrayana* and Zen.

Joanna Macy maintains that about five centuries after the Buddha there was a turning point represented by the scriptures called the *Perfection of Wisdom*, or *Prajnaparamita* which heralded Mahayana Buddhism. The hero figure of the Bodhisattva appears, no longer limited to previous lives of the Buddha, but is extended to all beings which are able to perceive the interdependent nature of reality. This saving insight is personified and emerging in the same era as her Mediterranean counterpart Sophia. She too is female. She is Perfection of Wisdom, the Mother of All Buddhas. Macy describes the *Mother of All Buddhas* or *Buddhist Sophia* as follows:

> She presents an archetypal structure very different from the feminine attributes we have inherited from patriarchal thought. Freed from the dichotomies which oppose earth to sky, flesh to spirit, the feminine appears here clothed in light and space as that pregnant zero point where the illusion of ego is lost and the world, no longer feared or fled,

is re-entered with compassion.[14]

Macy states that "The texts which bear her name are central to all major developments in later Buddhism, from Madhyamiki philosophy to Vajrayana and Zen".[15] These scriptures called *Perfection Wisdom, or Prajnaparamita* sutras, reiterate tirelessly her difference from earlier, more conventional notions of wisdom.

EARLY CHINESE TAOISM also has similarities with Sophianic wisdom. Jay Williams maintains that the *I-Ching*, the Confucian classic which virtually all the great thinkers of traditional China have turned to for understanding, has something to contribute to our understanding of *philo-sophia*:

> The I-Ching acts upon us therapeutically by denying at the outset the
> separation of soul and body, thought and nature, God and the world.
> The classic is neither Idealist nor Materialist, for both these options
> begin with Plato's bifurcation. In the *I* – soul is indistinguishable from
> body, thought from nature, *Tai Chi* from cosmos. Everything is in flux;
> yet the forms of flux remain constant and contain within them the
> seeds of change.[16]

For the third millenium, concludes Williams, "there is only philosophy, a love of wisdom...which points the way to a common humanity".[17]

Sophia of the Rg Veda

SOPHIA IS ALSO FOUND in the Hindu *Rg Veda*. The Hindu *Vak*, personified feminine vibration of universal creation, speaks of herself in the *Rg Veda*:

> I move with roaring, howling, and radiant might.
> I move with the infinite and nature's powers.
> I hold the love of the Lord of Lords.
> I hold the fire of the soul.
> I hold life and healing.

and:

> In the beginning I bring forth the Father.
> My source is in the water's ocean deep.
> From there I move out toward every creature.
> And with my stature I reach the sky above.
> R.V.X. 125.7

This compares with the later Ecclesiasticus:

> Alone I circled the vault of the sky and I walked
> on the bottom of the deeps over the waves
> of the sea and over the whole earth

and over every people and every nation
I have held sway. (Ecclesiasticus 24:8-20).[18]

Gnosticism and Sophia

AS WE SHALL SEE, Sophia and the Wisdom tradition was a problem for Judaism and
was suppressed. Sophia eventually disappeared from the development of the
mainstream monotheistic traditions of Judaism, Christianity and Islam. In reality,
however, the Sophia Wisdom archetype went underground and remained a vital force
in religious visions, esoteric traditions and schools of philosophy.[19] Sophia was a
prominent figure in early Gnosticism.

Greek 'gnosis' is usually translated as *'insight'*. Gnosticism broadly means 'religion of
(secretive) knowledge'. In Gnosticism, Sophia appeared as the two Sophias – the *world
soul* and the *embodied soul.*

Some Gnostics also believed that Jesus was Sophia; the "word" or logos that would
come to birth within the person.[20]

The Gnostic movement was made up of diverse sects and movements around the
same time as early Christianity. Some rejected organised religion, claimed that priests
were unnecessary, and that the individual could actualize the inner spiritual reality
independent of a leader or organised hierarchy. Such Gnostics showed that the
traditional idea of God inherited from Judaism did not satisfy many of the new
converts to Christianity.[21]

The Gnostics believed the creation and salvation accounts were *symbolic expressions* of
inner truth and not to be taken literally.[22] This spiritual search inwards is very much a
characteristic of Sophianic Wisdom. Damiani argues:

> The Gnostics seized eagerly and joyfully upon Sophia, making her the
> central point of the transfiguration of self and creation in their doctrine
> of the liberation of soul from the coils of ignorance and superstition".[23]

The beliefs that were to become orthodox Christianity in contrast, were those of
literalism and historicity – Christ's humanity; his literal suffering and death.

While some Christians in the early orthodox tradition saw Jesus as connected to
Sophia, Sophia was increasingly ignored in order to disassociate from their rivals, the
Gnostics. It is unsurprising that in the second century CE Gnosticism was declared a
heresy and this was "followed by a fierce campaign by the Church Fathers to seek out
and burn every trace of Gnostic teaching".[24] Sophia, however, remained as a central
figure in the Eastern (Orthodox) Church.[25]

Wisdom Esoteric Traditions

HOWEVER, ANCIENT SOPHIA remains hidden in the *Torah* or Old Testament,
'wisdom stream' and within the *New Testament* by virtue of being identified with Jesus

and his 'wisdom teachings'. Sophia is also identified with the Virgin Mary, the Mother of God, in esoteric mystical teachings where she is attested as Mother of *all creation*, including the patriarchal God-Father. She incorporates both male and female elements and hence she is primary. Sophia is also central to the Islamic Sufi mysticism of al-Suhrawardi and Ibn-al-Arabi.

So, while suppressed and distorted by the monotheistic patriarchal religions, Sophia reappears nonetheless in various guises and sometimes under other names in the esoteric wisdom traditions.

Damiani points out "Sophia was a central figure in the visionary philosophies of Jacob Boehme, Mother Anne Lee of the Shakers, Rudolf Steiner's anthroposophical movement and in the nineteeth century Russian School of Sophiology, represented by Vladmir Soloviev, Pavel Florensky and Sergei Bulgakov".[26] In The Bahir (c.1200), one of the earliest Kabbalistic texts, the Shekinah becomes identified with the Gnostic figure of Sophia. In the Talmud, the Shekinah was neutral, having neither sex nor gender. In the Kabbalah, however, the Shekinah becomes the female aspect of God.[27]

HENRY CORBIN discovered the ancient cosmology and Sophianic Wisdom imagined anew in the work of twelfth century Persian mystic, Master of Illumination, and highly skilled metaphysician, Shihab al-Din Yahya al-Suhrawardi. Suhrawardi's objective was to fuse Zoroastrian angelology, the theological study of angels, with Platonic and Neoplatonic cosmology and with the prophetic revelation of Islam. Indeed, it was "Suhrawardi who first articulated a clear grasp of the world of the Imagination, the world intermediary between sensation and intellect that Corbin was to call the *imaginal* world".[28] Considered even more influential than Suhrawardi was Muid ad-Din Ibn al-Arabi (1165-1240):

> In 1201, while making the circumambulations around the Kabah, Ibn al-Arabi had a vision which had a profound and lasting effect upon him; he had seen a young girl, named Nizam, surrounded by a heavenly aura and he realised that she was an incarnation of Sophia, the divine Wisdom. This epiphany made him realise that it would be impossible for us to love God if we relied only on the rational arguments of philosophy... 'If you love a being for his beauty, you love none other than God, for he is *the* Beautiful Being'.[29]

Sapientia or Sophia Alchemical Wisdom

SOPHIA ALSO PLAYS a major role in alchemy. Many centuries before Christ, alchemy was articulated in the Hermetic tradition of Hellenic Egypt but was not written down because of its sacred status. It reached its peak in the sixteenth and seventeenth centuries when many alchemical texts were printed. The Latin word for wisdom, the language of many alchemical texts, is "Sapientia".

SAPIENTIA, OR SOPHIA, is alchemical wisdom and "is a personified figure which is the goal, the secret, the inner essence of prima materia".[30] In alchemy Sophia, or

Sapientia, was equated with the Holy Ghost. She was also associated with the tree, which shines like lightning – signifying 'sudden rapture and illumination'and connects heaven and earth, spirit and body…a symbol of soul".[31] Sapientia or Sophia was associated with salt, the psychic form of the body which is the "objective intersection between the human microcosm and the macrocosm".[32]

JUNG REGARDED ALCHEMY as the link between Greek philosophy, the Christian Middle Ages, and modern Europe.[33] Alchemy enabled modern man to reconnect to the past (Gnosticism) and enabled an opening up to the future through the recovery of images and interpretations which have been demonised in Christianity. Damiani states:

> Sophia re-emerged in the Middle Ages, not only in the underground wisdom traditions, but also as the Black Madonna, whose images across Europe drew thousands of pilgrims for centuries. Sophia appeared in philosophy in the writings of scholars, poets, and mystics: John Scotus Erigena (A.D 810-77); Boethius (A.D. 480-524); Jakob Boehme; Dante; and many others. She was the impulse behind the troubadours, whose devotion to the feminine had such an impact on society that the status of women was actually raised for a time. She was the image of the Liberal Arts in the Middle Ages and was the inspiration for the Grail Legend and the Cathar Church of the Holy Spirit, Sophia. The Knights Templar were apparently devoted to Sophia: they were said to worship an image – "Baphomet" – which concealed in cryptographic form, its secret meaning – Sophia.[34]

Sophia Exiled by Patriarchy

THE SOPHIA ARCHETYPE PRE-DATES JUDAISM. When papyrus texts dating from the third millennium BCE were discovered in Egypt it was found that they were in places, word for word identical to passages in Proverbs (Prov. 22:17-23.11). In Damiani's words:

> It was clear from this discovery that wisdom was not an invention of post-exilic Israel but was widespread throughout the ancient world, with a history dating back thousands of years before the birth of Judaism… Wisdom was not an invention of Judaism, but symbolized a shared vision of practical spirituality that was common and prevalent. It was borrowed, not created, by the ancient Israelites and incorporated into religious texts.[35]

The problem for Yahwhism was that Sophia and the Sophia Wisdom Archetype undermined the *authority* and *pre-eminence* of the one and only Heavenly God-Father and '*his chosen*'. As Damiani puts it:

> Sophia was a problem because she was the voice that spoke for attributes and teachings that might have appeared antithetical or even threatening to the religious agenda of the men who shaped the

direction of Judaism. As monotheism took root in Hebrew religious consciousness, Yahwism directed itself towards revelation and salvation history. Traditional Yahwism regarded history as the sphere of divine action. God created the world and remains active in the everyday affairs of his chosen people. He intervenes and reveals himself to his people through his prophets and later in his law, the Torah.[36]

THE WISDOM TEACHINGS, spoken through the figure of Sophia, focused on a spirituality which was very different from Yahwism, which did not itself allow for a female presence.

Rather, "the wisdom teachings focused on engagement with one's own character and taking responsibility for one's spiritual development" and hence did not rely on prophets or rabbis for revelation and salvation.[37] Indeed, wisdom "was not to be discovered in any one book, dogma or teacher, but ... requires clear perception and discernment while Yahwism demands the ascertainment of God's will and obedience to God's laws".[38]

IT WAS A CLASH OF ARCHETYPES – the patriarchal, demanding, authoritarian, God-Father Yahweh was a jealous monotheistic God who demanded exclusive obedience to 'His Law' from His 'chosen people'; versus Sophia, the democratic and egalitarian Wisdom Goddess, who was available to *all* who sought inner autonomous wisdom and enlightenment.

Sophia De-Sacralising by Patriarchy

YAHWISM TRIED TO USURP THE WISDOM traditions of the Middle East by maintaining that wisdom was not Greek cleverness but rather the *fear* of Yahweh; that wisdom was *not a divine being*, rather it was *created by Yahweh* and was the *first of his creatures*; and that the *independent Goddess of Wisdom* was *rendered the breath or power of Yahweh*.

Within Judaism Sophia is reduced to wandering through the streets, calling on people to *fear* Yahweh. In the 'Wisdom of Solomon' Jews are warned to resist the seductive Hellenic culture around them and remain true to their traditions – hence it is not Greek philosophy but it is *fear of Yahweh* which is true wisdom.[39] In fact, while Wisdom is personified so that she seems to be a separate person (see for example, Proverbs 8.22,23,30,31), she was no longer an independent Divine Being.[40] Nevertheless, a personified Wisdom (Sophia) could not be separated from the Jewish God:

> [Sophia] is the breath of the power of God,
> pure emanation of the glory of the Almighty;
> hence nothing impure can find a way into her.
> She is a reflection of the eternal light,
> untarnished mirror of God's active power,
> image of his goodness.
> (The Wisdom of Solomon 7:25-6)

In the end, the monotheistic God-Father religion usurped the spiritual dimension of 'Wisdom' and Sophia. Whereas the Greeks believed that the *gift of reason* made human beings *kin* to God and they could therefore reach inwards to God by their own efforts, the Jews believed that their God Yahweh, only made himself known by means of revelation to his chosen.

Philo Rewrites Sophia

YET WHENEVER monotheists fell in love with Greek philosophy, they tried to adapt its God to their own. This was the case of Philo of Alexandria, the eminent Jewish philosopher (c.30 BCE–45 CE) who was a Platonist and had a distinguished reputation as a rationalist philosopher in his own right.[41] According to Joan Chamberlain Englesman:

> Sophia went from a position of divine status to removal from the hearts and minds of the early Christians and Jews of the first century because of one man. Philo, a renowned Hellenic Jewish scholar in Alexandria identified Sophia with the divine word "Logos". In place of the alive, speaking presence of the feminine Sophia, Philo substituted the masculine "Logos". First he makes Sophia the same as Logos, then Sophia gradually is excluded and forgotten. Finally, the masculine personified Logos assumes the divine roles of Sophia, including the firstborn image of God, the principle of order, and even the intermediary between God and humanity.[42]

Christians Lost the Goddess

EARLY CHRISTIANS CONCURRED with Philo's view. With the supplanting of Pagan religions which had kept alive the reverence and memory of the great Neolithic Goddesses and their attributes of wisdom, the active, living and immediate Sophia became a mere abstraction. Damiani states: "After Sophia became identified with Christ as Logos, the Word of God, the ancient association of wisdom with the powerful Goddesses of antiquity was lost and forgotten".[43] In the words of Baring and Cashford:

> [T]he archetypal feminine is finally 'deleted' from the image of the divine, and the Christian image of the deity as a trinity of Father, Son and Holy Spirit becomes wholly identified with the masculine archetype. Because of a sequence of theological formulations – grounded on the assumption that nature was inferior to spirit, and that whatever pertained to the female was inferior to the male – the image of the Holy Spirit lost its former association with the feminine Hokhmah, or Sophia, and was assimilated, first in Judaism, and then in Christianity, to the concept of the masculine Logos, the Divine Word. This theological development effectively erased the ancient relationship between Wisdom and the image of the goddess.[44]

The Sophia Gnostic Problem

WHILE IT WAS NECESSARY for the New Testament writers to link Jesus to Sophia in order to establish their new Christian sect, they had a problem with the Gnostics. As already discussed, the Gnostics downplayed or questioned the *literal and historical* humanity and death of Jesus, preferring to emphasise his universal divine nature, accessible as an *inward state of consciousness* in every individual. Sophia was "the central point of transfiguration of self".[45]

The Christians later stopped talking about Sophia in order to disassociate themselves from their rivals the Gnostics and they insisted on the historical literalness of Christ's humanity, suffering and death. Gnosticsm was declared a heresy in the second century CE and the Church Fathers sought to burn every trace of Gnostic teachings.

Sophia Wisdom Streams Reappear

THE ARCHETYPE OF THE DIVINE SOPHIA Wisdom Goddess was deliberately desacrilised, usurped, erased and forgotten, first by Judaism (the Yahwist or Israelite tradition) and then by Christianity (Messianic)

However, not all evidence of her presence was wiped out. The 'Wisdom stream' mystical trails remained as we have seen, albeit often in conflict and suppressed within the traditional, patriarchal monotheistic religions.

Recently within mainstream theological discourse and debate these 'Wisdom streams' have again reappeared for consideration. For example, theologian Lloyd Geering maintains that Jesus of Nazareth stood in the Wisdom tradition more than anything else; hence Jesus was a secular sage, a healer, a teacher and a man rather than a King or Messiah.[46] Geering points out that it can be legitimately claimed that humanistic or non-theistic Christianity is the genuine heir to the Wisdom stream of ancient Israel and that this Wisdom stream is firmly grounded in the Jesus tradition – whether this is called 'humanistic Christianity', 'non-theistic Christianity' or 'post-Christianity'.

IN THE MODERN, SECULAR AND HUMANIST WORLD, Geering argues that the Wisdom streams are at last coming into their own. Throughout biblical history the sages relegated God-talk to the periphery of their concerns. Unlike the Prophets, they did not appeal to God to solve their problems nor expect to hear any direct message. For the sages religion had more to do with how people lived. People had to take full responsibility for their lives and problems, first by study and then by courage and determination to do what is right. Geering states:

> The humanist tradition of Hebrew Wisdom did not look to Yahweh to deliver people by miraculous interventions in either nature or human history. It taught people to pursue the way of Wisdom and it relegated God to the role of an impersonal creative force which had shaped the world to be as it was. The world was awe-inspiring, it could not be changed and reverence for its structure was the beginning of wisdom. All these facts placed the sage in considerable tension with the loyal Yahwist of Israelite tradition, whether prophet, priest, or royalist....It is the same tension amounting at times to animosity, which exists today

between secular humanists and fundamentalists.[47]

While many Christians still accept without question that Jesus claimed to be 'the Messiah','the Saviour', 'the Way', 'the Truth' and 'the Life' – biblical scholarship tells a different story. Jesus did *not* make these assertions about himself; rather they were made by the early Christians and put in the mouth of Jesus. Jesus never spoke of himself as divine nor did he talk of God as a personal being – rather he referred to God in the same way as the sages.

THIS JESUS OF THE WISDOM STREAM, exemplified by Jesus of Nazareth and reflected in James, in the *Didache* (the Teachings of the Twelve Apostles, an early Christian treatise) and partially in Matthew's Gospel, was eventually overshadowed by the Pauline Gospel with the emphasis on the Saviour Christ, crucified, risen and glorified.[48] However Geering, along with other theologians, concludes that the long neglected stream of wisdom tradition is at last coming into its own, with the realisation that there is no Divine being in heaven to control human affairs and put things right. This is the advent of the modern, secular and humanist world.[49]

Whether or not one agrees with Geering, that *both* Christianity and its Wisdom stream can be salvaged and resurrected as well as be separated from the Heavenly God-Father – it is clear, that for many, the exclusivist, monotheistic, literalist Heavenly God-Father is no longer credible or desirable.

Why Sophia Must Return

CAITLIN MATTHEWS ARGUES that "Sophia is the great lost Goddess who has remained intransigently within orthodox spiritualities"[50] and summarises the case for why Sophia must return:

> The reemergence of the Divine Feminine – the Goddess – in the twentieth century has begun to break down the conceptual barriers erected by orthodox religion and social conservatism. For the first time in two millennia, the idea of a goddess as the central pivot of creation is finding a welcome response. The reasons are not difficult to find: our technological world with its pollution and unbalanced ecology have brought our planet face to face with its own mortality; our insistence on the transcendence of Deity and the desacrilization of the body and the evidence of the senses threaten to exile us from our planet. The Goddess appears as a corrective to this world problem on many levels. In past ages she has been venerated as the World Soul or spirit of the planet as well as Mother of the Earth. Her wisdom offers a better quality of life, based on balanced nurture of both body and spirit, as well as satisfaction of the psyche.[51]

Goddess Spirituality and Ecological Sanity

USA GREEN PARTY co-founder and ecofeminist philosopher Charlene Spretnak points out that since the mid-1970s "a movement of spiritual renewal that honors nature, the female, and the body has flourished in our society: the reclaiming of Goddess spirituality".[52] Spretnak maintains that the renewal of Goddess spirituality rejected the patriarchal dualism from the outset. Culture is not a struggle in opposition to nature but is a potentially harmonious extension of nature, with all its diversity, subjectivity, adaptability and inter-relatedness. This can be called ecological sanity:

> The central understanding in contemporary Goddess spirituality is that
> the divine – creativity in the universe, or ultimate mystery – is laced
> throughout the cosmic manifestations in and around us. The divine is
> immanent, not concentrated in some distant seat of power, a
> transcendent sky-god. Instead of accepting the notion in patriarchal
> religion that one must spiritually transcend the body and nature, it is
> possible to apprehend divine transcendence as the sacred whole, or the
> infinite complexity of the universe.[53]

Divine Immanence Within Nature

THE GODDESS, IN SHORT, is a metaphor for divine immanence - the theory that the divine is *within* or encompasses the material world, in contrast to *transcendence* in which the divine is seen *outside* the material world - and the transcendent sacred whole.

Betty Roszak, ecofeminist writer, concludes that the women's movement and ecology movement have come together as two powerful streams of dissent and protest against patriarchal domination and exploitation of Nature: "Feminist spirituality rejects the dualisms of the scientific mode in favour of a sense of the unity of all living things, for a worldview of organic process and dynamic change, of the interrelatedness of all beings. Not *mere* matter, but the divine in matter".[54]

Symbols are as important as technologies. The feminist and ecological ethic is one of relationship and interrelationship and inner and outer worlds: "What ecofeminism has to offer is just this promise of connection: the inner with the outer, the self with the other, the ordinary with the sacred, the person with the planet".[55]

A "process of re-imagining" the divine, which is ongoing, is argued by ecofeminist Carol P. Christ. Situating her work within process theology she points out, "I was moving in the direction of process philosophy even before I knew it existed".[56] She acknowledges, in particular, fellow travellers such as the early environmentalist Rachel Carson, process theologians and environmentalists John B. Cobb Jnr; A. N. Whitehead, and Charles Hartshorne and Carl Jung. All these philosophers were pro-feminist, before feminism. All concerned with relationality, interconnection, embodiment, spirituality – both within the psyche and the 'outside' world; they were concerned with the state of the earth and its creatures, flora and fauna, intuition, emotion, the unconscious, change, creativity, co-creation, symbolism, re-imagining. Carol P. Christ argues that "like other feminists who are participating in the process of re-imagining, she has found "alternative symbols, in my case through the feminist spirituality and Goddess movements".[57]

Psychologists Predict Sophia's Return

SOPHIA'S RETURN IS ALSO FORECAST from the psychoanalytic archetypal perspective. While still couched in terminology of the God-Father archetypal framework, as if this archetype has not yet had its day and is still a potent force, Lawrence Jaffe, Carl Jung and Gerhard Adler all predicted the return of the feminine principle. Jaffe argued a high valuation of the feminine principle:

> In the feminine principle I include the following values which may
> occur in either women or men, but with which in the past women have
> been more identified: the heart, the personal, feeling (in particular
> introverted feeling, as exemplified by Mary Bethany), the body, life,
> relatedness, nature, matter, particularity, ordinariness, egohood.[58]

For Jaffe, "Sophia (Wisdom) is God's feminine counterpart, forgotten during the Hebrew and Christian dispensations" but now "in the psychological dispensation" is "destined to reappear".[59] In the new Psychological dispensation we are all to be incarnations of the divine. For Jung, Sophia (Wisdom) the "Mother of God"; was with God before the creation:[60]

> The reappearance of Sophia in the heavenly regions points to a coming
> act of creation. She is indeed the "master workman"; she realizes God's
> thoughts by clothing them in material form, which is the prerogative of
> all feminine beings. Her coexistence with Yahweh signifies the
> perpetual *hieros gamos* from which worlds are begotten and born. A
> momentous change is immanent.[61]

This heralded momentous change; a transformation in consciousness. It is nothing less than the "individuation process".[62] In other words individuation (or wisdom, which is associated with Sophia will be an inner psychological truth and an inner spiritual quest – rather than a belief in the literal or factual, fundamentalist truth of an exterior authoritarian religion.

Indeed, Adler argues that "God's Sophia appears as the principle of the future, as highest authority, that which can revitalize and transcend an obsolescent and rigidifying concept of God".[63] Adler believed that Jung's emphasis on the feminine (Yin, Eros), and operating from it, "has initiated an historic change of accent, the importance of which we can as yet hardly grasp".[64]

Jaffe concludes: "An outstanding characteristic of the coming age of the Psychological dispensation will be the enthronement of the feminine principle and the revaluation of its primary carrier, woman".[65]

"Patriarchy's Time is Running Out"

PERHAPS NO ONE has described Sophia's return more profoundly and eloquently in our times than Edward C. Whitmont (1912-1998). Whitmont, author of the seminal *Return of the Goddess* (1982), was a Viennese born doctor exiled from Nazi Europe, who became a Jungian psychoanalyst and founder and chairman of the C. G. Jung Training Center of New York:

At a low point of cultural development that has led us into a deadlock of scientific materialism, technological destructiveness, religious nihilism and spiritual impoverishment, a most astounding phenomenon has occurred. A new mythologem is arising in our midst and asks to be integrated into our modern frame of reference. It is the myth of the ancient Goddess who once ruled earth and heaven before the advent of the patriarchy and of patriarchal religions. The Goddess is now returning. Denied and suppressed for thousands of years of masculine domination, she comes at a time of dire need. ... Mother Earth herself has been pressed to the limits of her endurance. How much longer can she withstand the assaults of our rapacious industrial and economic policies? The patriarchy's time is running out. What new cultural pattern will secure for humanity a new lease on earth? Amidst tremendous transition and upheaval, the Goddess is returning. ...In the depths of the unconscious psyche, the ancient Goddess is arising. She demands recognition and homage. If we refuse to acknowledge her, she may unleash forces of destruction. If we grant the Goddess her due, she may compassionately guide us toward transformation.[66]

Trimorphic Protennoia – Prophecy of Sophia

THE RETURN OF SOPHIA was arguably foretold centuries ago in the Gnostic, Nag Hammadi, Coptic Manuscripts. These were discovered in 1945 at the base of the Jabal at-Tarif cliffs, north of the Nile River, opposite Nag Hammadi.

Prophecy of Sophia, Trimorphic Protennoia

And I came for a second time, in the manner of a woman;
and I spoke with them.
And I shall instruct them about the coming of the end of the realm.
And I shall instruct them about the beginning of the coming realm,
which does not experience change,
and in which our appearance shall change.[67]

In the translation of John D. Turner this reads:

Trimorphic Protennoia

I am Protennoia, the Thought that dwells in the Light.
I am the movement that dwells in the All,
she in whom the All takes its stand,
the first-born among those who come to be,
she who exists before the All.
She (Protennoia) is called by three names,
although she dwells alone, since she is perfect.
I am invisible with the Thought of the Invisible One.
I am revealed in the immeasurable, ineffable (things).
I am incomprehensible, dwelling in the incomprehensible.
I move in every creature...

Now I have come the second time
in the likeness of a female,
and have spoken with them.
And I shall tell them of the coming
end of the Aeon and teach them
of the beginning of the Aeon to come,
the one without change,
the one in which our appearance will be changed.
We shall be purified within those Aeons
from which I revealed myself in the Thought
of the likeness of my masculinity.
I settled among those who are worthy
in the Thought of my changeless Aeon. [68]

Sophia's 'Answer to Job'

HENRY CORBIN COMMENTED that the "Sophianic idea and the guiding principles of sophiology could yield some precious insights into the hermeneutics of religious phenomena which, up to now, have not paid much attention to the recurrence of the Sophia Archetype".[69] In other words, Sophia had a moral and spiritual contribution. In particular Corbin looked at the moral, spiritual and authority problems and challenges posed by C.G Jung in his paper 'Answer to Job'.

The character of Job in the Old Testament raises questions about the *exterior, authoritarian, imposed, morality* of the tyrannical *Yahweh* – the Heavenly God-Father - who, while being inordinately emotional in his fury and admitting that anger and jealousy are devouring him, demands love, worship and praise for justice from Job.

Job's problem with Yahweh, Corbin suggests, is not only a moral one, but one requiring Wisdom. Indeed, it is *interior* Wisdom, Sophia, that Job was seeking.[70] In other words, what is needed by Job is the birth of a new archetype and therefore a new God and morality – Sophia Wisdom - where the divine wisdom acts through the psyche.

This is also a fundamental concept in the psychology and therapy of Jung – hence, full consciousness, individuation, demands a confrontation of consciousness with unconsciousness and the reaching of balance. 'God' is found not only in the unconscious but in the self.[71]

A Tragedy – but Feminism not the Answer

CORBIN REGARDED IT AS A TRAGEDY in Iranian thought and consciousness that when Persia became Muslim – during the first centuries following the collapse of Sassanid power in the seventh century CE –   Sophianist consciousness was taken over by Yahweh/Allah.

However while Sophianic consciousness remains in the form of Fatima, who is often called Fatima-Sophia – for Corbin, Sophianic consciousness should not be equated with Western feminism in modern times. Rather, Corbin argues, while it is:

[T]rue to say that the female priesthood of the pre-hellenic peoples and of the mystery religions is no longer in existence… What has been called 'feminism' in our modern society does nothing but recognize the priority of masculine values, even to the point of caricature. In total opposition to this, what we are concerned with is a world where socialization would not wrench from the soul its individuality nor its spontaneous perception of the life of things and of the religious beauty of living beings; a world where love would precede all knowledge and where the sense of death would be only a nostalgic yearning for the resurrection.[72]

Interiority, *I-Thou relation*, individuation, conscience, Self, self-realisation, Soul, heart, a spirituality which is ecocentric and redemptive of the scapegoat, are all central to the concept of Sophianic Wisdom.

Sophianic "Divinity Within"

WHITMONT DESCRIBES the new Sophianic morality and spirituality this way:

The Goddess is guardian of human interiority. The patriarchy regulated the externals of human behavior but devalued individualized instinct, feeling, intuition, emotion, and the depth of the feminine, except in the service of the collective. How significant that "effeminate" was coined as a pejorative term. In the new orientation, each individual needs to discover the indwelling source of authentic conscience and spiritual guidance, the divinity within. Jung called this transpersonal center the Self… The Goddess's coming does not mean a rejection of ethics though, but a new ethics more deeply rooted in individual conscience.[73]

Matthews also recognises the imperative of the interior, heart-felt nature of Sophianic Wisdom and morality – as opposed to the exterior authoritarianism of patriarchal monotheism and the rationalized consensus of the philosophers: "Wisdom is not part of any deistic schema; she is central to our understanding of spirituality".[74] Thus:

Amid the desacrilization of our world, ancient wisdom returns out of the dark to lead us to our future. But it is as the streetwise wisdom of the wandering, exiled Sophia, not the safely enthroned Wisdom of the philosophers and theorists that we see her. And those who receive her have the parched thirst of those who deeply desire the nurture of the real, living wisdom.[75]

Symbolized by "integrity, honesty and clear perception" Sophianic Wisdom is particularly characterised by the ability to see metaphorical and symbolic truths.[76] "Wisdom is an effect of seeing not only the literal but the metaphorical (symbolic)".[77] And Sophia is "related to the source of creative inspiration, poetry and art. Wisdom and creativity paired!"[78]

Sophianic Ecopiety Interior Landscapes

THE POSTMODERN ECOLOGIST'S perception (wisdom) in the natural environment is frequently metaphorical, symbolic, poetic, inspirational and could be described as aesthetic or artistic. Through interior wisdom we are enabled to perceive the interior nature of our exterior landscapes. This understanding enables care and moral action.

Inner imagination is vital to Sophianic Wisdom and also points to interiority. As we have seen, imagination is also inherent in how the postmodern ecologists perceive their landscape and natural environment. Indeed, imagination "is a valid way of gaining knowledge about reality ... a way of knowing won through total relationship, not conceptual knowledge 'about' something when the knower is not implicated in the known".[79]

"Total relationship" epistemology (holism) is another description of the *I-Thou* relationship. This characterises Sophianic Wisdom, morality and spirituality (or ecopiety) as well as postmodern ecology.

Hwa Yol Jung has distinguished the new postmodern ecocentric ethics and ecopiety from anthropocentric and economic or consumer morality:

> As *pietas* (piety) represents unconditional reciprocity, that is, a circle of giving and receiving, man has the obligation or duty to reciprocate and take care of "Mother Nature" as his/her natural nurturer. ... In essence, we must *redefine* the good life beyond the escalating psychology of "economism" and "consumerism" which is by necessity anthropocentric rather than ecocentric. The idea of *ecopiety* is an attempt to define a *new ethics of the future* based on "ecological man" (*homo ecologicus*)in place of "economic man" (*homo oeconomicus*). The idea of ecopiety, in sum, is indeed subversive: the end of *homo oeconomicus* is the beginning of *homo ecologicus*.[80]

Postmodern ethics are ecocentric. As Hwa Yol Jung states: "It is the discovery of the ecological chain of Being whose ethics cultivates the sense of ecopiety. Consequently postmodern ethics is ecocentric, that is, it is an *ethics as if the earth really matters*".[81]

Sophianic Morality – Individuation and I-Thou

THE DUALISTIC '*I-IT WORLD*' of anthropocentrism (God Father morality) and modernism (Trickster morality) is challenged by the epistemology of postmodern ecology (Sophia Wisdom morality). As Charlene Spretnak has pointed out, now "the divine is immanent" and "Goddess spirituality ... rejected the patriarchal dualism from the outset".[82]

The *I-Thou relation* inherent in Sophianic Wisdom and ecological perception is expressed reverentially, as befits the archetypal Sophia. Sophianic wisdom is an attitude towards the unknown and provides a bridge between the known and unknown.[83]

If morality and spirituality have their source in a 'state of being' or development of the individual psyche, Sophianic morality and spirituality are associated with, and are derived from, 'individuation', 'self', 'soul', 'conscience' and 'heart'. All of these concepts and terms are inherent in the Sophia Wisdom Archetype. As Corbin notes:

> What is new here is the scrutiny throwing light into the depths and discovering the similar dynamics which underlie the various manifestations of the archetype. It is the soul facing what happens and what is called for when the figure of Sophia appears on the horizon, and how the soul can realize individuation when it is suggested by this *living* and liberating symbol.[84]

Sophia, or individuation, is to embrace the whole, both the known and the unknown in one's Self. Sophianic Wisdom is associated with the realisation of self. As Matthews states, "The process of Jungian individuation is nothing other than the personal recognition of the indwelling spark of Sophia, a realisation that enables the individual to act in a self-aware but unselfish manner".[85]

New Ego a Seeker and Explorer

THE EGO ALSO CHANGES within the Sophia Archetype: "The new ego is affirmative. It accepts what formerly has been rejected: body sensuality and enjoyment, but also woundedness, pain, discomfort, and imbalance".[86]

The patriarchal habit of control, repression and expulsion is no longer relevant in the new holistic consciousness, whereby human existence is perceived as an aspect of a unitary, cosmic organism. Consciousness is no longer seen as a quasi-accidental by-product of man-made culture; rather it is an inherent potentiality which underlies existence.

The new ego under the Sophianic Archetype becomes a seeker and an explorer. Life and relationships are seen as processes, not as fixed forms. Whitmont argues that for men and the animus the new demand is for "the courage to let go of their firm ego position of control over self and others" with the consequence that:

> These new ego values necessitate a radical change in the masculine value system of both sexes. The heroic striving for dominance, conquest, and power, the topdog – underdog order of things, the rule of authority and rank, of right or wrong, my way or your way, will have to be modified by the capacity to endure simultaneous, seemingly mutually exclusive opposites. We must learn to appreciate shadings and a spectrum of colors rather than black-and-white systems... The new masculine values must respect a variety of different gods or ideals, rather than only one dominant God who is lord and king.[87]

The ego, as conquering king or Hero under the God-Father Archetype and the Trickster Archetype, becomes more of a seeker or discoverer, a revealer, guardian and challenger. In the Sophianic Archetype the ego is a mediator, a priestess of life's values and mysteries. The courage to be is focussed inwards, towards seeking individuation and realisation of Self, as much as it is the heroic struggle in the outer world.

Sophia's Shadow – Redemption of the Scapegoat

SOPHIANIC WISDOM is to recognise that the outer world is often a reflection of the inner. In the new Sophianic morality the scapegoat "demands to be found within ourselves and redeemed".[88] Individuation and self-realisation require that, in the words of Whitmont:

> The formerly rejected shadow problems – our secret weaknesses,
> shames, "perverted" urges and feelings, everything that makes us feel
> "guilty" – are now to be accorded recognition and value as balance and
> indispensible aspects of life, aspects of the transformative power of the
> Goddess.[89]

While the first step in consciousness is discrimination between what is "felt as good or evil, pleasurable or painful, beautiful or ugly, morally acceptable or unacceptable"; scapegoating, that is, "projecting the negative aspect of those dualities onto the other", belongs to the patriarchal phase of this evolutionary development. Now, however, the scapegoat demands to be found in ourselves and redeemed.[90]

This has particular relevance to the debate over the acceptance of gays and the feminine within the patriarchal religious hierarchies and the acceptance of the *Anima*, the *Eternal Feminine* in man. Acknowledging one's differences, real and imagined imperfections and perceived weaknesses, accepting one's pain and that of others, is part of the new moral and spiritual quest. For Whitmont:

> The questing explorer can never feel himself to be perfect, nor can he
> expect others to be...the wound underlies and motivates the search. The
> wound is part of that intensification of consciousness which, if it is to
> know the good, must also incur the pain of the bad. While striving for
> the good, the questing knight realizes that on the way, he cannot hope
> to avoid the bad. He will find it in his own soul. For it is there that the
> Grail is to be found.[91]

Whitmont argues that while the patriarchal ego wanted to "hold tight, to be perfect and guiltless, and never ashamed of itself", this caused it to become "self-righteous, rigid, hard and judgemental". In the new Sophianic morality the "searcher faces up to inner conflict and moves through pain and joy in expectation of change. Pain is accepted in self; others are allowed to have theirs".[92] The Grail seeker responds to the question of life and finds his/her individual trail.

A New God – Sophia Inner Wisdom

HENRY CORBIN once asked: "How many men, today, can claim to be truly the 'representatives' of *themselves*, when they represent nothing but collective standards, official dogmas, and ready-made opinions?"[93]

He points out that in the theology of Schleiermacher, the terms 'individuation' and 'incarnation' are joined.[94] 'Incarnation' here is not a belief in the external 'historical fact' of one saviour God, but the inner Wisdom and psychic truth of *Sophia within each individual.*

Job comes to know God, no longer by heresay but through his own eyes. It is anamnesis, a recalling to the 'here and now', of a deeper God of Wisdom.

As Corbin argues, at the heart of Jung's most personal exegesis on 'Job', is the creation of a new God; which is the pre-existing Sophia, pushed out by Yahweh - and now returned.[95] In other words it points to a new God, a new world and a new archetype – or rather the re-realisation of an old archetype – Sophia Wisdom, within the new Postmodern Ecological Landscape.

Restoring Sophianic Soul to the World

THE NEW ARCHETYPE OR SOPHIANIC GOD brings forth a new landscape and vice versa. Damiani concludes that Sophianic Wisdom within has the power to change the world, to restore soul to a barren world of competition and consumerism:

> Then we become capable of breaking the silence that protects the world from an encounter with soul. We voice the integrity within; our voice is the bridge across which Sophia moves to return to the world.[96]

Sophianic Quantum Spacetime

SOPHIA'S INTERIORITY shows remarkable similarities with the quantum physics concepts of *relative spacetime*, *hyperspace* and *holographic implicate* spacetime. This is the *inner reality* posited *behind* the everyday exterior, explicate 'reality' of measurable linear time and fixed place and space.

Sophianic Wisdom could be argued to originate from an *implicate order* or *inscape*, perhaps even a *spiritual* or *conscious spacetime*.

Postmodernism has also been described as synonymous with the inner: the imagination, metaphorical reality, imagistic truth. Inherent to postmodernism is the appreciation of the interpenetration of dimensions, the unfolding in which the transcendent is immanent. As geographer Denis Cosgrove concluded:

> [T]he post-modern experience heralds the possibility of a new world, or rather, once again, the possibility of penetrating an old one, largely submerged by the excesses of Modernism; the world of synchronicity, the monad, of Renaissance Environmentalism.[97]

Inherent to the *Postmodern Ecological Landscape* is Sophianic holism and a conscious awareness of the importance of the imagination, both of which have resonances with *relative* spacetime, hyperspace, holographic spacetime, implicate orders and inscape.

'Spacetime' is found in both the special theory of relativity and the general theory of relativity, where space and time are bound together. The universe has an overall architecture, which is "*dynamic*, with an almost organic history": Space, in effect, "becomes like a living thing".[98] As Margaret Wertheim points out *hyperspace* is the picture which emerged in the 1990s. Matter like force would not be an independent entity, rather:

> a secondary by-product of the totalizing substrate of space. Here, everything that exists would be enfolded into the bosom of hyperspace… every particle that exists would be described as a vibration in the microscopic manifold of the extra hidden dimensions. Objects would not be *in space*, they would *be space*. Protons, petunias, and people – we would all become patterns in a multidimensional hyperspace we cannot even see.[99]

In this 'inner reality' as well as strange things happening to matter, strange things happen to time. In the hyperspace physicists' world, time becomes just another dimension of space. Particle accelerators have become the tools for exploring higher-dimensional space.[100]

A TIMELESSNESS, or escape from the trammels of the passage of linear time, which has fascinated mystics and religious thinkers throughout the ages, is most characteristic of the Sophia Wisdom Archetype. The writings of some quantum physicists could almost be interchanged with that of the mystics. For example, "pure consciousness is *freed of time*. To the highly evolved mind, which has filtered out ego noise, reality appears as a *timeless* continuum".[101]   Known for his loop of time metaphor, physicist Stephen Hawking recognises that *imaginary time* may be a door to a higher level of insight:

> This might suggest that so-called imaginary time is really the real time and that what we call real time is just a figment of our imaginations. In real time, the universe has a beginning and an end at singularities that form a boundary to space-time and at which the laws of science break down. But in imaginary time, there are no singularities or boundaries. So maybe what we call imaginary time is really more basic, and what we call real is just an idea that we invent to help us describe what we think the universe is like.[102]

The conscious awareness of the importance of the *imagination*, as we have seen, is inherent to inner Sophianic Wisdom and the *Postmodern Ecological Landscape*. It is plausible it operates within and derives from the field of *imaginary time*.

Other scientists have been fascinated with the implications of quantum spacetime. For example, is it possible to have *a memory of the future*? Electromagnetic waves can propagate in both time directions. Fred Hoyle and Paul Davies would say "Yes" and others, such as John Wheeler, consider it a serious possibility. If so, then perhaps this is further support for an inner Sophianic Wisdom Archetype. Wisdom to some extent is the ability to apprehend the future and its ramifications.

THE HOLOGRAPHIC UNIVERSE posited by David Bohm and Karl Pribram, has inherent multiple dimensions, multiple realities and parallel universes – and consciousness is not fundamentally separate from matter.

> As David Bohm sees it, if the universe is nonlocal at a subquantum
> level, that means that reality is ultimately a seamless web, and it is only
> our own idiosyncrasies that divide it up into such arbitrary categories
> as mind and body. Thus consciousness cannot be considered as
> fundamentally separate from matter, any more than life can be
> considered as fundamentally separate from nonlife.[103]

The Sophianic Wisdom Archetype and the *Postmodern Ecological Landscape* are also inherently *holistic* or *holographic*. As we have seen Sophianic Wisdom is opposed to the dualistic split between elevated spirit and denigrated natural world and physical body. In the *Postmodern Ecological Landscape* inspiration, meaning, creativity and vitality are derived from this perception of spiritual holism.

The flow of time, in the Holographic Universe, is the product of a constant series of *unfoldings* and *enfoldings*. This suggests that as the present enfolds, becoming the past, it returns to the cosmic storehouse of the implicate. In other words, as Bohm puts it, "The past is active in the present as a kind of implicate order".[104]

On the Holographic Universe theory, the tangible reality of our everyday lives is like a holographic image. Underlying is a deeper order of existence, that gives birth to all the objects and appearances of our physical world – in much the same way that holographic film gives birth to a hologram. "Bohm calls this deeper level of reality the *implicate* (which means 'enfolded') order, and he refers to our own level of existence as the *explicate*, or unfolded, order".[105] It is likely that the *inner* Wisdom of the Sophia Archetype and the perceptions and insights of the *Postmodern Ecological Landscape* derive from, or tap into, this implicate order.

INDEED 'INSCAPE', so described by David Peat, is perhaps talking about the perception of this *implicate order*. Peat argues:

> It is also possible to see nature as *inscape*. With inscape, one attempts
> to enter into the heart of a thing. This involves a sense of dissolution of
> boundaries and of a merging of one's personal horizons with that of the
> object. To see the world as inscape is to believe that every thing, from
> tree to stone, star to atom, has its own unique being and authenticity.
> Inscape involves a direct experience of that inner voice.[106]

Entering "into the heart of a thing"; "dissolution of boundaries"; "merging of one's personal horizons with the object"; perceiving "unique being and authenticity" is characteristic of the *I-Thou* relation. This is clearly a Sophianic archetypal mode of perception, characteristic of the *Postmodern Ecological Landscape.*

Similarly, Peat argues that any truly great scientist must also be sensitive to *'inscape'* and he relates the vision of Heisenberg. Heisenberg, at the moment of his discovery of quantum theory had what could be called an experience of *'inscape'*. He was on holiday in Helgoland and had an insight into problems that had been puzzling him about an earlier theory of the atom. In great excitement, working out the implications of his idea, he had the following experience – "At first, I was alarmed" he relates; "I had the feeling that, through the surface of atomic phenomena, I was looking at a strangely beautiful interior, and felt almost giddy at the thought that I now had to probe this wealth of mathematical structures nature had so generously spread out before me".[107]

The idea of 'inscape' leads on to the idea of a 'conscious universe', an 'enspirited world', a 'World Soul' and a 'Soul of the World'. It is to a consideration of Sophia as Anima Mundi/World Soul that we now turn.

Evolution of Sophia Anima Mundi

THE *SOUL OF THE WORLD*, the *Anima Mundi* is synonymous with the Sophia Wisdom Archetype. The idea of a '*conscious universe*', an '*enspirited world*', a '*world soul*', a '*soul of the world*' or a '*world ensouled*', is both a very ancient philosophy and an inherently postmodern, quantum physicist theory. It is also a view shared by archetypal psychologists, postmodern geographers and postmodern ecologists.

As we have seen, in the Mother Earth Archetype and the *Nature/Earth Landscape* the world is also regarded as alive, enspirited and animistic. To some extent there is an intertwining of the Mother Earth Archetype and the Sophia Wisdom Archetype.[108] Many of the ancient goddesses showed characteristics of both archetypes and in other cases it could be argued that Sophia devolved or specialised out of the Mother Earth Archetype.

Erich Neumann, for example, maintains that at a very much higher level the Mother reveals herself anew as Sophia:

> Only at a very much higher level will the "good" Mother appear again.
> Then, when she no longer has to do with embryonic ego but with adult
> personality matured by rich experience of the world, she reveals herself
> anew as Sophia, the "gracious" Mother, or, pouring forth her riches in
> the creative fullness of true productivity, as the "Mother of All
> Living."[109]

Further, Neumann argues that at the highest level of spirituality is Sophia Wisdom:

> The feminine vessel as vessel of rebirth and higher transformation
> becomes Sophia and the Holy Ghost... Just as in the elementary phase
> the nourishing stream of the earth flows into the animal and the phallic
> power of the breast flows into the receiving child, so on the level of
> spiritual transformation the adult human being receives the 'virgin's
> milk' of Sophia. This Sophia is also the spirit and the bride of the
> Apocalypse, of whom it is written: 'And let him that is athirst come.
> And whosoever will, let him take the water of life freely'. ... And at this
> highest level there appears a new symbol in which the elementary
> character and transformative character of nourishment achieve their
> highest spiritual stage: the heart spring of Sophia, the nourishment of
> the middle. This central stream flows from Sophia in our
> Philosophia... A new organ becomes visible, the heart that sends forth

> the spirit-nourishing 'central' wisdom of feeling, not the 'upper'
> wisdom of the head. ... Thus modern man, on a different plane,
> discovers what primordial man experienced through an overpowering
> intuition; namely, that in the generating and nourishing, protective and
> transformative, feminine power of the unconscious, a wisdom is at
> work that is infinitely superior to the wisdom of man's waking
> consciousness, and that, as source of vision and symbol, of ritual and
> law, poetry and vision, intervenes, summoned or unsummoned, to save
> man and give direction to his life.[110]

Joanna Macy makes similar arguments to Erich Neumann about the evolution of consciousness and in so doing it could be said she distinguishes the Mother Earth Archetype from the Sophia Wisdom Archetype.

Macy argues that in our infancy as a species we were not separated from the natural environment. Trees, rocks and plants surrounded us with a living presence. We were enveloped in a primal intimacy or "participation mystique" as the anthropologists describe it. We were as at one with our world, as a child is in its Mother's womb. Then self-consciousness arose and we distanced ourselves in order to measure, judge, exercise free-will and engage in the lonely journey of the heroic age.

Today however we yearn to reclaim the sense of wholeness with nature. We are ready to return. "The third movement begins. Having gained distance and sophistication of perception, we can turn and recognize who we have been all along. Now it can dawn on us: we are our world knowing itself".[111]

However Matthews is somewhat more critical of the philosophical unpicking of the original Goddess myths in pursuit of "the pure archetypal idea of what the Goddess and indeed, Deity, really are":

> The ancient notion that the whole earth partook of the Goddess's
> substance was subtly altered, producing the philosophy of the World
> Soul or *Anima Mundi*. The goddessly metaphors are stripped of their
> mythological garments and reduced to skeletal and sometimes
> deformed frameworks.[112]

Whether one agrees with Neumann and Macy, or Matthews – the difference is primarily that Sophia is inherently *wisdom* and the Mother Earth is inherently *nurturance*. The Sophia Wisdom Archetype has many elements of *postmodernism* and postmodern concerns, while the Mother Earth Archetype was most influential, pervasive and essentially *premodern* in her historical heyday. This being the case, both archetypes are *universal* and, as in the nature of archetypes, outside of time, or *ahistorical*.

Sophia is the divine presence in our World, the Celestial Earth. Both the mystical theosophists and Jacob Boehme posit an *intermediate world* between the sensory or sensible and intellectual, or the transcendent and the world of man, "a 'spiritual corporeity' which represents the Dwelling, the Divine Presence for our World. This Dwelling is Wisdom itself, Sophia".[113]

Sophia *Anima Mundi-World Soul* is found in early Greek philosophy, including the philosophy of Plato[114]. She is also found in Buddhism, the *Rg Veda* of Hinduism, the *I-Ching* of Taosim, the Wisdom streams of the mystical strands of Judaism, Christianity and Islam. Sophia *anima mundi* is found in the writings of mystic visionaries as diverse as Julian of Norwich and William Blake, and in the very ancient and very modern scientific – hence James Lovelock's hypothesis of the living Earth as Gaia. In essence Sophianic Wisdom is hidden and bound within matter, the Celestial Earth.[115]

Sophia and Quantum Physics

THE ANCIENT DESCRIPTIONS which point to Sophia as *Anima Mundi/World Soul* – hence "wisdom that lies hidden or bound within matter"; "the reconciliation of nature and spirit"; "the pre-terrestrial vision of the celestial world" – have strong similarities with the descriptions made by quantum physicists about the quantum realities behind and within matter, the world and the universe.

Quantum physicists describe symmetries and archetypes beyond matter and enfolded in the material world. They speak of wholeness of matter and mind at the quantum level and nonlocal space-time. They describe consciousness within matter; active information directing matter. They talk of archetypes, acausal orderedness, as a basis for science, and quantums of information applicable to both mind and matter.

Some quantum physicists have explicitly acknowledged a return to the concept of *Anima Mundi/World Soul* with the discovery in science of quantum phenomena.

Shortly before his death Werner Heisenberg argued that what is fundamental in nature is not particles but the *symmetries* which lie beyond them. These symmetries can be thought of as the archetypes of all matter and the ground of material existence.[116]

Bohr's theoretical physics emphasis on wholeness and the *nonlocal* nature of spacetime is compatible with Sophianic *Anima Mundi/World Soul*. This deeper nonlocal order has been found to be essential to thought processes. Here mind and matter appear to have something in common. "Indeed this leads to the general proposal that mind and matter are not separate and distinct substances but that like light and radio waves they are orders that lie within a common spectrum".[117]

Bohm's theory that quantum processes could be interpreted as having what could almost be called a *"mental" side* - is also in accord with Sophianic *Anima Mundi/World Soul* – whereby active information has a directing effect on quantum processes, playing a formative role in unfolding the elementary particles out of their grounding quantum field.[118]

Carl Friedrich Von Weizsacker is one who argued for the re-emergence of the *World Soul* motif on the basis that, indeed, quantum theory is to be understood as a *theory of information* – a holism that encompasses all that exists in both the realms of mind and matter:

In his recent discussion of implications of his theory of ur-alternatives, von Weizsacker has drawn attention to the possibility for the re-emergence of the World Soul: he has argued that if quantum theory may be understood to be a theory of information, then it applies to information about mental events as well as physical events. According to the ur theory, *res cognitans* and *res extensa* must then enter into appearance together, and thus Cartesian dualism is theoretically strictly refuted. The consequence of this is a holism that encompasses all that exists in both the realms of mind and of matter that brings forth the question of the possibility of a World Soul.[119]

Sophia World Soul – Celestial Light

JUNG WAS EXPLORING along similar lines to the quantum physicists when he introduced the idea of a psychoid archetype (*unus mundus*) which he said contains both mind and matter and yet goes beyond them both. Jung coined the term 'psychoid unconscious' to account for the unitary nature of psyche and world.[120] It is rooted in the unconscious, rather than being unified by an external metaphysical being or reality.

More precisely, "the 'psychoid unconscious' can be considered a further gradation of the unconscious where self and world meet, and where all opposites are reconciled".[121] The *Anima Mundi/World Soul* is very similar to the psychoid archetype or *unus mundus*.

The physicist Wolfgang Pauli took up Jung's psychoid archetype because he saw it as a major contribution to understanding the 'laws' of nature:

> For Pauli, the psychoid archetype represented a sort of 'missing link' between the world which is the legitimate study of science, and the mind of the scientist who studies it. Jung's postulate was not just 'the bridge to matter in general' but to 'a cosmic order independent of our choice and distinct from the world of phenomena'.[122]

Sophianic Wisdom and individuation, as we have seen, are closely identified, if not identical. Individuation, to embrace the whole, both the known and the unknown in oneself, is also associated with *Anima Mundi/World Soul* and Jung's psychoid archetype, or *unus mundus*.

In alchemy Sophia is associated with the evolution of one's conscious. This transformation process is individuation. Sophia is here associated with symbols which express the depths of the self, psyche and soul in the world, where body becomes spirit and spirit becomes body.

One of these symbols is of Sophia as a Tree, another is of Sophia as Salt.[123] *Light, lightning, illumination, shining, gold, 'incarnated light'*, are also associated with Sophianic Wisdom and individuation; where body becomes spirit and spirit body, where heaven and earth are connected in the depths of self, psyche and soul in the World, World Soul.[124]

Henry Corbin describes Sophianity from Mazdean to Shi'ite Iran, as "for the human being to accede here and now to the Celestial Earth, to the world of Hurqalya, world of 'celestial corporeity', which is that of the subtle bodies of Light".[125]

In a strikingly similar description, scientist Darryl Reanney also writes of light and consciousness. Reanney points out that those rare moments when consciousness breaks free of ego are described as "moments of illumination"; the "inbreaking of light" and "the metaphor of consciousness as a light-bringing agent is widespread in all mystical literature".[126]

Individuation is a breaking free of ego consciousness into a realisation of *Anima Mundi/World Soul*: "Individuation does not shut one out from the world, but gathers the world to one's self".[127] Individuation here is self-realisation which involves the psychoid archetype – unus mundus – in other words, *Anima Mundi/World Soul*.

The enfolded and implicate in *Anima Mundi/World Soul* becomes unfolded and explicit. Individuation becomes the self-realisation of the psychoid archetype. Whitmont describes it this way:

> The new Aquarian view, ushered in by twentieth-century physics, no longer thinks in terms of discrete objects; rather it conceives of a continuous flux of process, vibrational fields, quantum pulses of an undefinable, nonmaterial substratum. This is a universal consciousness, perhaps, yet prior to what *we* call consciousness. Prior to energy and matter, it results in both. It is a self-directed flow that gives form. The dynamics of our world, in the view of the modern myth, do not flow from a maker or director outside of it, who manipulates it like an object. The world is inner or self-directed, an immanense groping for self-realization in the three dimensions of space, and in the fourth dimension of time as well. Consciousness and conscience now discover self-direction. They find themselves in relation to the newly emerging Feminine – the Yin – as inner-directed awareness, with its growing transformative aspect – time.[128]

This is a description of the new, yet at the same time ancient, Sophia *Anima Mundi/World Soul* Archetype.

Archetypal Philosopher James Hillman maintains that we need "an aesthetic response to the world. This response ties the individual soul immediately with the world soul"; indeed they are inseparable as "(a)ny alteration in the human psyche resonates with a change in the psyche of the world".[129] The return of the *Anima Mundi/World Soul* should therefore be a therapeutic goal both for the individual and the world.

Geographer Peter Bishop influenced by archetypal psychology, maintains that the study of a country or a place and its people should be a task that contributes "towards the return of soul to the world, to an anima mundi psychology".[130] While there has been a long tradition of locating the psyche somehow within both the individual and the world, this has been lost in recent centuries. However, as Hillman warns, "the more we concentrate on literalizing interiority within my person the more we lose the sense of soul as a psychic reality... within all things".[131]

In his study of Tibet, for example, Bishop found that the place had a logic and coherence of its own, its genius loci: it was not a 'silent other' but alive, substantial and compelling. "It was part of the world calling attention to itself, deepening our soulful appreciation of mountains, of deserts and rivers, of light and colour, of time and space, of myriad peoples and their cultures, of fauna and flora, of the plurality of imaginative possibilities".[132]

This is an instance of a return of perception of *Anima Mundi/World Soul*, and a return of the Sophianic Wisdom Archetype. In short, spirituality is to be sought in individuation, the opening up to the unus mundus; or in other words the Sophianic *Anima Mundi, World Soul*. This deep realisation of Self lies at the heart of all religious intimations of the essential oneness of life.

Sophia and Ecospirituality

INHERENT TO the *Postmodern Ecological Landscape* are concepts of holism, wisdom, participatory consciousness and a new spirituality which informs, or imbrues together the individual psyche and the outside world. This is the archetypal climate and province of Sophianic *Anima Mundi/World Soul*.

In archetypal psychology it is posited that at a deep level "the human psyche merges with the outer world"; archetypal psychology accords with Deep Ecology in recognising that nature is a part of 'the Self'.[133]

The ancient Sophianic *Anima Mundi/World Soul* reappears in contemporary times in the works of environmental psychologists. One environmental psychologist, Jim Swan, suggests that some places may be capable of acting as "triggers" to mystical experiences, creative and inspirational experiences.[134]

While living in harmony with nature is not a new notion, the scientific study of human-environmental relations, especially in psychology as it applies to environmental matters is relatively recent. Mystical or transcendental experiences have their origins in the mental 'set' of the individual and also in the environmental setting.

Transcendent experiences of place include the feeling of a linkage with nature and/or a comprehension of being a part of everything; the ability to communicate with nature in its many forms; waking visions of mythical beings or objects; the ability to influence the weather; dreams of an unusual nature; a feeling of unusual energy in a place.[135] The ancient *Anima Mundi/World Soul* is being reborn in the *Postmodern Ecological Landscape* era as a merging of the fields of ecology and psychology.

Fritjof Capra argues that the two fields of ecology and psychology have only recently been connected:

> The link between ecology and psychology that is established by the
> concept of the ecological self has recently been explored by several
> authors. Deep ecologist Joanna Macy writes about 'the greening of the
> self,' philosopher Warwick Fox has coined the term 'transpersonal

ecology', and cultural historian Theodore Roszak the term 'eco-psychology' to express the deep connection between these two fields, which until very recently were completely separate.[136]

Theodore Roszak also draws attention to the psychological connection between an ecological perception of the world and behavioural ethics in *ecopsychology*.[137] What is agreed is that there is a need for a new paradigm; for a holistic worldview or ecological view, which recognises that at a fundamental level we and all phenomena are interdependent.[138]

Also arguing for a paradigm shift, Morris Berman, more than twenty-five years ago, held that "Western life seems to be drifting toward increasing entropy, economic and technological chaos, ecological disaster, and ultimately, psychic dismemberment and disintegration".[139] Western industrial society will likely be remembered for the power and failure of the Cartesian paradigm. Like Capra, Berman has predicted that there will be an increasing shift towards holism. Indeed "Some type of holistic, or participatory consciousness and a corresponding sociopolitical formation have to emerge if we are to survive as a species".[140]

For biologist Rupert Sheldrake a 'new form of animism' is the organismic or holistic new paradigm which is superseding humanism: "The organismic or holistic philosophy of nature which has grown up over the last sixty years is a new form of animism. It implicitly or explicitly regards all nature as alive".[141]

Sheldrake argues that in its strongest form the Gaia hypothesis recognises that Gaia herself is purposeful and this raises the difficult question of what that purposive organizing principle, traditionally regarded as the soul or spirit of the Earth, is: "the soul of the Earth may best be thought of in terms of the unified field of Gaia".[142] For Sheldrake this is rather like the primal unified field in modern evolutionary physics.

In Sheldrake's opinion the "old dream of a progressive humanism is fading fast ... there is a shift from humanism to animism, from an intensely man-centred view to a view of a living world. We are not somehow superior to Gaia; we live within her and depend on her life".[143]

Charlene Spretnak describes the need for a new alternative to the modernist paradigm. She maintains that the core teachings of the "great wisdom traditions" have much to offer, with revelations of ecological communion and dynamic oneness. Spretnak goes on to add, however, that to appreciate these core spiritual insights we will have to do this independently of the institutional religions that may have grown around them. We will also need to explore possibilities across parochial boundaries. If we can cross these dividing lines and search openly and honestly, "the wisdom traditions illuminate central issues of our time".[144]

The new postmodern paradigm, it is generally agreed, is ecological; more specifically it is Deep Ecology. And the "essence of deep ecology, is to ask deeper questions".[145] In other words, deeper wisdom comes from asking deeper questions – as Capra points out:

> This is also the essence of a paradigm shift. We need to be prepared to
> question every single aspect of the old paradigm… So, deep ecology
> asks profound questions about the foundations of our modern,
> scientific, industrial, growth-oriented, materialistic worldview and way
> of life. It questions this entire paradigm from an ecological perspective:
> from the perspective of our relationships to one another, to future
> generations, and to the web of life of which we are a part.[146]

Sophianic Wisdom, like Deep Ecology, is about the asking of deeper questions and the perception of deeper realities. Belden C. Lane describes this deep questioning "If there is hope for a rediscovery of the spirit, it will not be found in looking back to an innocence once lost, a simplistic return to the paradise of Eden. It will demand a reaching through and beyond the harshest criticisms levelled by the whole of the western spiritual tradition."[147]

While 'Shallow Ecology' and some other forms of environmentalism are anthropocentric or human-centred – hence viewing humans as above, or outside nature and the source of all value, with only 'instrumental' or 'use' value to nature – Deep Ecology does not separate humans or anything else from the natural environment. The world is seen as a network of phenomena interconnected and interdependent at a fundamental level.[148] Thus Spretnak describes *Anima Mundi/World Soul* in postmodern ecological terms:

> Ecological postmodernism recognises not only that all beings are
> structurally related through our cosmological lineage, but also that all
> beings are internally constituted by relations with others, even at the
> molecular level. We are not the fixed, thoroughly self-contained
> entities of the modern model. At subtle levels of perception, we are ever
> changing and ever aware of our connectedness with other humans, the
> rest of nature on Earth and the whole of the universe.[149]

DEEP ECOLOGY has a spiritual, religious and ethical orientation which is at core identical to the archetypal Sophianic *Anima Mundi/World Soul* spirituality and ethics. Capra argues:

> Ultimately, deep ecology awareness is spiritual or religious awareness.
> When the concept of the human spirit is understood as the mode of
> consciousness in which the individual feels a sense of belonging,
> connectedness, to the cosmos as a whole, it becomes clear that
> ecological awareness is spiritual in its deepest essence.[150]

All living things as members of ecological communities are bound in a network of interdependencies. With this realisation comes a radically new ethics. Some might call it a spiritual ethics of care.[151]

Deep ecological awareness means care flows naturally; the protection of nature is protection of ourselves. Just as we need no morals to breath, so one needs no moral exhortation to show care. For the ecological self, behaviour follows naturally and beautifully the norms of strict environmental ethics. "What this implies is that the connection between an ecological perception of the world and corresponding behaviour is not a logical but a *psychological* connection".[152]

As Peter Russell argues; "One is, in effect, in touch with a universal level of the self. If there is any identity at all in this state, it is of an at-one-ness with humanity and the whole of creation".[153]

"that tree was bathed in an eerie light ...there were eternal sounds"

FROM THE UNIVERSAL to the particular, as they say in philosophy, let us take New Zealand as a particular country in which the new ecospirituality, the *Postmodern Ecological Landscape* and Sophia spirituality, can be illustrated in the recent writings of a number of eminent New Zealanders.

Tohunga and theologian Maori Marsden, steeped in the lore of ancient Maori traditional ecospirituality, writes interchangeably from his Maori cultural background perspective, as well as for a postmodern multicultural New Zealand society.

> Imminent within all creation is 'mauri' – the life-force which generates,
> regenerates and upholds creation. It is the bonding element that knits
> all the diverse elements within the universal 'Procession' giving
> creation its unity in diversity. It is the bonding element that holds the
> fabric of the universe together.[154]

This could be a description of *Anima Mundi/World Soul*, not unlike the descriptions given by quantum physicists - that there are forces, like light or radio waves or consciousness, which lie beyond the material world and which at quantum levels, act as a bonding of matter and non-matter.

Postmodern Deep Ecology and Sophianic *Anima Mundi/World Soul* is further indicated when Marsden argues for a departure from the modern ideology of the human being as the centre of the universe, to a spirituality where the destiny of humanity and earth is bound. In an echo of Teilhard de Chardin and James Lovelock, Marsden states:

> The function of humankind as the envelope of the noosphere –
> conscious awareness of Papatuanuku is to advance her towards the
> omega point of fulfilment. This will mean a radical departure from the
> modern concept of man as the centre of the universe towards an
> awareness that man's destiny is intimately bound up with the destiny of
> the earth.[155]

Marsden reinforces deep ecology and archetypal psychology when he states from his Maori perspective that "the universe has a spirit and life of its own – a spirit and life (wairua and mauri) imminent within creation which must be respected and supported.

Man's well-being corresponds with the well-being of earth".[156]

In what could be a description of Sophianic Wisdom, for Marsden the highest form of spiritual tohunga, or priesthood, is a realisation or knowledge of the *mauri* – that life-force which impels the cosmic process towards fulfillment. This is to recognise the *atuatanga divinity* or god within

> Mauri as life-force is the energy within creation which impels the cosmic process onwards towards fulfillment. The processes within the physical universe and therefore 'pro-life' and the law of self-regeneration latent within creation will, if not interfered with, tend towards healing and harmonising the eco-systems and biological functions within Mother Earth. From the Maori point of view that... transition and transformation will result in the perfect comprehension of the higher spiritual laws ever sought by the ancient seers (tohunga) to enable mankind to flow in union with the universal process and thereby become fully creative. This is man's transition from the purely human into atuatanga (divinity whose manifestation has already become evident in the lives of the saints and seers of various peoples and religions. This atuatanga will mean the perfect blend and union of mind and spirit in which the gift of matakite (enlightenment) will allow man to exercise mana (authority, power) responsibility in perfect wisdom and freedom. Thus, will he creatively lift up and transform creation itself.[157]

Ranganui Walker – academic historian, writer, radical, and urbane political and social observer – also gives a description of spirituality which fits very much with postmodern deep ecology, individuation and Sophianic Wisdom. When asked "What is your spiritual belief?" Walker answered simply:

> I suppose the nearest would be animism or naturalism, which are denigrated by anthropologists. I feel a close presence to something greater than me when I am with nature. When I am in a forest I feel I am in the temple of Tane. For instance, one evening we went to see Tane-mahuta in the Waipoua forest. It was dark enough for owls to be flying around and yet that tree was bathed in an eerie light. I knew I was in a superior presence to myself, there were eternal sounds. It's not agnosticism, not a denial of God.[158]

Ngaio Marsh, internationally renowned writer and theatre director, in 1934 wrote that landscape "can be felt through the spiritual and mental experiences of human beings. If these are realised it may be that the shapes of mountains and rivers will appear, not as so many theatrical properties, but inevitably, so that the story could have enfolded in no other setting".[159]

Charles Brasch, poet, intimates Sophianic perception when he writes:

> I was struck by the grand simplicity of the landscape, disposed in the

> vast masses which are its elements – Cecil, Walter, Bayonet, the
> Remarkables, huge initial letters of an alphabet of countless signs, or
> the thunderous opening notes of a symphony in which every leaf, grass
> and stone had its own distinct vibration".[160]

Anne Hadfield, Presbyterian Church elder, describes similarities between pre-Christian Celts and pre-Christian Maori, both of whom had a close relationship with the sea and the land and "celebrated the mystery of life in the heat of the sun, the light of the moon, refreshment of water, and the abundance of the harvest".[161] Hadfield concludes that Maori and Pakeha are not so different in their pre-Christian spiritual roots. Further, she argues for a contemporary spirituality in which "we are co-creators, and therefore profoundly linked with the life birthing energy of God and of each other".[162] She could be talking about Sophia.

Michael King, celebrated journalist and New Zealand historian, both redefines the *Heavenly God-Father* Archetype of his Catholic childhood and gives what could be described as a moving description of the *Postmodern Ecological Landscape*, the archetypal Sophianic Wisdom. Describing the regeneration of "a landscape which has been logged, burned over and mined" he apprehends:

> [W]hat I would now call God. Not the image of our childhood: the old
> man with a long beard in the sky who intervened in human affairs
> when necessary to unleash floods, deliver tablets of stone or deposit his
> son. That was a metaphor that sought to make sense of the
> complexities of the human psyche, an image made in our own likeness.
> The God I discern now is infused in the host of good honest men and
> women who make up the underlying fabric that holds communities
> like ours together; and in the regenerative power of the natural world.
> In the rise of mist from the estuary and the fall of rain, in the
> movements of the incoming and outgoing tides, I see a reflection of the
> deepest mystery and most sustaining pattern of all of life: that of arrival
> and departure, of death and regeneration. And in seeing them, I feel
> satisfaction. I am thankful that this piece of earth exists and we upon it,
> to see and to experience these things; and – thanks to the miracle of
> human consciousness – to *know* that we experience them.[163]

This is the archetypal climate and province of Sophianic Wisdom – *Anima Mundi/World Soul* and the new *Postmodern Ecological Landscape*. Sophia has returned.

NINE

Sophia Geography

Sophia rules the eighth clime, the
archetypal world of images, the world in
which the forms of our thoughts and
desires, of our presentiments and of our
behavior and all works accomplished on
earth subsist.

– C.G. Jung

[U]ltimately what we call physics and
physical is but a reflection of the world of
the Soul; there is no pure physics, but
always the physics of some definite psychic
activity.

The earth is then a vision, and geography a
visionary geography… the categories of the
sacredness "which possesses the soul" can
be recognised in the landscape with which it
surrounds itself and in which it shapes its
habitat, whether by projecting the vision on
an ideal iconography, or by attempting to
inscribe and reproduce a model of the
vision on the actual earthly ground.

– Henry Corbin

A Hymn to Sophia

I N THIS CHAPTER I explore, however tentatively and inadequately, the Sophianic *inner landscape* – the *Imaginal*, the *Mundus Imaginalis*, Sophianic harmonic perception or *Ta'wil*, and the Sophianic visionary geography of the soul.[1] In the *Postmodern Ecological Landscape* and under the Sophia Wisdom Archetype we become more aware of the imagination in creating landscape. The inner landscape becomes as important as the outer landscape.

As Lopez observes, to "inquire into the intricacies of a distant landscape ... is to provoke thoughts about one's own interior landscape, and the familiar landscapes of memory. The land urges us to come around to an understanding of ourselves".[2]

Lynn Ross-Bryant argues that "For Lopez the landscape we imagine is also that *other* that exists beyond and outside of human language *and* that shapes human language and experience..."[3]

Postmodern ecological writers indicate, often implicitly rather than explicitly, that there is a vital interaction between inner landscapes, imagination and outer landscapes.

In many cases it is the outer landscape which stimulates our imagination and creates the realisation of a deeper inner wisdom and inner Being. In other cases, it would seem that it is the inner landscapes of the psyche, from which the imagination springs that creates the outer landscapes of our Being-in-the-world.

Sophia's Inner Landscapes

SOPHIA IS THE archetype of inner landscapes. Sophia is identified with *Anima Mundi/World Soul* and *Mundus Imaginalis* – the inner landscapes of forms and archetypes from which our outer landscapes are a manifestation and a materialisation.

The Sophia archetype, as *Anima Mundi/World Soul* and the divine feminine, perfect nature, also embodies a holistic view of humans, nature and spirit. The mysterious otherness of nature in which the sacred is revealed is characteristic of Sophianic Wisdom and perception.

Sophianic perception is *ta'wil* harmonic perception. It is participatory, mystical and consciously archetypal – recognising the ability to perceive on several levels simultaneously. It is the antithesis of Cartesian objectification, the *I-It world*, materialist reduction and dualism.

Behind and within the *Postmodern Ecological Landscape* is the Sophia Wisdom Archetype. Postmodern ecological writers indicate that it is the *inner landscape* of the psyche from which the imagination springs, that creates the outer landscapes of our being in the world.

As will be shown, these are also the arguments of the Sophianic Mazdean and Sufi mystics and their archetypal 'visionary geography', as translated and interpreted by Henry Corbin. Inherent to *mundus imaginalis/imaginal landscapes* and Sophianic harmonic perception (*ta'wil*) are the inner archetypal landscapes of the soul.

"How do people imagine the landscapes?"

IMAGINATION IN THE *Postmodern Ecological Landscape* is the key to the relations and interactions between the natural world and human beings. Barry Lopez asks:

> How do people imagine the landscapes they find themselves in? How
> does the land shape the imaginations of the people who dwell in it?
> How does desire itself, the desire to comprehend, shape knowledge?
> These questions seemed to me to go deeper than the topical issues, to
> underlie any consideration of them.[4]

These are Sophianic epistemological questions. They predominate in the *Postmodern Ecological Landscape* and the *I-Thou relation* with the land and the landscape. Descriptors of this relationship are mystical, emotional, lyrical and reverential. These are also descriptors inherent to Sophianic Wisdom, morality, perception and spirituality. For example, Lynn Ross-Bryant maintains that Lopez is an exemplar of postmodern ecological writers who offer a holistic view of humans, nature and spirit.

The mysterious otherness of nature is allowed to present itself and in the process the sacred is revealed. Thus, "Lopez joins postmodern thought in general and neopragmatism in particular in discounting the Cartesian project of knowing the world objectively, in itself. Humans have no privileged position from which they can observe the world".[5]

The Celestial Earth – "subtle bodies of Light"

CORBIN DESCRIBES SOPHIA, the divine presence of wisdom for our world in an intermediate imaginal world – the *Celestial Earth*, as follows:

> Between the intellectual and the sensible… [is] a 'spiritual corporeity'
> which represents the Dwelling, the Divine Presence, for our world.
> This Dwelling is Wisdom itself, Sophia.[6]

Sophia is "the imaginal place of the Divine Presence in our world". Sophia as the Celestial Earth is typified in the Shi'ite gnosis by Fatima, "the Sophia of the Shi'ite theosophy and cosmology".[7] Thus Sophianity is for the human being to accede here and now to the Celestial Earth, to the world of Hurqalya, world of 'celestial corporeity', which is that of the subtle bodies of Light.[8]

"the Soul of the Perceiver"

THE QUANTUM WORLD of nonmaterial symmetries and archetypes also requires new ways of envisioning the world, description and language.

The importance of the imagination and an inner non-physical reality behind our physical external world is understood by quantum physicists; in particular Wolfgang Pauli, F. David Peat and David Bohm.

Pauli argued that the psychologist and the physicist are engaged in a complimentary quest. Hence he advocated that the:

> [I]nvestigation of scientific knowledge directed outwards should be supplemented by an investigation of this knowledge directed inwards. The former process is directed to adjusting our knowledge to external objects; the latter should bring to light the archetypal images used in the creation of our scientific theories. Only by combining both these directions of research may complete understanding be obtained.[9]

Psychiatrist Anthony Stevens states: "The relationship between the physical world we perceive and our cognitive formulations concerning that world is predicated upon the fact that the soul of the perceiver and that which is recognised by perception are subject to an order thought to be objective."[10]

Stevens notes that, for Pauli, "…the archetypes which order our perceptions and ideas are *themselves* the product of an objective order which *transcends* both the human mind *and* the external world."[11]

Inscape

FOLLOWING ON from Pauli, quantum physicist F. David Peat has also called for changes in our language which apply to both 'inscape' and 'landscape'. This postmodern language draws upon metaphor, allusion, ambiguity and values:

> [T]here can be no single explanation, theory or level within nature. We must seek complementary descriptions rather than the single, all-embracing, complete and logically consistent rational accounts which attempt to answer all questions and close all doors. We must seek to engage nature using all the richness that is possible within human language, by drawing upon metaphor, allusion and ambiguity in order to create coherent yet complementary accounts… the science of inscape and landscape requires a degree of creativity within its language, including the ability to deal with metaphor and ambiguity and to accommodate the qualities and values of our experience.[12]

By 'inscape' Peat is referring to the authentic voice, or inner-dwellingness of things and our experience of them; hence he argues … "By inscape I wish to suggest the inexhaustible nature of each human being, tree, rock, star and atom, and that there is no most fundamental level, no all embracing account or law of a perception or encounter. Rather one attempts to engage in the inner authenticity of the world".[13]

This is the '*I-Thou*' poesis of the artist and Sophianic Wisdom. As in the Sophia Wisdom Archetype, where there is no dualism, Peat questions the fragmentation within our current (modernist) worldview between inner and outer and "the desire for an objective science which has no room for values, qualities and the nature of subjective experience".[14]

Implicate Order

DAVID BOHM has argued similarly that there is "no fundamental distinction between the processes of the imagination and perception".[15] Bohm distinguishes between *primary* imagination, *creative* imagination and *reflexive* imagination. Thus, "the reality which you perceive is affected by your thought. Thought is working as a kind of imagination being infused into your perception. It becomes part of what you see. And that imagination is necessary".[16] According to Talbot, Bohm uses the idea of implicate order to echo the idea that:

> Every action starts from an intention in the implicate order. The imagination is already the creation of the form; it already has the intention and the germs of all the movements needed to carry it out. And it affects the body and so on, so that as creation takes place in that way from the subtler levels of the implicate order, it goes through them until it manifests in the explicate.[17]

In other words, in the implicate order, imagination and reality are ultimately indistinguishable.

Home of Archetypes – Mundus Imaginalis and Alam-al-mithal

THIS THINKING by postmodern ecologists and quantum physicists on the imagination and a seminal, inner non-physical reality has precedent in Sophianic *mundus imaginalis,* the *archetypal imaginal* and *visionary landscapes* of the Mazdean and Sufi mystics of Persian antiquity, as recounted and interpreted by Henry Corbin.[18]

Gilbert Durand (1921-2012), the eminent French philosopher and Professor of Sociology and Anthropology, a follower of Bachelard, Corbin and Jung, notes that Corbin "pointed out that the world of images is quite real; it retains the rich and diverse manifestations of the tangible world. …At the same time, they are removed from the world of fixed time and the limitations of space".[19]

Durand argues that Western culture is dying from an emphasis on positivism and rationalism and a minimization of images and myths.   However, beyond this fragmented self lies the modality of *mundus imaginalis* (*Alam- al-mithal*), the gigantic net of woven dreams and desires of the species.

Durand explains that it was Jung, Bachelard, Levi-Srauss and Henry Corbin who recognized the neglected feminine anti-history of philosophy – an inner place of spiritual revelation – revealed by dreams, symbols and visions. This was the feminine guide of the imagination, the active Sophia inner wisdom.

Sophianic *mundus imaginalis,* of the imaginal inter-world, *Alam-al-mithal,* is where the dynamic patterns of archetypes are embedded and they in turn spiritualize the tangible world.

The Imaginal

DURAND COMPARES the exploratory "Sophianic approach of the Orient", with its emphasis on the imaginal with the more recent didactic approach of the West, which he describes as shortsighted – "the mutilated, down-graded, intellectual attitude of narrow-minded rationalism and simple-minded historicism" – those frustrating blindspots of

Western genius – have been thrown off by the exploratory exegesis of the imaginal". [20]

Like the postmodernists, Henry Corbin also criticises the limitedness of Western rationalist epistemology:

> It is a long time… since western philosophy, let us call it 'official philosophy', drawn along in the wake of the positive sciences, has admitted only two sources of Knowledge (*Connaitre*). There is sense perception which gives the data we call empirical. And there are the concepts of understanding (*entendement*), the world of the laws governing these empirical data. Certainly, Phenomenology has modified and overtaken this simplificatory epistemology (*gnoseologie*). Yet the fact remains that between the sense perceptions and the intuitions or categories of the intellect there has remained a void. That which ought to have taken its place between the two, and which in other times and places did occupy this immediate space, that is to say the Active Imagination, has been left to the poets. [21]

Corbin maintains that "The very thing that a rational and reasonable scientific philosophy cannot envisage is that this Active Imagination in man should have its own noetic or cognitive function, that is to say it gives us access to a region and a reality of Being which without that function remains closed and forbidden to us. [22]

For a long time Corbin divided his time between Paris and Teheran and searched "like a young philosopher, for the key to this world as a real world, which is neither the sensible world nor the world of abstract concepts". [23]

Through his translations he was to discover that in the spiritual world of ancient Mazdean and Shi'ite Persia, the Imagination is a mediating power between the inner spiritual world and the outer sensory world of our being.

The imagination "is a cognitive power in its own right". [24] Corbin describes this epistemology – foreign to dualism and the disappearance of which has brought on a catastrophe of spirit:

> It is essentially a median and mediating power, in the same way that the universe to which it is regulated and to which it gives access, is a median and mediating universe, an intermediate world between the sensible and the intellectual (*intelligible*), an intermediate world without which articulation between sensible and intellectual (*intelligible*) is definitely blocked. And then pseudo-dilemmas pullulate in the shadows, every escape or resolution closed to them. [25]

The Imaginal versus the Image

IN THE SCIENTIFIC CIVILISATION in which we live we are thought to have gained mastery over images – hence "It is quite commonplace to refer to our present day civilisation as a "civilisation of the image" (to wit our magazines, motion pictures, and television)".[26] However this contains a radical misunderstanding.

Corbin argues that "instead of the image being raised to the level of the world to which it belongs, instead of it being invested with a *symbolic function* that would lead to inner meaning, the image tends to be reduced simply to the level of sensible perception and thus to be definitely degraded."[27]

He asks "Might one not have to say then that the greater the success of this reduction, the more people lose their sense of the *imaginal* and the more they are condemned to producing nothing but fiction?"[28]

The form of the imagination (the imaginal) as talked about by Corbin and the philosophers of Persia have nothing to do with the imaginary, the unreal or fiction.[29] In other words one could argue that it has nothing to do with advertising, branding, logos and consumerism. Corbin states:

> "The seriousness of the role of the Imagination is stressed by our
> philosophers when they state that it can be 'the Tree of Blessedness' or
> on the contrary 'the Accursed Tree' ....that which means Angel or
> Demon in power. The imaginary can be innocuous; the *imaginal* never
> can be so."[30]

Similarly, David Bohm also warns of the power of the imagination. It can be creative and it can be destructive, because the fantasy realm can merge with reality and create resistance to seeing that it is a fantasy... perception is all basically of the same nature as the imagination.[31]

Corbin maintains that; "Whenever imagination strays and is wasted recklessly, when it ceases to fulfill its function of perceiving and producing the symbols that lead to inner intelligence, the *mundus imaginalis* (which is the realm of the *Malakut*, the world of the soul) may be considered to have disappeared."[32]

In order to distinguish the intermediate world of the Imagination from the merely fictitious and unreal, Henry Corbin searched for a new term. The Latin language came to his assistance and he designated *mundus imaginalis* as the key term which has a literal equivalent to the Arabic *'alam al-mithal, al-'alam al-mithali*.

Intermediate Universe – "world of the Soul"

MUNDUS IMAGINALIS circumscribes a very precise order of reality "which corresponds to a precise mode of perception".[33]

It is the intermediate universe which the scholars of Islam designate as the "eighth clime, that is, is "the kingdom of "subtle bodies", the "spiritual bodies" – threshold of the Malakut or the world of the *Soul*

It is "a clime *outside* all climes, a place *outside* all places, outside of *where (Na-Koja-Abad)*."[34] The *"alam al-mithal, the mundus imaginalis,* the world of the mystical cities such as Hurqalya" is "where time is reversed and where space, being only the outer aspect of an inner state, is created at will."[35] This is very much comparable to quantum space-time theories where space and time are strange (to our present physical and linear ways of thinking), mobile and relative conceptions.

Corbin gives a concise definition: "More exactly still: this *mundus imaginalis*, world of Hurqalya, world of Malakut or world of Soul, is the 'Celestial Earth' and the 'Celestial Corporeity'." [36]

Corbin points out that such an intermediate world was "ceaselessly mediated, particularly in Islamic Iran, both by the masters of Sufism, the adepts of the Suhrawardian philosophy of light, and the adepts of Shaikhism" and that, indeed, this "intermediate world is … the centre of *the worlds*."[37]

The world of the Imaginable, of imaginative Reality, the *world of archetype – Images*, is established as mediator between the world of the pure intelligible essences and the sensory universe. This world is the *eighth* keshvar, the eighth climate the "Earth of the emerald cities", the mystical Earth of Hurqalya

It is "from the soul itself, from the celestial Earth of the Soul, that the "spiritual flesh" is constituted – the suprasensory and at the same time perfectly concrete, *caro spiritualis*".[38]

Interworlds and Nonlocal Reality

IN THE TEXTS this theme is repeated and amplified, forming "a progression from one octave to the other of the Iranian spiritual universe repeating and amplifying the same theme".[39]

Corbin maintains that "Something in the nature of harmonic perception is needed in order to perceive a world of many dimensions".[40] It may be that this world is the "lost continent":

> The spatial distances between humans are being more and more reduced
> in our day, at least if measured in terms of time; concurrently we hear
> talk of an "acceleration of history." On the other hand, the *real* universes
> – those by which and for which men live and die, which can never be
> reduced to empirical data because their secret reality exists before all our
> projects and predetermines them – those universes, it would seem, have
> never been so far from being able to communicate with each other, from
> being penetrable by one another. It may be that the first and last reason
> for this impenetrability is to be sought in the loss of the *interworld*, in the
> vanished consciousness of this assembly of universes which our authors
> call the "world of Hurqalya". [41]

It is interesting to compare this mystical view of a spiritual Earth of many universes and an inter-world behind the physical and material Earth of our senses, with David Bohm's view of a nonlocal level of reality beyond the quantum. Bohm proposes that the universe should no longer be viewed as a machine but rather as a stupendous multi-dimensional hologram. He suggests that at the super-holographic level the universe may have as many dimensions as there are subatomic particles in our three-dimensional universe, a staggering 10^{89}. This level may be a "mere stage" beyond which is "an infinity of further development."[42] As Michael Talbot points out:

It would no longer be correct to speak of the multidimensional level of the universe as a material plane. Rather, Bohm concludes, "it could equally well be called Idealism, Spirit, Consciousness. The separation of the two – matter and spirit – is an abstraction. The ground is always one".[43]

As to where or how this higher ground is perceived, Bohm states only that " ...we are led to propose further that the more comprehensive, deeper, and more inward actuality is neither mind nor body but rather a yet higher – dimensional actuality, which is their common ground and which is of a nature beyond both."[44]

In harmony with this, Henry Corbin stated, prior to Bohm, that:

> ...[W]hat we call *physics* and physical is but the reflection of the world of the Soul; there is no pure physics, but always the physics of some definite psychic activity. So, to become aware of it is to see the world of the Soul, to see all things as they are in the Earth of Hurqalya ... which is the surrection and the resurrection of the world of the Soul.[45]

and, further:

> *Hurqalya is the Earth of the soul, because it is the soul's vision.* "To see things in Hurqalya" is to see them as they are as events of the soul, and not as constituted into the autonomous material realities, with a meaning detached from and independent of the soul, as our positive science constitutes and "objectifies" them. Finally, it is a way of meditating the Earth and transfiguring it by this meditation.[46]

Harmonic Perception – Ta'wil and Hurqalya

ACCESS TO THE WORLD of Hurqalya is difficult, Corbin concedes. One can not penetrate this world by "house breaking, one does not move around mentally in the world of Hurqalya by the assistance of a formal logic or of a dialectic which leads from one concept to the next by deduction. Passage from one imaginal Form to another does not obey any conceptual dialectic". [47]

It requires mental and inner vision. It is a way of perceiving and meditating the Earth which is "linked with a psycho-spiritual structure which we have to rediscover in order to bring out the value of the means of knowledge it offers". [48] Corbin states that:

> [To] come face to face with the Earth not as a conglomeration of physical facts but in the person of its Angel is an essentially psychic event which can "take place" neither in the world of impersonal abstract concepts nor on the plane of mere sensory data. The Earth has to be perceived not by the senses, but through a primordial Image and, in as much as this Image carries the features of a personal figure, it will prove to "symbolize with" the very Image of itself which the soul carries in its innermost depths. The perception of the Earth Angel will come about in an intermediate

universe which is neither that of the Essences of philosophy nor that of the sensory data on which the work of positive science is based, but which is a universe of archetype-Images, experienced as so many personal presences. In recapturing the intentions on which the constitution of this universe depend, in which the Earth is represented, meditated, and encountered in the person of its Angel, we discover that it is much less a matter of answering questions concerning essences ("what is it?") than questions concerning persons ("who is it?" or "to whom does it correspond?"), for example, *who* is the Earth? *who* are the waters, the plants, the mountains? or, to *whom* do they correspond? The answer to these questions causes an Image to appear and this Image invariably corresponds to the presence of a certain state."[49]

In other words, the emphasis on; *inner vision*, a *psycho-spiritual structure*, personalized questions as to "*who*" rather than the "*what*" of the Earth and geography, an *Image* which appears when these personalized questions are asked and the *correspondence of this Image with a state* (presumably emotional and psychological) – indicate a mode of perception and epistemology which could best be described as *imaginal-archetypal.* This is very far from our current objectivist and scientific way of seeing the Earth and geography.

"To see or perceive things in Hurqalya", or the earth in its pure state, what is required is a faculty of perception "designated by the "technical term *ta'wil,* which etymologically means "to bring back" the *data* to their origin, to their archetype, to their *donor*".[50] Hence *ta'wil* clearly has similarities with postmodern and archetypal epistemological analysis and hermeneutics.

Corbin argues "*Ta'wil* presupposes the super-position of worlds and interworlds, as the correlative basis for a plurality of meanings in the same text."[51]

This "technique" was once known in the West but rapidly degenerated into an artificial technique because it was cut off from its *theosophia* of which it is the correlative and because it was deprived of spontaneity by a dogmatic authority. "The *ta'wil* without question, is a matter of *harmonic perception,* of hearing an identical sound (the same verse, the same *hadith* even an entire text) on several levels simultaneously."[52]

Here again, one is reminded of similarities with Bohm's sub-quantum inner multi-dimensional, super-holographic universe (worlds and inter-worlds); an "enfolding-unfolding universe and consciousness"[53]

Bohm also draws on parallels between consciousness, the implicate order and music (harmonic perception). He argues that the activity in consciousness of listening to music, constitutes a striking parallel to the activity proposed for the implicate order in general and in listening to music one is directly perceiving an implicate order.

Again, in the mystical world Henry Corbin describes, Sophia is the *World Soul,* *Anima Mundi*, the *Divine Feminine* and *Perfect nature*. Sophia is the Philosophers' Angel and the Visionary organ of the Soul. Sophia is the "*imaginal* place of the Divine Presence in our world".[54] Sophianity is to accede to the Celestial Earth, the world of "'celestial corporeity', which is that of the subtle bodies of Light".[55]

It is through the active imagination that we perceive and show an Earth which is other than the Earth seen by ordinary sensory experience.[56] It requires extraordinary perception, *ta'wil* – harmonic perception, archetypal perception.

A "Visionary Geography"

THUS, IN SOPHIANIC mystical philosophy, the Earth is both a vision and geography, indeed, a visionary geography.

To perceive the soul of the earth is to perceive one's own soul. As Corbin states:

> We can therefore say this: the *Imago Terrae*, while it is the organ of perception itself, also signifies those aspects and figures of the Earth that are perceived, no longer simply by the senses nor as sensory empirical data, but by the archetype-Image, the Image *a priori* of the soul itself. The Earth is then a *vision*, and geography a *visionary geography*. Hence it is the Image of itself and its own Image that the soul rediscovers and meets.[57]

In other words and to reiterate, the:

> [P]erception of the Sophianic mystery of the Earth, of geosophy, obviously cannot take place in the framework of positive geography. It presupposes a visionary geography, what has been rightly called a "landscape of Xvarnah"… [This landscape] is not spread over profane, previously determined space, but is concentrated or concentrates a sacred space… and this space does not need to be *situated*, since it is of itself *situative*.[58]

The psyche and the landscape have become one.

> Geographical features, mountains for instance, are here no longer merely physical features; they have a significance for the soul; they are psycho-cosmic aspects. The events that take place there consist in the very seeing of these aspects; they are psychic events.[59]

In a visionary geography plants, water, mountains are transmuted into symbols. The mountain tops of the Earth are the mountain tops of the soul. "The mountain tops of the Earth of visions are the mountain tops of the soul. The two archetypal Images, the *Imago Terrae* and the *Imago Animae*, correspond to one another: the *mountain of visions is the psycho-cosmic mountain*."[60]

The hierophanies of visionary geography offers an example of a case of psycho-geography unlike any other.[61] Corbin points out that visionary geography creates a mental iconography that offers *Spenta Armaiti*, the *Sophia* and *Feminine Angel of the Earth* support for meditation on what we previously called *geosophy* – the Earth in its spiritual form, – and is inseparable from eschatology (theology concerned with the end of the world) because its function is "essentially to prepare the birth of the earthly human being to his celestial "I," which is Daena, the daughter of Spenta Armaiti-Sophia".[62]

To recognise oneself as a son or daughter of the Spiritual Earth (or Angel of the Earth) is to have one's soul awakened to consciousness of a celestial kinship. It is to undertake in one's own being Sophianity, Sophia. By assuming this nature the human being is in a true sense the child of the Earth Angel and is so able to have a mental vision of her.[63]

One is no longer a person "imprisoned between the boundaries of terrestrial birth and death, but a human being in his totality, including the past of his pre-existence and the future of his superexistence".[64]

Corbin maintains that "the active Imagination of the celestial Earth, is not a "fantasy"; it is a power capable of "substantiating" and "vivifying".[65]

As we have seen, many explorers of the natural world and the psyche, postmodern ecologists, mountaineers and lovers of the natural Earth would agree, that contact with the Earth does have a substantiating and vivifying effect and that the Earth does seem to have a 'soul' with which we can become attuned 'in soul'.

For example John Bierman, in his biography of Laszlo Almasy, writes of Almasy's consuming passion for the desert where "Almasy believed, one could escape the tensions and temptations of modern living and find one's real self. There, body and soul were cleansed and man felt 'nearer to the Creator'… 'The desert is terrible and it is merciless,' he would write, 'but to the desert all who once have known it must return' ".[66]

Opening up of Soul

DEVOTION TO THE SPIRITUAL EARTH tends to cause the opening up of the anima, the secret presence of the Eternal feminine in man – Sophianic Wisdom.[67] Sophia is associated with both the *Anima* and the *Soul – the opening up of consciousness and hence Wisdom*. Sophia as *Soul* and *Anima*, preceding male and female differentiation, is the *imaginative consciousness* in the form of an archetypal feminine being:

> [E]ternally Feminine, preceding even terrestrial woman because
> preceding the differentiation of male and female in the terrestrial
> world, just as the supracelestial Earth rules over all the Earths, celestial
> and terrestrial, and exists before them. Fatima-Sophia is in fact the
> Soul: the Soul of creation, the Soul of each creature, that is, the
> constitutive part of the human being that appears essentially to the
> imaginative consciousness in the form of a feminine being, *Anima*. She
> is the eternally feminine in man, and that is why she is the archetype of
> the heavenly Earth; she is both paradise and intuition into it…[68]

A "Psychological Geography"

IN 1953, HENRY CORBIN argued for a *psychological geography*, a new line of study in which the "intention is to discover the psychological factors that come into play in the conformation given to a landscape". Thus:

> Out of geographical studies, a new line of study, described as
> *psychological geography,* has developed in our day: The intention is to
> discover the psychological factors that come to play in the conformation
> given to a landscape. The phenomenological presupposition implicit in
> research of this kind is that the essential functions of the soul, the *psyche,*
> include the projection of a nature, a *physis;* conversely, each physical
> structure discloses the mode of *psycho-spiritual* activity that brings it into
> operation. In this sense, the categories of the sacredness "which possess
> the soul" can be recognized in the landscape with which it surrounds
> itself and in which it shapes its habitat, whether by projecting the vision
> on an ideal iconography, or by attempting to inscribe and reproduce a
> model of the vision on the actual earthly ground.[69]

Corbin concludes: "This is why each of the hierophanies of our visionary geography
offers an example of a case of psycho-geography unlike any other".[70]

We are defined by our landscapes. The categories of sacredness "which possess the
soul" can be recognized in the archetypal landscape(s) with which it surrounds itself.
This is the essence of the inner Sophianic Wisdom Archetype – within the *Postmodern
Ecological Landscape.*

Perhaps no other postmodernist ecological writer, explorer of the psyche and lover
of the natural world, gives a better lyrical working illustration of the Sophia Wisdom
Archetype (*Anima Mundi/World Soul* and *Mundus Imaginalis*) – the *inner landscape*
perception within the *Postmodern Ecological Landscape* in our time, than does Barry
Lopez in this passage from *Arctic Dreams:*

> I bowed. I bowed to what knows no deliberating legislature or parliament,
> no religion, no competing theories of economics, an expression of
> allegiance with the mystery of life. I looked out over the Bering Sea and
> brought my hands folded to the breast of my parka and bowed from the
> waist deeply toward the north, that great strait filled with life, the ice and
> the water. I held the bow to the pale sulphur sky at the northern rim of the
> earth. I held the bow until my back ached, and my mind was emptied of its
> categories and designs, its plans and speculations. I bowed before the
> simple evidence of the moment in my life in a tangible place on the earth
> that was beautiful. When I stood I thought I glimpsed my own desire. The
> landscape and the animals were like something found at the end of a
> dream. The edges of the real landscape became one with the edges of
> something I had dreamed. But what I had dreamed was only a pattern,
> some beautiful pattern of light. The continuous work of the imagination, I
> thought, to bring what is actual together with what is dreamed is an
> expression of human evolution.[71]

Afterword

I WANTED to finish here, leaving you the reader with intimations and intuitions of Sophia – that great lost continent of the psyche; that Henry Corbin spent his life searching for – Hurqalya, the "eighth clime" or a "clime outside all climes", the forgotten Soul of the Spiritual Earth and the geography of the soul. Also Sophia's other ways of knowing – ta'wil, harmonic perception, archetypal perception and inner wisdom. However I was issued with a challenge, one professor was not happy to be left with a phenomenological exploration and demanded answers to his questions – "So what?" and "What does this mean for me?" He wanted personal, existential answers. So, rising to the challenge, here is this author's tentative summary and personal conclusions. You must draw your own conclusions.

It was Carl Jung, on the trail of the ancient Gnostics, who reintroduced the idea that all religious experience is psychic in nature. Archetypal and Depth Psychology established this tradition once more in the twentieth century. Spirituality is inherent to the psyche (soul) and *all* the Gods are archetypes inherent within the psyche.

Individuation is an inner spiritual quest or process towards the fullest possible realisation of the self and the *Imago dei*, the God-image within the psyche or soul.

Like 'spirituality', 'landscape' is an inner concept originating in the psyche. It manifests as a '*focus of perception*'.

Geographers have long recognised a link between mind, imagination and landscape. This is exemplified in sacred landscapes. Arguably these spiritual landscapes are both *timeless*, insofar as our understanding of, and our potentiality to participate in, different imaginal-sacred landscapes is historically transcendent; and *historical* – insofar as there are clearly discernable historical changes in imaginal-visionary landscapes and the historical periods wherein particular imaginal-visionary landscapes predominate.

This leads on to a consideration of archetypes within landscapes. Archetypes are also timeless (historically transcendent) yet historically situated.

We are all possessed by our archetypes and their shadowside. Unlike Mercia Eliade who saw archetypes as, in a very real sense, man's (sic) salvation – leading man out of an unreal, profane, time-bound, meaningless existence – for Jung "the archetypes alone are not our salvation. Instead, they can be our damnation. They can be just as dangerous as they can be healing, just as blinding as enlightening."[1]

To lose oneself completely in an archetype – in other words to be absorbed into an archetype to such an extent that one loses one's individuality, ego and powers of independent thought and decision making – is extremely dangerous and to invite disaster.[2]

What is important is that there is such a balance between ego and archetype that healing, wholeness and individuation can occur. The process of conscious realization of the shadowside, the redemption of the scapegoat in ourselves and in our archetypes is found in individuation, which is the fullest possible realization of the self. This process requires Sophianic wisdom and is a characteristic of the Sophianic Wisdom Archetype.

We have arrived at a point in history where we need to examine honestly our landscapes and the archetypes which possess, inform and govern these landscapes, and hence our being, spirituality and values that we live by – for they relate to the very landscape we inhabit.

The future of our spiritual exploration is thus inward and towards conscious value-fulfilment and enhanced individuation.

We can no longer with honesty and integrity adhere, for example, to outworn, authoritarian, religious dogmas – especially those fundamentalist religions of the self-believing 'chosen', who marginalize and scapegoat others, and objectify and defile the world leading to destruction and war. We can no longer exploit and pillage our earth with Tricksterish abandon.

More than ever in our world, at this historical time point, the imperative is to perceive and realise a new landscape and archetype – Sophianic Wisdom (*Anima Mundi/World Soul, Mundus Imaginalis*); the inner archetype and spiritual landscape within the *Postmodern Ecological Landscape*.

As Henry Corbin states "what we call *physics* and the physical is but the reflection of the world of the Soul; there is no pure physics, but always the physics of some definite psychic activity. So to become aware of it is to see the world of the Soul…"[3]

Corbin describes *mundus imaginalis* – a world as ontologically real as the world of the senses and the intellect. In order to perceive this Sophianic *inner landscape* (*Mundus Imaginalis*) – this imaginal *inner* archetypal landscape and visionary geography of the soul, what is required is a special form of perception – *ta'wil.*

This is Sophianic harmonic archetypal perception, which is to bring data back to their origin, their archetype, their donor. In this, *ta'wil* has similarities with postmodern archetypal epistemological analysis and hermeneutics.

Like Bohm's postulated holographic universe, *ta'wil* presupposes the super-position of worlds and inter-worlds. It is the ability to perceive an identical sound or meaning on several levels simultaneously. In other words, the personal search for meaning can be a Gnostic quest, for ultimately the search for meaning is a personal process and an inner one.

The psyche or soul is "not a finished product" as Jane Roberts and *Seth* says, but a "process of becoming."[4] The search for meaning in one's life is an expression of individual creativity and the asking of deeper questions.

No guru or religion can provide the short-cut to what is an individual imperative and process. Ultimately *you* must choose *your* way and realise your value fulfillment.

Meaning may be sought in the '*outwards*' direction of a science which encompasses search questions and concepts of consciousness within matter, symmetries behind matter, and synchronicities and quantum processes which have a 'mental side', an 'inscape' or holographic 'implicate' order.

On the other hand, the personal search for meaning may involve the *inwards* personal altered state, perceptual orientation of the yogi; the meditation disciplines of the Buddhist; the mystical illuminations, symbols and synchronicities of those journeying into the dream, terrors and depths of the psyche or soul, such as was revealed in Jung's own self-journeying explorations.

Personal meaning may be sought from the speakers or channelers such as Jane Roberts and *Seth*, or the aphorisms of the Gnostic sage Jesus of the wisdom tradition[5] and the New Testament 'Sermon on the Mount'– who said "Seek and you shall find", "Ask and you shall receive", "Knock and the door shall be opened", "Love thy neighbour as thyself" and "Love your enemies".

Personal meaning may also be found in an aesthetic inwhich is perceived beauty, light, love and 'God' [*Imago Dei*] in the *Sophianic Soul of the World and Universe* and recognizes that our outer landscapes and inner archetypes are but a reflection of our inner selves and our spiritual evolution.

Appendix Notes

Science and Spirituality

The issue of science and spirituality, or religion, is a significant theme running throughout this book. It may be helpful, therefore, to summarize the position taken in the chapters. **Chapter 1** shows that science has undergone a sea-change. While in the modernist first half of the twentieth century, dominated by logical positivism, 'spirituality' appeared to be on very tenuous ground as regards meaning – in the most recent postmodern era, positivists and sceptics brandishing scientism have themselves come under critique. Indeed there have been significant conceptual changes in science – for while spirituality has made a return in 'secular' society, science itself has, in many regards, become more 'spiritual'. For example, theoretical biologist and complexity theory pioneer Stuart Kauffman argues that the "process of reinventing the sacred requires a fresh understanding of science that takes into account complexity theory and the idea of emergence. It will require a shift from reductionism, the way of thinking that still dominates our scientific world view."[1] James Lovelock is also critical of reductionism and talks of the need for a better balance in science with ideas of self-regulation, the circular logic of systems and emergence.[2] Lovelock, as well as Lynn Margulis, Humberto Maturana and Francisco Varela, Rupert Sheldrake, David Bohm, Murray Gell-Mann, Roger Sperry and John Hitchcock, are just a few of the more notable scientists cited who have challenged the traditional reductionist axioms of science, revolutionizing perception of the world in such a way that the holistic, the complex and arguably the spiritual and immaterial are allowed a foot in the door. Arguably, a new postmodern science is called for; indeed postmodernism, process theology, quantum physics and spirituality are closely intertwined. This is pursued in detail in **Chapter 4** where the evidence for archetypes is also explored at length.

Anthony Stevens has argued that "One of the most congenial attributes of Jung was his Janus head which enabled him to look at and comprehend both the imaginal life of the spirit and the organic processes of biology and thus transcend the Cartesian divide."[3] Hence in his 'theory of archetypes' Jung was both modernist and postmodernist, thus avoiding biological fundamentalism and physical or biological reductionism. Also in **Chapter 4** it is argued that just as Darwin found homologues in anatomy and the ethologists demonstrated homologues in patterns of behaviour, Jung traced homologues in symbols – hence universal occurrences of symbols and myths pointing to the existence of universal structures within the human mind.[4] While a legitimate scientific perspective can be made for Jung's 'theory of archetypes', and a case can be made for scientific evidence for archetypes from the point of falsifiablity, as analysed by Walter Shelburne in depth, for example[5] – the theory of archetypes fits better into the realm of quantum physics and emergence theory.

While classical physics could shed no light on the nature of consciousness, quantum physics possesses many characteristics reminiscent of consciousness – hence uncertainty and non-measurement; wave-particle complementarity, indeterminacy, non-locality and holism inter-relatedness, and participant-observer entanglement. In short, there are fundamental links between consciousness and the quantum world, as numerous quantum physicists have pointed out. In **Chapters 8 and 9** the theories of Carl Friedrich von Weizsacker, Wolfgang Pauli, Darryl Reanney, F. David Peat and David Bohm are addressed. Most notably, the lifelong collaboration between Jung and Pauli, which as a result of perceiving parallel developments in depth psychology and quantum physics, led to the development of the following propositions: physics and the psyche represent complementary aspects of the same transcendent unitary reality; archetypes acting as fundamental dynamic patterns whose various representations characterize all processes whether mental or physical; archetypes acting simultaneously in both realms of matter and mind accounting for synchronistic phenomena.[6] More recently the argument for the re-emergence of 'emergence' theory – which involves the shift from materialist, mechanistic reductionism towards mental causation, not reducible to physical causation – gives further support for archetypal theory and spirituality.[7]

Postmodernism and Jung

Despite being challenging and disquieting for orthodoxy, postmodernism is here to stay.[8] Not only does postmodernism make sense, it makes scientific sense, as the quantum physicist David Bohm argued.[9] Postmodernism is closely associated with quantum physics, process philosophy and process theology.[10] For postmodern geographers like Denis Cosgrove, the crisis of modernism is "ultimately a crisis of nature and our relations with it".[11] Many environmentalists, ecologists and other scientists would be in agreement.[12] As is pointed out by David Ray Griffin and David Bohm, constructive or revisionary postmodernism is not *anti*-modernism or *anti*-science, rather it seeks to go beyond modernism.[13]

For some, Jung is deeply suspect, lacking academic integrity, credibility and simply outdated. Yet Jung is seminal in the development of archetypal theory, although he is not the only archetypal theorist, nor necessarily the most important. For example, Henry Corbin, Anthony Stevens, James Hillman, Wolfgang Pauli, Erich Neumann, and Edward C. Whitmont also make very important contributions. Nevertheless, Jung's huge body of research and philosophical work continues to fascinate academics from many disciplines and cannot be ignored. Jung's theory spans both modernism and postmodernism.

As is elaborated in **Chapter 4** academic support for Jung and his work on archetypes comes from scholars at the forefront of their fields in psychiatry, depth-psychology, archetypal psychology, theology, religious studies, philosophy, sociology, anthropology, history, theoretical quantum physics and geography. Jung's scientific credibility is undoubtedly widely accepted. His lifelong collaborator on the archetypal hypothesis was quantum physicist Wolfgang Pauli (1900-1958) who was awarded the Nobel Prize for physics in 1945. Jung's scientific and academic credibility has been analysed in detail by Walter A. Shelburne, a founding member of the Applied Philosophy Institute, California.[14]

Jung's most popularist and virulent detractor in recent times has been the widely publicised Jesuit-educated Richard Noll, Professor of Psychology at De Salles University.[15] However, Noll's books have themselves been critically dissected at length by Anthony Stevens.[16] Stevens, an archetypal theorist and research psychiatrist, concludes that both Noll's books "are masterpieces of intellectual distortion" and "carefully contrived, scholarly and heavily detailed works of misinformation, designed to fill out [Noll's] own prejudiced and somewhat paranoid vision of Jung's achievement. It is unfortunate that so much valuable research should be used as ammunition in what looks like a purely personal vendetta."[17] In short, Jung is accused of 'pseudo-science' by some detractors; such objections and challenges are also countered in **Chapter 4**.

The theory of *Consilience* of the evolutionary biologist Edward O. Wilson is in some quarters regarded as providing a much better academic, and more up to date foundation for archetypes, than Jung. However, Wilson's theory is no less controversial, nor does it amount to a better, updated foundation for archetypal theory than does the life work of Carl Jung.

Wilson, raised a fundamentalist Christian, tries to effect a rapprochement between evolutionary science and fundamentalist Christianity. As an entomologist he is world-renowned for a life-time's work and his expertise in the study of ants. Only relatively late in his career did he attempt to reduce culture and human nature to evolutionary biology, which helped spawn the concepts of *'sociobiology'*, *'evolutionary psychology'* and *'evolutionary psychiatry'*. All these conceptual frameworks are controversial because they are, in essence, reductionist: of human nature and culture to genes and Darwin's theory of biological evolution. The scientific validity is empirically tenuous and has been questioned by evolutionary biologists, neurobiologists, social scientists, philosophers and others, and is something which Darwin himself, probably would have questioned.[18]

Wilson's theory of Consilience aims to unite the sciences with the humanities.[19] 'Consilience' is the synthesis of knowledge from different fields of specialized endeavour. Human nature is a collection of epigenetic rules– genetic patterns of mental development. In this Wilson could almost be describing the *'form'* of archetypes as described by Carl Jung – similar points are made by other reviewers of Wilson's theory, epigenesis, and Jung's earlier theory.[20] However, despite a brief reference to archetypes,[21] nowhere does Wilson acknowledge or even mention the seminal and lifelong work of Carl Jung on archetypes.[22] Wilson has, for the most part, a narrow, evolutionary reductionist and fundamentalist determinist perspective on human nature and culture.[23]

Interestingly, Wilson is vehemently anti-postmodernism.[24] Wilson has also at some points argued scientific evolutionary support for religious tribalism[25]; not exactly helpful in a world of warring religious fundamentalists, although later he *seems* to have resiled from this position. Most recently Richard Dawkins, who argues that "What matters is gene selection", has been critical of Wilson's theory of kin selection as a form of group selection. For Dawkins, Wilson thinks kin selection "is a special, complex kind of natural selection, which it is not."[26] There have been acrimonious public debates where Wilson has been accused of racism, misogyny and eugenics.

Fellow Harvard biologists Stephen Jay Gould and Richard Lewontin have been particularly critical of his science, as has neuroscientist Steven Rose.[27]

The 'Shadow'

Because of the likelihood of potential confusion of understanding, it is perhaps helpful at this juncture to discuss what is meant by the use of the 'shadow'. Jung argued that the shadow is the aspect of the Self which remains unconscious, because it is repressed by the superego, or else it is not activated by the environment. This often has negative connotations because it is found to be morally unacceptable by the individual or group; hence it becomes projected on to others. On the one hand it can be argued that the "shadow aspect" is a part of each individual. Jung for example argued that "Everyone carries a shadow and the less it is embodied in the individual's conscious life, the blacker and denser it is." [28] On the other hand, it can be argued that the shadow is a quality of all archetypes, as Jung recognized and as is emphasized by James Hillman. Because we are all possessed by archetypes and vice versa there does not appear to be any contradiction or problem with accepting both these views – hence the shadow is both within the individual and within archetypes. Unlike Eliade, who saw archetypes as in a very real sense man's salvation – leading man out of an unreal, profane, time-bound, meaningless existence – for Jung "the archetypes alone are not our salvation. Instead, they can be our damnation. They can be just as dangerous as they can be healing, just as blinding as enlightening."[29] To lose oneself completely in an archetype – in other words to be absorbed into an archetype to such an extent that one loses one's individuality, ego and powers of independent thought and decision making – is extremely dangerous and is to invite disaster.[30]

What is important is that there is such a balance between ego and archetype that healing, wholeness and individuation can occur. The process of conscious realization of the shadowside, the redemption of the scapegoat in ourselves and in our archetypes is found in individuation, which is the fullest possible realization of the Self.

As described in **Chapter 8**, this process requires Sophianic Wisdom and is a characteristic of the Sophianic Wisdom Archetype. Thus ego individuation is associated with the Sophianic Wisdom Archetype. We all have a shadowside and we can understand, hold, and be possessed by not just one archetype but many archetypes. The crucial issue of the shadow in the Sophianic Wisdom Archetype is that we take ownership of our individual shadowside and the shadow-sides of our archetypes, hence that which we often scapegoat in others becomes consciously realized as a possibility in ourselves. In this way the shadowside comes to have a new meaning which is not totally negative, but developmental, educative, redemptive and increases compassion and complexity.

Spirit, Soul and Spirituality

Both *spirit* and *soul* are used interchangeably, as is *psyche* and *soul*. All can be encompassed within the concept of *spirituality*. In **Chapter 1** the equivalence of psyche and soul is demonstrated. Jung, after 1933, tended to the use of *psyche* [31] and believed it could be the subject of scientific phenomenological investigation, primarily through the exploration of universal symbols, images, metaphors, myths and archetypes. James Hillman has a preference for *soul* over psyche and maintains soul has more metaphysical and romantic overtones and shares frontiers with religion.[32] Hence while psyche has more worldly physical connotations – soul, for Hillman at least, is more closely connected with metaphysics and religion. Hillman's books tend to use 'soul' rather than 'psyche'. 'Soul' is the dominant theme in his entire work.

It should be noted however that Jung, as well as being a psychiatrist and medical scientist, is also regarded as a postmodernist with his emphasis on the image as the root of the psyche, the importance of *poesis* and deferring to poetics, and his suspicion of overarching metaphysical language.[33] In this Jung was more at home with phenomenological spirituality than the metaphysical formulations of orthodox monotheistic religion.

It is my contention that psyche and soul are interchangeable. They are a part of a continuous interpenetrating whole, imbued by and under the overarching concept of spirituality. Soul or psyche could be termed a "highly individualized spiritual energy".[34]

It could be argued that, in its broad outline, the argument for the separation of spirit/spirituality from soul is the result of an overt or unconscious hierarchal, dualistic sacred/profane, spirit/earth mindset as is a characteristic of patriarchal monotheism. In contrast, the animistic, pagan and Gnostic view is that spirituality is not up there somewhere remote and separate, but is a given, inherent within all living beings and at the quantum level – hence the holographic interpenetration of worlds, inter-worlds and planes. Thus spirituality is within all matter.[35] As described in detail in **Chapter 1** this is the view held by Jung, where spirituality is inherent in the individual psyche/soul or Self. In this respect Jungian Depth Psychology accords with Deep Ecology in recognizing that nature is a part of 'the self', hence the terms 'psychoid unconscious' and 'psychoid archetype'.

As is also shown in **Chapter 1** when spirituality is intrinsic to the psyche, from the viewpoint of Jung and the Gnostics as well as some physicists – for example John Hitchcock – the realization of the Self or individuation becomes paramount and spirituality is both a process and a goal. Spirituality is a distillation and a refinement of spirit-matter. The God image, or *Imago Dei*, is an archetype which comes from *within* the psyche/soul and displays the struggle of the psyche for self-realisation. This view that spirituality is inherent in the psyche, hence God or Gods are archetypes inherent within our psyche/soul, constitutes an enormous challenge to orthodox religious monotheism.[36]

Spirituality is particularly a postmodern issue and conceptually it is no longer exclusive to what many regard as an outmoded or discredited patriarchal monotheism. Hence spirituality is not confined to orthodox religious hierarchical and dualistic metaphysical systems. Spirituality is real; arguably in all great creativity and art spirituality is an enigma, but nonetheless a reality. It can manifest as a consciously sought and impelled inner journey, or it can suddenly confront us, as in beauty and light, as we go about our everyday lives.

Conceptual Clarification of 'Inner' and 'Outer'

At this point it may be useful to clarify the notions of 'interior', 'inner', 'innerness' (and 'outer'). It could be argued that 'locating spirituality or *Imago Dei*/God within the individual' is not the same as interiority, either within the landscape let alone within the *Anima Mundi*. However, if one accepts Jung's *psychoid archetype* or *psychoid unconscious* and a holistic enspirited view of the world and universe, then this is precisely the case. The realisation of this is simply a matter of degree or penetration – hence how far one desires or allows ones psyche/soul, that "highly individualized spiritual energy", to consciously expand, permeate, and adventure. The psyche or soul is "not a finished product" but a "process of becoming".[37]

For example, in **Chapter 1** it is shown that the material empirical scientific world view has been undermined by biologists who challenge the independent nature of cognition. Complexity theory and the idea of emergence allow for this new view of the world, which is spiritual, relational and holistic. As David Bohm argues, a postmodern science would not separate matter and consciousness – meaning and value are as integral aspects of the world as they are of us.[38] Bohm proposes the notion of *implicate orders* – complex non-local levels of reality beyond the quantum in which separateness dissolves.[39] For Bohm this is a realm of consciousness which can't be considered fundamentally separate from matter.[40] Similarly Roger Sperry talks of molecules and atoms moved by higher level forces – mental, vital and spiritual forces, not reducible to fundamental laws of physics and long excluded by materialist philosophy – which become reinstated in non-mystical form.[41]

A broad concept of *inner* spirituality, unconfined to conventional religions, is also held by quantum physicist John Hitchcock who argues that spirit is inherently within matter and as scientific "models" evolve towards greater depth and subtlety the case amounts to a spiritual imperative, even for physics itself.[42] The point of this is that some quantum scientists now give support to the arguments of Jung and the Gnostics who saw spirituality as an intrinsic *inner*, *interior* property of the psyche. The *outer* world is but a reflection of the *innerness* of the psyche or soul. To realize the psyche is a basic drive, a psychological need, and the basis of religious meaning. It is to realize ones interconnectedness with all things. At the furthest reaches of the self-realisation process the boundary between psyche and world blurs to the point of extinction. Hence the psyche /soul is a part of a continuum forming an indivisible whole and is simultaneously universal and particular.[43]

In **Chapter 2** it is shown that landscape is an *inner* conception. It is a perceptual concept and in particular it is a 'focus of perception'. The literary, existential, phenomenal and imaginal in the archetypal depths of the psyche/soul are relevant here. Phenomenological epistemology and methodology are most appropriate for landscape exploration. 'Geography of religion' has become 'geography of spirituality'.

In **Chapter 3** it is argued that landscapes are imaginal and visionary. The role of the imagination in creating landscape is increasingly a focus of postmodern geography. There has been a revival of interest in the image, the imagination and the imaginal. The point is that all these are *interior*, *inner* properties and concepts of the psyche or soul which are being used to explore the '*outer*' landscape maps of our world. It is shown that geographers have long recognized a link between mind, imagination and landscape. As John Kirtland Wright once commented, "The most fascinating *terrae incognitae* of all are those that lie within the minds and hearts of men".[44] David Lowenthal is one who has made a strong case for personal and collective cultural imagination and creativity as underlying our images and ideas of the world and earth.[45]

In **Chapter 4** the case is made for archetypal landscapes.

In **Chapters 5 to 9**, by showing and exploring the archetypes within and informing historical and ahistorical (historically transcendent) paradigm landscapes, the relationship between spirituality and landscape is illustrated. Hence the *'interior'*, *'inner'*, *'innerness'* of archetypes of our psyche /soul are shown to be linked with the *'outer'* world via our landscapes.

In particular the notions of 'interior', 'inner' 'innerness' and the 'outside' world are explored in **Chapters 8 and 9** – hence the Sophia Wisdom Archetype (*Anima Mundi/World Soul*) within the *Postmodern Ecological Landscape*, and the concepts of a Sophianic *inner landscape* (*Mundus Imaginalis*: Sophianic *harmonic archetypal perception Ta'wil*) and the *visionary geography* of the soul.

It is shown that the ancient descriptions which point to Sophia as *World Soul* or *Anima Mundi* – hence "wisdom that lies hidden or bound within matter"; the "reconciliation of nature and spirit"; the "pre-terrestrial vision of the celestial world" – have strong similarities with descriptions made by quantum physicists about the quantum realities behind and within matter, the world and the universe. In this regard Werner Heisenberg's theories are to be taken as the archetypes of all matter and the ground of material existence.[46] To these are added Bohr's emphasis on wholeness and the non-local nature of space-time, Bohm's theory that quantum processes could be interpreted as having what would almost be called a "mental" side,[47] and Carl Friederich von Weizsacher view of the re-emergence of the *world soul* motif on the basis that quantum theory is to be understood as a theory of information. His theory of *'ur-alternatives'* points to a holism that encompasses all that exists in both the realms of mind and matter and brings forth the possibility of a World Soul.[48]

For Wolfgang Pauli the psychoid archetype, or the unconscious, represents a sort of 'missing link' between the world which is the legitimate study of science and the mind of the scientist who studies it.[49] Notions of an *inner, interior, innerness* spirituality and soul/psyche within the *outer* world are not only to be found in the theory of quantum physicists but are shown to be inherent in archetypal psychology and postmodern ecology.

The role of *inner landscapes* in the formation of the *outer* landscape is illustrated in the arguments of postmodern ecologists such as Barry Lopez.[50] Lynn Ross-Bryant argues that "For Lopez the landscape we imagine is also that *other* that exists beyond and outside human language *and* that shapes human language and experience…"[51]

In **Chapter 9** the Sophianic *inner landscape* – viz., the imaginal, the *Mundus Imaginalis*, Sophianic harmonic perception or *Ta'wil* and the Sophianic visionary geography of the soul is explored. In many cases it is the perception of *outer* landscape which stimulates our imagination and creates the realisation of a deeper *inner* wisdom and *inner* Being. In other cases it would seem that it is the *inner* landscapes of the psyche, from which the imagination springs that creates the *outer* landscapes of our being-in-the-world. Whether the *outer* landscape becomes the *inner* landscape or the *inner* landscape the *outer* landscape is a matter of perception turned inwards or outwards.

The importance of the *imagination* and *inner* non-physical reality behind our physical *external* world is argued by quantum physicists Wolfgang Pauli, F. David Peat and David Bohm. For example, for Pauli "the archetypes which order our perceptions and ideas are themselves the product of an objective order which transcends both the human mind and the external world".[52] And Peat talks of '*inscape*', the authentic voice, an *inner*-dwellingness of things and our experience of them; the "inexhaustible nature of each human being, tree, rock, star and atom and that there is no most fundamental level, no all embracing account or law of a perception or encounter. Rather one attempts to engage in the *inner* authenticity of the world.[53] David Bohm argues similarly that there is "no fundamental distinction between the processes of the imagination and perception."[54]

Henry Corbin stated prior to Bohm "what we call *physics* and the physical is but the reflection of the world of the Soul; there is no pure physics, but always the physics of some definite psychic activity. So to become aware of it is to see the world of the Soul…"[55] Corbin describes *Mundus Imaginalis* as a world as ontologically real as the world of the senses and the intellect. In order to perceive this Sophianic *inner landscape* (*Mundus Imaginalis*), this imaginal *inner* archetypal landscape and visionary geography of the soul, what is required is a special form of perception – ta'wil. This is Sophianic harmonic archetypal perception, which is to bring data back to their origin, their archetype, their donor. In this, *ta'wil* has similarities to postmodern archetypal epistemological analysis and hermeneutics. Like Bohm's postulated holographic universe *ta'wil* presupposes the super-position of worlds and inter-worlds. It is the ability to perceive an identical sound or meaning on several levels simultaneously.[56] The exploration of 'spirituality, landscape and archetypes' could be described as essentially an exploration of the '*interior*', the '*inner*', '*innerness*' and the '*outer*'.

It is argued that locating spirituality within the individual psyche or soul is in the same continuum as recognizing spirituality within the landscape and within anima mundi/world soul. It is *inner* related, inter-related and realized by *ta'wil* –Sophianic *inner* archetypal perception.

Form Versus Content of Archetypes

As the reader considers the chapters on the archetypes behind landscapes, it must be kept in mind that the *form* of an archetype and the *content* of an archetype are two different things. Archetypes are not determined as to their content but only as regards their form and then only to a limited degree. As will be explained the *content* of an archetype is contextual, conjectural, contestable, culturally and historically mobile and phenomenologically selective and subjective on the part of the perceiver. With this in mind let us consider some possible objections and justifications to way that the author handles the archetypes described in this book. 1) It might be objected that there is an imbalance in the treatment of individual archetypes in **Chapters 5 to 8** - hence '*Mother Earth*' is treated somewhat more leniently, than the '*Heavenly God-Father*' and the '*Trickster*'. But the Mother Earth Archetype is treated so because after centuries of being ignored, negated and derogated there has been a resurgence of appreciation of the perspective of primal, polytheistic and ancient matriarchal religions, especially towards the natural environment.⁵⁷ 2) It might be argued that **Chapters 6 and 7** are too negative. However, **Chapter 6** is a critique concerned with landscape and the natural environment, as it is found in the Anthropocentric Landscape 'focus of perception' of patriarchal monotheism. The Heavenly God-Father Archetype is that of mainstream Western orthodox patriarchal monotheism. This archetype is the predominant one in the West and is both contemporary and historical. It is the fundamentalist, all powerful Heavenly God-Father of Orthodox Judaic monotheism, Christian monotheism and Islamic monotheism. It is *not* to be confused with the suppressed, scarcely visible Heavenly God-Father concepts of polytheistic primal indigenous peoples, pagans, the mystical, Gnostics or the Gnostic Jesus, who have been regarded as heretical by orthodox monotheism and driven underground.⁵⁸ The author writes, not as an apologist for orthodox religion, but as a concerned environmentalist and feminist in an increasingly secular world. This is the author's perspective and it relies heavily on the sources, citations and critiques of theologians and philosophers, at the vanguard of religious, environmental and spiritual thinking.⁵⁹ As postmodernist and ecofeminist theologians recognize, a re-visioning of the divine and a new theology in light of contemporary experience – especially woman's experience is required. Since the middle of the twentieth century the feminist contribution to theology has finally been accepted amongst all but the most conservative academic theologians, and in all but the most conservative university religious studies departments. It is established as one of the critiques, and has an important and vibrant pedigree of university scholarship, playing a vanguard role especially in the areas of postmodernism, process theology and ecospirituality. Given the nature of orthodox patriarchal monotheism and the nature of feminism, it could hardly be other than critical.

As regards the Trickster Archetype of **Chapter 7** many will endorse this perspective. The Trickster Archetype can provide critical insights into advertising and corporate culture and the objectification of the natural world in a world of objective 'I-It' relations and perceptions. This chapter is meant to be provocative; but hopefully it is also fun! Above all the Trickster is fun – this is despite the brilliance and shadow–side of this archetype. In this *Technological/Materialist Landscape* we are all imbued with the Trickster and 'his' exploits – both angelic and devilish. We partake in his exuberance, ambitions, boundary exploration, trickery, games, sleights-of-hand, personas commercial success, communications expertise, technological genius, liminality and in his shadowside – if not in actuality then certainly in fantasy. We both applaud him and are appalled by him. We live vicariously through the Trickster and his shadow via entertainment – films, video games and the mass communications of television, magazines, and books. As Anthony Stevens states "Perception and understanding are, after all, largely matters of selection and interpretation in the light of archetypal preparation and individual experience." ⁶⁰

In conclusion, it is most important to reiterate the distinction between the *form* of an archetype and the *content* of an archetype. This distinction has been ignored, misunderstood and simply not realized by many theorists. Jung was to write "Again and again I encounter the mistaken notion that an archetype is determined in regard to its content, in other words that it is a kind of unconscious idea (if such an expression be permissible). It is necessary to point out once more that archetypes are not determined as to their content, but only as regards their form, and then only to very limited degree. A primordial image is determined as to its content only when it has become conscious and is therefore filled out with the material of conscious experience."[61] To put it another way, the content of an archetype cannot be reductionist or fundamentalist. It is in a continual state of becoming. The content of an archetype – as postmodernists will immediately recognize – is contextual, conjectural, contestable, culturally and historically mobile and phenomenologically selective and subjective on the part of the perceiver. It is an on-going process of evolving consciousness.

Certainly there will be other views, some very much more positive, on the contemporary cultural content of these archetypes, which also have validity. It is impossible, in the compass of a single book, to encapsulate and describe phenomenologically all perspectives.

Finally, it needs to be noted that the process of consciously realizing the negative and the shadowside of our archetypes is a mark of individuation and Sophianic Wisdom. The shadow is thus transmuted from being something entirely negative into something which could be termed developmental.

Glossary

Anima The feminine principle or archetype. Jung emphasized the soul as the feminine principle or archetype within man.

Animism Belief that all things in the world (including stones, plants, the wind etc) are imbued with some kind of spiritual or psychological presence. Things are 'ensouled' or 'animated' by a universal 'world soul'; or by individual spirits of various kinds. Animism is inherent to **Paganism**. Also related to **Panpsychism**, the view that there is some spark of consciousness in all things and **Pantheism**, that everything there is constitutes a unity and that this unity is divine.

Animus The male principle or archetype within woman.

Archetypal Psychology First named as such by James Hillman, this has the intention of moving beyond clinical inquiry within the consulting rooms of psychotherapy in favour of being situated within Western culture and imagination. Affiliated to the arts, history of ideas, and culture, it refers to a deep theory in Jung's later work. To be distinguished from **Analytical Psychology**, clinically based analysis associated with medical and empirical psychologies, founded by Jung as a result of disagreements with Freud and the usual appellation for Jung's earlier psychology.

Archetypes These supply motifs with which to structure the chaos of experience, and structure the developing psyche itself. Archetypes are basic universal structures of the psyche and patterns of relational modes – cultural, mythical, metaphorical and imaginal aspects. Carl Jung argued that they are the hidden foundations of the conscious mind and inherited mental images as the content of the collective unconscious. These are roots which the psyche has sunk in the earth and in the world generally. Archetypes comprise systems of readiness for action and at the same time images and emotions. The language of archetype is found in the metaphorical discourse of mythology. Archetypes function analogously to Platonic forms.

Collective Unconscious This term is used by Carl Jung to designate those aspects of the psyche which are common to all humankind. Unlike the personal unconscious which is made up of memories, the collective unconscious is made up of propensities or originating patterns, which Jung called archetypes.

Consilience Literally a 'jumping together' of knowledge, consilience has roots in the ancient Greek concept of intrinsic orderliness governing the cosmos as inherently comprehensible by logical process. Edward O. Wilson's theory of consilience aims to unite the sciences with the humanities; hence 'consilience' is the synthesis of knowledge from different fields of specialized endeavour. Wilson asserts that the sciences, humanities and arts have a common goal: to give a purpose to understanding the details, to lend to all inquirers the conviction, which is far deeper than a mere working proposition, that it is an orderly world able to be explained by a small number of natural laws.

Constructive Postmodernism This seeks to go beyond modernism while yet accepting that modernism and its mechanistic reductionist program has produced unparalleled advances in science. Constructive postmodernism is both a critique and rejection of modernism that also offers proposals for conceptual reconstruction. The term was coined by David Ray Griffin. Alfred North Whitehead and David Bohm belong to this camp, as do many environmentalists, ecologists and ecofeminists. Whitehead's philosophy gives the earliest, most systematic account of the assumptions of constructive postmodernism.

Depth Psychology An archetypal psychology of image, James Hillman argues this is the modern field whose interest is in the unconscious levels of the psyche – that is the deeper meanings of the soul, which is itself no modern term. It assumes a *poetic* basis of mind and is a psychology that "starts neither in the physiology of the brain, the structure of language, the organization of society, nor in the analysis of behaviour, but in the processes of the imagination" (Hillman).

Ecofeminism This has been at the forefront of the ecology, environmental and ecospirituality movements. Ecofeminists have challenged traditional philosophy and theology by advocating a holistic understanding and epistemology, recognizing the spiritual interconnectedness of all creation. They advocate co-responsibility for the world. Ecofeminists have combined a critique of the destructiveness of patriarchal attitudes to nature and women with an affirmation of a spiritual search which is nature-centred rather than having an anthropocentric focus.

Ecospirituality This refers to the experience of the Divine Presence or Divine Reality in the natural world, which is often argued to be more important as a movement than any one of the great World religions.

Ego A part of the Self and of an archetypal nature, it is the part of the personality which one consciously realises as 'I' or 'me'.

Epigenesis The unfolding development of an organism. Aristotle originated the theory. Edward O Wilson and Charles Lumsden argue that epigenesis is the sum of all the interactions between genes and the environment, creating the distinctive traits of an organism.

Epigenetic rules These are hereditary regularities of mental development that animate and channel the acquisition of culture.

Epistemology Taken from Greek, meaning "knowledge, understanding". It is the branch of philosophy concerned with the nature and scope of knowledge. It questions what knowledge is, how it is acquired, and the possible extent a given subject or entity can be known.

Existentialism The problem of being must take precedence over that of knowledge in philosophical investigations. Being cannot be made the subject of objective inquiry; it is revealed by reflection on one's own unique concrete existence in time and space.

Gnosticism From Greek feminine 'gnosis' translated as 'insight'. Knowledge of a mystical or esoteric experiential nature, participation with the divine. Gnosticism is a process of inwards "knowing", self exploration and associated with 'Light'. 'Gnostic' has a precedent in several ancient philosophical traditions. The origins of Gnosticism are obscure and debated but argued to be in ancient Persia, Platonism and Buddhism, pre-dating Judaism. Gnosis also has a hermetic understanding and in the Hellenic world gnosis and hermetic understanding were exclusively Pagan. Gnostic teachings are found in a family of sects flourishing from the second to the fourth centuries AD, combining elements of Christianity with Platonism. The discovery of the Nag Hammadi Library of Gnostic texts by a farmer in Upper Egypt in 1945, reveals how varied this movement was and has stimulated renewed interest. Outlawed by the Christian Roman Emperors, declared heresy by the early orthodox Christian Church Fathers and suppressed by the bishops , Gnosticism survived in Syria-Egypt and the Persian Schools (Babylonia) unrelated to Judaism and Christianity. Sophia and the spiritual search inwards towards a transfiguration of self are inherent in Gnosticism. Sophia remains central in the Eastern (Orthodox) Church, Wisdom traditions and mystical spiritual schools. There is a French Gnostic Church. Gnosticism has influenced a number of thinkers eg. Madame Blavatsky, Arthur Schopenhauer, Henry Corbin, Carl Jung , Alfred North Whitehead – also writers W. B. Yeats, Lawrence Durrell, Jorge Luis Borges , Hermann Hesse, Rene Guenon, Albert Camus and Allen Ginsberg.

Heavenly God-Father An archetype found universally, but most prominently and essentially in Western patriarchal monotheism – Judaism, Christianity and Islam. It denotes a transcendent deity, apart from nature, dominant and masculine in conceptual form and content.

Hermeneutics From Hermes, 'to interpret' language signs. Initially a theory of text interpretation, especially wisdom literature, philosophical texts and biblical texts. More recently it has become a theory of human existential understanding and knowledge (Schleiermacher, Dilthey, Heidegger). Comprehension through foreknowledge. Circularity of understanding and reciprocity between whole and parts. Words point beyond themselves. Involves analogies and imaginative sympathy. Understanding through grammatical and psychological interpretation as well as dialogue and ongoing cultural discourse.

Hero Of an archetypal nature, which in mythology refers to a being or entity of extraordinary strength and courage, the hero is often the offspring of a mortal and a god, celebrated for his exploits.

Hierophany and hierophanies Is from the Greek root *'hieros'* meaning "sacred" or " holy" sign; "to reveal" or " to bring to light"; signifies a manifestation of the sacred.

I-Thou "*I-Thou*" describes the world of relations. This is the "*I*" that does not objectify any "It" but rather acknowledges a living relationship. "*I-Thou*" relationships are sustained in the spirit and mind of an "*I*" for however long the feeling or idea of relationship is the dominant mode of perception. It can refer to a relationship with a tree, an animal, or the sky, as well as the relationship between two human individuals. In contrast "*I-It*" is better described as the primary word of experiencing and using and is characterized by objectification and lacking mutuality. See Martin Buber's book, *I and Thou*.

Imaginal Of, relating to, or resembling an imago or image, this is used most notably by such thinkers as Henry Corbin and Gilbert Durand. Corbin distinguishes *imaginal* from superficial images of the modernist material world of sensible perception, e.g., advertising and consumerism, where it is derogated to 'fantasy', 'fiction', 'imaginings'. Rather, *imaginal* as Corbin uses it is a spiritual and epistemological concept of great importance.

Imago Dei This names the God-image archetype. Jung argues that the God–image or Imago Dei comes from within the psyche. The idea of an all-powerful divine Being is present everywhere, unconsciously if not consciously. The God-image archetype displays the struggle of the psyche for self-realisation.

Individuation Term used by Jung to designate the process of personality development which leads to the fullest possible actualization of the Self; a 'coming to selfhood' or 'self-realization'.

Mother Earth An archetype found mythically, trans-historically and universally, even in technological, materialist 'sophisticated' societies.

Mundus Imaginalis The world where ideas, e.g., the pure spiritual forms of Platonism, or archetypes, are embodied. Here objects of the tangible world are spiritualised, acquiring meaning by way of semantic and eschatological extension. A "world that is as ontologically real as the world of the senses and that of the intellect" and which "requires its own faculty of perception, namely imaginative power, a faculty with a cognitive function, a *noetic* value which is as real as that of sense perception or intellectual intuition" (Corbin).

Myth A theme or character type which embodies an idea, allegory, or parable.

Objectivism and **Objectivity** 'Objectivity' is a central philosophical concept, especially in science, related to reality and truth. Generally it is the state of being true outside the subject's individual biases and interpretations. 'Objectivism' – theories that various kinds of judgement are objective ie. pertain to objects, as opposed to 'subjectivism' pertaining to subjects (people). Describes a branch of philosophy originating in the early nineteenth century. Often associated with modernism and reason. It is challenged by postmodernism and a relational view of reality.

Paganism Nature-based religion associated with animism, polytheism and sacred feminine, Goddess(es). Includes Primal indigenous religions, historical polytheistic religions and contemporary Neopagan religions. Worldview that is pantheistic, polytheistic and animistic. Pre-dates monotheism and Abrahamic religions and is subject of anthropology and archaeological study.

Persona The mask used by an actor in classical times to represent his role; used by

Jung to designate the characteristic roles humans individually adopt in their relating to others.

Phenomenology School of philosophy inspired by the work of Edmund Husserl (1859-1938) that seeks to examine and describe conscious experience and events without any recourse to explanation, metaphysical assumptions, traditional philosophical questions or preconceptions about their causation, in order to discover their essential structures and relationships.

Pneuma Breath, sometimes equated by the Greeks with air, the breath of the cosmos, and in a religious context for 'spirit' or 'soul'.

Positivism and **Logical Positivism** A philosophy of science based on the view that in the social as well as natural sciences, information derived from sensory experience, logical and mathematical treatments and reports of such data, are together the exclusive source of all authoritative knowledge . Positivism assumes that there is valid knowledge (truth) only in scientific knowledge.

Postmodernism 'After modernism', this refers to the consequences of the breakdown of the 'Enlightenment project' that had been aimed at getting all the world's diverse peoples to see things the same way – the rational way. It rejects epistemological foundationalism of reason – i.e., universal rationality. Instead, reason is contextual and relative. Emphasis is placed on perspective, plurality and metaphor.

Process Philosophy is the doctrine that what is, is becoming; or that what is ultimately consists in change, or both. A process is a sequence of changes. This line of thinking is associated with the philosophy of Alfred North Whitehead. The ancient Greek philosopher, Heraclitus, is identified as the originator with the doctrine of change being central to the universe.

Process Theology The tenets of process philosophy applied to theology, in particular through the work of Alfred North Whitehead. Charles Hartshorne, John B. Cobb Jr., and David Ray Griffin have expanded Whitehead's work into the realm of theology, and each rejects metaphysics that privileges 'being' over 'becoming'.

Psyche / Soul The terms *psyche* and *soul* can be used interchangeably. While soul has metaphysical and religious overtones, psyche has a more naturalistic, biological usage and is more associated with mind. James Hillman tends to soul; Jung settled for psyche.

Psychoid Archetype At a deep level the human psyche or soul merges with the outer world. Jung coined the term to account for the unitary nature of psyche and world. It is sometimes referred to as the psychoid unconscious.

Self An archetype that for Jung comprises a dynamic concept at the heart of personality development and individuation – it is the centre which embraces both the conscious and the unconscious.

Shadow Jung's term for that aspect of the Self which remains unconscious, because it is repressed by the superego, or else it is not activated by the environment. This often has negative connotations because it is found to be morally unacceptable by the individual or group hence it becomes projected on to others.

Sophia The Greek word for wisdom, this is also an archetype. The eternal Sophia Wisdom Goddess Archetype is identified with *Anima Mundi/World Soul; Anima,* the feminine principle or archetype within man; *Soul,* preceding the differentiation of male and female; *Wisdom* behind and within the Gods and the creator God; *Mundus Imaginalis,* the *Imaginal* inner archetypal landscape and visionary geography of the soul; and *Ta'wil –* harmonic archetypal perception.

Sophianic This term means that which relates to Sophia. For example, Sophianic Wisdom refers to the realm of divine action upon and through the psyche, to prompt it towards individuation and self–realization.

Superego The term introduced by Freud to designate the inner moral authority, or ethical complex, which monitors individual behaviour in such a way as to make it acceptable first to the parents and later society.

Synchronicity The coincidence in time of two or more causally unrelated events which have the same or similar meaning. In synchronicity, phenomena exist which are unable to be explained causally. The metaphors of synchronicity are those of harmony and correspondence. They cannot be grasped through empirical observation or measurement but are apprehended phenomenologically.

Ta'wil Meaning 'to bring back', it refers data to their origin, to their archetype, to their donor. It is a faculty of perception, specifically harmonic perception, which "presupposes the super-position of worlds and interworlds, as the correlative basis for a plurality of meanings in the same text" (Corbin). It refers to the capacity to hear and perceive on several levels simultaneously.

Trickster Otherwise known as the God Hermes, this is an archetype found universally in the mythologies of many peoples. The Trickster has a long association with the marketplace, trickery, boundaries, crossroads, heroic exploits, transformation and communications.

Unus Mundus For Jung, this term refers to an indivisible continuum of "psychoid events".

Uroborus The ancient symbol of a serpent bent in a circle and biting its own tail: considered by Erich Neumann (1954) to represent the primordial Self out of which ego-consciousness is born.

Notes

Foreword

1 Sir Arthur Conan Doyle, *A Study in Scarlet and the Sign of Four*. (New York: Dover Thrift edition, 2003), p.29.

2 Lord Alfred Douglas, "Two Loves", Reprinted from *The Chameleon*, December, 1894, accessed April 16, 2013, from: http://law2.umkc.edu/faculty/projects/trials/wilde/poemsofdouglas.htm.

Introduction

1 Billy Graham, *World Aflame* (United Kingdom: World's Work: Kingswood, 1965).

2 Rachel Carson, *Silent Spring* (United States: Houghton Mifflin, 1962).

3 See Tariq Ali, *The Clash of Fundamentalisms: Crusades, Jihads and Modernity* (United Kingdom: Verso, 2002).

4 Richard Dawkins, *The God Delusion* (London: Bantam Press, 2006).

5 Philip Wheelwright, *Heraclitus* (Princeton, N.J: Princeton University Press, 1959), Fragment 42.

6 See J. Douglas Porteous, *Landscapes of the Mind – Worlds of Sense and Metaphor* (University of Toronto Press, 1990), 4.

7 Belden C. Lane, *Landscapes of the Sacred – Geography and Narrative in American Spirituality* (New York: Paulist Press, 1988).

8 Barry Lopez, Arctic Dreams – *Imagination and Desire in a Northern Landscape* (London: The Harvill Press, 1998), 256-7.

9 See Denis Cosgrove, *Social and Symbolic Landscape* (London & Sydney, Croom Helm, 1984), 35. See also Donald Meinig ed., *The Interpretation of Ordinary Landscapes* (Oxford University Press, 1979), 6.

10 Theodore Roszak, *The Voice of the Earth* (New York: Simon & Schuster, 1992), 138.

11 Thomas Berry, *The Dream of the Earth* (San Francisco: Sierra Club, 1988), 149.

12 Eric Davis, *Techgnosis – Myth, Magic and Mysticism in the Age of Information* (London: Serpents Tail, 1999), 15-16.

13 Edward C. Whitmont, *Return of the Goddess* (New York: Crossroad Pub. Co.,1984), vii-viii.

14 Henry Corbin, *Spiritual Body and Celestial Earth – From Mazdean Iran to Shi'ite Iran* (New Jersey: Princeton University Press, Bollingen Series XCI: 2, 1989 edition), 30.

Spirituality Comes of Age

1 See *The Press*, Christchurch, New Zealand, March 12, 2010.

2 Richard Dawkins, *The God Delusion* (London: Bantam Press, 2006), 19.

3 See Walter Principe, 'Toward Defining Spirituality', *Studies in Religion* v.12, no.2 (1983),127-141., and Donald Evans, *Spirituality and Human Nature* (State University of New York, 1993), 1.

4 Peter H. Van Ness, *Spirituality, Diversion, and Decadence* (State University of New York, 1992), 12.

5 See Peter H. Van Ness, 'Bonhoeffer, Nietzsche, and Secular Spirituality', *Encounter: Creative Theological Scholarship* v.52, no. 4. Autumn (1991), 327-341. Also John L.. Elias, 'The Return of Spirituality: Contrasting Interpretations', *Religious Education* v. 86, no.3 (1991), 455-466. See also Jon Alexander, 'What Do Recent Writers Mean by Spirituality?', *Spirituality Today* v. 32, no. 3. Sept (1980), 247-256.

6 See Peter H. Van Ness (1991) *Spirituality, Diversion, and Decadence*, 327-328, 330; John Elias (1991) 'The Return of Spirituality: Contrasting Interpretations', 456-8; Jon Alexander (1980) 'What Do Recent Writers Mean by Spirituality?' 250-254.

7 Steven G. Smith *The Concept of the Spiritual* (Philadelphia: Temple University Press, 1988), 21.

8 For a humanist and premodern view of spirituality see Donald Evans, *Spirituality and Human Nature* (Albany: State University of New York Press, 1993), viii.

9 Steven G. Smith (1988) *The Concept of the Spiritual*, 21-22.

10 Ibid, 22.

11 Ibid, 23.

12 Ibid, 25. Note: Leibniz and Berkeley tried to remove the embarrassment by deriving the appearances of matter from spiritual substance, while Hume and Kant tried to resolve the problem by rejecting the notion of spiritual substance. This was to make the status of soul more mysterious than ever.

13 Ibid, 26.

14 Ibid, 29.

15 Ibid, 36.

16 Ibid, 36.

17 Ibid, 37.

18 Ibid, 37-38.

19 Ibid, 38.

20 Lloyd Geering, *Religious Trailblazers* (Wellington: St. Andrew's Trust for the Study of Religion and Society, 1992), 26.

21 Ibid, 26.

22 James N. Lapsley (1990) 'Spirit and Self', *Pastoral Psychology*, v.38 (3), Spring (1990), 136.

23 Ibid, 135-7.

24 Ibid, 135-7.

25 Donald Evans (1993) *Spirituality and Human Nature*, 102.

26 Philip Simpson interview, 'Exploring the Gaia Hypothesis' in *Nga Kaitiaki*, no. 21. August/ September (1989), 10.

27 Jon Alexander (1980) 'What Do Recent Writers Mean by Spirituality?', 247.

28 John L. Elias (1991) 'The Return of Spirituality: Contrasting Interpretations', 457.

29 Cf. Walter Principe (1983) 'Toward Defining Spirituality', 139.

30 Peter H. Van Ness (1991) 'Bonhoeffer, Nietzsche and Secular Spirituality', 331.

31 See Dietrich Bonhoeffer, *Letters and Papers from Prison*, trans. Reginald Fuller et al, ed. Eberhard Bethge, rev. ed. (New York: Macmillan Company, 1972), 341. Note: Nevertheless,"God is the beyond in the midst of our life", 282.

32 Ibid, 337.

33 Ibid, 338.

34 Ibid, 339.

35 Simone de Beauvoir, *The Second Sex* (London: New English Library, 1970), 352.

36 Merlin Stone, *When God Was a Woman* (New York: Harvest/Harcourt Brace Jovanovich, 1976).

37 See Changing of the Gods – Feminism and the End of Traditional Religions (Boston:Beacon Press, 1979), 5.

38 Mary Daly, *Beyond God the Father –Toward a Philosophy of Women's Liberation* (Boston: Beacon Press, 1973); *Gyn/Ecology – The Metaethics of Radical Feminism* (Boston: Beacon Press, 1978); *Pure Lust – Elemental Feminist Philosophy* (London: The Women's Press, 1984).

39 Irshad Manji, The Trouble With Islam: A Muslim's Call for Reform in Her Faith (Canada: Random House, 2003).

40 Carol P. Christ, *She Who Changes – Re-imagining the Divine in the World* (New York: Palgrave MacMillan, 2003).

41 Ellen Leonard, 'Experience as a source for theology: A Canadian and feminist perspective', *Studies in Religion* v.19, no.2 (1990), 146.

42 See Rosemary Radford Ruether, *New Women, New Earth* (New York: Seabury, 1975) and 'Ecology and Human Liberation: A Conflict between the Theology of History and the Theology of Nature?' in *To Change the World: Christology and Cultural Criticism* (New York: Crossroad, 1981), 57-70. See also Marsha Hewitt, 'Women, Nature and Power; Emancipatory Themes in Critical Theory and Feminist Theology', *Studies in Religion* v.20, no.3 (1991), 271.

43 See Merlin Stone, *When God Was a Woman* (1976); William G. Dever, 'Women's popular religion, suppressed in the Bible, now revealed by archaeology', *Biblical Archaeology Review*, v.17, no.2 (1991), 64-65; Marija Gimbutas, *The Gods and Goddesses of Old Europe* (London: Thames and Hudson, 1974); – *Myths, Legends and Cult Images* (Berkeley: University of California Press, 1974); Charlene Spretnak, ed., *The Politics of Women's Spirituality: Essays on the Rise of Spiritual Power Within the Feminist Movement* (Garden City, N.Y: Anchor Press / Doubleday, 1982).

44 Marsha Hewitt (1991) 'Women, Nature and Power; Emancipatory Themes in Critical Theory and Feminist Theology', 157.

45 See Sally Mcfague, *Models of God: Theology for an Ecological, Nuclear Age* (Philadelphia: Fortress Press, 1987); Rosemary Radford Ruether, *New Women , New Earth* (New York: Seabury, 1975); Susan Griffin, *Woman and Nature: the Roaring Inside Her* (New York: Harper & Row, 1978); Carolyn Merchant, *The Death of Nature: Women, Ecology, and the Scientific Revolution* (New York: Harper & Row, 1980);

Charlene Spretnak, *The Spiritual Dimension of Green Politics* (Santa Fe: N.M. Bear & Co, 1986); Carol P. Christ, *She Who Changes – Re-Imagining the Divine in the World* (2003).

46 See Thomas Berry, *The Dream of the Earth* (San Francisco: Sierra Club, 1988) ,160-161.

47 Ariel Salleh, 'The Ecofeminism/Deep Ecology Debate: A Reply to Patriarchal Reason', *Environmental Ethics* v.14, no.3 (1992), 215.

48 Wayne Teasdale, 'Nature-Mysticism as the Basis of Eco-Spirituality', *Studies in Formative Spirituality*, v.12, no.2 (1991), 218-219. Note: Teasdale refers to Evelyn Underhill's *Mysticism: A Study in the Nature and Development of Man's Spiritual Consciousness* (New York: Dutton, 1961), 234.

49 Ibid, 230.

50 Stuart Kauffman, 'God of Creativity', *New Scientist*, 10 May (2008), 52. See reference to Stuart Kauffman, *Re-inventing the Sacred: A New View of Science, Reason and Religion* (New York: Basic Books, 2008).

51 For example see Humberto R. Maturana and Francisco J. Varela, *The Tree of Knowledge – The Biological Roots of Human Understanding* (Boston: New Science Library, 1987), 241.

52 David Bohm, 'Postmodern Science and a Postmodern World' in: David Ray Griffin ed., *The Re-enchantment of Science – Postmodern Proposals* (State University of New York Press, 1988), 57-68

53 Ibid, 68.

54 David Bohm, *Wholeness and the Implicate Order* (London: Routledge & Kegan Paul, 1981).

55 Roger Sperry, 'Changed Concepts of Brain and Consciousness: Some Value Implications', *Zygon* v.20. no.1 (1985), 41-57.

56 Ibid, 56.

57 John Hitchcock, *The Web of the Universe: Jung, the "New Physics" and Human Spirituality* (New York: Paulist Press, 1991), 45.

58 Ibid, 45.

59 Behaviourism is a school of psychology that regards objective observable aspects of the behaviour of organisms as the only valid subject of study; cf. *Collins English Dictionary*, eds., Hanks, P., Long, T.H., Urdang, L. (London: Collins, 1977),132. See also; *A Dictionary of Philosophy,* eds., Speake, J., Isaacs, A. (London: Pan Books, 1979), 37; *The Oxford Companion to the Mind,* ed., Richard L. Gregory (Oxford University Press, 1987), 71-74 ; *The Oxford Companion to Philosophy,* ed., Ted Honderich (Oxford University Press, 1995), 81-2.

60 J.B. Priestly, *Sunday Telegraph.* See review C.G. Jung, *Memories, Dreams, Reflections* (Great Britain: Fount Paperbacks, 1977. First published, 1961)

61 Donald Broadribb, *The Mystical Chorus – Jung and the Religious Dimension* (Australia: Millenium Books, 1995), 127.

62 John Pennachio, 'Gnostic Illumination and Carl Jung's Individuation', *Journal of Religion and Health* v.31, no.3, Fall (1992), 245.

63 Curtis D. Smith, 'Psychological Ultimacy: Jung and the Human Basis of Religious Meaning', *Religious Humanism* v.25, no.4 (1991), 174.

64 Ibid, 178.

65 R. Melvin Keiser, 'Postcritical Religion and the Latent Freud', *Zygon* v.25. no.4 (1990), 433.

66 Karen Armstrong, *A History of God* (London: Mandarin Paperbacks, 1994), 115.

67 Hippolytus, *Heresies* 8.15. 1-2 as cited in Armstrong, Ibid, 114.

68 Karen Armstrong (1994) *A History of God*, 287.

69 Ibid, 275.

70 Donald Broadribb (1995) *The Mystical Chorus*,122.

71 Karen Armstrong (1994) *A History of God*, 244.

72 Ibid, 253.

73 Ibid, 245.

74 James Hillman, *ReVisioning Psychology* (New York:Harper & Row Publishers, 1975), xi.

75 Ibid, xi.

76 Ibid, xi. & 231 notes. See reference to Philip Wheelwright, *Heraclitus* (Princeton, NJ:Princeton University Press, 1959), Fragment 42.

77 Thomas Moore(ed.) & James Hillman, *The Essential James Hillman – A Blue Fire* (London: Routledge, 1990), 20. Note: Hillman's books tend to use 'soul' rather than 'psyche'. 'Soul' is the dominant theme in his entire work.

78 James W. Heisig, *Imago Dei – A Study of C.G. Jung's Psychology of Religion* (London: Associated University Presses, 1979), 159-160.

79 James Hillman, *Archetypal Psychology – A Brief Account* (Dallas: Spring Publications, Inc. 1993), 16.

80 Lloyd Geering (1992) *Religious Trailblazers*, 30.

81 C.G. Jung, 'Mind and Earth', in: *The Collected Works of C.G. Jung*,(1953-78). vol.10, para. 53.

82 See James W. Heisig (1979) *Imago Dei – A Study of C.G. Jung's Psychology of Religion,* 137.

83 James Hillman, (1993) *Archetypal Psychology*, 2.

84 Ibid, 1.

85 Ibid, 3.

86 Ibid, 3.

87 Ibid, 4.

88 See Donald Broadribb (1995) *The Mystical Chorus*, 248.

89 C.G. Jung , 'Mysterium Conjunctionis' in: *The Collected Works of C.G. Jung*, vol.14: paras, 552 and 788.

90 Curtis D. Smith, 'Psychological Ultimacy: Jung and the Human Basis of Religious Meaning', *Religious Humanism*, v.25, no.4 (1991), 177.

91 Lawrence W. Jaffe, *Liberating the Heart* (Toronto: Inner City Books, 1990), 73; see also Ferne Jensen, (ed.), *C.G. Jung, Emma Jung and Toni Wolff* (San Francisco: Analytical Psychology Club of San Francisco, 1982), 62 & 65.

92 C.G. Jung, *The Collected Works of C.G. Jung*, vol.12. para.9. See also *The Collected Works of C.G. Jung*, vol.11, 'Psychology and Religion: West and East'.

93 James W. Heisig (1979) *Imago Dei*, 138-9.

94 John P. Dourley, 'The Challenge of Jung's Psychology for the Study of Religion', *Studies in Religion*, v.18, no.3 (1989), 302-3.

95 Ibid, 310.

96 Ibid, 297 & 310. See also Dourley, 'The Jung, Buber, White Exchanges: Exercises in Futility', *Studies in Religion*, vol.20. pt.3.(1991), 299-309; 'Some Implications of Jung's Understanding of Mysticism', *Toronto Journal of Theology*, vol.6. pt.1, (1990), 15-26.

97 Jung states; "Religious experience is absolute, it cannot be disputed. You can only say that you have never had such an experience, whereupon your opponent will reply: 'Sorry, I have.' And there your discussion will come to an end." (C.G. Jung (1953-78). *The Collected Works of C.G. Jung*, (London: Routledge & Kegan Paul), vol.7, para 167; see also Anthony Stevens (1986) 'Thoughts on the Psychobiology of Religion and the Neurobiology of Archetypal Experience', *Zygon*, v. 21. no.1 (1986), 21.

98 Jung, Ibid, para 110; cf Stevens, Ibid, 20.

99 James W. Heisig (1979) *Imago Dei*, 134.

100 Curtis D. Smith, 'Psychological Ultimacy: Jung and the Human Basis of Religious Meaning', *Religious Humanism* v.25, no.4(1991), 174.

101 Ibid, 178-9.

102 John Pennachio, 'Gnostic Inner Illumination and Carl Jung's Individuation', *Journal of Religion and Health* v.31, no.3, Fall (1992), 238.

103 Ibid, 239. See also Elaine Pagels, *The Gnostic Gospels* (New York: Vintage, 1979).

104 Ibid, 245.

105 John P. Dourley (1989) 'The Challenge of Jung's Psychology for the Study of Religion', 297-311. Dourley argues that "possibly the most significant implication of Jung's thought for religious studies and theology remains his challenge to those who engage in either to experience individually and immediately the energies that birth the material with which they deal. In doing so Jung's approach could cultivate a newer and more extended empathy in the study of religion itself through the transformation of the consciousness of those who engage in it" (p.311).

Landscapes of Geography

1 Denis E. Cosgrove, *Social and Symbolic Landscape* (Croom Helm, London & Sydney, 1984), 261.

2 Ibid, 260-261.

3 Carl Sauer, (1925) 'The Morphology of Landscape' (University of California Publications in Geography 2), 19-54. See Peter Jackson, (1989) *Maps of Meaning – An Introduction to Cultural Geography* (London: Unwin Hyman), 13. 'Landscape' was defined as 'the unit concept of geography', a 'peculiarly geographic association of facts'. Genetic morphology was used in historical, cultural and physical geography, all of which have employed the landscape concept extensively.

4 Denis E. Cosgrove (1984) *Social and Symbolic Landscape*, 17. Cosgrove refers to Carl Sauer's 1926 printing of '*The Morphology of Landscape*' reprinted in J. Leighly (ed.), *Land and Life: Selections from the Writings of Carl Ortwin Sauer* (University of California Press, 1963). Cosgrove argues that "Carl Sauer (1926) … acknowledges … that there remains an aspect of meaning in landscape which lies 'beyond science', the understanding of which cannot be reduced to formal processes"(p.17).

5 Ibid, 17-18. Peter Jackson (1989) *Maps of Meaning*, is in agreement. According to Jackson, cultural geographers who followed Sauer adopted an unnecessarily truncated view of their subject and confined themselves to mapping the distribution of culture traits in the landscape. (p.19). Jackson argues that an extreme version of this disciplinary myopia is found in Wagner and Mikesell's introduction to their very influential *Readings in Cultural Geography* (1962). Since the 1970s, this Saurian view of cultural geography has been extended in new directions.

6 Cosgrove (1984)*Social and Symbolic Landscape*, 11.

7 Most notable in this regard was Ley and Samuels (eds.) *Humanistic Geography* (London: Croom Helm, 1978).

8 Jackson (1989) *Maps of Meaning*, 20.

9 J. Douglas Porteous, *Landscapes of the Mind – Worlds of Sense and Metaphor* (University of Toronto Press, 1990), 8.

10 See Yi-Fu Tuan, *Space and Place* (University of Minnesota Press, 1977); 'Sign and Metaphor', *Annals of the Association of American Geographers*, 68, (1978), 362-72.

11 J. Douglas Porteous (1990) *Landscapes of the Mind*, 9. See also D.C.D. Pocock, 'Place and the Novelist', *Transactions, Institute of British Geographers* NS 6, (1981), 337-47.

12 See Peter Jackson (1989) *Maps of Meaning*, 20.   As Jackson points out, geographers have recently shown an interest in literary analysis and other conceptions of geography besides traditional forms of landscape interpretation. See: E. Soja, 'The Postmodernization of Geography: a Review', *Annals, Association of American Geographers,* 77, (1987), 289-94; S.J. Daniels, 'Arguments for a Humanistic Geography' in: R.J. Johnson (ed.), *The Future of Geography* (London: Methuen, 1985), 143-58; P. Lewis, 'Beyond Description', *Annals, Association of American Geographers* 75, (1985), 465-77; D. Gregory, 'A Real Differentiation and Post-modern Human Geography' in: D. Gregory & R. Walford (eds.), *New Horizons in Human Geography* (London: Macmillan, 1989); and D. Gregoru & D. Ley, 'Culture's Geographies', *Society and Space* 6, (1988), 115–16. See also: Denis Cosgrove, 'Environmental Thought and Action: Pre-modern and Post-modern', *Transactions of the Institute of British Geographers*, v.15 (1990), 344-358; Peter Bishop, 'Rhetoric, Memory, and Power: Depth Psychology and Postmodern Geography', *Environmental and Planning D: Society and Space*, vol.10 (1992), 5-22.; D. Matless, 'An Occasion for Geography: Landscape, Representation, and Foucault's Corpus', *Environment and Planning D: Society and Space*, v.10 (1992), 41-56.

13 Yi-Fu Tuan, 'Language and the Making of Place: A Narrative-Descriptive Approach', *Annals of the Association of American Geographers* v.81, no.4 (1991), 694.

14 Jackson(1989) *Maps of Meaning*, 181.

15 Ibid, 177.

16 Barry Lopez, *Arctic Dreams – Imagination and Desire in a Northern Landscape* (London: The Harvill Press, 1998), 256.

17 See Te Maire Tau, 'Ngai Tahu and the Canterbury Landscape – A Broad Context' in: Cookson, John & Dunstall, Graeme (eds.), *Southern Capital Christchurch – Towards a City Biography 1850- 2000* (Canterbury University Press, 2000) 41-60; Geoff Park, *Nga Uruora The Groves of Life – Ecology & History in a New Zealand Landscape* (Wellington: Victoria University Press, 1995); Trudie McNaughton, *Countless Signs – The New Zealand Landscape in Literature* (New Zealand: Reed Methuen, 1986); Harry C. Evison, *Te Wai Pounamu The Greenstone Island – A History of the Southern Maori during the European Colonization of New Zealand* (Christchurch: Aoraki Press, 1993); Hong-Key Yoon, *Maori Mind, Maori Land* (Berne & New York: Eratosthene Interdisciplinary Series, Peter Lang, 1986); Philip Temple (ed.), *Lake, Mountain, Tree: An Anthology of Writings on New Zealand Nature and Landscape* (New Zealand: Godwit, 1998).

18 Cosgrove(1984) *Social and Symbolic Landscape*, 13.

19 Yi-Fu Tuan, 'Language and the Making of Place: A Narrative-Descriptive Approach', *Annals of the Association of American Geographers*, v.81, 4 (1991)', 697.

20 David Lowenthal, 'Geography, Experience, and Imagination: Towards a Geographical Epistemology', *Annals of the Association of American Geographers,* v. 51, no.3, September (1961), 251.

21 Cosgrove (1984) *Social and Symbolic Landscape*, 269.

22 Martin Heidegger, *On the Way to Language*, Trans. Peter Hertz (San Francisco: Harper & Row, 1971), 63.

23 Saroj Chawla, 'Linguistic and Philosophical Roots of Our Environmental Crisis', *Environmental Ethics*, v.13, no.3 (1991), 253.

24 Ibid, 262.

25 Sallie B. King, 'Two Epistemological Models for the Interpretation of Mysticism', *Journal of American Academy of Religion*, LVI / 2, Summer (1988), 266.

26 Ibid.

27 Lopez (1998) *Arctic Dreams*, 275.

28 Ibid, 313-4.

29 Takeshi Yamagishi, 'Landscape and the Human being', *Human Studies,* 15, (1992).

30 See Cosgrove (1984) *Social and Symbolic Landscape.*

31 Ibid, 15.

32 J. Douglas Porteous, *Landscapes of the Mind – Worlds of Sense and Metaphor* (University of Toronto Press, 1990), 4.

33 Lopez (1998) *Arctic Dreams*, 257.

34 Roger S. Ulrich, 'Aesthetic and Affective Response to Natural Environment', *Behaviour and the Natural Environment*, Irwin Altman and Joachim F. Wohlwill, eds., (Vol. 6 of *Human Behaviour and Environment*, Plenium Press, New York, 1983), 85.

35 Ibid, 89.

36 Ibid, 110.

37 Ibid, 109.

38 Ibid, 117.

39 See for example Harry Heft and Joachim F. Wohlwill, 'Environmental Cognition in Children' in: Daniel Stokols and Irwin Altman (eds.), *Handbook of Environmental Psychology* (Malabar Florida: Krieger Publishing Co., 1991), 175-203; Rachel Sebba, 'The Landscapes of Childhood – The Reflection of Childhood's Environment in Adult Memories and in Children's Attitudes', *Environment and Behavior* Vol.23, no.4, July (1991), 395-422. As Sebba finds from research(p.395), "the environment which an adult remembers as significant in childhood was personally experienced without adult mediation and the related experiences were only found in childhood. The child's sensory perception remains in adult memory as a central childhood experience because its relative importance is at its peak at this stage of life. The adult recalls the natural environment due to qualities that are substantially different from those of the man-made environment".

40 Cf. William Barrett, *Irrational Man – A Study in Existential Philosophy* (London: Heinemann, 1967).

41 Yi-Fu Tuan, 'Geography, Phenomenology, and the Study of Human Nature', *Canadian Geographer*, v.15 (3), (1971), 184.

42 Ibid, 183.

43 Ibid.

44 Ibid, 191.

45 See Cosgrove(1984) *Social and Symbolic Landscape*, 19.

46 Mark Johnson, The Body in the Mind – The Bodily Basis of Meaning, Imagination and Reason (University of Chicago Press, 1987), 205.

47 Takeshi Yamagishi, 'Landscape and the Human being', *Human Studies,* 15 (1992), 101.

48 Ibid, 97.

49 Ibid, 106.

50 Ibid, 113.

51 Edmunds V. Bunkse, 'Saint-Exupery's Geography Lesson: Art and Science in the Creation and Cultivation of Landscape Values', *Annals of the Association of American Geographers*, v.80 (1990), 96-97.

52 Ibid, 97-98.

53 Ibid, 100.

54 Ibid.

55 Ibid, 101.

56 Ibid, 102.

57 Ibid.

58 Ibid, 106.

59 Ibid, 104.

60 Lopez (1989) *Arctic Dreams*, 199-200.

61 Ibid, 200.

62 Cindy Katz and Andrew Kirby, 'In the Nature of Things: The Environment and Everyday Life', *Transactions – Institute of British Geographers,* v.16, no. 3 (1991), 259.

63 Ibid, 261.

64 Ibid, 262-263.

65 Ibid, 263.

66 Ibid, 265.

67 Mark Johnson, *The Body in the Mind – The Bodily Basis of Meaning, Imagination and Reason* (University of Chicago Press, 1987), x.

68 Ibid, 207.

69 Ibid, 212.

70 Humberto R. Maturana and Francisco J. Varela, *The Tree of Knowledge – The Biological Roots of Human Understanding* (New Science Library, Shambhala Publications, Inc. 1987), 214.

71 Ibid, 241.

72 Steve Odin, 'The Japanese Concept of Nature in Relation to the Environmental Ethics and Conservation Aesthetics of Aldo Leopold', *Environmental Ethics,* v.13, no. 4 (1991), 350.

73 Ibid, 346; see also Aldo Leopold, *A Sand Country Almanac: With Essays on Conservation from Round River* (N.Y: Ballantine Books, 1966).

74 J. Baird Callicott and Roger T. Ames (eds.) *Nature in Asian Traditions of Thought – Essays in Environmental Philosophy* (State University of New York, 1989), 58.

75 Ted Honderich (ed.), *The Oxford Companion to Philosophy*, (Oxford University Press, 1995), 909-910.

76 Steve Odin, 'The Japanese Concept of Nature in Relation to the Environmental Ethics and Conservation Aesthetics of Aldo Leopold', 350.

77 Ibid, 360.

78 Henryk Skolimowski, *The Participatory Mind – A New Theory of Knowledge and of the Universe* (Arkana, Penguin Group, 1994), xviii-xix.

79 Ibid, xvii.

80 Lopez (1998) *Arctic Dreams*, 274.

81 Buber's *I and Thou* (*Ich und Du*) was first published in German in 1923 and translated into English in 1937. The edition referred to here is Martin Buber, *I and Thou,* trans. W. Kaufmann (Edinburgh: T & T Clark, 1970).

82 Ibid, 5.

83 Ibid, 54.

84 Maurice Friedman, *Martin Buber – The Life of Dialogue* (N.Y: Harper & Row, 1960), 57.

85 Ibid.

86 Lloyd Geering, *The World of Relation – An Introduction to Martin Buber's I and Thou* (New Zealand: Victoria University Press, 1983), 16.

87 Ibid, 20.

88 Buber (1970) *I and Thou*, 84.

89 Geering (1983) *The World of Relation*, 27.

90 See Friedman (1960) *Martin Buber*, 73-76.

91 Bunkse (1990) 'Saint-Exupery's Geography Lesson', 100-102.

92 Ibid, 106. Bunkse states: "What is valuable is a certain ordering of things. Civilisation is an invisible tie, because it has to do not with things but with the invisible ties that join one thing to another in a particular way."

93 See Cindy Katz and Andrew Kirby (1991) 'In the Nature of Things', 259-265.

94 Lopez (1998) *Arctic Dreams*, 228.

95 Lily Kong, 'Geography and Religion: Trends and Prospects', *Progress in Human Geography,* v.14 (1990), 355-371. Kong gives a succinct description of historical development of geography and religion – delineating 'religious geography', 'ecclesiastical geography' and 'biblical geography' and an 'environmentally deterministic' approach all prior to the twentieth century. For Kong the development of the geography of religion in the twentieth century can be characterised as "undergoing a thesis – antithesis – synthesis cycle" (p. 358). Initially focus has been on religion as determined by its

environment. In the second stage of antithesis, the geography of religion has moved to a focus on the moulding influence of religion on its environment .(p.359).

96 C.J. Glacken, *Traces on the Rhodian Shore* (CA: University of California Press, 1967), 35.

97 Yi-Fu Tuan, 'Humanistic Geography', *Annals of the Association of American Geographers*, 66, (1976), 271.

98 M. Buttner, 'Survey Article on the History and Philosophy of the Geography of Religion in Germany', *Religion*, v.86 (1980), 100-104.

99 David E. Sopher, 'Geography and Religions', *Progress in Human Geography,* v.5 (1981), 510.

100 Erich Isaac, 'The Act and the Covenant: The Impact of Religion on the Landscape', *Landscape* 11, (1962), 12-17.

101 Sopher, 'Geography and Religions', *Progress in Human Geography*, v.5 (1981), 519.

102 Lily Kong, 'Geography and Religion: Trends and Prospects', *Progress in Human Geography,* v.14 (1990), 355-371.

103 Ibid, 359.

104 Ibid, 367.

105 A. Cooper, 'New Directions in the Geography of Religion', *Area*, v.24, no.2 (1992) 123.

106 J. Kay, 'Human Dominion over Nature in the Hebrew Bible', *Annals of the Association of American Geographers,* v.79 (1989), 214-232.

107 See S. Bhardwaj, *Sentimental Journeys: Thoughts on the Nature of Pilgrimage.* Conference paper, Department of Geography, Kent State University, Ohio, 1990.

108 Cooper (1992) 'New Directions', 127.

109 Peter Bishop, *The Myth of Shangri-La – Tibet, Travel Writing and the Western Creation of Sacred Landscape* (University of California Press, 1989).

110 Ibid, vii.

111 Ibid.

112 Ibid, 9.

113 Ibid, 18.

114 Ibid, 18. Bishop states that "the aim is not to achieve a theoretical reconciliation but to open up a field of ideas that has both the width and the capacity to endure contradictions".

115 Ibid, 19.

116 Ibid, 251.

Imaginal-Visionary Landsacpes

1 The term *imaginal* means relating to, or resembling an image (Cf. *Collins English Dictionary,* London (1979), 731). The term is used most notably by such thinkers as Henry Corbin and Gilbert Durand.

2 Gilbert Durand 'Exploration of the Imaginal', *Spring* (1971), 88.

3 John Kirtland Wright, 'Terrae Incognitae: The Place of the Imagination in Geography', *Annals, Association of American Geographers*, vol.37 (1947), 15.

4 David Lowenthal, 'Geography, Experience, and Imagination: Towards a Geographical Epistemology', *Annals of the Association of American Geographers*, v. 51, no.3, September (1961), 260.

5 David Lowenthal and Martyn J. Bowden (eds.), *Geographies of the Mind – Essays in Historical Geosophy* (Oxford University Press, 1975), 3.

6 Yi-Fu Tuan, 'Geography, Phenomenology, and the Study of Human Nature', *Canadian Geographer*, v.15 (1971), 181.

7 See Denis Cosgrove, *Social and Symbolic Landscape* (Croom Helm, London & Sydney, 1984), 35. See also Donald Meinig (ed.), *The Interpretation of Ordinary Landscapes* (Oxford University Press, 1979) 6. Note: Both refer to the seminal importance of the writings of J.B. Jackson and to his journal *Landscape*.

8 Hong-Key Yoon, 'On Geomentality', *Geo Journal*, v.25, no.4 (1991), 392.

9 Ibid, 387.

10 D. Matless, 'An Occasion for Geography: Landscape, Representation, and Foucault's Corpus', *Environment and Planning D: Society and Space*, v.10 (1992), 44-45.

11 Denis Cosgrove, 'Environmental Thought and Action: Pre-modern and Post-modern', *Transactions of the Institute of British Geographers*, v.15 (1990), 345.

12 Ibid, 352.

13 Ibid, 353.

14 Ibid, 345.

15 K. Harries, 'Metaphor and Transcendence' in: S. Sacks (ed.), *On Metaphor* (Chicago: Chicago University Press, 1978), 72.

16 Cosgrove(1990) 'Environmental Thought and Action', 345.

17 Ibid, 345.

18 Ibid, 357.

19 Peter Bishop, 'Rhetoric, Memory and Power: Depth Psychology and Postmodern Geography', *Environmental and Planning D: Society and Space,* v.10 (1992), 5.

20 See Lynn White Jr., 'The Historical Roots of Our Ecological Crisis', *Science,* 155, March (1967), no. 3767, pp. 1203-1207; Yi-Fu Tuan, 'Geopiety: A Theme in Man's Attachment to Nature and Place' in: David Lowenthal and Martin J. Bowden, (eds.), *Geographies of the Mind: Essays in Historical Geography in Honor of John Kirkland Wright* (N.Y: Oxford University Press, 1976), 13-14; Yi-Fu Tuan, 'Sacred Space: Explorations of an Idea' in: K. Butzer (ed.), *Dimensions of Human Geography* (Chicago: University of Chicago Press, 1978), 87-100; Belden C. Lane, *Landscapes of the Sacred -- Geography and Narrative in American Spirituality* (New York/Mahwah: Paulist Press, 1988); Peter Bishop, *The Myth of Shangri-La – Tibet, Travel Writing and the Western Creation of Sacred Landscape* (University of California Press, 1989): William Irwin Thompson, *Imaginary Landscape: Making Worlds of Myth and Science* (New York: St Martin's Press, 1989).

21 See James G. Cowan, 'Aboriginal Solitude', *Parabola Magazine,* vol.17, no. 1 (1992), 62-67.

22 Wendell, C, Bean & William G. Doty (eds.), *Myths, Rites, Symbols: A Mircea Eliade Reader* (New York: Harper & Row, 1975), I, 128.

23 Andree Collard and Joyce Contrucci, *Man's Violence Against Animals and the Earth* (Indiana University Press, 1989), 8.

24 Ibid, 7.

25 H. and H.A. Frankfort, John A. Wilson, Thorkild Jacobsen and William A. Irwin, *The Intellectual Adventure of Ancient Man – An Essay on Speculative Thought in the Ancient Near East* (Chicago: University of Chicago Press, 1946), 4-7.

26 C.M.G. Gudgeon, 'Mana Tangata'. *The Journal of Polynesian Society,* v.14, no.54 (1905), 57. Cf. Hong-Key Yoon, *Maori Mind, Maori Land*, Eratosthene Interdisciplinary Series (Bern & New York: Peter Lang, 1986), 58.

27 William Martin, *The Taranaki Question* (London: W.H. Dalton, 1961), 39. Cf. Hong-Key Yoon(1986) *Maori Mind, Maori Land*, 57 & 59.

28 Elsdon Best, *The Maori* (Polynesian Society, Wellington (1941 [1924]) vol.1), 397.

29 Erich Isaac, 'Religion, Landscape and Space', *Landscape* v.9, no.2 (Winter, 1959-60), 14-15.

30 Ibid, 16-17.

31 Ibid, 17.

32 Yi-Fu Tuan, 'Sacred Space: Explorations of an Idea', in: K. Butzner (ed.), *Dimensions of Human Geography* (Chicago: University of Chicago Press, 1978), 86.

33 Ibid, 86.

34 Belden C. Lane, *Landscapes of the Sacred – Geography and Narrative in American Spirituality* (New York: Paulist Press, 1988), 189.

35 Samuel Terrien, *The Elusive Presence: The Heart of Biblical Theology* (San Francisco: Harper & Row, 1978).

36 Lane (1988) *Landscapes of the Sacred,* 18.

37 Jeanne Kay, 'Human Dominion over Nature in the Hebrew Bible', *Annals of the Association of American Geographers,* v. 79 (1989), 214ff.

38 Yi-Fu Tuan, 'Geopiety', 26.

39 Lane (1988) *Landscapes of the Sacred,* 187.

40 Ibid.,187- 188. Cf. *Confessions of St. Augustine,* X, viii, 5.

41 Ibid, 187-188.

42 Lane(1988) *Landscapes of the Sacred,* 19. See also: Walter Harrelson, *From Fertility Cult to Worship* (Garden City, New York: Doubleday & Co., 1969), especially Chapter One; Harvey Cox, *The Secular City* (New York: Macmillan, 1965), Chapter One; Walter Brueggemann, *The Land* (Philadelphia: Fortress Press, 1977), 184-5.

43 Yi-Fu Tuan, 'Geopiety', 26.

44 Geoff Park, *Nga Uruora – The Groves of Life* (Victoria University Press, 1995), 134.

45 Trudie McNaughton (ed.), *Countless Signs -- The New Zealand Landscape in Literature* (Auckland: Reed Methuen Ltd., 1986), 8.

46 Park (1995) *Nga Uruora*, 134-135.

47 Ibid, 134.

48 Letters from James and Hamilton McIlwrath (Canterbury: September 8, 1862 and December 1, 1863) to parents John and Jane Logan McIlwrath and brothers in County Down, Ireland.

49 McNaughton(1986) *Countless Signs*, 6-7.

50 Lynn White, Jr 'The Historical Roots of Our Ecological Crisis", *Science*, v.155, no. 3767 (10 March 1967), 1203-1207.

51 Ibid, 1205.

52 Ibid, 1206.

53 Ibid, 1207.

54 Peter Bishop, 'Note to the author', September, 2009.

55 Erich Isaac 'Religion, Landscape and Space', *Landscape*, v.9, no.2, Winter (1959-60),18.

56 Ibid.

57 Ibid.

58 Yi-Fu Tuan, 'Sacred Space: Explorations of an Idea' in: Butzer, K. (ed.), *Dimensions of Human Geography*, (Chicago: University of Chicago Press, 1978), 94.

59 Ibid, 98-99.

60 Lane(1988) *Landscapes of the Sacred*, 190-1.

61 Ibid.

62 Ibid.

63 Ibid, 191.

64 Cindy Katz and Andrew Kirby, 'In the Nature of Things: The Environment and Everyday Life', in: *Transactions – Institute of British Geographers*, v.16, no.3 (1991), 259-271.

65 William Irwin Thompson, *Imaginary Landscape: Making Worlds of Myth and Science* (New York: Saint Martin's Press, 1989),169.

66 Lynn Ross-Bryant, 'Of Nature and Texts: Nature and Religion in American Ecological Literature', *Anglican Theological Review*, v.73, no.1 (1991), 38.

67 Lopez, *Arctic Dreams*, xxvii.

68 Ibid, 228.

69 Ibid, xxii.

70 Ibid, 398-399.

71 Lynn Ross-Bryant, 'Of Nature and Texts: Nature and Religion in American Ecological Literature', 39.

72 Ibid, 39.

73 Ibid, 41.

74 Ibid, 49.

75 Lopez(1998) *Arctic Dreams*, 414.

76 P. Bishop, 'Rhetoric, Memory, and Power: Depth Psychology and Postmodern Geography', *Environment and Planning D: Society and Space*, v.10, no.1 (1992), 17.

77 William Irwin Thompson, *Imaginary Landscape: Making Worlds of Myth and Science*, 52.

78 Ibid, 130; see also 123.

79 Ibid, 131.

80 Ibid, 50-51.

81 Ibid, xviii.

82 Ibid, xix.

83 Ibid, 130.

84 Ibid, 84.

85 Ibid, 80.

86 Ibid, 83.

87 Ibid, 84.

88 Ibid, 83.

89 Ibid, 169.

Towards Archetypal Landscapes

1 David Harvey, The Condition of Postmodernity: An Enquiry into the Origins of Cultural Change (Cambridge: Basil Blackwell, 1989), 27.

2 Kevin J. Vanhoozer, 'Theology and the Condition of Postmodernity: A Report on Knowledge of God' in: Kevin J. Vanhoozer (ed.), *The Cambridge Companion to Postmodern Theology* (Cambridge: Cambridge University Press, 2003), 10.

3 Cf. Dan R. Stiver, 'Theological Method' in: *The Cambridge Companion to Postmodern Theology*, (Cambridge University Press, 2003),170-173.

4 Richard Bernstein, *Beyond Objectivism and Relativism: Science, Hermeneutics and Praxis* (Philadelphia: University of Pennsylvania Press, 1985), 8.

5 Graham Ward (ed.), *The Postmodern God – A Theological Reader* (Oxford: Blackwell Publishers, 1997), xxix.

6 David Ray Griffin, 'Reconstructive Theology' in: *The Cambridge Companion to Postmodern Theology* (2003), 92.

7 Timothy E. Eastman and Hank Keeton (eds.), *Physics and Whitehead: Quantum, Process and Experience*, SUNY Series in Constructive Postmodern Thought (State University of New York, 2004), 260.

8 David Bohm, 'Postmodern Science and a Postmodern World' in: David Ray Griffin, ed., *The Re-enchantment of Science* (State University of New York Press, 1988), 57-68.

9 Ibid, 61.

10 Griffin (1988) *The Re-enchantment of Science*, x-xi.

11 Bohm (1988) 'Postmodern Science and a Postmodern World', 60.

12 Walter Truett Anderson(ed.),*The Fontana Postmodern Reader* (London:Fontana Press, 1966), 8.

13 Vanhoozer (2003) *The Cambridge Companion to Postmodern Theology*, xiii-xiv.

14 Dan R. Stiver (2003) 'Theological Method' in: *The Cambridge Companion to Postmodern Theology*, 172-179.

15 Vanhoozer(2003) *The Cambridge Companion to Postmodern Theology*, 23.

16 Carol P. Christ, 'Rethinking Theology and Nature', in: Judith Plaskow and Carol P. Christ (eds.), *Weaving the Visions – New Patterns in Feminist Spirituality* (Harper: San Francisco, 1989), 314.

17 Frederick Mark Gedicks, 'Spirituality, Fundamentalism, Liberty: Religion at the End of Modernity', *De Paul Law Review*, (2005), Abstract. See 'Social Science Network': http://papers.ssrn.com/sol3/papers.cfm? abstract id=634262.

18 Gordon D. Kaufman, *In the Face of Mystery – A Constructive Theology* (Cambridge, Massachusetts: Harvard University Press, 1993), ix.

19 Ibid, 40.

20 Cf. Sheila Davaney (ed.), *Theology at the End of Modernity: Essays in Honor of Gordon D. Kaufman.* (Philadelphia: Trinity Press International, 1991).

21 Peter Bishop, 'Rhetoric, Memory and Power: Depth Psychology and Postmodern Geography', *Environmental and Planning D: Society and Space,* vol. 10 (1992), 5-22; Denis Cosgrove, 'Environmental Thought and Action: Pre-modern and Post-modern', *Transactions of the Institute of British Geographers*, v.15 (1990), 344-358.

22 Ibid, 10-11.

23 Ibid, 11.

24 C.G. Jung, 'Symbols of Transformation', in: *The Collected Works*, vol.5. para. 11-33.

25 Denis Cosgrove, 'Environmental Thought and Action: Pre-modern and Post-modern', 353.

26 Edward S. Casey, 'Jung and the Post-Modern Condition', *Spring* (1987), 100-101.

27 Ibid, 105.

28 Ibid.

29 James Hillman, *Re-Visioning Psychology* (New York: Harper & Row, 1975), xiii.

30 Ibid, xii.

31 James Hillman, *Archetypal Psychology – A Brief Account* (Dallas: Spring Publications,Inc. 993), 2.

32 Ibid, 4.

33 Carl Jung, 'Two Essays in Archetypal Psychology', in: *Collected Works*, vol. 7, 188.

34 Richard Noll, The Jung Cult: *Origins of a Charismatic Movement* (Princeton University Press, 1994); *The Aryan Christ: The Secret Life of Carl Jung* (New York: Random House, 1997).

35 Anthony Stevens, 'Critical Notice', *Journal of Analytical Psychology*, no. 42 (1997), 671-689, and Anthony Stevens, *Archetype Revisited: An Updated History of the Self* (London: Brunner-Routledge, 2002).

36 Ibid, xii.

37 Cf. Hilary Rose and Steven Rose (eds.), *Alas, Poor Darwin – Arguments Against Evolutionary Psychology* (London: Vintage, 2001); R.C. Lewontin, Steven Rose and Leon J. Kamin, *Not in Our Genes – Biology, Ideology and Human Nature* (New York: Pantheon Books, 1984).

38 Stevens, 'Critical Notice', 681; Cf. Carl Jung, 'The Concept of the Collective Unconscious', *Collected Works*, vol.9, para. 155.

39 Anthony Stevens (2002) *Archetype Revisited*, 348.

40 Note: (1) Reductionism generally means the best scientific strategy to understanding complex things is by attempting to explain them in terms of interactions of their parts and to reduce them to simpler minute and fundamental things. Complex systems are the sum of their parts. Mentality is reducible to matter and material processes.(2) Emergence theory describes the way complex systems and patterns arise out of a multiplicity of relatively simple interactions – without the 'emergent' being reduced to their sum or difference. 'Emergence' is neither predictable from nor reducible to its simpler or lower level characteristics. It evolves from the rules - an analogy is a game of chess - but can not be reducible to the rules. While the concept has been around since Aristotle it has recently had renewed interest.

41 Philip Clayton and Paul Davies (eds.), *The Re-Emergence of Emergence – The Emergentist Hypothesis from Science to Religion* (Oxford University Press, 2006), xiii.

42 Anthony Stevens(2002) *Archetype Revisited*, 24.

43 Ibid.

44 Ibid, 25. Note: *Homologues* means having related or similar positions, structures, roles or functions.

45 Walter A. Shelburne, *Mythos and Logos in the Thought of Carl Jung – The Theory of the Collective Unconscious in Scientific Perspective* (State University of New York Press, 1988), 10.

46 Stevens, *Archetype – A Natural History of the Self*, 47.

47 See Guilford Dudley, 'Jung and Eliade: A Difference of Opinion', *Psychological Perspectives*, vol.10, Part 1 (1979), 41.

48 Anthony Stevens (1982) *Archetype – A Natural History of the Self*, 39; Cf. C.G. Jung, 'The Structure and Dynamics of the Psyche', *Collected Works*, 8, 154.

49 Dudley (1979) 'Jung and Eliade: A Difference of Opinion', 42.

50 Ibid, 45.

51 Ibid, 46.

52 Ibid, 47.

53 Anthony Stevens, 'Thoughts on the Psychobiology of Religion', *Zygon*, vol.21, no.1 (1986), 13.

54 Ibid, 12.

55 Ibid, 19.

56 Walter A. Shelburne, *Mythos and Logos in the Thought of Carl Jung - The Theory of the Collective Unconscious in Scientific Perspective* (State University of New York Press, 1988), 88. See also James Hillman, The Myth of Analysis: Three Essays in Archetypal Psychology (New York: Harper and Row, 1972), 179; and Re-Visioning Psychology (New York: Harper and Row, 1975), 152.

57 Ibid, 141.

58 Ibid, 123.

59 Stevens(1986) 'Thoughts on the Psychobiology of Religion', 12.

60 Stevens (1982) *Archetype – A Natural History of the Self,* 23.

61 Joseph Campbell, *The Inner Reaches of Outer Space – Metaphor as Myth and as Religion*, 12. (New York: Harper & Row, 1986), 11.

62 Shelburne (1988) *Mythos and Logos in the Thought of Carl Jung*, 126-131.

63 Ibid, 130.

64 C. G. Jung, 'The Symbolic Life', in: *The Collected Works* (1976), vol. 18, 657- 658.

65 Shelburne (1988) *Mythos and Logos in the Thought of Carl Jung*, 131.

66 Ibid, 132.

67 Ibid, 133.

68 Ibid, 135.

69 Ibid, 136; See also C. G. Jung, 'Researches into the Phenomenology of the Self' in: *The Collected Works*, vol. 9, part 2 (2nd. ed. 1968), 50.

70 Ibid, 137.

71 Ibid, 136; see R.E.L. Masters and Jean Housten, *The Varieties of Psychedelic Experience* (New York: Dell, 1966).

72 Ibid, 138; see Stanislav Grof. *Realms of the Human Unconscious: Observations from L.S.D. Research* (New York: Dutton, 1976).

73 Charles R. Card, 'The Emergence of Archetypes in Present-Day Science and its Significance for a Contemporary Philosophy of Nature', *Dynamical Psychology – An International, Interdisciplinary Journal of Complex Mental Processes*, (1996), 1-20.

http://goertzel.org/dynapsyc/1996/natphil.html.

74 Ibid, 10.

75 Ibid, 13.

76 Ibid.

77 Ibid.

78 Shelburne (1988) *Mythos and Logos in the Thought of Carl Jung,* 11.

79 Ibid, 10.

80 Ibid, 11.

81 Ibid.

82 See David F.Peat *Synchronicity – The Bridge Between Matter and Mind* (New York & London: Bantam Books, 1988).

83 Charles R. Card and Vasile V. Morariu, 'The Archetypal Hypothesis of C.G. Jung and W. Pauli and the Number Archetypes: An Extension of the Concept to the Golden Number.'

http:/ www.geocities.com/paideusis/n 1cm.html, 1.

84 Christian de Quincey, 'Deep Spirit: Quantum Consciousness?' (2005); http: //www.deepspirit.com/sys-tmpl/quantumconsciousness/, 3. Note: De Quincey cites as examples the quantum concepts of uncertainty and non-measurement; wave-particle complementarity; indeterminacy; non-locality and holism inter-relatedness; participant-observer interaction.

85 Peat (1988) *Synchronicity*, 17.

86 Ibid, 22.

87 Ibid, 34.

88 Ibid, 23.

89 Denis Cosgrove, 'Environmental Thought and Action: Pre-modern and Post-modern', *Transactions of the Institute of British Geographers*, vol. 15 (1990), 352.

90 Ibid, 352. Cf. C.G. Jung, *Synchronicity - An Acausal Connecting Principle* (Princeton, N.J., 1973).

91 Ibid.

92 Charles R. Card, 'The Emergence of Archetypes in Present-Day Science and its Significance for a Contemporary Philosophy of Nature', 14.

93 Michael Talbot, *The Holographic Universe* (London: Harper Collins Publishers, 1996).

94 Christian de Quincey, 'Deep Spirit: Quantum Consciousness?', 5.

95 Talbot (1996) *The Holographic Universe,* 71; Cf. Stanislav Grof, *Beyond the Brain* (Albany, N.Y: State University of New York Press, 1985).

96 Peat, 'Time, Synchronicity and Evolution', 3.
http://www.fdavidpeast.com/biography/essays/text/saur.txt.

97 Peat (1988) *Synchronicity*, 103.

98 Ibid, 104.

99 See Christopher Isham, 'Space and Time at the Edge of Mind', Royal College of Psychiatrists: http://www.repsych.ac.uk/college/specialinterestgroups/spirituality/publications/newsletter"/

100 See Philip Clayton and Paul Davies, *The Re-Emergence of Emergence – The Emergentist Hypothesis from Science to Religion* (Oxford University Press, 2006).

101 Christopher Hauke, *Jung and the Postmodern – The Interpretation of Realities* (Routledge, London, 2000).

102 See C.G.Jung, 'Mind and Earth', *The Collected Works of C.G.Jung*, vol.10. para. 53.

103 C.G. Jung (ed.), *Man and His Symbols* (London: Picador, Pan Books, 1978), 87.

104 Ibid.

105 Ibid, 88.

106 Anthony Stevens (1982) *Archetype – A Natural History of the Self,* 67.

107 Jung(1978) *Man and His Symbols*, 87.

108 Thomas Moore (ed.), and James Hillman, *The Essential James Hillman – A Blue Fire* (London: Routledge, London, 1990), 23.

109 Ibid.

110 Ibid.

111 James Hillman (1993) *Archetypal Psychology – A Brief Account* (Dallas: Spring Publications, Inc., 1993), 13.

112 Ibid,7; Cf. Edward Casey, 'Towards an Archetypal Imagination', *Spring* (1974), 1-32.

113 Denis E. Cosgrove, *Social and Symbolic Landscape* (London & Sydney: Croom Helm, 1984), 13.

114 Hillman(1993) *Archetypal Psychology*, 7. Jung argued that in the wider meaning of psychology, creative fantasy is given prior place. See C.G. Jung, *The Collected Works*, vol.6; para, 84.

115 James Hillman, *The Dream and the Underworld* (New York: Harper & Row, 1979), 130.

116 Hillman(1993) *Archetypal Psychology*, 12.

117 Ibid, 13.

118 Moore (ed.), and James Hillman (1990) *The Essential James Hillman*, 24.

119 Dudley(1979) 'Jung and Eliade', 43.

120 Ibid.

121 Moore (ed.) and James Hillman(1990) *The Essential James Hillman*, 24.

122 Ibid.

123 Hillman(1993) *Archetypal Psychology*, 35.

124 Ibid.

125 Ibid.

126 James Hillman, *Re-Visioning Psychology* (New York: Harper and Row, 1975), 22.

127 Ibid, 35.

128 Ibid.

129 Ibid, 23.

130 Hillman (1993) *Archetypal Psychology*, 53.

131 Moore (ed.) and James Hillman(1990) *The Essential James Hillman*, 23.

132 Ibid.

133 Hillman(1975) *Re-Visioning Psychology*, 23.

134 Peter Bishop(1989) *The Myth of Shangri-La*, 18.

135 Ibid, 19.

136 Peter Bishop(1992) 'Rhetoric, Memory and Power', 13.

Mother Earth

1 Andree Collard and Joyce Contrucci, *Rape of the Wild – Man's Violence Against Animals and the Earth* (Indiana University Press, 1989), 8.

2 Rupert Sheldrake, *The Rebirth of Nature – The Greening of Science and God* (London: Random Century, 1990), 4.

3 Ibid.

4 Maori Marsden, 'The Natural World and Natural Resources: Maori Value Systems and Perspectives', in: *Resource Management Law Reform Core Group Working Paper*, Part A, No.29, (Wellingotn: Ministry for the Environment, July 1989), 21.

5 See D.R. Simmons, *Iconography of New Zealand Maori Religion* (Leiden, The Netherlands: E.J. Brill, 1986); Elsdon Best, *Maori Religion and Mythology*, Part 1 (New Zealand: Dominion Museum Bulletin 10.\ (1924): 33); R. Taylor, *Te Ika a Maui. New Zealand and its Inhabitants* (London: Wertheim & McIntosh, 1855).

6 Marsden (1989) 'The Natural World and Natural Resources ', 22.

7 Carolyn Merchant, *The Death of Nature – Woman, Ecology, and the Scientific Revolution* (San Francisco: Harper & Row, 1980), 2.

8 Ibid, 23-24.

9 Ibid, 25-26.

10 Harold Turner, 'The Primal Religions of the World and their Study', in: Victor Hayes (ed.), *Australian Essays in World Religions* (The Australian Assn. for the Study of Religions, 1977), 30.

11 Annie L. Booth and Harvey M. Jacobs, 'Ties that Bind: Native American Beliefs as a Foundation for Environmental Consciousness', *Environmental Ethics,* vol. 12, no.1 (1990), 32.

12 John G. Neihardt, *Black Elk Speaks: Being the Life Story of a Holy Man of the Oglala Sioux* (New York: Pocket Books, 1975), 6.

13 Ibid, 113.

14 Carolyn Merchant, *The Death of Nature,* 28.

15 David Suzuki and Peter Knudtson, *Wisdom of the Elders – Honoring Sacred Native Visions of Nature* (New York: Bantam Books, 1992), 53.

16 Ibid, 53.

17 Sheldrake(1990) *The Rebirth of Nature,* 123.

18 Ibid, 55.

19 Ibid, 56.

20 James Lovelock, *The Ages of Gaia – A Biography Of Our Living Earth* (Oxford University Press, 1989), 3.

21 Merchant, ibid, xv.

22 Ibid, xvi.

23 K.W. Kelly,(ed.), *The Home Planet* (Reading, Mass.: Addison- Wesley, 1988), 109.

24 Sandra Lee, 'Cherishing Papatuanuku' – Interview with Powhiri Rika-Heke in: *Nga Kaitiaki,* no.21, August/September (1989), 9.

25 John Patterson, *Exploring Maori Values* (New Zealand: Dunmore Press Ltd., 1992), 157.

26 Ibid, 158.

27 Ibid, 48.

28 Marsden(1989) 'The Natural World and Natural Resources: Maori Value Systems and Perspectives', 22.

29 Ibid.

30 Ibid, 20.

31 Ibid, 21.

32 Sheldrake(1990) *The Rebirth of Nature,* 9.

33 Anthony Stevens, *Archetype – A Natural History of the Self* (London: Routledge & Kegan Paul, 1982), 89.

34 C.G. Jung, 'Psychological Aspects of the Mother Archetype', *The Collected Works,* vol.9, Part 1, para.158 (Routledge & Kegan Paul, London, 1959), 82. See also C.G. Jung, *Four Archetypes,* (Routledge & Kegan Paul, London, 1972), 15.

35 Ibid, para. 156, 81.

36 Erich Neumann, *The Origins and History of Consciousness* (Princeton: Princeton University Press, Bollingen Series XLII, 1973), 43.

37 Ibid, 40.

38 Sheldrake (1990) *The Rebirth of Nature,* 9.

39 Ibid, 8.

40 Ibid, 13.

41 Ibid, 8.

42 'Maori Values and Environmental Management', (New Zealand: Natural Resources Unit, *Manata Maori,* 1991), 2.

43 Ibid.

44 Elsdon Best, *Some Aspects of Maori Myth and Religion* (Wellington: Dominion Museum Monograph No.1. Government Printer, Wellington, 1954), 13-14.

45 Ibid, 14. (transl. "A Mother's love of her infant clinging to her bosom".)

46 Alfonso Ortiz, 'Why Nature Hates the White Man', *Omni,* March (1990), 77.

47 Donald Broadribb, *The Mystical Chorus – Jung and the Religious Dimension* (Australia: Millennium Books, 1995), 196.

48 Ortiz (1990) 'Why Nature Hates the White Man', 78.

49 Broadribb (1895) *The Mystical Chorus,* 182.

50 Ortiz (1990) 'Why Nature Hates the White Man', 78.

51 Ibid, 97.

52 Ibid, 78.

53 H. and H.A. Frankfort, John A. Wilson, Thorkild Jacobsen and William A. Irwin, *The Intellectual Adventure of Ancient Man – An Essay on Speculative Thought in the Ancient Near East* (The University of Chicago Press, Chicago, 1946), 4.

54 Broadribb, ibid, 262.

55 J. Baird Callicott, 'Traditional American Indian and Western European Attitudes Toward Nature: An Overview', *Environmental Ethics*, vol.4 (1982), 293.

56 J. Donald Hughes and Jim Swan, 'How Much of the Earth is Sacred Place' *Environmental Review*, vol.10, no.4, Winter (1986), 247. See also W.C. Vanderwerth (ed.), *Indian Oratory: Famous Speeches by Noted Indian Chieftains* (Norman, 1971), 120-1.

57 Ibid, 247.

58 See Annie L. Booth and Harvey M. Jacobs, 'Ties that Bind: Native American Beliefs as a Foundation for Environmental Consciousness', *Environmental Ethics*, v.12, no.1 (1990),38.

59 Ibid, 40.

60 Ibid.

61 Ibid, 41.

62 Andree Collard and Joyce Contrucci, *Rape of the Wild – Man's Violence Against Animals and the Earth*, 8.

63 Suzuki and Knudtson(1992) *Wisdom of the Elders*, 242.

64 Te Maire Tau, *Nga Pikituroa o Ngai Tahu – The Oral Traditions of Ngai Tahu* (Dunedin: University of Otago Press, 2003), 86.

65 Ibid, 299.

66 Ortiz (1990) 'Why Nature Hates the White Man', 77.

67 Ibid, 94.

68 James G. Cowan, 'Aboriginal Solitude', *Parabola Magazine,* vol.17, Part 1 (1992), 63.

69 Annie L. Booth and Harvey M. Jacobs, 'Ties that Bind: Native American Beliefs as a Foundation for Environmental Consciousness', 31-32.

70 Lovelock(1989) *The Ages of Gaia*, 212.

71 Theodore Roszak, *The Voice of the Earth* (New York: Simon & Schuster, 1992),137.

72 Stevens(1982) *Archetype – A Natural History of the Self*, 90.

73 Jung, *The Collected Works*, vol.9, Part 1. Para, 158, 82.

74 Rupert Sheldrake(1990) *The Rebirth of Nature*, 3.

75 Ibid, 10.

76 Erich Neumann (1973) *The Origins and History of Consciousness*, 58.

77 Ibid, 63.

78 Ibid, 83.

Heavenly God-Father

1 What we are to talk about is not the multi-God archetypal concepts of the 'Wisdom Stream' Gnostics, mystics or heretics. For them God was a supra-gender, androgynous, universal pantheistic force to be explored and revealed within the psyche. Nor are we talking of the God Father archetypal concepts of the polytheistic pagans, primal peoples or early matriarchal religions. For them the Sky God Father is just one in a pantheon of equally powerful Gods. What we are talking about is the exclusivist Heavenly God-Father Archetype of the *monotheistic*, great Western orthodox religions of Judaism, Old Testament fundamentalist Christianity and Islam.

2 Andree Collard and Joyce Contrucci, *Rape of the Wild – Man's Violence Against Animals and the Earth* (Indiana University Press, 1989), 15.

3 Theodore Roszak, *The Voice of the Earth* (New York: Simon & Schuster, 1992), 236.

4 Collard and Contrucci (1992) *Rape of the Wild*, 16-17. Cf. Gen.1:28 which "presents the view that God created everything and gave it to man to dominate. The degrees of his domination range from benevolent stewardship, to conquest … and outright oppression". (p.17).

5 H. and H.A. Frankfort, John A. Wilson, Thorkild Jacobsen, William A. Irwin, *The Intellectual Adventure of Ancient Man* (Chicago: University of Chicago Press, 1948), 230.

6 Lloyd Geering, *Christianity Without God* (Wellington: Bridget Williams Books, 2002), 138.

7 Ibid, 138.

8 Ibid, 139.

9 J. Donald Hughes and Jim Swan, 'How Much of the Earth is Sacred Space?', *Environmental Review,* vol.10. no.4, Winter (1986), 249.

10 H. and H.A. Frankfort, et.al.,(1948) *The Intellectual Adventure of Ancient Man,* 235.

11 Ibid.

12 Moana Jackson, 'The Treaty and the Word: The Colonization of Maori Philosophy', in: Graham Oddie and Roy Perret (eds.), *Justice, Ethics and New Zealand Society* (Oxford University Press, 1992), 3-5.

13 Hughes and Swan (1986) 'How Much of the Earth is Sacred Space?', 248-249.

14 Ibid, 249.

15 Ibid, 250.

16 John Passmore, *Man's Responsibility for Nature* (Great Britain: Unwin Brothers, 1974), 10.

17 H. and H.A. Frankfort et. al., (1948) *The Intellectual Adventure of Ancient Man,* 244.

18 Ibid, 247-248.

19 Thomas Berry, *The Dream of the Earth* (San Francisco: Sierra Club Nature and Natural Philosophy Library, 1988), 149.

20 Collard and Contrucci (1989) *Rape of the Wild,* 17.

21 Robert Faricy, *Approaches to a Theology of Nature* (London: SCM Press, 1982), 7.

22 Charlene Spretnak, *States of Grace – The Recovery of Meaning in the Postmodern Age* (San Francisco: Harper Collins Publishers, 1991), 162.

23 Edward F. Edinger, *Ego and Archetype – Individuation and the Religious Function of the Psyche* (Baltimore: Penguin Books, 1973), 155.

24 Lawrence W. Jaffe, *Liberating the Heart – Spirituality and Jungian Psychology* (Toronto: Inner City Books, 1990), 20.

25 John Passmore (1974) *Man's Responsibility for Nature,* 6.

26 Hebrew scriptures and teachings; first five books of the Old Testament. Bible.

27 Walter Gulick, 'The Bible and Ecological Spirituality', *Theology Today,* v.48, no.2 (1991), 188.

28 John Biggs, 'Towards a Theology for the Environment', *Baptist Quarterly,* v. 34. no.1 (1991), 37.

29 Ibid.

30 Edward C. Whitmont, *Return of the Goddess* (New York: The Crossroad Publishing Company, 1982), 98-99.

31 Cf. Max O. Hallman, 'Nietzsche's Environmental Ethics', *Environmental Ethics,* v.13, no.2 (1991), 102.

32 Ian McHarg, 'Values, Process, Form', in: Robert Disch (ed.), *The Ecological Conscience: Values for Survival* (New Jersey, Englewood Cliffs: Prentice-Hall, 1970), 98. Cf. J. Baird Callicott, 'Traditional; American Indian and Western European Attitudes Toward Nature: An Overview', *Environmental Ethics,* v. 4 (1982), 307.

33 See Lloyd Geering (2002) *Christianity Without God ,* 141.

34 Lynn White, Jr., 'The Historical Roots of Our Ecological Crisis', *Science,* vol. 155, no. 3767 (10 March 1967), 1205.

35 Hallman (1991) 'Nietzsche's Environmental Ethics', 100-101.

36 Robert Faricy, *Approaches to a Theology of Nature,* 5. Note: In this regard see also Mike Holderness, 'Enemy at the Gates', *New Scientist* (8 October, 2005) who reports that Christian fundamentalist individuals, groups, think-tanks, 'research' organizations and foundations appealing to a renewal of the faith of their fathers and forefathers are advocating a faith-based approach to science and an economy ruled by spirit and faith. This has led to a dismissal of "ideas such as global warming, pollution problems and ozone depletion. And that unsurprisingly, has political ramifications, including climate-change denial and the pursuit of ruthless free-market economics" (p. 48).

37 Collard and Contrucci (1989) *Rape of the Wild,* 26.

38 Hallman (1991) 'Nietzsche's Environmental Ethics', 105.

39 Lynn White, Jr., (1967)'The Historical Roots of Our Ecological Crisis', 1205.

40 Edward C. Whitmont (1982) *Return of the Goddess,* 79.

41 Edward C. Whitmont (1982) *Return of the Goddess,* 100.

42 Jane Roberts, *The Unknown Reality,* vol.1 (London: Prentice Hall International, Inc., 1977), 112.

43 Ibid, 142.

44 Ibid, 141.

45 Ibid, 142.

46 Ibid, 269.

47 Ibid, 112-113.

48 Erich Neumann, *The Origins and History of Consciousness* (New York: Princeton University Press, Bollingen Series XLII, 1973), 127.

49 Ibid, 131.

50 Edward C. Whitmont (1982) *Return of the Goddess*, 83.

51 Edward Edinger (1973) *Ego and Archetype* , 152.

52 Donald Broadribb, *The Mystical Chorus – Jung and the Religious Dimension* (Alexandra NSW, Australia: Millenium Books, 1995), 67.

53 Anthony Stevens, *Archetype – A Natural History of the Self* (London: Routledge & Kegan Paul, 1982), 105.

54 Whitmont (1982) *Return of the Goddess*, 90.

55 Erich Neumann (1973) *The Origins and History of Consciousness*, 143.

56 Ibid, 147.

57 Collard and Contrucci (1989) *Rape of the Wild*, 26.

58 Ibid, 26-27.

59 Gulick (1991) 'The Bible and Ecological Spirituality', 188. "When one examines the legal content of the Torah, one finds that it regulates relationships between people (and between people and God) so as to establish a just society in which privileges are protected but exploitation is prohibited. Thus the covenant establishes a publicly known standard by which to secure moral behavior. Priest and prophet, Yahwist and Deuteronomist alike judge events and people in light of this standard. Many are they who experience the guilt of falling short of the standard. Hence, the second creation story, with its account of disobedience and punishment, eventually comes to be used as a paradigm to assess those who attempt to fulfill the law and who fail. As a result of the first human disobedience, the ground is cursed so that it yields thorns and thistles. Nature is viewed and judged from a highly anthropocentric perspective. It is to be managed either by God or by God's representatives on earth: human beings".

60 Thomas Berry (1988) *The Dream of the Earth*, 150.

61 Collard and Contrucci (1989) *Rape of the Wild*, 27.

62 Whitmont (1982) *Return of the Goddess*, 90.

63 Ibid, 91.

64 O.W. Markeley and Willis W. Harman, (eds.), *Changing Images of Man* (London: Pergamon Press, 1982), 22.

65 Donald Broadribb (1995) *The Mystical Chorus – Jung and the Religious Dimension*, 73.

66 Ibid, 73.

67 H. and H.A. Frankfort et. al., (1946) *The Intellectual Adventure of Ancient Man*, 263.

68 Whitmont (1982) *Return of the Goddess*, 86-87.

69 Broadribb (1995) *The Mystical Chorus*, 74.

70 H. and H.A. Frankfort et. al.,(1946) *The Intellectual Adventure of Ancient Man*, 227.

71 Charlene Spretnak (1991) *States of Grace*, 159.

72 Collard and Contrucci (1989) *Rape of the Wild* , 26.

73 Erich Neumann (1973) *The Origins and History of Consciousness*, 127.

74 Walter B. Gulick (1991) 'The Bible and Ecological Spirituality', 184.

75 Lloyd Geering, *About Time* (Wellington: St. Andrew's Trust for the Study of Religion and Society, 1989), 27.

76 Ibid, 4-5.

77 Whitmont (1982) *Return of the Goddess*, 105.

78 Ibid.

79 Ibid, 106.

80 Ibid, 110.

81 Spretnak(1991) *States of Grace*, 162.

82 Donald Broadribb(1995) *The Mystical Chorus*, 83-4.

83 Muriel Porter, *Sex, Power and the Clergy* (Australia: Hardie Grant Books, 2003)

84 Ibid, 84-5.

85 Irshad Manji, *The Trouble With Islam – A Muslim's Call for Reform in Her Faith* (Canada: Random House, 2003).

86 Robert Fisk (2007)'The Forgotten Holocaust', Independent News and Media Limited.

87 See Derek Hastings, *Catholicism and the Roots of Nazism* (Oxford University Press, 2010) also Wikipedia for '*Religious Views of Adolf Hitler*' and '*Catholic Church and Nazi Germany*'.

88 Notes: According to Hitler's chief architect, Albert Speer, Hitler remained a formal member of the Catholic Church until his death and even ordered his chief associates to remain members. (Albert Speer, *Inside the Third Reich:Memoirs* (New York: Simon and Schuster, 1997),p.96); Biographer John Toland argues that Hitler was "a member in good standing of the Church of Rome" and "carried within himself its teaching that the Jew was the killer of God. The extermination, therefore, could be done without a twinge of conscience since he was merely acting as the avenging hand of God" (John Toland, *Adolf Hitler: The Definitive Biography* (New York:Anchor Books, 1976), p.703) ; Historian, Richard Steigmann-Gall notes that "Hitler gave no indication of being an atheist or agnostic or of believing in only a remote, rationalist divinity. Indeed, he referred continually to a providential, active deity." (Richard Steigmann-Gall, *The Holy Reich* (Cambridge: Cambridge University Press, 2003, p.26). He argues Christianity was fused into Hitler's thinking (p. 46); Nazi General Gerhard Engel reported in his diary that in 1941 Hitler stated, "I am now as before a Catholic and will always remain so."(John Toland, *Adolf Hitler* (New York: Anchor Publishing, 1992),p.507); According to Hitler's personal photographer, Heinrich Hoffmann, the Catholic priest Bernhard Stempfle was a prominent member of Hitler's inner circle and frequently advised him on religious issues(Derek Hastings, *Catholicism and the Roots of Nazism* (Oxford University Press, 2010), p.119); Catholic historian Jose Sanchez argues that Hitler's anti-semitism was explicitly rooted in Christianity. (Jose M. Sanchez, *Pius XII and the Holocaust: Understanding the Controversy* (Washington, D.C: Catholic University of American Press, 2002), p.70); Feminist Gloria Steinem draws parallels between the recent Christian Right, the Roman Catholic Church and Nazism – particularly in regard to women's rights to contraception, work outside the family, their role in the family and society as breeders, mothers and wives; and issues such as abortion, homosexuality and feminism. For example; "In 1933, feminists were removed from teaching and other public posts by the same law that removed "non-Ayrans" from such jobs. All women were banned from the Reichstag, from judgeships, and from other decision-making posts".(Gloria Steinem (1982) 'The Nazi Connection' (from research done at the Woodrow Wilson Center of the Smithsonian Institution; published in Herbert F. Vetter (ed.), *Speak Out Against the New Right* (Boston: Beacon Press, 1982)); Further notes: While there is evidence that at times Hitler was certainly ambivalent of, critical and disenchanted with the Christianity of his times (not surprising because there was very brave opposition to the Nazis from individual theologians and the clergy, in many instances where individuals put their lives on the line and were killed by the Nazis), – Hitler's advocacy of a genetically superior and pure, master race, created by God, has definite parallels with patriarchal monotheism and the concepts of the Heavenly God-Father's '*chosen*'. The Nazi patriarchal military hierarchy bore some comparisons with the patriarchal hierarchical structure of the Roman Catholic Church. Also, in order to justify Nazi aggression, Hitler drew a parallel with militanism and the rise to power of Christianity as the Roman Empire's official state religion. Hitler advocated a "positive Christianity" – militant , non-denominational and emphasizing Christ as an active preacher, organizer and fighter opposed to institutionalized Judaism – infused with nationalism and anti-Semitism. Hitler often associated atheism with Bolshevism, Communism and Jewish materialism. (Norman H. Baynes, (ed.), *The Speeches of Adolf Hitler*, Vol 1. (Oxford University Press, 1942),p.240) For references and a general discussion of the issue see 'Religious Views of Adolf Hitler' and 'Catholic Church and Nazi Germany' *Wikipedia* .

89 Stevens(1982) *Archetype,* 238.

90 Jenny Gibbons, 'Recent Developments in the Study of The Great European Witch Hunt', *Pomegranate* (Lammas, 1998) Issue No.5. http://www.cog.org/witch-hunt-html. pp. 1-20.

91 Martha Reineke, "'The Devils Are Come Down Upon Us" – Myth, History, and the Witch as Scapegoat', *Union Seminary Quarterly Review*, v.44, no.1/2 (1990), 78.

92 Edward C. Whitmont (1982) *Return of the Goddess*, 184, states: "The tragedy of the male, as he aspired to the heroic ideal, was represented as a faltering in his resistance to wily woman; letting himself be deceived or seduced into accepting from her hands the forbidden fruit of desire, passion, and bodily urges. The more the patriarchal culture came to stress the life-denying ascetic ideal, the more were the repressed passions – the vulnerable as well as the lustful sides of existence – projected upon women. Consequently, women needed to be kept in subordinate positions, if not quarantined in harems or hidden beneath disguising or disfiguring clothes, veils or *skeitels* (wigs worn by Orthodox Jewish women). Femininity was to be limited to obedient passivity, domesticity, and maternal nurturance. Women themselves had to learn to distrust the tides of their emotions and to suspect the voices of their bodies."

93 Cf. Mary Daly, *Beyond God the Father – Toward a Philosophy of Women's Liberation* (Boston: Beacon Press, 1973).

94 Lloyd Geering (2002) *Christianity Without God*, 139.

95 Theodore Roszak, *The Voice of the Earth* (New York: Simon & Schuster, 1992), 236-7.

Trickster

1 See for example Paul Radin, *The Trickster – A Study in American Indian Mythology*, with commentaries by Karl Kerenyi and C.G. Jung (London: Routledge and Kegan Paul, 1956).

2 Alan Combs and Mark Holland, *Synchronicity – Science, Myth and the Trickster* (New York: Paragon House, 1990), 82.

3 C.G. Jung, *Four Archetypes* (London: Routledge & Kegan Paul, 1980),142-3. (Note: The internet throws up almost 13,000 associations between Trickster and Hermes).

4 Allan Combs and Mark Holland, *Synchronicity – Science, Myth and the Trickster* (New York: Paragon House, 1990), 82.

5 George P. Hansen, *The Trickster and the Paranormal* (Philadelphia: Xlibris Corporation, 2001).

6 Allan Combs and Mark Holland, *Synchronicity – Science, Myth and the Trickster* (New York: Paragon House, 1990), 97.

7 Ibid, 79.

8 Carl Jung (ed.), *Man and His Symbols* (London: Picador, Pan Books, 1978).

9 Joseph L. Henderson, 'Ancient Myths and Modern Man' in: Carl Jung (ed.), *Man and His Symbols*, 101.

10 Erich Neumann, *The Origins and History of Consciousness* (New York: Princeton University Press, Bollingen Series XLII, 1973), 160-161.

11 Ibid, 340-341.

12 Ibid, 340-341.

13 Ibid, 390.

14 Ibid, 177.

15 Dudley Young, *Origins of the Sacred* (London: Little, Brown and Co., 1992), 198.

16 Combs and Holland(1990) *Synchronicity*, 93.

17 Norman O. Brown, *Hermes the Thief* (New York: Vintage Books, 1969) as cited in Combs and Holland, 93.

18 Combs and Holland(1990) *Synchronicity*, 93.

19 Erik Davis, *Techgnosis – Myth, Magic and Mysticism in the Age of Information* (London: Serpents Tail, 1999), 16.

20 Dudley Young (1992) *Origins of the Sacred*, 197.

21 Ibid.

22 Ibid, 204.

23 Ibid, 205.

24 Joel Bakan *The Corporation – The Pathological Pursuit of Profit and Power* (New York: Free Press, Simon & Schuster, 2004), 5.

25 Erik Davis (1999) *Techgnosis*, 3.

26 Ibid, 3.

27 Ibid, 1.

28 Ibid, 14.

29 Ibid, 14-15.

30 Ibid, 15.

31 Ibid.

32 Ibid, 16.

33 Ibid, 17.

34 Keith Ward, *The Times*, December 1984. See James Lovelock, *The Ages of Gaia – A Biography of our Living Earth* (Oxford University Press, 1984), 209-210.

35 Richard Dawkins, *The God Delusion* (London: Transworld Publishers /Bantam Press, 2006), 31.

36 See Christopher Hitchens, *God is Not Great: How Religion Poisons Everything* (USA: Twelve/ Hachette Warner Books, 2007); Sam Harris, *The End of Faith* (United States: W.W. Norton, 2004); Daniel Dennett, *Breaking the Spell: Religion as Natural Phenomenon* (London: Penguin, 2006).

37 Carl Jung, *Man and his Symbols* (London: Picador, 1964), 295.

38 Ibid.

39 Anthony Stevens, *Archetype – A Natural History of the Self* (Routledge & Kegan Paul, London, 1982), 284.

40 Ibid, 121.

41 Gaby Hinsliff of *The Observer*, 'Not so much about God in Classes on Religion', reprinted in *The Press*, Christchurch, Feb. 16, 2004. A. 11.

42 Ibid.

43 Karen Armstrong, *A History of God* (London: Mandarin, 1994), 397.

44 Ibid, 409.

45 Ibid, 406.

46 Ibid, 409-410.

47 John Macquarrie, *In Search of Deity* (London: SCM Press, 1984), 17.

48 Lloyd Geering, *Christianity Without God* (Wellington: Bridget Williams Books, 2002), 131-147.

49 Ibid, 138.

50 Karen Armstrong(1994) *A History of God*, 454.

51 Ibid, 456.

52 Geering(2002) *Christianity Without God*, 132.

53 Margaret Wertheim, *The Pearly Gates of Cyberspace – A History of Space from Dante to the Internet* (New York: W.W. Norton & Company, 1999), 37.

54 Ibid, 118-9.

55 David Holt, 'Jung and Marx', *Spring* (1973), 55.

56 Neil Postman, *Technopoly – The Surrender of Culture to Technology* (New York: Alfred A. Knopf, 1992), 54.

57 Neil Postman, *Amusing Ourselves to Death – Public Discourse in the Age of Show Business* (London: Heinemann, 1986), 116-117.

58 Ibid, 122.

59 Wertheim(1999) *The Pearly Gates*, 263.

60 Ibid, 265.

61 Ibid, 271.

62 Ibid, 281-282.

63 Davis (1999) *Techgnosis*, 38.

64 Ibid, 1.

65 Ibid, 38.

66 Ibid, 22.

67 Ibid, 9.

68 Stevens (1982) *Archetype*, 121.

69 Joel Bakan (2004) *The Corporation*, 125-126.

70 Ibid, 127.

71 Ibid, 53-54.

72 Ibid, 35.

73 Ibid, 56-57 Note: a definition of "psychopathic" is an antisocial personality characterised by the failure to develop any sense of moral responsibility and the capability of performing violent or antisocial acts.

74 Robert D. Sack, 'The Consumer's World: Place as Context', *Annals of the Association of American Geographers*, vol.78 (1988), 659.

75 Ibid, 661.

76 Ibid, 657.

77 Ibid, 659.

78 Ibid, 658.

79 Bakan (2004) *The Corporation*, 26.

80 Sack (1988) 'The Consumer's World', 659.

81 Michael Heim, *The Metaphysics of Virtual Reality* (Oxford University Press, 1993), 79-80.

82 Sherry Turkle, *Life on the Screen – Identity in the Age of the Internet* (New York: Simon & Schuster, 1995), 255.

83 Wertheim (1999) *The Pearly Gates*, 242-243.

84 Ibid, 236-237. See also Turkle (1995) *Life on the Screen*, 12. Note: a definition of MUD is Multi-User Domains, combining role-playing games, player vs player, interactive function and online chat.

85 Turkle(1995) *Life on the Screen*, 268.

86 Heim (1993) *The Metaphysics of Virtual Reality*, 89.

87 Dominic J. Balestra, 'Technology in a Free Society: The New Frankenstein', *Thought: A Review of Culture and Idea*, vol.65, no.257 (June 1990), 163.

88 Robert L. Thayer, Jr., 'Pragmatism in Paradise – Technology and the American Landscape', *Landscape*, v.30. no.3 (1990), 4.

89 Postman(1986) *Amusing Ourselves to Death*, 77.

90 Ibid, 78-80.

91 Leo Bogart, 'Media Habits of Media Tycoons', *Transaction Social Science and Modern Society*, vol.30, no. 5, July/August (1993), 52.

92 Postman(1986) *Amusing Ourselves to Death*, Forward, viii.

93 Ibid, 155-156.

94 Combs and Holland(1990) *Synchronicity*, 84.

95 Ibid, 93.

96 Ibid, 94.

97 Marcus Chown, 'Clock-Watchers', *New Scientist*, 1 May 2004, 34.

98 Combs and Holland (1990) *Synchronicity*, 101.

99 Sack(1988) 'The Consumer's World', 659 & 661.

100 Wertheim (1999) *The Pearly Gates*, 229-230.

101 Ibid, 231.

102 Ibid, 232.

103 C.G. Jung, *Four Archetypes* (London: Routledge & Kegan Paul, 1980), 147.

104 Lloyd Geering, *The World of Relation – An Introduction to Martin Buber's I and Thou* (New Zealand: Victoria University Press, 1983), 21-22.

105 See Dudley Young (1992) *Origins of the Sacred*, 193-4, who describes the Trickster of the American Indians. One can make interesting similarities and comparisons with the modern Trickster. The same descriptors apply.

106 Jung (1980) *Four Archetypes*, 143.

107 Ibid, 150.

108 Bakan (2004) *The Corporation*, 69.

109 Ibid, 60.

110 Ibid, 61.

111 Ibid,180.

112 Ibid, 70.

113 Ibid, 64.

114 Ibid, 69.

115 Ibid, 138.

116 Loretta Napoleoni, *Rogue Economics – Capitalism's New Reality* (Australia & New Zealand: Allen & Unwin, 2008).

117 Ibid, Greg Palast, back page.

118 Ibid.

119 See Neil Postman, 'The Age of Show Business', in: *Amusing Ourselves to Death*, 80-105, for a critique of the beginnings of 'Reality TV'.

120 Alison Hearn, CBC Radio's COMMENTARY, 12/4/04, http://www.cbc.ca/insite/COMMENTARY/2004/4/12.html.

121 George Will, "Reality television: oxymoron" June 21,2001. http://www.townhall.com/columnists/georgewill/gw20010621.shtml.

122 Ziauddin Sardar, 'alt. Civilizations. faq: Cyberspace as the Darker Side of the West' in: Ziauddin Sardar and Jerome R. Ravetz, (eds.), *Cyberfutures – Culture and Politics on the Information Superhighway* (Pluto Press, London, 1996), 14-15.

123 Ibid, 24.

124 Ibid.

125 See Tony Allen-Mills, 'Chilling Report of Abuse', *The Press*, Christchurch, May 24, 2004, B4. Reprinted from *The Sunday Times* May, 2004.

126 Sardar and Jerome R. Ravetz (eds.),(1996) *Cyberfutures*, 24.

127 Dudley Young (1992) *Origins of the Sacred*, 193-4.

128 Catherine Itzin (ed.), *Pornography – Women, Violence and Civil Liberties* (Oxford University Press, 1992), 3.

129 'Child Porn Sites Increase', *The Press*, Christchurch, January 20, 2004, C5.

130 Itzin, passim.

131 Susan Griffin, *Pornography and Silence: Culture's Revenge Against Nature* (New York: Harper & Row, 1981), 82.

132 Ibid, 83.

133 Peter Baker, 'Maintaining Male Power: Why Heterosexual Men Use Pornography', in Catherine Itzin (ed.), *Pornography – Women, Violence and Civil Liberties*, 134; cf.139-140.

134 Susan Griffin(1981) *Pornography and Silence*, 47.

135 Ibid, 49; cf. 228.

136 Dominic J. Balestra, 'Technology in a Free Society: The New Frankenstein', *Thought: A Review of Culture and Idea*, vol.65, no.257 (1990), 160.

137 Carolyn Merchant, *The Death of Nature: Women, Ecology, and the Scientific Revolution* (San Francisco:Harper & Row Publishers, 1980), 164.

138 Ibid, 186-187.

139 Ibid, 188.

140 Ibid, 189 .

141 Ibid, 189-192.

142 Ibid, 216.

143 Ibid, 228.

144 Michael Heim (1993) *The Metaphysics of Virtual Reality,* 55.

145 Paul Crowley, 'Technology, Truth and Language: The Crisis of Theological Discourse', *The Heythorp Journal*, vol.32, no.3 (1991), 324-325.

146 Michael Heim (1993) *The Metaphysics of Virtual Reality*, 61.

147 Eric Katz, 'The Call of the Wild: The Struggle Against Domination and the Technological Fix of Nature', *Environmental Ethics*, vol. 14, no.3 (1992), 265 –267.

148 Hwa Yol Jung, 'Marxism and Deep Ecology in Postmodernity: From Homo Oeconomicus to Homo Ecologies', *Thesis Eleven*, vol. 28 (1991), 90.

149 Ibid, 90-91.

150 Bakan(2004) 'Interview with Noam Chomsky', *The Corporation*, 134-5.

151 Ibid, 135; 'Interview with Mark Kingwell'.

152 Ibid, 85; 'Interview with Anita Roddick'

153 Ibid, 71; 'Interview with Robert Monks'.

154 Ibid, 149.

155 Balestra(1990) 'Technology in a Free Society', 166-167.

156 See Bakan(2004) 'Interview with Ray Anderson', *The Corporation*, 106.

157 Frank Fisher, 'Technology and the Loss of Self: An Environmental Concern', *Environments*, vol.20, no.2 (1989), 5.

158 Theodore Roszak, *The Voice of the Earth* (Simon & Schuster, New York, 1992), 239.

159 Ibid, 242.

160 Ronald Fletcher, 'Hearth and Home', *Transaction Social Science and Modern Society*, vol.31, no. 1, Nov/Dec (1993), 58; 60.

Sophia's Return

1 Note: As if in precognition of his life's work, Henry Corbin wrote this haunting meditation in 1932, at the edge of Lake Siljan in Sweden, when he was 29 years old. Corbin called it *Theology by the Lakeside.* "Everything is but revelation; there can only be re-velation. But revelation comes from the Spirit, and there is no knowledge of the Spirit. It will soon be dusk, but for now the clouds are still clear, the pines are not yet darkened, for the lake brightens them into transparency. And everything is green

with a green that would be richer than if pulling all the organ stops in recital. It must be heard seated, very close to the Earth, arms crossed, eyes closed, pretending to sleep. For it is not necessary to strut about like a conqueror and want to give a name to things, to everything; it is they who will tell you who they are, if you listen, yielding like a lover; for suddenly for you, in the untroubled peace of this forest of the North, the Earth has come to Thou, visible as an Angel that would perhaps be a woman, and in this apparition, this greatly green and thronging solitude, yes, the Angel too is robed in green, the green of the dusk, of silence and of truth. Then there is in you all the sweetness that is present in the surrender to an embrace that triumphs over you. Earth, Angel, Woman, all of this in a single thing that I adore and that is in this forest. Dusk on the lake, my Annunciation." (Henry Corbin, 'Theologie au bord du lac', in *Christian Jambet*, ed. Henry Corbin. Paris: *Cahier del' Herne*, no.39 (1981), 62.)

2 Kathleen Granville Damiani, *Sophia: Exile and Return* (Ann Arbor, MI: UMI Co., 1998), 57.

3 Karen Armstrong, *A History of God* (London: Mandarin Paperbacks, 1994), 49.

4 Erich Neumann, *The Origins and History of Consciousness* (Princeton: Princeton University Press, 1973), 355.

5 Ibid, 355-356.

6 Henry Corbin, *Spiritual Body and Celestial Earth – From Mazdean Iran to Shi'ite Iran* (Princeton: Princeton University Press, Bollingen Series XCI:2, 1989) 66.

7 Ibid, 40.

8 Caitlin Matthews, *Sophia – Goddess of Wisdom, Bride of God* (Illinois: Quest Books, 2001), xxxii.

9 Ibid.

10 Henry Corbin, *Creative Imagination in the Sufism of Ibn Arabi* (Princeton: Princeton University Press, 1969), 327.

11 See Damiani (1998) *Sophia: Exile and Return*, 78-84.

12 Anne Baring and Jules Cashford, *The Myth of the Goddess: Evolution of an Image* (London: Viking Arkana, 1991), 610-611.

13 Damiani (1998) *Sophia: Exile and Return*, 83-84.

14 Joanna Macy, *World as Lover, World as Self* (Berkley, CA: Parallax Press, 1991), 106.

15 Ibid, 107.

16 Jay G. Williams, 'Return to the Roots: Platonic Philosophy and the I-Ching', *Ching Feng*, v.34:1, January (1991), 13.

17 Ibid, 15.

18 Damiani (1998) *Sophia: Exile and Return*, 64.

19 Ibid, 78.

20 Ibid, 71.

21 Armstrong (1994) *A History of God*, 115.

22 Ibid, 114.

23 Damiani (1998) Sophia: Exile and Return, 70.

24 Ibid, 71; cf. Elaine Pagels, *The Gnostic Gospels* (New York: Random House, 1979).

25 Damiani (1989) *Sophia: Exile and Return*, 57.

26 Kathleen Granville Damiani (2004), 'Sophia, Soul of the World', http:azothgallery.com/alchemical/k-damiani-sophia soul.html

27 Armstrong (1994) *A History of God*, 286-287.

28 Tom Cheetham, *Green Man, Earth Angel – The Prophetic Tradition and the Battle for the Soul of the World* (Albany, N.Y: State University of New York Press, 2005), 65.

29 Armstrong (1994) *A History of God*, 270.

30 Damiani (1998) *Sophia: Exile and Return*, 73-74.

31 Ibid, 76.

32 Ibid, 77.

33 Ibid, 75.

34 Ibid, 78-79.

35 Ibid, 64-5. See reference to Gerhard von Rad, Wisdom of Israel (Nashville: Abingdon Press, 1972), 10.

36 Ibid, 67.

37 Ibid.

38 Ibid.

39 Armstrong (1994) *A History of God*, 81.

40 Ibid, 82.

41 Ibid, 83.

42 Joan Chamberlain Englesman, *The Feminine Dimension of the Divine* (Philadelphia: The Westminster Press, 1979), 119.

43 Damiani (1998) *Sophia: Exile and Return*, 70.

44 Anne Baring and Jules Cashford, *The Myth of the Goddess: Evolution of an Image* (London: Viking Arkana, 1991), 611.

45 Damiani (1998) *Sophia:Exile and Return*, 70-71.

46 Lloyd Geering, *Christianity Without God* (Wellington: Bridget Williams Books, 2002), *passim*.

47 Ibid, 115.

48 Ibid, 129.

49 Ibid, 130.

50 Caitlin Matthews (2001) *Sophia – Goddess of Wisdom, Bride of God*, xxv.

51 Ibid, xxix.

52 Charlene Spretnak, *States of Grace: The Recovery of Meaning in the Postmodern Age* (San Francisco: Harper Collins, 1991), 127.

53 Ibid, 136.

54 Betty Roszak, 'The Spirit of the Goddess', *Resurgence*, no. 144, Jan-Feb (1991), 28.

55 Ibid, 29.

56 Carol P. Christ, *She Who Changes – Re-imagining the Divine in the World* (New York: Palgrave MacMillan, 2003), 18.

57 Ibid, 20.

58 Lawrence Jaffe, *Liberating the Heart - Spirituality and Jungian Psychology* (Toronto: Inner City Books, 1990), 135.

59 Ibid, 136.

60 Ibid.

61 C. G. Jung, 'Answer to Job', *Psychology and Religion* in: *The Collected Works* , vol.11, par. 624.

62 Ibid, par. 755.

63 Gerhard Adler, 'Aspects of Jung's Personality and Work', *Psychological Perspectives*, vol.6, no.1 Spring (1975), 19.

64 Ibid, 20.

65 Lawrence Jaffe(1990) *Liberating the Heart*, 137.

66 Edward C. Whitmont, *Return of the Goddess* (New York: Crossroad Pub. Co., 1984), vii-viii.

67 Caitlin Matthews (2001) *Sophia – Goddess of Wisdom, Bride of God*, 327.

68 John D. Turner, edited and trans., 'Trimorphic Protennoia', in *The Nag Hammadi* Library, revised edition (San Francisco: Harper Collins, 1990).

69 Henry Corbin, 'The Eternal Sophia', *Harvest,* vol.31 (1985), 20.

70 Ibid, 17-18. Note: Corbin states "The *filius Sapientiae* is the one through whom the Holy Spirit brings about the divine anthropomorphic, a God of love into a man of gentleness. He is begotten by an 'unknown father' and by the Sophia-Sapientia. 'Christian virtues' are required for this to happen, but they are not enough, the problem is not only moral; Wisdom is needed, the wisdom that Job was seeking and, until her anamnesis, remained hidden to Yahweh... The final Sophianic hierogamy in the Apocalypse and the Assumption of the Virgin, namely, the Exaltation of Maria-Sophia warrants the divine Incarnation, not in the sense of a repetition of the birth of God, but in the sense of the Incarnation, begun by Christ, and continuing in the human creature... No doubt this birth is eternal, in the pleroma; but birth in time can only happen if it is perceived and acknowledged by man. The *historicity* of the Event is its psychic reality, and the relation of time with eternity... God is born to man and man is born to God as *Filius Sapientiae*, son of Sophia. It is not only the Anamnesis of Sophia, as in the Old Testament, but her reign and her exaltation with her work of *mediation*, she who is 'the defender and witness in Heaven', and that is *the* answer to Job."

71 Ibid.

72 Ibid, 22.

73 Whitmont (1982) *Return of the Goddess*, ix-x.

74 Matthews (2001) *Sophia – Goddess of Wisdom, Bride of God*, xxxi.

75 Ibid, 351.

76 Damiani (1998) *Sophia:Exile and Return*, 18.

77 Ibid, 268.

78 Ibid, 9.

79 Baring and Cashford(1991) *The Myth of the Goddess: Evolution of an Image*, 678.

80 Hwa Yol Jung, 'Marxism and Deep Ecology in Postmodernity: From Homo Oeconomicus to Homo Ecologicus', *Thesis Eleven,* vol 28 (1991), 92-3.

81 Ibid, 94.

82 Spretnak (1991) *States of Grace*, 136.

83 Damiani (1998) *Sophia: Exile and Return*, 18.

84 Corbin (1985) 'The Eternal Sophia', 8.

85 Matthews (2001) *Sophia – Goddess of Wisdom, Bride of God*, 329.

86 Whitmont (1982) *Return of the Goddess*, 187.

87 Ibid, 190-191.

88 Ibid, 188.

89 Ibid.

90 Ibid.

91 Ibid, 194-195.

92 Ibid, 195.

93 Corbin (1985) 'The Eternal Sophia', 8.

94 Ibid, 9.

95 Ibid, 13. Note: Corbin argues "The establishment of a patriarchal society is due to the absence and forgetting of Sophia – a male dominated society in which woman plays a secondary role…implying the contempt or forgetting of all those sophianic 'values' and feelings….Fear and trembling, absence of Eros; Yahweh has no concern for man, but only for a goal in which man serves as his auxiliary. In this critical development, Job marks the point of culmination… 'Because man feels that he is exposed to the arbitrary whims of the divine, he needs Sophia, as opposed to Yahweh who, up to this point had only man's void to confront'. And because Job had seen this face of God, men in the last pre-christian centuries were able to achieve the anamnesis of the pre-existing Sophia whose light touch compensates Yahweh's attitude, and reveals to human beings the only luminous and tender, benevolent and just aspect of their God… We are now at the heart of Jung's most personal exegesis. It reaches heights of emotional expression disclosing the contained passion of a soul for whom no rigid, ready-made interpretation, however hallowed by time, could create an insuperable obstacle, nor stop him reaching the ultimate and unremitting truth of the 'alone to the alone'. In the pages that follow, one can hear the secret vibrations of a sophianic hymn, hailing the arrival of the eternal Virgin; this points to a new creation, not of a new world but of a new God."

96 Damiani (1998) *Sophia: Exile and Return*, 282.

97 Denis Cosgrove, 'Environmental Thought and Action: Pre-modern and Post-modern', *Transactions of the Institute of British Geographers*, vol. 15 (1990), 353.

98 Margaret Wertheim, *The Pearly Gates of Cyberspace – A History of Space from Dante to the Internet* (New York: W.W. Norton & Company, 1999), 174-175.

99 Ibid, 213.

100 Ibid, 211-217.

101 Darryl Reanney, *The Death of Forever – A New Future for Human Consciousness* (Melbourne: Longman Cheshire, 1991), 202.

102 Stephen Hawking, *A Brief History of Time* (London: Bantam Press, 1988), 147.

103 Michael Talbot, *Beyond the Quantum* (N.Y & London: Bantam Books, 1988), 53.

104 Michael Talbot, *The Holographic Universe* (London:Harper Collins, 1996), 200.

105 Ibid, 46.

106 F. David Peat, *The Philosopher's Stone* (United States: Bantam, 1991), 48.

107 Ibid, 49.

108 Traditionally *Anima Mundi, World Soul* has also been associated with the Mother Earth Archetype and more recently, modern science-based Gaia philosophy; for example, see Theodore Roszak, *The Voice of the Earth* (New York: Simon & Schuster, 1992), 136-159.

109 Erich Neumann (1973) *The Origins and History of Consciousness*, 15.

110 Erich Neumann, *The Great Mother: An Analysis of the Archetype* (Princeton: Princeton University Press, 1963), 329-330.

111 Joanna Macy (1991) *World as Lover, World as Self*, 13-14.

112 Matthews (2001) *Sophia – Goddess of Wisdom, Bride of God Sophia*, 76.

113 Henry Corbin, 'Towards a Chart of the Imaginal', *Temenos*, 1 (1981), 31.

114 See Matthews (2001) *Sophia – Goddess of Wisdom, Bride of God Sophia*, 76-77.

115 Note: the word 'Sophianic' can best be translated as 'that which pertains to the image and likeness of Sophia', a particularisation of one aspect of the feminine archetype; the wisdom that lies hidden or bound in matter and, hence, the *Sapientia, Scientia* or *Philosophia* of the alchemists. See Henry Corbin (1985) 'The Eternal Sophia', 7.

116 F. David Peat, *Synchronicity -- The Bridge between Matter and Mind* (N.Y & London: Bantam Books, 1988), 94.

117 Ibid, 185-186.

118 Ibid, 186-187.

119 Charles R. Card, 'The Emergence of Archetypes in Present-Day Science and its Significance for Contemporary Philosophy of Nature', *Dynamical Psychology* (1996), 26-27.

120 C.G. Jung, 'Mysterium Conjunctions' in: *The Collected Works*, vol.14, para. 552.

121 Curtis D. Smith, 'Psychological Ultimacy: Jung and the Human Basis of Religious Meaning', *Religious Humanism,* vol.25: 4 (1991), 177.

122 Stevens (1982) *Archetype,* 74.

123 Damiani (1998) *Sophia: Exile and Return*, 76-77.

124 See Titus Burckhardt, *Alchemy: Science of the Cosmos, Science of the Soul.* (London: Stuart & Watkins, 1967), 82-83.

125 Henry Corbin (1981) 'Towards a Chart of the Imaginal', 32-33.

126 Darryl Reanney(1991) *The Death of Forever – A New Future for Human Consciousness*, 220.

127 C.G. Jung, 'The Structures and Dynamics of the Psyche' in: *The Collected Works,* vol. 8, para, 226.

128 Whitmont (1982) The Return of the Goddess, 221.

129 Hillman, 'Anima Mundi – The Return of the Soul to the World' , *Spring: An Annual of Archetypal Psychology and Jungian Thought* (1982),79.

130 Peter Bishop, *The Myth of Shangri-La – Tibet, Travel Writing and the Western Creation of Sacred Landscape* (University of California Press, 1989), 251.

131 Ibid.

132 Ibid.

133 Donald Broadribb, *The Mystical Chorus – Jung and the Religious Dimension* (Australia: Millennium Books, 1995), 247-248.

134 Jim Swan, 'Sacred Places and Transcendental Experiences', *Theta: Journal of the Society for Psychic Research*, Spring (1983), 67-68.

135 Ibid, 67-68.

136 Fritjof Capra, *The Web of Life – A New Synthesis of Mind and Matter* (London: Harper Collins, 1996), 12.

137 Theodore Roszak, *The Voice of the Earth* (New York: Simon & Schuster, 1992), 320-321.

138 Macy (1991) *World as Lover, World as Self,* 12.

139 Morris Berman, *The Reenchantment of the World* (United Kingdom: Cornell University Press, 1981), 15.

140 Ibid, 23.

141 Sheldrake, *The Rebirth of Nature – The Greening of Science and God* (London: Random Century, 1990), 125.

142 Ibid, 131.

143 Ibid, 174.

144 Spretnak (1991) *States of Grace*, 23.

145 Capra (1996) *The Web of Life*, 7.

146 Ibid, 7-8.

147 Belden C. Lane, *Landscapes of the Sacred – Geography and Narrative in American Spirituality* (New York/Mahwah: Paulist Press, 1988), 191.

148 Capra (1996) *The Web of Life*, 7.

149 Spretnak (1991) *States of Grace*, 20.

150 Capra (1996) *The Web of Life*, 7.

151 Ibid, 11.

152 Ibid, 12.

153 Peter Russell, *The Global Brain – Speculations on the Evolutionary Leap to Planetary Consciousness* (Los Angeles: J.P. Tarcher, 1983), 136.

154 Maori Marsden, 'The Natural World and Natural Resources: Maori Value Systems and Perspectives', in: *Resource Management Law Reform Core Group. Working Party, No.29. Part A.* (Wellington: Ministry for the Environment, July 1989), 20.

155 Ibid, 23.

156 Ibid, 28.

157 Ibid, 26.

158 Ranganui Walker, *Nga Tau Tohetohe: Years of Anger* (Auckland: Penguin books, 1987), 78.

159 Trudie McNaughton, *Countless Signs – The New Zealand Landscape in Literature* (Auckland: Reed Methuen, 1986), 13.

160 Charles Brasch, *Indirections: A Memoir, 1903-1973* (Wellington:Oxford University Press, 1980), 321.

161 Anne Hadfield, 'A Spirituality for Aotearoa – A Personal Viewpoint' (Unpublished paper, Presbyterian Church of New Zealand, March, 1987), 4.

162 Ibid, 11.

163 Michael King, *Being Pakeha Now – Reflections and Recollections of a White Native* (Penguin Books, 1999), 240-241.

Sophia Geography

1 Note: It is impossible here to do justice to the concepts of the *Imaginal, Mundus Imaginalis* and *Ta'wil* as is evidenced by the complexity and life-time's work on translations and interpretation by Henry Corbin. At most, it is possible here only to give a very superficial indication and generalised view of some of the main themes, without differentiating them and sourcing them in detail to their particular mystical strands and esoteric historical originations.

2 Barry Lopez, *Arctic Dreams - Imagination and Desire in a Northern Landscape* (London: The Harville Press, 1998), 247.

3 Lynn Ross-Bryant, 'Of Nature and Texts: Nature and Religion in American Ecological Literature', *Anglican Theological Review*, v.73, no.1 (1991), 40.

4 Lopez (1988) *Arctic Dreams*, xxvii.

5 Ross-Bryant (1991) 'Of Nature and Texts', 40.

6 Henry Corbin, 'Towards a Chart of the Imaginal', *Temenos* 1 (1981), 30.

7 Ibid, 31.

8 Ibid, 32-33.

9 Wolfgang Pauli, 'The influence of archetypal ideas on the scientific theories of Kepler' in: C.G. Jung and W. Pauli, *The Interpretation of Nature and the Psyche* (London: Routledge & Kegan Paul, 1955), 208.

10 See Anthony Stevens, *Archetype – A Natural History of the Self* (London: Routledge & Kegan Paul, 1982), 74.

11 Anthony Stevens, 'Thoughts on the Psychobiology of Religion and the Neurobiology of Archetypal Experience', *Zygon*, v.21, no.1 (1986), 19.

12 F. David Peat, *Synchronicity – The Bridge Between Matter and Mind* (New York & London: Bantam Books, 1988), 6-7.

13 Ibid, 6.

14 Ibid.

15 David Bohm, *Thought as a System* (London: Routledge, 1994), 151.

16 Ibid, 152.

17 Michael Talbot, *The Holographic Universe* (London: Harper Collins Publishers, 1996), 84.

18 Tom Cheetham, *Green Man, Earth Angel – The Prophetic Tradition and the Battle for the Soul of the World* (Albany, N.Y: State University of New York Press, 2005), 63-64.

19 Gilbert Durand, 'Exploration of the Imaginal', *Spring* (1971), 98.

20 Ibid, 98-99.

21 Henry Corbin, 'Towards a Chart of the Imaginal', *Temenos,* 1 (1981), 23.

22 Ibid.

23 Ibid, 24.

24 Ibid.

25 Ibid.

26 Henry Corbin, 'Mundus Imaginalis or the Imaginary and the Imaginal', *Spring* (1972), 17.

27 Ibid.

28 Ibid.

29 Corbin (1981) 'Towards a Chart of the Imaginal', 24.

30 Ibid, 26.

31 David Bohm(1994) *Thought as a System*, 153.

32 Corbin(1972) 'Mundus Imaginalis, or the Imaginary and the Imaginal', 14.

33 Corbin(1972) 'Mundus Imaginalis, or the Imaginary and the Imaginal', 1.

34 Ibid, 7.

35 Ibid, 13.

36 Corbin (1981) 'Towards a Chart of the Imaginal', 31.

37 Henry Corbin, *Spiritual Body and Celestial Earth – From Mazdean Iran to Shi'ite Iran* (N.J.: Princeton University Press, 1989), 50.

38 Ibid, Prologue xxiii.

39 Ibid.

40 Ibid, xxviii.

41 Ibid, xxi.

42 David Bohm, *Wholeness and the Implicate Order* (London: Routledge & Kegan Paul, 1981), 213.

43 David Bohm and Renee Weber 'Nature as Creativity', *Revision,* 5, no.2, Fall (1982) 40. See Michael Talbot, *Beyond the Quantum* (New York: Bantam Books, 1988) 55.

44 Bohm (1981) *Wholeness and the Implicate Order*, 209.

45 Henry Corbin (1989) *Spiritual Body and Celestial Earth*, 81.

46 Ibid, 88-9.

47 Corbin(1981) 'Towards a Chart of the Imaginal', 36.

48 Corbin(1989) *Spiritual Body and Celestial Earth*, 4.

49 Ibid, 4-5.

50 Ibid, 53.

51 Ibid, 54.

52 Ibid, 54.

53 Bohm (1981) *Wholeness and the Implicate Order*, chapter 7.

54 Corbin(1981) 'Towards a Chart of the Imaginal', 31.

55 Ibid, 32-33.

56 Corbin(1989) *Spiritual Body and Celestial Earth*, 29.

57 Ibid, 29-30.

58 Ibid, 16.

59 Ibid.

60 Ibid, 35.

61 Ibid, 30. Note: Hierophany and hierophanies is from the Greek root *'hieros'* meaning "sacred" or " holy" sign; "to reveal" or " to bring to light"; signifies a manifestation of the sacred.

62 Ibid, 36.

63 Ibid, 37.

64 Ibid, 36.

65 Ibid, 40.

66 John Bierman, *The Secret Life of Laszlo Almasy – The Real English Patient* (London: Viking, 2004) 38.

67 Corbin (1989) *Spiritual Body and Celestial Earth*, 40.

68 Ibid, 66.

69 Ibid, 30.

70 Ibid.

71 Lopez (1988) *Arctic Dreams*, 414.

Afterword

1 Guilford Dudley, 'Jung and Eliade: A Difference of Opinion', *Psychological Perspectives*, vol.10, part 1 (1979) 47.

2 Ibid, 46.

3 Henry Corbin, *Spiritual Body and Celestial Earth – From Mazdean Iran to Shi'ite Iran* (New Jersey: Princeton University Press, Bollingen Series XCI:2, 1989), 81.

4 Jane Roberts, *Seth Speaks – The Eternal Validity of the Soul* (New York: Bantam Books, 1981), 258.

5 See 'Gnosis: Self-Knowledge as Knowledge of God' in Elaine Pagels, *The Gnostic Gospels* (New York: Vintage Books, 1989), 119-141.

Appendix Notes

1 Stuart Kauffman, 'God of Creativity', *New Scientist*, 10 May, (2008), 52; see also Stuart Kauffman, *Reinventing the Sacred: A New View of Science, Reason and Religion* (New York: Basic Books, 2008).

2 James Lovelock, *Homage to Gaia: The Life of an Independent Scientist* (Oxford University Press, 2000), 263-4, 389-390.

3 Anthony Stevens, *Archetype Revisited – An Updated Natural History of the Self* (London: Brunner-Routledge, 2002),348.

4 See Anthony Stevens (2002) *Archetype Revisited*, 25

5 See Walter A. Shelburne, *Mythos and Logos in the Thought of Carl Jung –The Theory of the Collective Unconscious in Scientific Perspective* (State University of New York Press, 1988),126-133.

6 Charles R. Card and Vasile V. Morariu, ' The Archetypal Hypothesis of C.G. Jung and W. Pauli and the Number Archetypes: An Extension of the Concept of the Golden Number.'
http://www.geocities.com/paideusis/n lcm.html

7 See Philip Clayton and Paul Davies, *The Re-Emergence of Emergence – The Emergentist Hypothesis from Science to Religion* (Oxford University Press, 2006).

8 See for example, Kevin J. Vanhoozer, ed., *The Cambridge Companion to Postmodern Theology* (Cambridge University Press, 2003); Graham Ward, ed., *The Postmodern God – A Theological Reader* (Blackwell Publishers, 1997); *The Blackwell Companion to Postmodern Theology* (Oxford: Blackwell Publishers, 2001).

9 David Bohm, 'Postmodern Science and a Postmodern World' in David Ray Griffin, ed., *The Reenchantment of Science* (State University of New York Press, 1988), 57-69.

10 See Timothy E. Eastman and Hank Keeton, ed., *Physics and Whitehead: Quantum Process and Experience – Suny Series in Constructive Postmodern Thought* (State University of New York Press, 2004), pp. ix-xiii; 258-273.

11 Denis Cosgrove, 'Environmental Thought and Action: Premodern and Postmodern', *Transactions of the Institute of British Geographers*, v.15(1990), 355.

12 See, for example, Edmunds V. Bunkse, 'Saint-Exupery's Geography Lesson: Art and Science in the Creation and Cultivation of Landscape Values', *Annals of the Association of American Geographers*, v.80 (1990), 96-108. Cindy Katz and Andrew Kirby, 'In the Nature of Things: The Environment and Everyday Life', *Transactions – Institute of British Geographers*, v. 16, no. 3 (1991), 259-271.

13 David Ray Griffin ed., *The Reenchantment of Science* (State University of New York Press, 1988), pp. x-xi; 1-46, 57-69.

14 See Walter A. Shelburne, *Mythos and Logos in the Thought of Carl Jung- The Theory of the Collective Unconscious in Scientific Perspective* (State University of New York Press, 1988).

15 Richard Noll, *The Jung Cult: Origins of a Charismatic Movement* (Princeton University Press, 1994); *The Aryan Christ: The Secret Life of Carl Jung* (New York: Random House, 1997).

16 See Anthony Stevens, 'Critical Notice', *Journal of Analytical Psychology*, no.42 (1997),671- 689.

17 Ibid, 671 & 689.

18 See R.C. Lewontin, Steven Rose and Leon J. Kamin, *Not in Our Genes – Biology, Ideology and Human Nature* (New York: Pantheon Books, 1984); also Hilary and Steven Rose (eds.), *Alas, Poor Darwin – Arguments Against Evolutionary Psychology* (London: Vintage, 2001).

19 Edward O. Wilson, *Consilience – The Unity of Knowledge* (New York: Alfred A. Knoff, 1998).

20 See Walter A. Shelburne, *Mythos and Logos in the Thought of Carl Jung*, p. 139. See also Anthony Stevens, *Archetype Revisited – An Updated Natural History of the Self* (London: Brunner -Routledge, 2002), 175.

21 E.O. Wilson, *Consilience*, 223-224.

22 See reviews of *Consilience* and comparisons with Jung's theory by Jim Wilder
http://www.amazon.com/Consilience-knowledge-Edward-O-Wilson   and Anthony Campbell
http://www.accampbell.uklinux.net/bookreviews/r/wilson

23 Hwa Yol Jung, 'Edward O. Wilson's Theory of Consilience: A Hermeneutical Critique' *International Journal of Public Administration*, vol. 25, nos.9 & 10 (2002), 1171-1197.

24 Edward O Wilson, *Consilience*, 40-44; 214-215.

25 Cf. ibid, 245-247.

26 See Richard Dawkins, 'The Group Delusion' in *New Scientist*, 12 January (2008), 17.

27 See R.C. Lewontin, Steven Rose and Leon J. Kamin, *Not in Our Genes – Biology, Ideology and Human Nature* (New York: Pantheon Books, 1984); also Hilary and Steven Rose (eds.) *Alas, Poor Darwin – Arguments Against Evolutionary Psychology* (London: Vintage, 2001).

28 Carl Jung, 'Psychology and Religion' (1938), *The Collected Works*, vol.11: Psychology and Religion: West and East, 131.

29 Guilford Dudley, 'Jung and Eliade: A Difference of Opinion', *Psychological Perspectives*, vol.10, part 1 (1979), 47.

30 Ibid, 46.

31 James W. Heisig, *Imago Dei – A Study of C.G. Jung's Psychology of Religion* (London: Associated University Presses, 1979), 159-160.

32 James Hillman, *Revisioning Psychology* (New York: Harper & Row Publishers, 1975), xi; and Thomas Moore (ed.), *The Essential James Hillman – A Blue Fire* (London: Routledge, 1990), 20.

33 Edward S. Casey, 'Jung and the Post-Modern Condition', *Spring* (1987), 100-101.

34 Jane Roberts, *Seth Speaks – The Eternal Validity of the Soul* (New York: Bantam Books, 1981), 60.

35 John Hitchcock, *The Web of the Universe: Jung, the "New Physics" and Human Spirituality* (New York: Paulist Press, 1991).

36 John P. Dourley, 'The Challenge of Jung's Psychology for the Study of Religion', *Studies in Religion*, v.18, no.3 (1989), 172-180.

37 Roberts (1981) *Seth Speaks*, 258.

38 David Bohm, 'Postmodern Science and a Postmodern World', in David Ray Griffin, ed., *The Reenchantment of Science – Postmodern Proposals* (State University of New York Press, 1988), 57-68.

39 David Bohm , *Wholeness and the Implicate Order* (London: Routledge & Kegan Paul, 1981).

40 Michael Talbot, *Beyond the Quantum – How the Secrets of the New Physics are Bridging the Chasm Between Science and Faith* (New York: Bantam Books, 1988), 53.

41 Roger Sperry, 'Changed Concepts of Brain and Consciousness: Some Value Implications', *Zygon*, vol.20, no.1 (1985), 41-57.

42 Hitchcock (1991) *The Web of the Universe*, 45.

43 Curtis D. Smith, 178.

44 John Kirtland Wright, '*Terrae Incognitae*: the Place of the Imagination in Geography', *Annals , Association of American Geographers*, v.37 (1947), 15.

45 David Lowenthal, 'Geography, Experience and Imagination: Towards a Geographical Epistemology', *Annals of the Association of American Geographers*, v.51, no.3, September (1961), 260. See also David Lowenthal and Martyn J. Bowden (eds.), *Geographies of the Mind – Essays in Historical Geosophy* (Oxford University Press, 1975), 3.

46 F. David Peat, *Synchronicity – The Bridge Between Matter and Mind* (N.Y. & London: Bantam Books, 1988), 94.

47 Ibid, 185-7.

48 Charles R. Card, 'The Emergence of Archetypes in Present -Day Science and its Significance for Contemporary Philosophy of Nature', *Dynamical Psychology* (1996), 26-7.

49 Anthony Stevens, *Archetype – A Natural History of the Self* (London: Routledge & Kegan Paul, 1982), 74.

50 Barry Lopez, *Arctic Dreams – Imagination and Desire in a Northern Landscape* (London: The Harville Press, 1998), 247.

51 Lynn Ross-Bryant, 'Of Nature and Texts: Nature and Religion in American Literature', *Anglican Theological Review*, v.73, no.1 (1991), 40.

52 Anthony Stevens (1986) 'Thoughts on the Psychobiology of Religion and the Neurobiology of Archetypal Experience', 19.

53 F.David, Peat (1988) *Synchronicity*, 6.

54 David Bohm, *Thought as a System* (London: Routledge, 1994), 151.

55 Henry Corbin, *Spiritual Body and Celestial Earth – From Mazdean Iran to Shi'ite Iran* (New Jersey: Princeton University Press, Bollingen Series XCI:2, 1989), 81.

56 Ibid, 54.

57 See Chapter 1: section on feminist, ecofeminist theology and ecospirituality in general. See also David Suzuki and Peter Knudtson, *Wisdom of the Elders – Honoring Sacred Native Visions of Nature* (New York & London: Bantam Books, 1992).

58 See Elaine Pagels, *The Gnostic Gospels* (New York: Vintage Books, 1989).

59 It should be noted that some of the strongest critiques are made by theologians and thinkers who are not only academics but who also have come from within, or were brought up in, the institutions of patriarchal monotheism – for example, Mary Daly, Catholic educated and former Associate Professor of Theology at Boston College, and author of *Beyond God the Father* (1973); the late Thomas Berry, ecotheologian, Catholic priest and director History of Religions, Fordham University, who wrote *The Dream of the Earth* (1988); Edward C. Whitmont, brought up an orthodox Jew, and as a doctor and therapist was founder and chairman of the C. G. Jung Training Centre of New York and he wrote *Return of the Goddess* (1982); and in New Zealand, Lloyd Geering, Emeritus Professor of Religious Studies, Victoria University, former Professor of Old Testament Studies Knox Theological College and Moderator of the Presbyterian Church, who wrote *Christianity Without God* (2002) among many other titles. All make very strong critiques of patriarchal monotheism – as does Theodore Roszak, Emeritus Professor of History, California State University, and author of *The Voice of the Earth* (1992). Alternatives are offered by Charlene Spretnak, Professor of Philosophy and Religion at California Institute of Integral Studies, co-founder of the USA Green Party, and named by the British Government's Environment Department as one of the "100 Eco-Heros of All Time", and the author of *States of Grace – the Recovery of Meaning in the Postmodern Age* (1991); Dr. Carol P. Christ, former lecturer at Harvard Divinity School and Columbia University, ecofeminist and process theologian who wrote, among other titles, *She Who Changes: Re-imagining the Divine in the World* (2003).

60 Anthony Stevens, 'Thoughts on the Psychobiology of Religion and the Neurobiology of Archetypal Experience', *Zygon*, v.21, no.1 (1986), 16.

61 Carl Jung, 'The Concept of the Collective Unconscious', *The Collected Works*, vol.9, para.155.

Bibliography

Adler, Gerhard, 'Aspects of Jung's Personality and Work', *Psychological Perspectives*, vol.6, no.1, Spring (1979), pp. 11-21.

Alexander, Jon, 'What Do Recent Writers Mean by Spirituality?', *Spirituality Today*, v.32, no.3, Sept, (1980), pp. 247-256.

Alfonso, Ortiz, 'Why Nature Hates the White Man', *Omni*, March (1990), pp.75-97.

Allen-Mills, Tony, 'Chilling Report of Abuse', *The Press*, Christchurch, May 24, 2004, p.B.4. (Reprinted from *The Sunday Times*, May, 2004.)

Armstrong, Karen, *A History of God* (London: Mandarin Paperbacks, 1994).

Bakan, Joel, *The Corporation – The Pathological Pursuit of Profit and Power* (New York: Free Press, Simon & Schuster, 2004).

Baker, Peter, 'Maintaining Male Power: Why Heterosexual Men Use Pornography' in Catherine Itzin (ed.) *Pornography – Women, Violence and Civil Liberties* (Oxford Univesity Press, 1992), pp.124-165.

Balestra, Dominic J., 'Technology in a Free Society: The New Frankenstein', *Thought: A Review of Culture and Idea*, v.65, no.257, (June 1990), pp.155-168.

Baring, Anne and Jules Cashford, *The Myth of the Goddess: Evolution of an Image* (London: Viking Arkana, 1991).

Barrett, William, *Irrational Man – A Study in Existential Philosophy* (London: Heinemann, 1967).

Bean, Wendell C., and William G. Doty (eds.), *Myths, Rites, Symbols: A Mircea Eliade Reader* (New York: Harper & Row, 1975).

Berman, Morris, *The Reenchantment of the World* (United Kingdom: Cornell University Press, 1981).

Bernstein, Richard, *Beyond Objectivism and Relativism: Science, Hermeneutics and Praxis* (Philadelphia, PA: University of Pennsylvannia Press, 1985).

Berry, Thomas, *The Dream of the Earth* (San Francisco: Sierra Club, 1988).

Best, Elsdon, *Some Aspects of Maori Myth and Religion*, Dominion Museum Monograph No.1., (Wellington: Govt. Printer, 1954).

Best, Elsdon, *Maori Religion and Mythology*, Part 1., (Wellington: Dominion Museum Bulletin, 10, 1924).

Best, Elsdon, *The Maori* (Wellington: Polynesian Society, 1941 [1924] vol. 1.)

Bhardwaj, S., *Sentimental Journeys: Thoughts on the Nature of Pilgrimage*. (Conference Paper: Department of Geography, Kent State University, Ohio, 1990).

Bierman, John, *The Secret life of Laszlo Almasy – The Real English Patient* (London: Viking, 2004).

Biggs, John, 'Towards a Theology for the Environment', *Baptist Quarterly*, v.34, no.1 (1991), pp.33-42.

Bishop, Peter, 'Rhetoric, Memory and Power: Depth Psychology and Postmodern Geography', *Environmental and Planning D: Society and Space*, v.10 (1992), pp. 5-22.

Bishop, Peter, *The Myth of Shangri-La – Tibet, Travel Writing and the Western Creation of Sacred Lasndscape* (Berkeley & Los Angeles. CA: University of California Press, 1989).

Bogart, Leo, 'Media Habits of Media Tycoons', *Transaction Social Science and Modern Society*, v.30, no.5, July/August (1993), pp. 49-56.

Bohm, David, 'Postmodern Science and a Postmodern World', in David Ray Griffin (ed.), *The Reenchantment of Science – Postmodern Proposals* (New York: State University of New York Press, 1988), pp. 57-68.

Bohm, David, and Renee Weber, 'Nature as Creativity', *Revision*, 5, no.2, Fall (1982), pp.35-40.

Bohm, David, *Wholeness and the Implicate Order*, (London: Routledge & Kegan Paul, 1981).

Bohm, David, *Thought as a System* (London: Routledge, 1994).

Bonhoeffer, Dietrich, *Letters and Papers from Prison*, trans. Reginald Fuller et al, ed. Eberhard Bethge, rev.ed.(New York: Macmillan Company,1972).

Booth, Annie, L. and Jacobs, Harvey, M, 'Ties the Bind: Native American Beliefs as a Foundation for Environmental Consciousness', *Environmental Ethics*, v.12, no.1 (1990), pp. 27-43.

Brasch, Charles, *Indirections : A Memoir, 1903-1973*. (Wellington NZ: Oxford University Press, 1980) .

Broadribb, Donald. *The Mystical Chorus – Jung and the Religious Dimension* (Australia: Millenium Books, 1995).

Brown, Norman O., *Hermes the Thief* (New York: Vintage Books, 1969).

Buber, Martin, *I and Thou* (Edinburgh: T&T. Clark, 1970).

Bunkse, Edmunds V., 'Saint-Exupery's Geography Lesson: Art and Science in the Creation and Cultivation of Landscape Values', *Annals of the Association of American Geographers*, vol. 80 (1990), pp. 96-108.

Burckhardt, Titus, *Alchemy: Science of the Cosmos, Science of the Soul* (London: Stuart & Watkins, 1967).

Buttner, M., 'Survey Article on the History and Philosophy of the Geography of Religion in Germany', *Religion*, vol.10 (1980), pp. 86-119.

Callicott, J. Baird and Ames, Roger, T. (eds.), *Nature in Asian Traditions of Thought – Essays in Environmental Philosophy* (New York: State University of New York Press, 1989).

Callicott, J.Baird, 'Traditional American Indian and Western European Attitudes Toward Nature: An Overview', *Environmental Ethics*, v.4 (1982), pp. 293-309.

Campbell, Joseph, *The Inner Reaches of Outer Space – Metaphor as Myth and as Religion* (New York: Harper & Row, 1986).

Capra, Fritjof, *The Web of Life – A New Synthesis of Mind and Matter* (London: Harper Collins,1996).

Card, Charles, R and Vasile V. Morariu, 'The Archetypal Hypothesis of C.G.Jung and W. Pauli and the Number Archetypes: An Extension of the Concept of the Golden Number.' http:/www.geocities.com/paideusis/n1cm.html

Card, Charles, R, 'The Emergence of Archetypes in Present-Day Science and its Significance for a Contemporary Philosophy of Nature', *Dynamical Psychology – An Interdisciplinary Journal of Complex Mental Processes* (1996), pp. 1-20. http://goertzel.org/dynapsyc/1996/natphil.html.

Casey, Edward, 'Towards an Archetypal Imagination', *Spring: An Annual of Archetypal Psychology and Jungian Thought* (1974), pp. 1-33.

Casey, Edward, S, 'Jung and the Post-Modern Condition', *Spring: An Annual of Archetypal Psychology and Jungian Thought* (1987), pp. 100-6.

Chawla, Saroj, 'Linguistic and Philosophical Roots of Our Environmental Crisis', *Environmental Ethics*, v.13, no.3, (1991), pp. 253-262.

Cheetham, Tom, *Green Man, Earth Angel – The Prophetic Tradition and the Battle for the Soul of the World* (Albany, NY: State University of New York Press, 2005).

'Child Porn Sites Increase', *The Press*, Christchurch, January 20, 2004, p.C.5.

Chown, Marcus, 'Clock-Watchers', *New Scientist*, 1 May (2004), pp. 34-37.

Christ, Carol, P, 'Rethinking Theology and Nature', in Plaskow, Judith and Christ, Carol, P. (eds.), *Weaving the Visions – New Patterns in Feminist Spirituality* (San Francisco: Harper, 1989), pp. 314-325.

Christ, Carol, P. *She Who Changes – Re-imagining the Divine in the World* , (New York: Palgrave McMillan, 2003).

Clayton, Philip and Paul Davies (eds), *The Re-Emergence of Emergence – The Emergentist Hypothesis from Science to Religion* (Oxford University Press, 2006).

Collard, Andree and Joyce Contrucci, *Man's Violence Against Animals and the Earth* (Indiana University Press, 1989).

Combs, Alan and Mark Holland, *Synchronicity – Science, Myth and the Trickster* (New York: Paragon House,1990).

Cooper, A., 'New Directions in the Geography of Religion', *Area*, v.24, no.2(1992), pp. 123-129.

Corbin, Henry, 'Mundus Imaginalis or the Imaginary and the Imaginal', *Spring: An Annual of Archetypal Psychology and Jungian Thought* (1972), pp.1-15.

Corbin, Henry, 'The Eternal Sophia', *Harvest*, vol.31 (1985), pp. 7-23.

Corbin, Henry, 'Towards a Chart of the Imaginal', *Temenos*, 1 (1981), pp.23-36.

Corbin, Henry, *Spiritual Body and Celestial Earth – From Mazdean Iran to Shi'ite Iran* (New Jersey: Princeton Univesity Press, Bollingen Series XCI:2, 1989). (Note: Fifth Printing with prelude to Second Edition, 1989. Copyright 1977 Princeton University Press. Originally published in French 1953 and 1960).

Corbin, Henry, *Creative Imagination in the Sufism of Ibn 'Arabi* (Princeton: Princeton University Press, 1969).

Cosgrove, Denis, 'Environmental Thought and Action: Pre-modern and Post-modern', *Transactions of the Institute of British Geographers*, v.15 (1990), pp. 344-358.

Cosgrove, Denis E., *Social and Symbolic Landscape* (London & Sydney: Croom Helm, 1984).

Cowan, James G., 'Aboriginal Solitude', *Parabola Magazine*, v.17. Part 1 (1992), pp. 62-67.

Crowley, Paul, 'Technology, Truth and Language: The Crisis of Theological Discourse', *The Heythrop Journal*, v.32, no.3 (1991), pp. 323-389.

Dallas, Ruth, 'Deep in the Hills', in Philip Temple (ed.), *Lake, Mountain, Tree – An Anthology of Writing on New Zealand Nature and Landscape* (Auckland: Godwit, 1998).

Daly, Mary, *Gyn/Ecology – The Metaethics of Radical Feminism* (Boston: Beacon Press, 1978).

Daly, Mary, *Pure Lust – Elemental Feminist Philosophy* (London: The Women's Press, 1984).

Daly, Mary, *Beyond God the Father – Toward a Philosophy of Women's Liberation* (Boston: Beacon Press, 1973).

Damiani, Kathleen Granville, *Sophia: Exile and Return* (Ann Arbor, MI: UMI Company, 1998).

Damiani, Kathleen, Granville, 'Sophia, Soul of the World' (2004), http://azothgallery.com/alchemical/ k-damiani-sophia soul.html.

Davis, Erik, *Techgnosis – Myth, Magic and Mysticism in the Age of Information* (London: Serpents Tail, 1999).

Dawkins, Richard, 'The Group Delusion', *New Scientist*, 12 January (2008), p.17.

Dawkins, Richard. *The God Delusion* (London: Transworld Publishers / Bantam Press, 2006).

de Qunicey, Christian, 'Deep Spirit: Quantum Consciousness' (2005), http://www.deepspirit.com/systmpl/quantumconsciousness.

de Beauvoir, Simone, *The Second Sex* (London: New English Library, 1970).

Dennett, Daniel, *Breaking the Spell: Religion as Natural Phenomenon* (London: Penguin, 2006).

Denver, William G, 'Women's Popular Religion Suppressed in the Bible, Now Revealed by Archaeology', *Biblical Archaeology Review*, v.17, no.2 (1991), pp. 64-5.

Dourley, John P, 'Some Implications of Jung's Understanding of Mysticism., *Toronto Journal of Theology*, v.6. pt.1 (1990), pp.15-26.

Dourley, John P., 'The Challenge of Jung's Psychology for the Study of Religion', *Studies in Religion*, v.18, no.3 (1989), pp. 297-311.

Dourley, John P., 'The Jung, Buber, White exchanges: Exercises in futility', *Studies in Religion*, v.20, part 3 (1991), pp. 299-309.

Dudley, Guilford, 'Jung and Eliade: A Difference of Opinion', *Psychological Perspectives*, vol.10, part 1 (1979), pp. 38-47.

Durand, Gilbert, 'Exploration of the Imaginal', *Spring: An Annual of Archetypal Psychology and Jungian Thought* (1971), pp. 84-100.

Eastman, Timothy E., and Hank Keeton (eds), *Physics and Whitehead: Quantum Process and Experience*, SUNY Series in Constructive Postmodern Thought, (New York: State University of New York, 2004).

Edinger, Edward F., *Ego and Archetype – Individuation and the Religious Function of the Psyche* (Baltimore: Penguin Books, 1973).

Elias, John L., 'The Return of Spirituality: Contrasting Interpretations', *Religious Education*, v.86, no.3 (1991), pp. 455-466.

Englesman, Joan Chamberlain, *The Feminine Dimension of the Divine* (Philadelphia: The Westminster Press, 1979).

Evans, Donald, *Spirituality and Human Nature* (New York: State University of New York Press, 1993).

Evison, Harry C., *Te Wai Pounamu The Greenstone Island – A History of the Southern Maori during the European Colonization of New Zealand* (Christchurch: Aoraki Press,1993).

Faricy, Robert, *Approaches to a Theology of Nature* (London: SCM Press, 1982).

Fisher, Frank, 'Technology and the Loss of Self: An Environmental Concern', *Environments*, v. 20, no.2 (1989), pp. 1-16.

Fletcher, Ronald, 'Hearth and Home', *Transaction Social Science and Modern Society*, v.31, no.1 Nov/Dec (1993), pp. 55-60.

Frankfort, H., H. A. Frankfort, John A. Wilson, Thorkild Jacobsen, and William A. Irwin, *The Intellectual Adventure of Ancient Man – An Essay on Speculative Thought in the Ancient Near East* (Chicago: University of Chicago Press, 1946).

Friedman, Maurice, *Martin Buber – The Life of Dialogue* (N.Y.: Harper & Row, 1960).

Gedicks, Frederick Mark, 'Spirituality, Fundamentalism, Liberty: Religion at the End of Modernity', *DePaul Law Review*, vol 54 (2005), pp.1193-231.

Geering, Lloyd, *Christianity Without God* (Wellington: Bridget Williams Books, 2002).

Geering, Lloyd, *About Time* (Wellington: St Andrew's Trust for the Study of Religion and Society, 1989).

Geering, Lloyd, *The World of Relation – An Introduction to Martin Buber's I and Thou* (Wellington: Victoria University Press, 1983).

Geering, Lloyd, *Religious Trailblazers* (Wellington: St. Andrew's Trust for the Study of Religion and Society,1992).

Gibbons, Jenny, 'Recent Developments in the Study of the Great European Witch Hunt', *Pomegranate* (Lammas, 1998) http://www.cog.org/witch-hunt.html 8 pp.

Glacken, C. J., *Traces on the Rhodian Shore* (CA: University of California Press, 1967).

Goldenberg, Naomi, *Changing the Gods – Feminism and the End of Traditional Religions* (Boston: Beacon Press, 1979).

Griffin, David Ray (ed.), *The Re-enchantment of Science – Postmodern Proposals* (New York: State University of New York Press,1988).

Griffin, Susan, *Woman and Nature: The Roaring Inside Her* (New York: Harper & Row, 1978).

Griffin, Susan, *Pornography and Silence: Culture's Revenge Against Nature* (New York: Harper & Collins, 1981).

Grof, Stanislav, *Beyond the Brain* (Albany, N.Y.: State University of New York Press, 1985).

Grof, Stanislav, *Realms of the Human Unconscious: Observations from L.S.D Research* (New York: Dutton, 1976).

Gudgeon, C. M. G., 'Mana Tangata', *The Journal of Polynesian Society*, v.14, no.54 (1905), pp. 49-66.

Gulick, Walter, 'The Bible and Ecological Spirituality', *Theology Today*, v.48, no.2 (1991), pp.182-194.

Hadfield, Anne, 'A Spirituality for Aotearoa – A Personal Viewpoint' (Unpublished Paper, Presbyterian Church of New Zealand, March, 1987).

Hallman, Max O, 'Nietzsche's Environmental Ethics', *Environmental Ethics*, v.13, no.2 (1991), pp.43-60.

Hansen, George,P., *The Trickster and the Paranormal* (Philadelphia: Xlibris Corporation, 2001).

Harrelson, Walter, *From Fertility Cult to Worship* (Garden City, New York: Doubleday & Co, 1969).

Harries, K, 'Metaphor and Transcendence', in S. Sacks (ed.), *On Metaphor* (Chicago: University of Chicago Press, 1978), pp. 71-88.

Harris, Sam, *The End of Faith : Religion, Terror, and the Future of Reason* (United States: W.W. Norton, 2004).

Harvey, David, *The Condition of Postmodernity: An Enquiry into the Origins of Cultural Change* (Cambridge: Basil Blackwell, 1989).

Hauke, Christopher, *Jung and the Postmodern – The Interpretation of Realities* (London: Routledge, 2000).

Hawking, Stephen, *A Brief History of Time* (London: Bantam Press, 1988).

Heft, Harry, and Joachim F. Wohlwill, 'Environmental Cognition in Children' in Daniel Stokols and Irwin Altman (eds.), *Handbook of Environmental Psychology* (Malabar Florida: Krieger Publishing Company, 1991), pp. 175-203.

Heidegger, Martin, *On the Way to Language* (San Francisco: Harper & Row, 1971).

Heim, Michael, *The Metaphysics of Virtual Reality* (Oxford University Press, 1993).

Heisig, James, W., *Imago Dei – A Study of C.G. Jung's Psychology of Religion* (London: Associated University Presses, 1979).

Henderson, Joseph, L., 'Ancient Myths and Modern Man', in Carl Jung (ed.), *Man and His Symbols* (London: Picador, 1964).

Hewitt, Marsha, 'Woman, Nature and Power: Emancipatory Themes in Critical Theory and Feminist Theology', *Studies in Religion*, v.20, no.3 (1991), pp. 267-279.

Hillman, James, *Archetypal Psychology – a Brief Account* (Dallas: Spring Publications Inc., 1993).

Hillman, James, 'Anima Mundi – The Return of the Soul to the World', *Spring: An Annual of Archetypal Psychology and Jungian Thought*, (1982), pp. 71-93.

Hillman, James, *The Dream and the Underworld* (New York: Harper & Row, 1979).

Hillman, James, *ReVisioning Psychology* (New York: Harper & Row, 1975).

Hinsliff, Gaby, 'Not so much about God in Classes on Religion', *The Christchurch Press*, Christchurch, Feb, 16 (2004), p. A.11.

Hitchcock, John, *The Web of the Universe: Jung, the "New Physics" and Human Spirituality* (New York: Paulist Press, 1991).

Hitchens, Christopher, *God is Not Great: How Religion Poisons Everything* (USA: Twelve/Hachette Warner Books, 2007).

Holderness, Mike, 'Enemy at the Gates', *New Scientist*, 8 October (2005), p. 48.

Holt, David, 'Jung and Marx', *Spring: An Annual of Archetypal Psychology and Jungian Thought*, (1973), pp. 52-66.

Hughes, J. Donald and Jim Swan, 'How Much of the Earth is Sacred Place?', *Environmental Review*, v.10, no.4 (Winter, 1986), pp. 247-259.

Irwin, Sally, *Between Heaven and Earth – The Life of a Mountaineer, Freda Du Faur* (Australia: White Crane Press, 2000).

Isaac, Erich, 'Religion, Landscape and Space', *Landscape*, v.9, no.2 (Winter, 1959-60), pp. 14-18.

Isaac, Erich, 'The act and the covenant: the impact of religion on the landscape', *Landscape*, 11 (1962), pp. 12-17.

Isham, Christopher, 'Space and Time at the Edge of Mind', Royal College of Psychiatrists: http://www.repsych.ac.uk/college/specialinterestgroups/spirituality/publications/newsletter"/

Itzin, Catherine (ed.), *Pornography – Women, Violence and Civil Liberties* (Oxford University Press, 1992).

Jackson, Moana, 'The Treaty and the Word: The Colonization of Maori Philosophy', in Graham Oddie and Roy Perret (eds.), *Justice, Ethics and New Zealand Society* (Oxford University Press, 1992).

Jackson, Peter, *Maps of Meaning – An Introduction to Cultural Geography* (London: Unwin Hyman, 1989).

Jaffe, Lawrence W., *Liberating the Heart – Spirituality and Jungian Psychology* (Toronto: Inner City Books, 1990).

Johnson, Mark, *The Body in the Mind – The Bodily Basis of Meaning, Imagination and Reason* (Chicago: University of Chicago Press, 1987).

Jung ,C.G, Unless otherwise stated, most quotations in the text originate from *The Collected Works of C.G. Jung*, edited by H. Read, M. Fordham and G.Adler, and published in London by Routledge & Kegan Paul, 1953-78. Because of a number of editions, quotation sources in the text are indicated by the volume number followed by the number of the paragraph from which the quotation is taken.

Jung , C. G., *Synchronicity – An Acausal Connecting Principle* (trans. R.F.Hull) (Princeton Paperback Edition, 1973).

Jung, C. G., 'Mind and Earth', in *The Collected Works of C.G.Jung*, vol.10 (1953-78).

Jung, C, G., ' Mysterium Conjunctionis', in *The Collected Works of C.G.Jung*, vol.14 (1953-78).

Jung, C,G, 'Psychology and Alchemy', in *The Collected Works of C.G. Jung*, vol.12 (1953-78).

Jung, C,G, ' Psychology and Religion: West and East', in *The Collected Works of C.G.Jung*, vol.11 (1953-78).

Jung, C,G, 'Two Essays on Analytical Psychology', in *The Collected Works of C.G.Jung*, vol.7 (1953-78).

Jung, C,G. 'The Structures and Dynamics of the Psyche', in *The Collected Works of C.G.Jung*, vol.8 (1953-78).

Jung, C,G, 'Researches into the Phenomenology of the Self' in *The Collected Works of C.G.Jung*, vol.9. part 2 (2d.ed 1968).

Jung, C,G, 'The Concept of the Collective Unconscious' in *The Collected Works of C.G.Jung*, vol.9 (1953-78).

Jung, C,G, 'Answer to Job'; 'Psychology and Religion' in *The Collected Works of C.G.Jung*, vol.11 (1953-78).

Jung, C,G, 'The Symbolic Life' in *The Collected Works of C.G.Jung*, vol.18 (1976).

Jung, C.G.,'Mysterium Conjunctionis' in *The Collected Works of C.G.Jung*, vol.14 (1963, 1970).

Jung,C.G, 'Psychological Aspects of the Mother Archetype', in *The Collected Works of C.G.Jung*, vol.9, Part 1 (1959).

Jung,C.G. 'Symbols of Transformation' in *The Collected Works of C.G.Jung*, vol.5 (1967).

Jung, C.G. (ed.), *Man and His Symbols* (London: Picador, Pan Books, 1978).

Jung, C.G., *Four Archetypes*, (Routledge & Kegan Paul, London, 1980).pb.

Jung, Hwa Yol, 'Edward O. Wilson's Theory of Consilience: A Hermeneutical Critique', *Journal of Public Administration*, vol.25, nos. 9 &10 (2002), pp.1171-1197.

Jung, Hwa Yol, 'Marxism and Deep Ecology in Postmodernity: From Homo Oeconomicus to Homo Ecologies', *Thesis Eleven* , v. 28 (1991), pp. 86-99.

Katz, Cindy and Andrew Kirby, 'In the Nature of Things: the Environment and Everyday Life', *Transactions – Institute of British Geographers*, v.16, no.3 (1991), pp. 259-271.

Katz, Eric, 'The Call of the Wild: The Struggle Against Domination and the Technological Fix of Nature', *Environmental Ethics*, v.14. no.3 (1992), pp. 265-273.

Kaufman, Gordon D., *In the Face of Mystery – A Constructive Theology* (Cambridge, MA: Harvard University Press,1993).

Kauffman, Stuart, 'God of Creativity', *New Scientist*, 10 May (2008), pp. 52-53.

Kauffman, Stuart, *Reinventing the Sacred: A New View of Scicnce, Reason and Religion,* (New York: Basic Books, 2008).

Kay, Jeanne, 'Human Dominion over Nature in the Hebrew Bible', *Annals of the Association of American Geographers*, v.79 (1989), pp. 214-232.

Keiser, Melvin R., 'Postcritical Religion and the Latent Freud', *Zygon*, v. 25, no.4 (1990), pp. 433-447.

Kelly, K.W. (ed.), *The Home Planet* (Reading, MA: Addison-Wesley, 1988).

King, Sallie B., 'Two Epistemological Models for the Interpretation of Mysticism', *Journal of the American Academy of Religion*, LVI/2, Summer (1988), pp. 257-279.

Kong, Lily, 'Geography and Religion: Trends and Prospects', *Progress in Human Geography*, v.14 (1990), pp. 355-371.

Lane, Belden C., *Landscapes of the Sacred – Geography and Narrative in American Spirituality* (New York/Mahwah: Paulist Press,1988).

Lapsley, James N., 'Spirit and Self', *Pastoral Psychology*, v.38, no.3, Spring (1990), pp. 135-146.

Lee, Sandra, 'Cherishing Papatuanuku'. Interview by Powhiri Rika–Heke, *Nga Kaitiaki*, no.21, August/September (1989), pp. 8-9.

Leonard, Ellen, 'Experience as a Source for Theology: A Canadian and Feminist Perspective', *Studies in Religion*, v.19, no.2 (1990), pp. 143-162.

Leopold, Aldo, *A Sand Country Almanac: With Essays on Conservation from Round River* (New York: Ballantine Books, 1966).

Lewontin, R.C., Rose, Steven, and Kamin, Leon, J., *Not in Our Genes – Biology, Ideology and Human Nature* (New York: Pantheon Books, 1984).

Ley, David & Samuels, Marwyn , S. (eds.), *Humanistic Geography* (London:Croom Helm, 1978).

Lopez, Barry, *Arctic Dreams – Imagination and Desire in a Northern Landscape* (London: The Harvill Press, 1998).

Lovelock, James, *Homage to Gaia: The Life of an Independent Scientist* (Oxford University Press, 2000).

Lovelock, James, *The Ages of Gaia – A Biography of our Living Earth* (Oxford: Oxford Univesity Press, 1989).

Lowenthal, David and Martyn J. Bowden (eds.), *Geographies of the Mind –Essays in Historical Geography* (Oxford University Press, 1975).

Lowenthal, David, 'Geography, Experience, and Imagination: Towards a Geographical Epistemology', *Annals of the Association of American Geographers*, v.51, no.3, September (1961), pp. 241-260.

Macy, Joanna, *World as Lover, World as Self* (Berkley, CA: Parallax Press, 1991).

Manji, Irshad, *The Trouble With Islam: A Muslim's Call for reform in her Faith* (Canada: Random House, 2003).

'Maori Values and Environmental Management', (New Zealand: Natural Resources Unit, *Manata Maori*, 1991), pp. 1-10.

Maquarrie, John, *In Search of Deity* (London: SCM Press, 1984).

Markeley, O.W. and Willis W. Harman (eds.), *Changing Images of Man* (London: Pergamon Press, 1982).

Marsden, Maori, 'The Natural World and Natural Resources, Maori Value Systems and Perspectives (Part A)' in *Resource Management Law Reform Core Group Working Paper no.29*, (Ministry for the Environment, Wellington, July, 1989).

Martin, William, *The Taranaki Question* (London: W.H. Dalton, 1961.)

Matless, D, 'An Occasion for Geography: Landscape, Representation and Foucault's Corpus', *Environment and Planning D: Society and Space*, v.10 (1992), pp. 41-56.

Matthews, Caitlin, *Sophia – Goddess of Wisdom, Bride of God* (Illinois: Quest Books, Theosophical Publishing House, 2001).

Maturana, Humberto R., and Francisco J. Varela, *The Tree of Knowledge – The Biological Roots of Human Understanding* (Boston: New Science Library, 1987).

McIlwrath, James and Hamilton, *Letters home to parents John and Jane Logan McIlwrath and brothers in County Down, Ireland*, (Canterbury, September 8,1862 & December 1, 1863).

McFague, Sally, *Models of God: Theology for an Ecological, Nuclear Age* (Philadelphia: Fortress Press, 1987).

McHarg, Ian, 'Values, Process, Form', in Robert Disch (ed.), *The Ecological Conscience: Values for Survival* (Englewood Cliffs, NJ: Prentice Hall,1970), pp.21-36.

McNaughton, Trudie (ed.), *Countless Signs – The New Zealand Landscape in Literature* (Auckland: Reed Methuen, 1986).

Meinig, Donald (ed.), *The Interpretation of Ordinary Landscapes* (Oxford University Press,1979).

Merchant, Carolyn, *The Death of Nature – Woman, Ecology, and the Scientific Revolution* (San Francisco: Harper & Row, 1980).

Moore, Thomas & James Hillman (eds.), *The Essential James Hillman –A Blue Fire* (London: Routledge, 1990).

Napoleoni, Loretta, *Rogue Economics – Capitalism's New Reality* (Australia & New Zealand: Allen & Unwin, 2008).

Neihardt, John G., *Black Elk Speaks: Being the Life Story of a Holy Man of the Oglala Sioux* (New York: Pocket Books, 1975).

Neumann, Erich, *The Great Mother: An Analysis of the Archetype* (Princeton: Princeton Univesity Press, 1963).

Neumann, Erich, *The Origins and History of Consciousness*, Bollingen Series XLII (Princeton: Princeton University Press, 1973).

Noll, Richard, *The Aryan Christ:The Secret Life of Carl Jung* (New York: Random House,1997).

Noll, Richard, *The Jung Cult: Origins of a Charismatic Movement* (Princeton University Press, 1994).

Odin, Steve, 'The Japanese Concept of Nature in Relation to the Environmental Ethics and Conservation Aesthetics of Aldo Leopold', *Environmental Ethics*, v.13, no.4 (1991), pp. 345-60.

Pagels, Elaine, *The Gnostic Gospels* (New York: Vintage, 1979).

Park, Geoff, *Nga Uruora – The Groves of Life: Ecology and History in a New Zealand Landscape* (Wellington: Victoria University Press, 1995).

Passmore, John, *Man's Responsibility for Nature* (London: Unwin Brothers, 1974).

Patterson, John, *Exploring Maori Values* (Palmerston North: Dunmore Press, 1992).

Pauli, Wolfgang, 'The Influence of Archetypal Ideas on the Scientific Theories of Kepler', in C.G. Jung and W.Pauli, *The Interpretation of Nature and the Psyche* (London: Routledge & Kegan Paul, 1955), pp. 147-240.

Peat, F. David, *Synchronicity – The Bridge Between Matter and Mind* (New York & London: Bantam Books, 1988).

Peat, F. David, 'Time, Synchronicity and Evolution', 3. http://www.fdavidpeat.com/biography/essays/text/saur.txt.

Peat, F. David, *The Philosopher's Stone* (United States: Bantam Books, 1991).

Pennachio, John, 'Gnostic Illumination and Carl Jung's Individuation', *Journal of Religion and Health*, v.31. no.3, Fall (1992), pp. 237-245.

Porteous, J. Douglas, *Landscapes of the Mind – Worlds of Sense and Metaphor* (University of Toronto Press, 1990).

Porter, Muriel, *Sex, Power and the Clergy* (Australia: Hardie Grant Books, 2003).

Postman, Neil, *Technopoly – The Surrender of Culture to Technology* (New York: Alfred, A. Knopf, 1992).

Postman, Neil, *Amusing Ourselves to Death – Public Discourse in the Age of Show Business* (London: Heinemann, 1986).

Principe, Walter, 'Toward Defining Spirituality', *Studies in Religion*, v.12, no.2, (1983), pp. 127-141.

Radin, Paul, *The Trickster - A Study in American Indian Mythology* – With commentaries by Karl Kerenyi and C.G.Jung (London: Routledge and Kegan Paul, 1956).

Reanney, Darryl, *The Death of Foreever – A New Future for Human Consciousness* (Melbourne: Longman Cheshire, 1991).

Reineke, Martha, ' "The Devils Are Come Down Upon Us" – Myth, History, and the Witch as Scapegoat', *Union Seminary Quarterley Review*, v.44, no.1/2 (1990), pp. 55-83.

Roberts, Jane, *Seth Speaks, the Eternal Validity of the Soul* (New York: Bantam Books, 1981).

Roberts, Jane, *The Unknown Reality*, vol.1 (London: Prentice-Hall, 1977).

Rose, Hilary and Steven Rose (eds.), *Alas, Poor Darwin – Arguments Against Evolutionary Psychology* (London: Vintage, 2001).

Ross-Bryant, Lynn, 'Of Nature and Texts: Nature and Religion in American Ecological Literature', *American Theological Review*, vol.73, no.1 (1991), p. 40.

Roszak, Betty, 'The Spirit of the Goddess', *Resurgence,* no.144, Jan-Feb (1991), pp. 28-29.

Roszak, Theodore, *The Voice of the Earth* (New York: Simon & Schuster,1992).

Ruether, Rosemary Radford, 'Ecology and Human Liberation: A Conflict between the Theology of History and the Theology of Nature', in *To Change the World: Christology and Cultural Criticism* (New York: Crossroad, 1981), pp. 57-70.

Ruether, Rosemary Radford, *New Women, New Earth* (New York: Seabury, 1975).

Russell, Peter, *The Global Brain – Speculations on the Evolutionary Leap to Planetary Consciousness* (Los Angeles, CA: J.P. Tarcher, 1983).

Sack, Robert D., 'The Consumers' World: Place as Context', *Annals of the Association of American Geographers*, v.78 (1988), pp. 642-644.

Salleh, Ariel, 'The Ecofeminism / Deep Ecology Debate: A Reply to Patriarchal Reason', *Environmental Ethics*, v.14, no.3 (1992), pp. 195-216.

Sardar, Ziauddin, and Jerome, R. Ravetz (eds.), *Cyberfutures – Culture and Politics on the Information Superhighway* (London: Pluto Press, 1996).

Sauer, Carl, 'The Morphology of Landscape', in: *Geography 2* (1925), pp. 19-54.

Sebba, Rachel, 'The Landscapes of Childhood – The Reflection of Childhood's Environment in Adult Memories and in Children's Attitudes', *Environment and Behavior*, v. 23, no.4, July (1991), pp. 395-422.

Shelburne, Walter A., *Mythos and Logos in the Thought of Carl Jung – The Theory of the Collective Unconscious in Scientific Perspective* (Albany: State University of New York Press, 1988).

Sheldrake, Rupert, *The Rebirth of Nature – The Greening of Science and God* (London: Random Century, 1990).

Simmons, D. R., *Iconography of New Zealnd Maori Religion* (Leiden: E.J. Brill, 1986).

Simpson, Philip, Interview: 'Exploring the Gaia Hypothesis', *Nga Kaitiaki*, no.21, August/September, (1989), p. 10.

Skolimowski, Henryk, *The Participatory Mind – A New Theory of Knowledge and of the Universe* (London: Arkana, Penguin Group, 1994).

Smith , Curtis D., 'Psychological Ultimacy: Jung and the Human Basis of Religious Meaning', *Religious Humanism*, v.25, no.4 (1991), pp. 172-180.

Smith, Steven G., *The Concept of the Spiritual* (Philadelphia, PA: Temple University Press, 1988).

Soja, E., 'The Postmodernization of Geography: A Review', *Annals of the Association of American Geographers*, 77 (1987), pp. 289-294.

Sopher, David E., 'Geography and Religions', *Progress in Human Geography*, v.5 (1981), pp. 510-524.

Sperry, Roger, 'Changed Concepts of Brain and Consciousness: Some Value Implications', *Zygon*, v.20, no.1 (1985), pp. 41-57.

Spretnak, Charlene, *The Spiritual Dimension of Green Politics* (Santa Fe: N.M. Bear & Co., 1986).

Spretnak, Charlene, *States of Grace – The Recovery of Meaning in the Postmodern Age* (San Francisco: Harper Collins, 1991).

Stevens, Anthony, 'Critical Notice', *Journal of Analytical Psychology*, no. 42 (1997), pp. 671-689.

Stevens, Anthony, 'Thoughts on the Psychobiology of Religion and the Neurobiology of Archetypal Experience', *Zygon*, v.21. no.1 (1986), pp. 2-29.

Stevens, Anthony, *Archetype Revisited – An Updated Natural History of the Self* (London: Brunner–Routledge, 2002).

Stevens, Anthony, *Archetype – A Natural History of the Self* (London: Routledge & Kegan Paul, 1982).

Stiver, D. R., 'Theological Method', in Kevin J. Vanhoozer (ed.), *The Cambridge Companion to Postmodern Theology* (Cambridge University Press, 2003), pp. 170-186.

Stone, Merlin, *When God was a Woman* (New York: Harvest/ Harcourt Brace Jovanovich, 1976).

Suzuki, David and Peter Knudtson, *Wisdom of the Elders – Honoring Sacred Native Visions of Nature* (N.Y & London: Bantam Books,1992).

Swan, Jim, 'Sacred Places and Transcendental Experiences', *Theta: Journal of the Society for Psychic Research*, Spring (1983), pp. 65-72.

Talbot, Michael, *Beyond the Quantum - How the Secrets of the New Physics are Bridging the Chasm Between Science and Faith* (N.Y & London: Bantam Books, 1988).

Talbot, Michael, *The Holographic Universe* (London: Harper Collins, 1996).

Tau, Te Maire, Rawiri, 'Ngai Tahu and the Canterbury Landscape – A Broad Context', in John Cookson & Graeme Dunstall, *Southern Capital Christchurch – Towards a City Biography 1850-2000*, (Christchurch: Canterbury University Press, 2000), pp. 41-60.

Tau, Te Maire, Rawiri, *Nga Pikituroa o Ngai Tahu – The Oral Traditions of Ngai Tahu* (Dunedin: University of Otago Press, 2003).

Taylor, R., *Te Ika a Maui, New Zealand and its Inhabitants* (London: Wertheim & McIntosh, 1855).

Teasdale, Wayne, 'Nature- Mysticism as the Basis of Eco-Spirituality', *Studies in Formative Spirituality*, v.12, no.2 (1991), pp. 215-213.

Temple, Philip (ed.), *Lake, Mountains, Tree: An Anthology of Writings on New Zealand Nature and Landscape* (Wellington: Godwit, 1998).

Terrien, Samuel, *The Elusive Presence: The Heart of Biblical Theology* (San Francisco: Harper & Row, 1978).

Thayer, Robert L. Jr., 'Pragmatism in Paradise – Technology and the American Landscape', *Landscape*, v.30, no.3 (1990), pp. 1-11.

Thompson, William Irwin, *Imaginary Landscape: Making Worlds of Myth and Science* (New York: St. Martin's Press, 1989).

Truett, Anderson Walter (ed.), *The Fontana Postmodern Reader* (London: Fontana Press,1995).

Tuan, Yi-Fu, 'Geopiety: A Theme in Man's Attachment to Nature and Place', in David Lowenthal and Martin J. Bowden (eds.), *Geographies of the Mind: Essays in Historical Geography in Honor of John Kirtland Wright* (New York: Oxford University Press, 1976), pp. 11-39.

Tuan, Yi-Fu, 'Geography, Phenomenology, and the Study of Human Nature', *Canadian Geographer*, v.15, no.3 (1971), pp. 181-192.

Tuan, Yi-Fu, 'Humanistic Geography', *Annals of the Association of American Geographers*, v.66, no.2 (1976), pp. 266-276.

Tuan, Yi-Fu, 'Language and the Making of Place: A Narrative–descriptive Approach', *Annals of the Association of American Geographers,* v.81, no.4 (1991), pp. 684-696.

Tuan, Yi-Fu, 'Sacred Space: Explorations of an Idea', in K. Butzer (ed.), *Dimensions of Human Geography* (Chicago: University of Chicago Press, 1978), pp. 84-100.

Tuan, Yi-Fu, 'Sign and Metaphor', *Annals of the Association of American Geographers*, v.68, no.3 (1978), pp. 362-372.

Tuan, Yi-Fu, *Space and Place* (Minnesota: University of Minnesota Press, 1977).

Turkle, Sherry, *Life on the Screen – Identity in the Age of the Internet* (New York: Simon Schuster, 1995).

Turner, Harold, 'The Primal Religions of the World and their Study', in Victor Hayes (ed.), *Australian Essays in World Religions* (The Australian Assn. for the Study of Religion, 1977), pp. 27-37.

Ulrich, Roger S, 'Aesthetic and Affective Response to Natural Environment', in Irwin Altman and Joachim F. Wohlwill (eds.), *Behaviour and the Natural Environment*, v.6 (New York: Plenium Press, 1983), pp. 85-125.

Van Ness, Peter H., 'Bonhoeffer, Nietzsche, and Secular Spirituality', *Encounter: Creative Theological Scholarship*, v.52, no.4, Autumn (1991), pp. 327-341.

Van Ness, Peter, H., *Spirituality, Diversion and Decadence* (New York: State University of New York Press, 1992).

Vanhoozer, Kevin J., 'Theology and the Condition of Postmodernity: A Report on Knowledge (of God)', in Kevin J. Vanhoozer (ed.), *The Cambridge Companion to Postmodern Theology* (Cambridge: Cambridge University Press, 200?), pp.3-25.

Vanhoozer, Kevin J. (ed.), *The Cambridge Companion to Postmodern Theology* (Cambridge University Press, 2003).

Walker, Ranganui, *Nga Tau Tohetohe: Years of Anger* (Auckland: Penguin Books, 1987).

Ward, Graham (ed.), *The Postmodern God – A Theological Reader* (Oxford: Blackwell Publishers, 1997).

Wertheim, Margaret, *The Pearly Gates of Cyberspace – A History of Space from Dante to the Internet* (New York: W.W. Norton & Company, 1999).

White, Lynn Jr., 'The Historical Roots of Our Ecological Crisis', *Science*, vol.155, March (1967), pp. 1203-1207.

Whitmont, Edward C., *Return of the Goddess* (New York: The Crossroad Publishing Company, 1982).

Williams, Jay G., 'Return to the Roots: Platonic Philosophy and the I-Ching', *Ching Feng*, v.34:1, January (1991), pp. 3-15.

Wilson, Edward O., *Consilience – the Unity of Knowledge* (New York: Alfred A. Knoff, 1998).

Wright, John Kirtland, 'Terrae Incognitae: the Place of the Imagination in Geography', *Annals of the Association of American Geographers*, v.37 (1947), pp. 1-15.

Yamagishi, Takeshi,'Landscape and the Human Being', *Human Studies*, v.15, no.1 (1992), pp. 95-115.

Yoon, Hong-Key, 'On Geomentality', *Geo Journal*, v.25, no.4 (1991), pp. 387-392.

Yoon, Hong-Key, *Maori Mind, Maori Land*, Eratosthene Interdisciplinary Series (Bern & New York: Peter Lang, 1986).

Young, Dudley, *Origins of the Sacred* (London: Little, Brown and Co., 1992).

Acknowledgments

THIS BOOK IS A CAULDRON of ideas by thinkers and writers on the subjects of spirituality, landscape, archetypes and Sophia. I have tried to acknowledge them all by referencing meticulously all sources. I owe a debt of gratitude and pay homage to these thinkers, divinely inspired. They have enriched my life and I hope that the interested reader will seek out and follow up on the original source books and articles, as well as their other writings.

A PhD '*Spirituality, Landscape and Archetypes*', completed at the University of Waikato in 2009 is the basis of this book. In fact it was begun about 16 years earlier, in the early 1990s at Victoria University, but it had to fit in with life, children and establishing a vineyard. This was not a PhD rattled off fast. However I don't think it suffered because of the length of its gestation. Because of my other commitments I was given time to think, explore, wonder and ponder.

While he bears no responsibility for the final contents of this book, I owe a debt of gratitude to Professor Douglas Pratt, University of Waikato, for his editing, cheerful professionalism, patience and competence in seeing the PhD through to completion. However without the recognition of the importance of the subject and the initiative by Professor Jim Veitch, Victoria University, the research project would not have been started. It was he who suggested the research should be turned into a book. Dr George Armstrong listened bemused and patiently in the initial gestation of my ideas and investigations.

Throughout, I could not have done without the on-going friendship and unfailing support, at crucial times, of Dr Heather Kavan, Massey University; also Julian Young my partner, who tirelessly gave invaluable technological support and encouragement. Professor Peter Bishop, University of South Australia gave valuable feedback on the original PhD. David Famularo, journalist, artist and Green environmentalist activist, gave personal encouragement, collegial support and editing. Without his belief in the importance of the ideas expressed here, they would not have reached book form.

CRUCIAL TO MY THINKING ABOUT SPIRITUALITY has been the second-to-none quality of academia, rigorous scholarship and teaching standards that I encountered years ago as a young student in the 1970s at the University of Canterbury. Colin Brown headed the thriving, exploratory Comparative Religious Studies Department, which viewed religions and spirituality in their broadest sense. He left a life-long legacy to the students who flocked to his department. Here as well as the standard fare of a 'History of Christian Thought', 'Philosophy of Religion', 'Islamic Theology', 'Judaism' and 'Martin Buber' – I was introduced by the mountaineer Dr Jim Wilson, to 'Maori Spirituality', 'Buddhism', 'Hinduism', 'Confucianism'; and of special fascination for me, Englishman Dr David Brewster introduced me to the philosophy, theology and translations of Sorbonne Professor, Henry Corbin and 'Eastern and Western Mysticism'. Some years later Dr Rawiri Te Maire Tau took an interest in my research and Ngai Tahu provided me with a scholarship to complete my PhD, for which I am very grateful. In Wellington I attended the Victoria University Continuing Education lecture series given by Emeritus Professor Lloyd Geering, a fearless theologian, scholar, original thinker and brilliant teacher of religious philosophy in its broadest sense. Geering rekindled my interest in religion. Much appreciation goes to research librarians Barbro Harris and Justin Caygill at Victoria University who fielded my many requests to libraries, and to Jean Sunko, Carolyn and Marie of the Victoria University creche, who looked after my precious little Elinore and Roald with such care.

Finally, heart-felt love and thanks to my Mother Alison Antill, naturalist, environmentalist, tramper, gardener and one of the world's great arguers; Frank Gillett, mountaineer, skier, botanist and humble lover of the spirituality of mountains; Elsie Locke, fearless social activist for justice, the natural environment, and tramper extraordinaire; Ruby McIlraith and Sylvia Gillett; and Elizabeth Richards, pioneering woman high country farmer, for a wonderful childhood in New Zealand's natural environment.

About the Author

Dr. J.P. Antill grew up between the *Te Wai Pounamu* (Greenstone Island) mountains of the Southern Alps of New Zealand and the Pacific Ocean. A sixth generation New Zealander with both Ngai Tahu Maori ancestry (Iwikau of Akaroa) and European Pakeha whaler and settler farmer ancestry, from Northern Ireland, Scotland and England – she was brought up by an extended family and friends, involved in farming, teaching, tramping, skiing and mountaineering. While making a living as a researcher, writer and editor at the National Art Gallery, the Public Service and more recently in the family vineyard – her fascination has always been with the natural landscapes and their deep interaction with the human mind, expressed in art and culture, and as well the human created landscapes – and how these landscapes are all manifestations of spirituality.

Index

Made in the USA
Lexington, KY
30 November 2015